THE ACADEMIC ACHIEVEMENT OF MINORITY STUDENTS

Perspectives, Practices, and Prescriptions

Sheila T. Gregory

University Press of America,® Inc.
Lanham • New York • Oxford

Copyright © 2000 by
University Press of America,® Inc.
4720 Boston Way
Lanham, Maryland 20706

12 Hid's Copse Rd.
Cumnor Hill, Oxford OX2 9JJ

Library of Congress Cataloging-in-Publication Data

The academic achievement of minority students : perspectives, practices, and
prescriptions / (edited by) Sheila T. Gregory.
p.   cm.
Includes bibliographical references and index.
1. Minorities—Education—United States. 2. Academic
achievement—United States. I. Gregory, Sheila T.
LC3731.A57   1999   371.829—dc21   99-053188 CIP

ISBN 0-7618-1579-1 (pbk: alk. ppr.)

*D*edication

I am a teacher. I dedicate/rededicate my professional life to the young people of the world. I will respect all students entrusted to me by their parents. Daily I will strive to show my students that I genuinely care about them. I will model life-long learning as I seek to expand my own knowledge and skills. I will find the gifts in all students, believing that each one is capable of making meaning and success in their lives. Finally, I accept as a moral duty and sacred trust my responsibilities as a teacher, knowing that I am amply rewarded by the differences that I will make in young lives.

Stanley J. Zehm, 1993

*T*able of *C*ontents

II. *Perspectives on High School Academic Performance*

III.   *Improving Learning in Postsecondary Education*

List of Contributors

Angela H. Brown is assistant professor and secondary education coordinator at Piedmont College where she teaches courses in mathematics methods, learning and cognition, advanced instructional methods, and group processes. Her research interests include teacher training and issues of equity in education.

Sou-Yung Chiu is professor of mathematics from the National Chang-Hwa University of Education, Republic of China.

Jim Cofer is vice president for finance of the University of Missouri System. He has been a chief fiscal officer at the campus, system, and state levels for higher education and researched financing for higher education and financial aid. He was an Eisenhower Fellow in Hungary.

Jill Fischer is a graduate student in the Graduate School of Education at the University of California, Santa Barbara.

Teresa Fisher is assistant professor in the Psychology in Education Department at Arizona State University. Research interests include academic and career motivation, resilient youth and school mobility issues/interventions.

Stephanie Freese is currently the educational Director at Community Reform Temple in Westbury, NY, overseeing both secular and religious education of students from preschool through seventh grades. She recently received her Ed.D. in Educational Administration from Hofstra University, Hempstead, NY.

Cheryl Getz is assistant dean in School of Education, at the University of San Diego. Research interests include the social context of education, race and schooling and African American student development. She recently received her Ed.D. from the University of San Diego.

Reginald L. Green is associate professor of educational leadership at the University of Memphis. He has served as a teacher, principal, deputy superintendent, and superintendent at levels of K-12 education. He has numerous book and article publications on inner-city education, educational restructuring, school leadership, primary grade restructuring, gang violence, and other K-12 educational issues.

Sheila T. Gregory is director of marketing and public relations, and assistant professor of higher education/educational leadership in the College of Education at the University of Memphis. In addition to co-authoring an article, she is also the editor of this book.

Margaret M. Hall is director of university relations and development at the University of Arkansas at Pine Bluff. She is a doctoral student in the higher education program at the University of Arkansas at Little Rock.

Otis O. Hill is vice president and chairperson of the department of student development and a professor in the department of counseling at Kingsborough Community College, in Brooklyn, New York. He has served as assistant dean of students, dean of students, and director of off campus facilities. A few of his major accomplishments include the *Wall of Fame*, the *Early Attrition* project, and the 1989 Retention Award from the Noel Levitz National Conference on Student Retention.

Hsiu-Zu Ho is a professor of education in the Graduate School of Education at the University of California, Santa Barbara. Her research interests include culture and gender variations in motivation and achievement, cross-cultural psychology, and multicultural literacy.

Dennis Holmes is professor and chair of the department of educational leadership at the George Washington University. He teaches social science research methods, program evaluation, and measurement and has conducted national evaluation studies in the United States, Europe and Asia.

Donna Mahler is principal of Halle Hewetson Elementary School in Las Vegas, Nevada. She was an elementary teacher for 16 years in Nevada and Ohio. She is the recipient of an "Excellent in Education Award" from the Clark County School District and recently completed her doctoral degree.

Dianne L. H. Mark is associate chair and assistant professor in the department of teacher education and professional development at Central Michigan University. Her research interests include the academic achievement of African American students, urban partnerships, charter schools and pre-service teachers.

William Maxwell is an associate professor at the Center for Higher Education Policy Analysis in the Rossier School of Education at the University of Southern California. He studies and teaches international comparisons of educational leadership for equity and diversity.

Hugh Mehan is professor of sociology and director of the Center for Research on Educational Equity and Teaching Excellence (CREATE) at the University of California, San Diego. Recently elected to the National Academy of Education, his recent research focuses on ways to close the achievement gap between poor and minority students and their well-to-do contemporaries.

Karen F. Osterman is associate professor and chairperson in the department of administration and policy studies at Hofstra University. Her teaching and research focus broadly on motivation in a social context with particular emphasis on organizational structures and processes that affect the workplace behavior of adults and students.

Ruby Peralta is a graduate student in the Graduate School of Education at the University of California, Santa Barbara with an emphasis in the cultural perspectives of education.

Pedro R. Portes is professor of educational and counseling psychology at the University of Louisville. His work focuses on the adaptation of immigrant youth, ethnic identity formation, comparisons of parent-child interaction, compensatory education, and intellectual development. He is the author of a new parenting book *Making Kids Smarter*

Jim Vander Putten is assistant professor of higher education at the University of Arkansas at Little Rock. He has served as coordinator of the master's program in higher and postsecondary education at the University of Michigan and director of student support services at Sonoma State University.

Hakim M. Rashid is associate professor in the department of human development and psycho-educational studies in the School of Education at Howard University. He is also a co-principal investigator at the Center for Research on the Education of Students Placed at Risk.

Philip Rodriguez is director of student affairs at Cerritos Community College. His research interests include student retention and the educational pipeline, learning communities, and staff development for supporting students in becoming independent learners.

Lawrence Sáez is a Ph.D. candidate in political science at the University of Chicago. He has taught at UC Berkeley, Georgetown University, and the New School for Social Research.

Lacreta Scott is professor of English at Cerritos Community College She has a special interest in assisting remedial students to progress through the composition curriculum to transfer level proficiency.

Deniz Senturk is a graduate student in the Graduate School of Education at the University of California, Santa Barbara with an emphasis in Research Methodology.

Patricia Somers is associate professor of higher education at the University of Missouri, St. Louis. As an early recipient of the Pell grants and student loans, she has a long-standing interest in financial aid and student persistence.

Ricardo Stanton-Salazar is on faculty in the department of sociology at University of California, San Diego. His research interests include the sociology of education, youth culture, race and ethnic relations, family studies and how various social forces in society affect the development of minority adolescent social networks and help-seeking behavior, and how these factors influence their receptivity to educational interventions.

Watson S. Swail is associate director for policy analysis of The College Board, a national association of over 3,400 schools, colleges, and educational associations. Swail's research agenda focuses mainly on issues relating to the educational opportunity low-income, disadvantaged students. In addition to his research projects, he directs and produces The College Board's annual *Trends in Student Aid, Trends in College Pricing,* and *Trends in Academic Preparation and Opportunity* reports.

Ramona Thomas is associate program officer for the Spencer Foundation. Her research interests focus on students' transition from high school to higher education, particularly among Black students and those in urban schools. Her other interests include pre-college programs and the extent to which students' academic and social experiences in high school influence their postsecondary decisions.

Donna P. Towns is senior research associate at the Center for Research on the Education of Students Placed at Risk at Howard University specializing in urban classroom ethnography. Her background includes experience in law, anthropological linguistics and Caribbean studies.

Olga A. Vásquez is an ethnographer of education in the department of communications at the University of California, San Diego and was previously a research fellow at the UCSB Center for Chicano Studies. She is the lead author of *Pushing Boundaries: Language and Culture in a Mexicano Community* from Cambridge University Press (1994).

Chang-Pei Wang is professor of education from the Beijing Institute of Education, People's Republic of China.

Angela Whipple is a graduate student in the Graduate School of Education at the University of California, Santa Barbara with an emphasis in Developmental Studies.

Michelle Young is an assistant professor in planning policy and leadership studies at the University of Iowa. Her research and teaching focuses on race, class, and gender as it relates to family-school relationships and educational leadership and, more generally, the study of administrator preparation and professional development.

Madelon F. Zady, is assistant professor of clinical laboratory science at the University of Louisville. Her work in education focuses on adult-child interaction in relation to school performance in science with early adolescents, specifically on the psychology of learning in instruction and curriculum in science studies.

Stanley Zehm passed suddenly in the Spring of 1999. Prior to his death, he was a highly distinguished professor of education in the department of curriculum and instruction at the University of Nevada, Las Vegas. He was the author of seven books and dozens of articles related to cultural diversity and the academic successes of at-risk students. He won a number of awards including and Outstanding Graduate Teaching Award from Heritage College on the Yakama (Washington) Indian Reservation and the Lilly Fong Distinguished Professor of the Year from the College of Education at the University of Nevada, Las Vegas. He served as the chair of Donna Mahler's doctoral dissertation committee whose study is reviewed in the chapter.

Jules Zimmer is a professor of education and dean of the Graduate School of Education at the University of California, Santa Barbara. Her research interests include early learning, school readiness and school change, and cross-national comparisons of mathematics learning and attitudes towards learning.

*F*oreword

This book is a timely and critical contribution to the literature concerning the academic achievement of minority students. It comes at a time when the nation is closely examining its policies of the past regarding affirmative action. Also, when minority admissions to higher education are continually being questioned, the federal courts are rendering decisions such as *Hopwood v. Texas,* and citizens are enacting measures like Proposition 209 in California, that severely restricts the enrollment of minorities in colleges and universities.

As a result, many education professionals are looking for ways to boost the achievement of minorities in academic skills to make them competitive in higher education. This is particularly crucial in light of the fact that minorities are rapidly becoming a greater segment of the American population and are expected to be a substantial and contributing proportion of the skilled workforce if America is to remain a viable and leading nation.

In the past, the work of Claude Steele, a psychologist at Stanford University, explained why minority students perform less well on standardized tests, and the work of Jaime Escalante, a former high school Calculus teacher in California, demonstrated that minority students could surmount stubborn barriers to their academic achievement. Several other educators have also augmented our understanding of these phenomena.

In the present volume, Sheila Gregory has gathered an outstanding group of educators and researchers who exhibit various methods of enhancing minority student academic achievement, as well as understanding that this does not occur in a vacuum, but requires cognizance of the students' relationship to the environment of the school, the psychological involvement of the teacher, and other complex relational phenomena that affect learning.

For example, in Section One, Dianne Marks demonstrates that high achieving African American elementary students are inhibited from reaching their goals due to negative teacher attitudes and poor communication between home and school. Michelle Young, studying Mexican American children, finds that they are helped to be successful in school by meaningful parent involvement. Angela Whipple and her colleagues, in assessing Asian students in three nations, finds a positive effect of evaluative Math self-concept on Mathematics achievement. Each contributor in this section stresses the importance of adult affect on elementary student learning.

Section Two, involving high school achievement, gives concrete suggestions for improving minority student attainment. Ricardo Stanton-Salazar and his colleagues summarize two educational interventions that show substantial evidence of contributing to educational success among low-status students. Teresa Fisher identifies predictors of achievement for African American adolescents and notes implications for future interventions.

In Section Three on postsecondary attainment, Angela Brown describes how African American women's learning of Mathematics translates into effective teaching that enhances the academic achievement of minority students. Indeed, in that regard, Sheila Gregory illustrates the dedication of these women in her first book, *Black Women in the Academy* (1995), when she stated that "some African American faculty women have been found to leave higher paying positions in private industry for the opportunity to teach where they can serve as role models and make a difference in the lives of minority students." Sheila Gregory and Otis Hill conclude the last paper in this section with a report of a three-year study of minority community college students with specific details of what institutional and programmatic factors contribute to the academic success of these students.

As William Sedlacek (1998) has said, "as admissions competition has grown at institutions nationwide, and as institutions raise their standards to respond to this competition, students face growing challenges in their efforts to pursue higher education opportunities." This volume will contribute greatly to educators meeting that challenge with their students.

Reginald Wilson, Ph.D.
Senior Scholar Emeritus
American Council on Education

Preface

In the United States and abroad students of color are subjected to school failure because of the way in which academic performance is measured, the lack of motivation, effort and encouragement, and a host of demographic, socioeconomic and cultural factors. This lack of achievement and persistence is reflected in lower scores on standardized tests, increasing rate of truancy and high-school drop-outs, and the declining number of college admissions and baccalaureate degrees for students of color. What are the profiles and characteristics of these students? What are the effects of attrition on academic planning and curriculum? What academic, instructional, and other related factors are associated with academic achievement and attrition? What nonacademic factors, such as teacher's attitudes, are associated with academic achievement and attrition? What strategies can be offered to enhance academic performance of students of color? And finally, what prescriptions can we recommend for the future?

This volume addressed these questions and is divided into three sections. *Section One* entitled, "School Achievement of K-8 Students" is dedicated to K-8 education and includes seven manuscripts. *Section Two* "Perspectives on High School Academic Performance" is a collection of seven works and contains research on high school students. Finally, *Section Three* "Improving Learning in Postsecondary Education" focuses on postsecondary education and includes five articles. The contents of each chapter are briefly discussed below.

SECTION ONE

In Dianne L. H. Mark's paper, *Discrepancies between aspirations and preparation of low SES elementary students*, examines the academic performance of high achieving African American elementary students as they matriculated into high school. The purpose of the study was to determine the extent to which these students were still high achievers and to examine what role mentors played in their lives. The evidence of her work suggested that many of the students did not reach their intended goals due to negative teacher attitudes, poor communication between home and school, and lack of resources in the home.

Michelle Young's piece, *Family involvement: learning from secondary schools in the Texas borderland*, finds that when families were involved in their children's education, children performed more successfully in school. However, she notes that while the involvement of parents at the elementary level was well documented, few had given careful consideration to the involvement of parents in secondary schools. Her manuscript provides a portrait of the involvement of Mexican-American parents in secondary schools located along the Texas-Mexico border. Furthermore, it delineates the ways in which successful schools--particularly those enrolling predominantly Mexican-American students from poor, limited English proficient, non-English speaking, and/or migrant backgrounds--develop and sustain meaningful parental involvement.

The article entitled, *Children's math self-concept and its relationship with mathematics achievement*, was co-written by Deniz Senturk, Angela Whipple, Hsiu-Zu Ho, Jules Zimmer, Sou-Yung Chiu, and Chang-Pei Wang. The study from which the paper was based utilizes a multi-item scales to assess mathematics self-concept in 6th grade students in three nations: China, Taiwan, and the United States. The results of confirmatory factor analyses indicated the presence of distinct affective and evaluative components across all three nations in the sample. Structural equation modeling analyses indicated a positive effect of evaluative math self-concept on mathematics achievement. However, affective math self-concept did not predict mathematics achievement when holding the evaluative math self-concept constant. The study was unique in terms of the assurance of the construct validity and the reliability of the math self-concept measure across China, Taiwan and the U.S. and offers new insights into the relationship between math self-concept and mathematics achievement.

The piece from Donna Penn Towns, Hakim Rashid, entitled *Hopes transcend fears: school transition in an urban school cluster system*, examines how anxiety over the transition from one school or grade level to another becomes a problematic factor in the academic performance of some school children. The results of this study of student and teacher perceptions, surrounding transition issues in grades three, five and eight, highlight the differences between their respective perceptions. These differences suggest that the issues may be different for African American students in an urban school cluster setting where school experience has not always been optimal and hope that life will be better in the future transcended the fears commonly associated with change.

The article, *A Cross-national study of children's perceived control: its dimensionality and relationship with achievement* by Hsiu-Zu Ho, Jules Zimmer, Deniz Senturk, Jill Fischer, Ruby Peralta, Sou-Yung Chiu, Chang-Pei Wang, compares gender differences in perceived control reported by a sample of sixth-grade students from China, Taiwan, and the United States. Inter-correlation among the three sources of perceived control ("internal," "powerful others," and "unknown") in the cognitive domain indicated that the patterns for U.S. girls were similar to those for the Chinese and Taiwanese boys and girls. Within the social domain, however, the patterns of inter-correlation of the Asian boys were more similar to U.S. students. Similarly, the correlation of sources of control in the cognitive domain with mathematics achievement varied across nation and gender.

Reginald Green wrote his piece entitled, *"The ABC's for effective schools: Creating a nurturing environment to enhance learning,"* as a result of John Goodlad's book, *A Place Called School.* The research focuses on the characteristics of schools in which students feel nurtured. Above all else, one thing was found to be profoundly clear; a better climate (ABC) is necessary if we are to have effective schools and the factors that inform that notion is the focus of the article.

Donna Mahler and Stan Zehm, co-wrote a piece entitled, *"Perspectives of African American parents of high achieving students regarding the home-school relationship."* This chapter describes the findings of a qualitative research study that explored African American parent's perceptions of their roles in the education of their children and how these perceptions translate into specific parent involvement practices both at home and at school. It also identifies the concerns that African American parents of high achieving elementary students have about their children's schooling and offers their suggestions for improving the home-school relationship.

SECTION TWO

Madeline Zady and Pedro Portes collaborated to contribute the article, *"Cultural differences in self-esteem: Ethnic variations in the adaptation of recent immigrant Asian adolescents."* The piece argues that self-esteem serves as a meaningful index of individual and group adaptation in terms of mental health, schooling and related areas. Such adaptations, when examined in the case of immigrant adolescents, are shown in this piece, to be of particular value and interest to the field. This paper examines the extent to which differences in self-esteem exist among four Asian groups at a time of collective transition or adaptation, during adolescence, itself a time of transition. Employing a cultural historical (CH) perspective, the study found differences in the self-esteem among Asian groups as measured by the Rosenberg (1979) scale. In two groups, the more typical predictors of depression and parent-child conflict were shown to be significant and gender dependent. Self-esteem in the other two groups is largely open to conjecture, as the instrument used to evaluate it may be more relevant to some cultures than to others.

Ricardo Stanton-Salazar, Olga Vasquez, and Hugh Mehan co-wrote, *"Re-engineering academic success through institutional support."* In this piece, the authors present a network-analytic framework which highlights a number of key concepts and theoretical processes, which are believed to have considerable utility for better understanding instances of academic success among ethnic and racial minority students from low-income communities. Summarized are two educational interventions that continue to show substantial evidence of facilitating educational success and advancement among low-status students. Using the framework presented, the authors identify and elaborate on the various relational and social network processes underlying these two notable interventions; they then proceed to show how these key processes could be successfully integrated in any current intervention directed at low-income minority students.

In the article, *"The persistence of African American college students: How national data inform a Hopwood-proof retention strategy,"* Patricia Somers, Margaret Martin Hall, Jim Cofer, and Jim Vander Putten examine a national study which compares the variables that affect African American and White college student persistence. The findings indicate that college experiences, current price, and accumulated debt-load influence persistence of both groups of students. The piece includes a social commentary on the results and proposed retention strategies for universities based on recent court cases.

Lawrence Saez's chapter entitled *"Academic Achievement of Latino Immigrants"* helps to explain the continuing discrepancy in financial success and educational attainment between Latinos and other racial/ethnic groups. Various issues with cultural explanations are examined for the comparative lack of financial success and educational attainment of Latinos in the United States. The author argues that cultural explanations fail to explain variance within the Latino community in the educational and financial success. The essay instead suggests that the socio-economic status of Latino immigrants is the principal variable to explain and predict the education and financial performance of Latinos in the United States. A set of policy recommendations are provided dealing with immigration reform.

Karen Osterman and Stephanie Freese's piece entitled, *Nurturing the mind to improve learning: Teacher caring and student engagement* examines a serious problem that manifests itself in various degrees of alienation from school and from the learning process, ranging from detachment or "going through the motions" to dropping out. This article explores the psychological underpinnings of disengagement and examines the important role that teacher caring and support play in facilitating student engagement. In the context of this research, the authors also consider the practical implications for policymakers, teacher preparation programs, and school educators.

In her article, *"Predictors of academic achievement among African American adolescents,"* Teresa Fisher identifies factors that help explain differences in the high and low achievement of African American adolescents. Sophomores and Juniors (n= 368) from three inner-city high schools were administered a questionnaire that assessed the following independent variables: socioeconomic status, gender, educational aspirations and expectations, occupational aspirations and expectations, perceived opportunity for success in school, academic self-concept, awareness of limited opportunity for the future, and perceived support from parents, teachers and peers. Anecdotal information is included, which was provided by interviews conducted with 30 randomly selected high and low achieving students. Multiple regression and ANOVA procedures revealed that the students' academic self-concept was the best predictor of academic achievement (as measured by grade point average). The students' perception of academic support from significant others as well as their perception of the opportunities for success in an academic environment, were also crucial factors in the academic achievement behavior of African American adolescents. Implications for educators, parents and future interventions are discussed.

"Black students' academic performance and preparation for higher education," written by Ramona Thomas, examines the relationship between Black students' academic preparation and performance in school, and the influence of these factors on their college enrollment. The goals are to: (1) describe the academic preparation and achievement of Black high school students, (2)

examine whether Black students who expect to pursue higher education enroll in college, and (3) examine the significance of students' academic preparation and achievement in their college participation. Data for this study came from the National Education Longitudinal Study of 1988-1994. The findings suggest that Black students are not as well prepared as they could be for college.

SECTION THREE

Angela Brown's chapter, *Creative pedagogy to enhance the academic achievement of minority students in mathematics: Lessons from African American women mathematics teachers,"* highlights the experiences of seven African American women post-secondary mathematics teachers and how their experiences as learners of mathematics translate into creative teaching strategies and philosophies to enhance the academic achievement of minority students. Results indicate that student's confidence in math aptitude is determined by teacher attitude and that student success is enhanced when students are educated in a conducive climate. Teaching was found to be more than educating; it was also nurturing and empowering. Recommendations are given to encourage teachers to more actively seek to make mathematics accessible for all students.

In the paper entitled, *"Minority student persistence: A model for colleges and universities,"* Watson Scott Swail and Dennis Holmes present a research-based model based on the Goal Five of the Goals 2000: Educate America Act that provide administrators and practitioners a menu of activities, policies, and practices to consider during the planning and implementation of a comprehensive campus-based retention program. The model provides practical considerations for the adoption of policies at the institutional level to help increase the persistence of students in science, engineering, and the mathematics disciplines. A five-component retention framework is discussed based upon an extensive review of current literature. The paper concludes with a discussion of the model in terms of institutional and public policy.

Philip Rodriguez, Lacreta Scott, and William Maxwell, co-wrote a chapter entitled, *"Feasible learning opportunities for urban Latino students in community colleges,"* where they interviewed Latino community college students. The study revealed many feasible strategies that would enable any teacher to do something important in improving learning opportunities for minorities. The students reported strategies of inclusion and validation, multicultural assignments, personalized feedback, collaborative learning and peer groups.

In her article, *"Observing the spirit of resilience: The relationship between life experiences and success in higher education for African American students,"* Cheryl Getz investigates the challenges that African American student's face as they attempt to successfully navigate the collegiate environment. This study found that the spirit of these individuals, were the source of their self-efficacy and it was this belief in themselves (self-efficacy) that was the source of their resiliency. It was this quality that continued to contribute to their success and determination to succeed, despite the barriers--real and perceived--that they continued to overcome. The data generated from this study confirmed that including students in the ongoing dialogue about race and schooling could be a powerful way to help educators examine the nature of students' experiences by reflecting on them in constructively critical ways. The major implication of the study was the following; if the inter-relatedness between students' life experiences and academic success are understood more clearly, educators may become more open to creating an educational setting in which both students and professors learn from one another--a setting that better fulfills the fundamental educational goal of preparing all students to be successful.

The final chapter in this volume entitled, *"Improving learning outcomes for at-risk community college students,"* comes from Sheila Gregory and Otis Hill. The paper is based on a three-year longitudinal study of 60 immigrant, foreign-born, and minority "at risk" community college students which analyzes the results of a new academic skill-based program designed to enhance reading, writing, and math skills, raise academic performance, motivate students, and encourage persistence and matriculation. Applying the Chickering Model of Student Development (1993), the paper explores: (1) the effect of the program on academic performance; (2) characteristics of students whose GPA significantly improved; (3) the academic motivations of students; (4) greatest academic and personal concerns, and problems of students; and 5) the major factors which contribute to various student learning outcomes. Finally, the paper provides recommendations on what to consider when developing an academic skill-based program and explains in detail what institutional and programmatic factors contribute to the academic and social success of students.

Each of these nineteen works provide supporting evidence that the academic performance of minority and other children can be enhanced through encouragement, caring and supportive attitudes on the part of teachers and parents, maintaining high standards, expecting academic improvement throughout the semester, creative pedagogy, a diverse curriculum, instructional support and resources for teachers, and utilizing various means to measure student performance, such as tests, projects, readings, exercises, papers, activities, drama, and other creative displays of knowledge. The purpose of the book was to examine the academic achievement of minority students (kindergarten through postsecondary education) to reveal effective practices for enhancing student performance and instruction, in an effort to provide creative practices and recommendations that can be modeled and duplicated in classrooms across the country. Each chapter in this volume provides compelling information that explores many of these areas to aid the reader, both in theory and in practice.

Sheila T. Gregory, Ph.D.
Editor

Acknowledgments

I am grateful to my family, friends, and colleagues who helped to make this book possible, including:

God almighty, who continues to give me the inner strength and tenacity to keep going;

my precious daughter, Courtney Gregory Jones, who graciously and kindly allowed me the time I needed in the evenings to write and reminds me each day what is really important in life;

my unborn baby, who encourages me through movement and inspiration, keep moving and rest myself from time to time;

my husband, Tony Jones, who pitched in more around the house and filled in as mom for a time so I could complete this volume;

my parents, Karl and Tenicia Gregory, and my siblings, Karin and Kurt Gregory who have always provided their love and support;

the many contributors who made this volume possible;

Reginald Wilson who graciously offered to write the foreword to this book;

Nathan Essex, Dean of the College of Education at the University of Memphis, who provided me the flexibility at work to finish this book;

and other relatives and friends. Thank you all!

I.

School Achievement

of K-8 Students

1. *Discrepancies Between Aspirations & Preparation of Low SES Students*

Dianne L. H. Mark

INTRODUCTION/BACKGROUND

Parents hold varying degrees of expectations for their children. When parents were asked *how far in school their children will go and what type of work they would like their children to do*, responses ranged from "finishing high school" and "finishing graduate school" to "being an engineer or a physician." Some expectations are forced upon children by their parents, either intentionally or unintentionally. As an adolescent, children may not understand the significance of their parent(s) "pushing them." Reflecting back to when I was in high school and starting college, there came a time when I questioned why I was traveling down a certain path. As a college sophomore, I realized that I had been trying to maintain high grades because my parents had expected that of me. And even though they wanted us to work in professional careers, they did not know what strategies would lead us down those expected paths. They had high expectations, but at that time neither my parents nor I had been exposed to professional career choices. It became evident to me, afterwards, that I needed to formulate my own expectations and goals if I wanted to succeed in school and in life.

Like many African Americans of my generation, I was the first to attend and graduate from college. While my parents hoped that all six of their children would go to college, receive degrees, and begin working in a high-paying professional career, we all chose different paths. Realistically, expense was an issue with four children only one to four years apart in age. Also, because my oldest sister and I graduated from high school the same year, sending both of us to college was almost impossible. However, if my sister had chosen that path, I know that my parents would have secured the financial resources to support both of us through college. Although, I did not understand that "push" exerted by my parents many years ago, I know now that they felt that if we were to be successful, we needed a good, solid education.

How do parents and children decide upon expectations and aspirations? Do parents place unrealistic high expectations on their children? Do students have aspirations that are unreachable and based on false hope? At what point should students begin working on their dreams? Marotz-Baden and Tallman (1978) conducted a comparative study of white and blue-collar parents' aspirations and expectations of pre-adolescent children living in Minnesota and Mexico. Their data suggested that conceptual and empirical distinctions are made between aspirations and expectations, and their discrepancies were advantageous. However, their study was limited because they were unable to control for the possible confounding effects of culture. Marjoribanks (1995) investigated adolescents' aspirations using data collected from 516 Australian families. In this longitudinal study which spanned over five years, he constructed a parental involvement model and evaluated the extent to which that model predicted variations in adolescents' aspirations. He found that:

> ...adolescents' perception of their parents' involvement in learning are so strongly associated with their own aspirations, but that the relationship only becomes significant after quite a substantial level of positive parental involvement is perceived (p. 82).

Consequently, children are affected by their parent(s) involvement to the extent that they consider the parent(s) involved.

A LONGITUDINAL STUDY
The intent of this study was to explore the factors that contributed to urban students' perceptions of how their learning environment impacts upon their achievement. In 1991-92, a study was conducted to explore the home learning environment of high achieving African

American elementary children in low income single parent families (Mark, 1992). The purpose of that study was to look at how parents were involved in their children's schooling in ways other than those traditional methods (e.g. volunteering in the classroom, chaperoning on trips, etc). I was especially interested in African American families who, historically, have had many obstacles to a successful schooling experience. The home learning environment of low income African American, single parent families with high achieving children were explored. Hare (1987) argued that the educational system, through its unequal skill giving, grading, routing and credentialing procedures, played a critical role in fostering structured inequality in the American social system. This evidence suggests that underrepresented students, particularly African Americans, will continue to be underachievers in spite of modest gains. Consequently, many African American students learn that education may not lead them toward social mobility and opportunities; this in turn develops into negative attitudes toward schooling (Ogbu, 1978).

The results of other studies (Clark, 1983; Lee, 1984; Matthew-Juarez, 1982; Norman-Jackson, 1982; Ortiz, 1986; and Shields & Dupree, 1983) strongly support the premise that high academic achievement is a function of good parenting skills and positive parent involvement in the student's academic progress. One facet of parental involvement was the impact of the home environment. Lalyre (1989, p. 175) defined "home environment" to include the places where students slept, ate and interacted with close family members, other relatives and peers. Leahy (1936) viewed the home as the most important predictor for determining academic success, because it was the home that affected the child's behavior most continuously. Also, the home, according to Dave (1963, p. 4), "produces the first, most insistent, and perhaps, most subtle influence on the educational development of the child." Researchers, if they are to study influences on academic achievement, should include those factors related to the learning environment in the home.

Another issue that had been investigated as it related to the home learning environment was that of family composition, specifically, single parenthood (Epstein, 1984; Finn & Owings, 1994; Keith et al., 1986; Voelkl, 1993). Finn & Owings (1994) conducted a study using NELS '88 data on 8th grade students. They focused on the relationship between family structure and students' academic performance, giving special attention to the confounding effects of poverty and ethnicity. They found that children from single parent homes reported less parental monitoring and less supervision, although more time was spent talking with parents than in two-parent families. Research has indicated that there has been a steady decline in the "nuclear" two-parent family and an increase in female-headed households, especially in the African American community. Single parents have been stigmatized for decades for their "deviance" from the two-parent norm (Macintyre, 1977; Page, 1984; Peter & deFord, 1986). Single-parent families have been a group whose difficulties seem to go unnoticed by the majority of the public. However, this group was increasing, especially in the United States, Great Britain and Australia (Chilman, 1988; Haskey, 1991) and those difficulties need to be addressed.

Single parent families from low socioeconomic backgrounds are often looked upon as dysfunctional. Based upon data from the Bureau of the Census 1990 data, one out of five children lived in a one-parent family and 67% of the mothers with children under 18 were working. "It is easy for single parents who are poor to be mistakenly perceived as 'poor parents,' just as single parents are especially vulnerable to the conflation of 'families with problems' and 'problem families'" (Hardey & Crow, 1991, p. 4). However, in a study conducted by Peters and deFord (1986), African American single mothers discussed several advantages of their family structure. They felt that: 1) their children were more independent and responsible; 2) their children no longer saw their parents in constant conflict; and 3) there was a strong sense that the family was closer, worked as a cooperative unit and that family life was more flexible and more reflective of what the mother or the children wanted to do.

Prom-Jackson and colleagues (1987) investigated academically talented African American students from low-income families and analyzed the relative effect of family size in single- and two-parent households. The evidence from this analysis did not support the conception of the devastating effects of the single-parent household on student achievement. Some of the literature suggested that the family structure was the critical factor determining whether children would succeed academically. White (1982) conducted a meta-analysis of 200 studies that investigated the relationships between socioeconomic status and academic achievement. He found that socioeconomic correlated about .22 with individual student achievement. There were so many families who were not "nuclear" and who were poverty-stricken, whose children successfully stay in school. Some of those African American students from these "dysfunctional" family structures were very successful students and became very successful adults. African American families of all social status have been remarkably effective and resilient at helping their children cope with the schooling process (Slaughter & Epps, 1987).

Because of the increasing diversity of the student population in urban schools, the rising number of single parent families, and the growing concern for the acquisition of basic academic skills for these students, it seems imperative to investigate learning environments outside of the school. Also, because of the changing nature of our society, the family and schools in urban areas; and "because we do not yet know precisely how family environments interact with the schooling process...the study of home environment and student achievement continues to be important" (Slaughter & Epps, 1987, p.6). The learning environment in the home has been considered one of the best predictors of academic achievement and, therefore, offers an appropriate area of research.

In 1992, the focus on the home learning environment was described through data received by examining students' records, and observing and interviewing 19 families. The findings, which are in part, reflective of the findings of other studies on high achievers (Clark, 1983; Henderson & Berla, 1994; Lee, 1984, Matthew-Juarez, 1982; Soto, 1992) revealed that those parents:

1. had high expectations for their children;
2. had good communication with their children;
3. had high regard for reading to/by their children;
4. monitored children's television programs;
5. maintained structured households; and
6. established a system of rewards and
   punishments for their children

In this follow-up study, I explored how these high school students' perceived their educational performance. The research questions guiding this qualitative study included:

1. What, if any, is the impact of students' home environment on their academic performance?
2. What are students' expectation levels, both educational and career, and are they consistent with parent expectations?
3. What individuals, if any, have affected their academic performance?

REVIEW OF LITERATURE

The review of literature for this current study centers around three issues: 1) The impact of the home/community environment and academic performance; 2) parents' academic and career expectations as they relate to their children's expectations; and 3) the impact that teachers have had on the student academic performance. Stevens (1993) found that the instructions provided by many urban teachers have contributed to the continued academic gap between minority students and their white counterparts. A report issued by the U. S. Education Department and the National Education Goals Panel stated that although the gap between 1977 and 1990 is closing, White children still outperformed African American and Hispanic youth at all age levels and in all subjects (Nation's Schools, 1991). Studies have also indicated differences in teachers' perceptions of children from single-headed households when compared to those from two-parent households (Guttmann, Geva, and Gefen, 1988; Hetherington, Cox and Cox, 1978). In general, many American public schools have allowed family composition, race, and social class to become barriers in establishing positive relationships (Davies, 1988; Goldenberg and Gallimore, 1991). Furthermore, building-level administrators may add to these barriers by not exhibiting the qualities of commitment to, compassion for, and confidence in the ability of all African American children to learn. These qualities were found among principals of successful African American schools (Lomotey, 1989).

Students' perceptions of the impact of their academic performance and their home environment, specifically their parents' expectations, were important as they related to their self-image. Hare (1985) suggested that from preadolescence to adolescence, African American youth experience a decline in self-concept and academic ability. The home and community environments greatly impact upon the academic performance of students and therefore, it is important to determine how youth interpret this impact. It is just as important to determine whether the educational expectations of parents are consistent with that of their children. Clark (1983) surmised that parents with high-achieving children held high expectations, despite their low socioeconomic status and deteriorating neighborhoods. Slaughter and Epps (1987) concluded that African American families, regardless of social status, had been extremely effective and resilient at helping their children deal with schooling. And although the high achieving students realized that obstacles were inevitable and the road could be paved with stumbling blocks, they worked hard to get that "good education." Solorzano (1992) conducted a study on the effects of race, class and gender on student and parent mobility aspiration. He found that African American students of varied socioeconomic levels had higher aspirations than compared to White students.

Marotz-Baden and Tallman (1978) define "aspiration" as idealistic or unrealistic goals and "expectations" as realistic goals. They discussed the importance of providing operational definitions of these terms as they are used interchangeably. Earlier studies suggested that African American mothers and low-income youth have had unrealistically high expectations (Bell, 1965; Dole, 1973; Sell, 1973; and Della Fave, 1974). Furthermore, the educational expectations that African American parents from single-headed households proclaim, may be unrealistic and not unlike the goals of middle class, white, two-parent households. These unrealistically high expectations were attributed to parents wanting their children to aspire to a "better" life. However, many parents and children had not been exposed to the multitude of career choices. Nor did many parents, especially low-income parents, realize the financial commitment needed in order to accomplish their goals. In general, the median income for African American families was 43% lower than that of White families (Morris, 1992). Unfortunately, one-parent families continue to increase in the United States, Great Britain and Australia (Chilman, 1988; Haskey, 1991) and the vast majority of African American female-headed households live in poverty (Powell, 1989) with limited resources in the home (Oakes, 1988).

METHODOLOGY

Sample. The student sample for the original study was drawn from a population of 76 African American students who were identified as high achievers and who attended Mary Street School (geographical areas, school districts and names of families are all fictitious).· Mary Street School is in the core of the city of Dexter, which is a major metropolitan area in the State of New York. Mary Street Elementary is one of three predominately African American neighborhood schools in Dexter. High achievers were defined by those students who were reading at grade level or above and whose accumulative grade point averages were in the 85th percentile or higher. Although the City of Dexter had a 27% poverty rate, over 95% of the students attending Mary Street participated in the free or reduced lunch program.

The total sample in 1992-93 consisted of 19 low-income African American children from single parent families and their parents. There were 7 males and 12 females from grades fifth through eighth. Fourteen of the caregivers interviewed were the students' biological mothers, while there was only one biological father. Three caregivers were grandmothers and there was one great grandmother. Even though 17 of the parents never received a college degree, 15 of them held jobs outside of the home. Single parenthood consisted of those never married (N=7), divorced (N=7), widowed (N=3), and legally separated (N=2). The selection was based upon the following criteria:

1. Students and families were African American;
2. Students resided in a one-parent household;
3. Students were from low-income families;
4. Students were recognized as high achievers as indicated from report cards and reading scores on the Comprehensive Testing of Basic Skills assessment; and
5. There was equal representation of males and females.

The initial parent interviews were conducted using a structured open-ended questionnaire. I used a questionnaire that was developed by Guiang (1980). After a pilot study, I revised it slightly to make it more relevant for my sample of African American families. The questionnaire was classified into several areas relating to the learning environment of the home. These included, but were not limited to academic guidance, achievement press, activeness of the family, intellectuality in the home, and work habits in the family. Follow-up interviews with the parents and interviews with the children took place approximately two weeks later. During the two-week period between the initial interviews and the follow-ups, each child completed an activity schedule and each parent completed a parent interaction schedule. The activity schedule was used to gather additional information regarding the student's daily routine outside of school and was used as an interview guide with the children. The parent interaction schedule was designed so parents could record daily communication with their children.

During the follow-up interviews, I reviewed the interaction and activity schedules with the parents and children, received clarification, asked additional questions and through a research grant, paid each parent $15.00 for his/her time and cooperation. One problem that arose during this process was scheduling interviews and follow-up interviews. One family moved twice within a six-week period, while two families had moved just prior to the initial interview. Also, several parents had more than one job and it was difficult to schedule an interview. Finally, there were some families that had no telephone. In those few cases, I stopped by their homes the day before an interview and reminded them of the appointment or sent a reminder card home from school with their child.

Students were again contacted during the summer of 1995. Out of the 19 students, nine students agreed to be part of the follow-up study. The remaining 10 students who were not part of this follow-up study was because of the following reasons: one did not wish to participate in the study; three had non-verifiable addresses; and six had non-working or unpublished telephone numbers. After the interviews began, however, one student dropped out and another did not provide academic records, which left seven participants. These seven students are listed in Table 1.

Table 1: Demographics of Student Participants, 1995-96 School Year

Name	Gender	Age	Grade
Darwin Carpenter	M	14	9
Leon Chimes	M	17	12
Ebony Curtis	F	14	9
Taylor Luke	F	15	10
Kayla Magsby	F	15	10
Shante Nichols	F	15	10
Talia Temple	F	15	10

Procedures. Packets were sent to students and parents which contained a Letter of Instruction, an Agreement Form, a Release of Academic Files Form, a form to Update Demographic Information and a self-addressed stamped envelope. Many calls were made to remind students/parents to return the information. Face-to-face interviews were scheduled with students in their home during the 1995-96 fall semester. Unfortunately, due to extremely bad weather conditions, face-to-face interviews were not conducted. Telephone interviews were conducted using an audio tape recorder. The structured open-ended questions were categorized into four areas: schooling, guardians, social, and self. These 31 questions guided me through the interviews, and as with qualitative research, themes began developing.

Analysis. Data were collected through students' academic files and interviews. This was a qualitative study making use of ethnographic methods, using cultural forms and patterns and the regularities of social behavior (Erickson, 1973; Fetterman, 1982; Spradley, 1979; Wolcott, 1975). From the transcribed field notes, categories and subcategories surfaced. This data, as well as 1992 data were analyzed and compared. Additional themes emerged that generated additional questions for respondents.

Reliability and Validity. Reliability addresses the issues of whether different researchers would discover similar findings or generate similar constructs in similar settings, and the degree to which these other researchers would be able to match them with data in the same way as did the original researchers. Even the most exact replication of research methods may fail to produce identical results (LeCompte & Goetz, 1982). And although these studies can not be duplicated in the true sense of the word, I have included detailed documentation displaying the thoroughness to the reader and other researchers as it opens the doors for theory testing in the areas of educational learning environments and aspirations among African American students. I also incorporated two strategies to reduce threats to internal reliability descriptors and mechanically recorded data.

Internal validity refers to the extent to which scientific observation and measures are authentic representations of some reality (LeCompte & Goetz, 1982). To this end, I had numerous opportunities to communicate with the families during the initial study and the subsequent one. These interactions allowed me to become very familiar with the students and their parent or caregiver. Themes were derived from the respondents and generated. The coding was a continuous re-evaluation of the data. Finally, ethnographic analysis incorporated a process of disciplined subjectivity. This exposed all phases of the research activity to continual questioning and re-evaluation (Erickson, 1973).

FINDINGS
The findings were categorized into two sections. The first section provides a case summary for each student. The second section probes emerging themes that arose from the data.

Students were all enrolled in high schools in an urban city in New York State. Six of the students were in schools that represented four of the public high schools, while one student was enrolled in a parochial school. The two vocational public schools represented, offered an array of courses in the trade areas, including advertising art, carpentry, electronic technology, plumbing, sheet metal, drafting, and horticulture. The one magnet high school offered a program in computers and the remaining public high school offered a general and college prep curriculum. The private high school provided a "Jesuit preparation for college - for life."

The Students. **Darwin Carpenter** lived with his mother and his 20-year-old brother. His father, a social studies teacher, had also been active in his life and assisted him on a regular basis with schoolwork. While only a 9th grader, Darwin was still becoming familiar with his new environment and he found climbing the stairs at high school about one of the worse things about school. His grade point average of a 64.5% may have been an indication of his adapting, and he left eighth grade with an 74.7% average. During his first interview in 1992, he had an overall GPA of 84.1%. Darwin was enrolled in a vocational high school in the Building Trades Program. In 1992, his mother talked about trying to get him enrolled in a magnet school. The magnet school encouraged students to be independent and Ms. Carpenter thought this would be a good place for Darwin because she considered him a "completer." She also felt that she would rather have Darwin attend a regular high school focusing on "academics," rather than a vocational high school. However, the reason for now enrolling him in the vocational school was attributed to the number of Darwin's friends attending the regular high school. Ms. Carpenter felt that his friends would have a negative influence on her son. Although he enjoyed the classes on air conditioning, sheet metal and plumbing, they did not relate to his family's goal of his being a physician.

Darwin had been active in the local Boys' and Girl's Club for several years. He enjoyed sports, especially basketball and baseball, and had visions of playing basketball for his high school team in a couple of years. Although he stated that he wanted to be a "doctor in the medical field," he was uncertain about how much schooling it would take or what would be his area of specialization. He said that he wanted to be a "doctor that helps people...maybe a surgeon or heart transplanter." Darwin had not thought about college, but responded that he wanted to attend one out of town and then return home after college.

Ebony Curtis lived with her four brothers and her mother. She also had an older brother who did not reside with them. Ebony, a twin, enjoyed the drill team, watching television, reading, and listening to the radio. She attended a vocational high school and was enrolled in a program called "Career Academy." This program combined the field of Avionics with the leadership of Jr. ROTC. The curricular tracks included electronic communications, telecommunications and radio and TV broadcasting. Although Ebony chose this program, she planned to go to college and become a pediatrician or a beautician. The Avionics program, however, might have encouraged her to become a pilot.

She held a 72.8% grade point average in her academic subjects. Ebony worked hardest in global studies, health, and algebra because those were "the ones she really liked." She considered herself an average achiever because she did not work as hard in school as she possibly could and sometimes she just did not try and said "forget it." She felt that her high school teachers only had "average expectations" for her, and that in elementary school, they paid more attention to the students. She continued by stating, "Now it is like, if you do it you do it, if you don't, they [teachers] don't really care." Actually, something that she really did not like about school was the teachers and their attitudes. She felt that they were insensitive and did not want students to ask questions. Ebony obtained an 86.0% GPA in 1992.

Unlike some, Ebony found her first year of high school enjoyable. "I like it because I have more freedom to do what I want," she stated. Several years earlier, Ms. Curtis, who worked as a floor supervisor at a hotel, indicated that Ebony would attend a Catholic high school. She hoped that her daughter would aspire to get a position in the medical field because of her "great interest in science." Nonetheless, Ebony struggled with Earth Science during the first marking period of the school year and dropped the class.

Taylor Luke, a sophomore in a computer science program, had ambitions of moving to Atlanta, Georgia after attending a historical Black college. Although she lived with her grandmother, who was originally from the state of Florida, she had other relatives in Georgia that she had visited and had enjoyed the weather. Ms. Luke was divorced and worked as a personal care aid. She was very supportive of Taylor's decision to pursue a career in computer technology and had encouraged her in that area. When Taylor was a sixth grader, Ms. Luke thought that she might go into the medical field, but gave her the opportunity to make her own decision. Ms. Luke, however, expressed concern that her granddaughter not be employed in the service industry. A cheerleader at her high school, Taylor enjoyed watching television videos and talking on the telephone. She was aware of her grandmother's disapproval regarding videos, but listened to them when she could. In 1992, Ms. Luke indicated that she did not approve of the music videos and banned that channel in her home.

Taylor held a 62.0% average for the first marking period, in comparison to an overall GPA of 84.3% in 1992. She found the high school classes more difficult than elementary classes, but also perceived the teachers as uncaring. She stated, "They [teachers] don't care, they are just there to teach. They are just there to do their job, not be a friend." Although she enjoyed being around her friends and having fun, Taylor realized the importance of high grades. She felt that you have to maintain good grades to get a good job. She also believed that high grades were more important than understanding a subject "because it goes on your report card and it helps you get into college and things like that." One of her short-term goals was to get higher grades; the other was to lose some weight. She found herself working the hardest in Geometry because it was the most difficult; she received a 62% for the first marking period. She worked the least in Physical Education, saying: "I don't like changing clothes and all that."

Kayla Magsby also resided with her grandmother most of the time. Because her mother worked more than one job, she and her younger brother spent most of their school days and weekends with Ms. Magsby. Ms. Magsby, the only participant with a four-year degree, wanted to see her granddaughter receive a terminal degree. She also thought that in order for Kayla to be successful in life, she would need to acquire more than a bachelor's degree. Kayla attended the same high school as Taylor and Talia but was not accepted into the law program. Her classes included: English, Biology, Applied Math, Global Studies, Spanish, Physical Education and Art. She worked the hardest in Applied Math because she found it "easy and fun." In her most difficult class, Global Studies, she worked the least. Her GPA in 1992 was an 87.9%.

Kayla disliked school rules, but liked the teachers, whom she felt held high expectations for her. Nonetheless, there had not been any educators she felt had played a positive significant role in her life and that she would consider a role model or mentor. There also had not been any adults, in general, that she perceived as having a positive influence on her academic performance. Kayla, who has also visited relatives in Atlanta, aspired to attend a college in Georgia and remain there afterward to pursue a career.

She had been tap dancing for a number of years and Ms. Magsby thought that her granddaughter should enroll in a school for the Performing Arts. She had taken dance privately, but it had to be discontinued. Because of her dance experience and the fact that many of her cousins attended a school for the Performing Arts, Ms. Magsby thought that it would also be good for Kayla. However, she ended up in a traditional high school.

Shante Nichols attended the same vocational high school as Ebony and was enrolled in the Career Academy Program. Shante did not want to be in this program. Her first choice was CAD/CAM (Computer Assisted Design/Computer Assisted Machinery). In that program, students learn robotic construction, machine operation, hydraulics, electronics, programming, operation and repairs. However, the program was full and she was placed in the Career Academy Program. Shante did not want to be a computer technician, but thought she would be a nurse. She felt that her experience in Jr. ROTC might lead her to become a nurse in the army. Her mother, a widow who worked in a residential facility as a nurse, had always wanted her daughter to have a career in the medical field.

While Shante found English and Geometry her most difficult classes in 10th grade, she also worked the hardest in these classes. Her first marking period grade point average was an 84% and she came to enjoy Geometry the most because she was finding it easier. She considered herself an average achiever in school, but felt that she did not work as hard as she could in her classes. In 1992 her GPA was 93.8%. Although she perceived that her teachers held high expectations for her, she also thought that they were somewhat unfair in their instructions. The example she gave dealt with a time when some of her classmates were disruptive and her teacher punished the entire class instead of dealing with the individual students.

Shante felt that she had been working toward her goal of going to college and enrolling in a nursing program. She stated that "[I] try to keep my grades up and listen, so I can get into a good college." She considered a "good" college as one somewhere in Georgia. Shante spent hours on the telephone, sometimes talking from 3 p.m. to 11 p.m. on school nights and until 3 a.m. on weekends. She also spent about two hours a day studying, depending on her daily assignments. Similar to Darwin, she was also involved in the Boys' and Girls' Club, an after school tutorial/activity program and a local university program. She considered many of the adults working in the after school program as having positively affected her academic performance.

Talia Temple had been on home instructions at the time of her interview in 1996. She and some other girls were accused of violence toward a teacher. This case was waiting to go to court. Regardless of the current situation, Talia attended a traditional high school and was not enrolled in any magnet or special program. Her ambition was to attend four years of college and become a hairdresser or a nurse. In 1992, her mother felt that her daughter would want to go to college out of state and that she would like to see her become an attorney. She stated, "She [Talia] is going through to college. She already has that set. She's going to Florida State...That is where her grandmother lives." However, Talia planned on staying in Dexter to attend college and start her career because she was already accustomed to that environment.

Although she had a 55% grade point average for the first marking period, compared to her 83.1% GPA in 1992, she was out of school frequently for illness. Her immediate goal was to be able to graduate 10th grade. She found Geography and English the most difficult classes, but worked the hardest in them. And while she found Biology easy, "because there really isn't any work, you just have to dissect a couple of things," she only received a 70% in the class. This, however, was her highest grade for that marking period.

Talia admitted that she thought the best thing about going to school was that it gave her an opportunity to learn about new and different people and to allow her to handle things on her own. She felt that the teachers in high school did not spend enough time with her and other students. She stated, "...the teachers don't really have as much time for me like they did when I was at Mary Street School." She did, however, have a 7th or 8th grade teacher that she felt had a positive impact on her schooling. Also, she included her mother as her role model for her. When asked, "Why your mom?", she responded, "I see things that she has gone through, the way she has struggled to help me keep my grades up...I see how she has to sacrifice."

The last student, **Leon Chimes** now a senior at a parochial high school, was actively applying for college. Leon lived with his mother and 10 year-old sister just several blocks from the elementary school he attended almost four years ago. His older sister, who had her own place, graduated from a private college with a degree in teaching and is now a substitute teacher. Ms. Chimes who is legally separated, is originally from Alabama and is employed as a secretary at one of the local hospitals. She always wanted Leon to attend private school feeling it would provide a good basis for him as he prepared for college. Although, not accepted yet, Leon wants to go to Rochester Institute of Technology and study in the mechanical engineer program. His mother's goals for him in 1992 were for him to receive at least a Bachelor's degree and to possibly go into the medical field. She did state, however, that she would support him in whatever he did, as long as he did a good job.

While Leon was an eighth grader, he maintained a 87.7% grade point average and was reading at a tenth grade reading level in the seventh grade (During the 1991-92 study, standard achievement test scores were only available for their previous year.) His first semester grade point average for the 1995-96 academic year was 73.8%. However, he felt that he was "bombarded by schoolwork" and he did not work as hard as he possibly could in school. Leon's classes included Pre-Calculus, Physics, English and American Government, where he was struggling because he found it "boring."

Table 2: Relationships between academic program and career aspirations.

Name	Parents' Expectation	Students' Aspirations	High School Program
Darwin Carpenter	Medical Field	Physician	Building Trades
Leon Chimes	Medical Field	Mechanical Engineer	College Prep
Ebony Curtis	Medical Field	Pediatrician or Beautician	Career Academy Avionics
Taylor Luke	Medical Field	Computer Technician	Computer Magnet
Kayla Magsby	Not indicated	Attorney	General Education
Shante Nichols	Medical Field	Nurse	Career Academy Avionics
Talia Temple	Attorney	Nurse or Hairdresser	General Education

The Themes. One of the most consistent themes appeared to be the relationship between the students' high school program and their career aspirations. Table 2 shows parents' career expectations, students' aspirations and the type of high school program in which they were enrolled. Many of the parents aspired for their children to hold positions in the medical field or as lawyers. Many of the students, too, aspired to become physicians. Only Leon and Taylor wanted careers outside of the medical fields. Even in the 1992 data regarding 'Occupations desired by parents,' ten parents desired positions in the judicial system, while five desired positions in the medical field. However, based upon the students' high school programs and their grade point averages, many of the students might have found it difficult to get accepted into the colleges in the areas of medicine or law.

Also, while students were considering careers in areas that demanded proficiency in math and science, their grades in math and science were often low to average (See Table 3). Many of these students did not work their hardest in math because they found it difficult and they did not understand the concepts. While science was not mentioned as much as math, in terms of difficulty in class, these students, for the most part, showed below average grades in that subject, as well. Also, many of the students were involved in after school activities and hobbies that were not associated with any of their future goals. Talia found a connection between being a nurse or a hairdresser with her enjoyment of talking on the telephone and socializing. She stated, "...Because the two careers that I want to be in, I'm dealing with people." And Leon, who likewise enjoyed talking on the telephone, playing basketball and attending parties, also was involved in volunteer work at the hospital where his mother was employed. He stated that he enjoyed the partying the best, but felt that the volunteering related to his goal to become a mechanical engineer. He responded as follows, "...It will look good on my [college] application. As far as sports, it helps me maintain a healthy body."

Another emerging theme that became evident from the data is the perception that students held in identifying role models and mentors. When asked if any educators had a positive influence on their academic performance, three of the students named their elementary teachers. These teachers "took time out when they [students] really need it" recalled Darwin. Talia talked about an elementary teacher helping her with Reading and Spelling. Taylor described her 8th grade teacher as someone who treated "...us like we were her daughters." Neither Ebony nor Kayla could identify any educators who had a positive effect on their academic performance. As mentioned earlier, they both felt teachers did not care about students.

Leon and Shante named individuals who worked outside of their school. Leon also praised his African American female elementary principal.

Table 3:   Math and Science Grades in Relationship to Class(es) Worked Hardest and Least In

Name	Grades[4]	Class(es) worked hardest	Class(es) worked least
Darwin Carpenter Biology Algebra	 66% 55%	 Algebra	 None
Leon Chimes Physics Pre calculus	 76% 72%	Physics Pre calculus	 Am. History
Ebony Curtis Earth Science Algebra	 65% 79%	 Global Studies Algebra	 English
Taylor Luke Biology Geometry	 50% 62%	 Geometry	 None
Kayla Magsby Biology Applied Math	 65% 90%	 Applied Math	 Global Studies
Shante Nichols Physics Geometry	 85% 86%	English Global Studies	 Geometry
Talia Temple Biology Geometry	 50% 50%	Geography English	 Biology

Parents were perceived as role models more than mentors, with the exception of Leon's mother. The children described them as reliable, intelligent and dedicated. Leon, however, not only saw his mother as a role model, but also as "a mentor at home" and "...constantly keeps

---

[4] A T-test was run indicating that there is not significant difference between the grades for science and math where $p=0.298$.

on him about making sure his work is done!" The four students, who did not consider their mother or grandmother as role models, stated that they had no role model or their role model was a sports figure. A 'role model' was defined to the children as a person you look up to, someone you respect. Other than Leon, none of the students identified any adult as a mentor. Besides his mother, Leon spoke highly of the coordinator of the university program, responding "...she is like a mentor. She provides resources for me, tutoring, takes me to plays and gives me rides. Whatever I need, basically."

DISCUSSION AND IMPLICATIONS
The data analyzed has led me to some preliminary observations. These observations focus on students' high school placement and counseling, student perceptions of the role of teachers, and students' perceptions of the role of parents in their education. All of the parents held high expectations of their children for high school. They expected that they would be enrolled in a college prep program or at least a program that would foster skills required of becoming a physician or lawyer. However, only two of the eight children in this study were not enrolled in a vocational track program. What happened to those aspirations? Why is it that are these students began their schooling as successful students, but most will be struggling to graduate? When did they change? According to Ms. Carpenter, she felt that the vocational school was better for her son because many of his friends were not there.

   The students, however, discussed that they just "ended up" in this particular track. Were their voices unheard? Was their parents a part of process? How much were the parents encouraged to provide input when counselors were assigning classes? Also, how much do parents and children, especially from low-income environments, understand the importance of being placed on "the right track"? Do they realize that these tracks are designed to lead children to college or discourage them along the way? How knowledgeable are counselors of the trends in higher education? There have been multitudes of research that discuss how positive relationships between schools, parents and communities can only aid with the academic performance of students. But while schools claim to encourage parental involvement, how many of these schools really encourage input from parents and provide "parent friendly" information regarding the curriculum, tracking and college? It would also appear that there needs to be better two-way communications between guidance counselors and parents, the kind of communication that addresses expectations versus aspirations and realities versus idealistic goals. It would appear that parent involvement must be encouraged by the schools to include more than just classroom volunteers and field trip chaperones.

Another observation that stemmed from the students was their negative portrayal of their teachers. A learning environment that implies that teachers are perceived as uncaring and holding low expectations can not be very productive. In actuality, it can be counterproductive. Urban youth continue to be stigmatized as "lackadaisical," unmotivated," and "emotionally unstable" (Schultz, Neyhart and Reck, 1996). How are teachers being held accountable for their counterproductive attitudes? How do we ensure that student' self-esteem are solid enough to overcome the negative attitudes of educators that may encounter? Could this be a "clash of cultures" (Cushner, et al., 1996) that exists between educators and our children? And if so, how can we change it? How much of the academic success can be contributed to the elementary school environment. For example, their elementary school population was predominately African American. It was a neighborhood school where students were familiar with the community and its surroundings. The school also had a significant number of African American role models--including an African American female principal, teachers and support staff. According to Hale-Benson (1989) because most teachers instill middle class values, most "Black children are particularly at risk for being overlooked because of a non-recognition of their culture and the strengths that emerge from that culture (91)".

Spindler (1963) discussed "communication codes" that are part of our educational environment, as well as society-at-large. These codes are like guidelines or benchmarks that are embedded in the mindset of many educators. For example, the fact that middle-class teachers give more attention to middle-class children and perceive them as the most "talented and ambitious" in their classrooms. This was a definite obstacle for children from lower socioeconomic status backgrounds. And our children continue through school, it will become more difficult, if not impossible "to give evidence of their intelligence in terms of the limited codes that teachers use for evaluating children" (Hale-Benson, 1989, p. 91).

Finally, while students indicated that many of their parents were their role models, they did not portray them as mentors -- someone to guide them toward their academic and/or professional dreams. Like my own parents, most of the parents in this study did not attend college and many did not complete high school. However, if parents are unable to directly provide the resources necessary for their children to aspire "the good life," they must be able to provide those resources indirectly. While Darwin and his mother aspired for him to be in the medical field, they had never talked to someone in the medical field, investigated the cost of college, or even read materials on this field. However, students also need to be responsible for their own academic achievement, and parents as well as other significant adults, must recognize this responsibility and communicate it to the children (Parham and Parham, 1989).

I believe that most parents want their children to have a better life than their own (more money, better housing, better cars, etc.), however, many parents and children hold unrealistic goals. For example, Lynn Rock, a student interviewed but not compared with the other students academic grades because her records were not available; defined a high achiever as her aunt because she had completed high school, was a registered nurse, and "has this gorgeous house, with three cars." Her immediate goal was to get her own apartment, get out of her grandmother's house, and get a job. Living with her mother was not an option and she felt that she could make it on her own at the age of thirteen. Many low-income parents do not know what is required of their children to fulfill that role and the expense that is associated with it. These parents have not been exposed to the multitude of career choices. By default, many parents rely on the education system to perform these services.

But isn't that what the educational system is suppose to be doing--providing a learning environment where all children can learn, not just those that represent the values and beliefs of mainstream society? There is a continued increase in white, middle class students and a consistent decline of African American students enrolled in teacher education programs across colleges and universities nationwide (Cushner, et al., 1996; Holms and Nations Johnson, 1994; Shultz, Neyhart and Reck, 1996; Zimpher, 1989). How will this trend affect the success of African American and lower class students in the new millennium? What strategies or prescriptions can be offered to increase the chances of our children becoming successful in schools and in life? My list is in no way exhaustive, but it represents suggestions that touch upon many of the stakeholders that will have a significant (directly or indirectly) affect on students.

School Districts: While administrators, teachers, support staff are primarily hired based upon their knowledge, skills and performance, consideration should also be given to their experience working in culturally diverse settings. Or prospective educators must be willing to exhibit high expectations for all students, regardless of color and socioeconomic status. This willingness of educators could easily be determined through a selection process that reflects the needs of all students. Teachers who are already established in the district, should be required to attend professional development sessions that will enable them to be more sensitive to the needs of diverse students, as well as introduce them to instructional methods to help ensure academic success of these students. Finally, while some school districts have incorporated site based management teams that involve input and decisions from teachers, parents, local businesses and other community-based organization; many schools districts have still not bought into this collaborative model. The more that schools, communities, parents and other stakeholders work collaboratively, the better chance students will have to succeed academically.

1. Colleges of Education. Research has indicated that, especially due to the background of prospective teachers, pre-service teachers need to graduate with the necessary skills to teach all students from diverse backgrounds and in diverse settings. Many colleges of education do not even require students to enroll in classes on multicultural education or diversity to all of their students. While offering multicultural courses is an avenue to make students aware and sensitive to the issues of diverse students, it is by far not the only one. Haberman (1994), Gomez (1996) and McCormick (1990) for example, encouraged a combination of methods that colleges of education should incorporate in their elementary and secondary programs. These methods include coursework, field placement in urban areas, allowing students to be also involved in the communities in which they are placed, and the opportunity to reflect upon these experiences.

2. Parents and caregivers. In our society, there is a disproportionate number of poor families that are African American and Hispanic American families. Most families, regardless of the socio-economic status, want to be a part of the educative process of their children. However, many need suggestions from teachers and counselors to help guide them in this endeavor. Therefore, parents and caregivers must be willing to communicate with schools and teachers on things they can do to assist them. While schools must connect with the community and parents, so must

parents connect with the schools and develop an ownership that their children will adopt. Hopefully, schools will begin to make that transition a smooth one for parents.

With school districts being more conscious and sensitive regarding the types of teachers, counselors and staff they employ, schools of education need to provide pre-service teachers with the necessary tools for teaching all students. Likewise, parents need to be willing to continue helping their children (even by seeking advice from teachers and counselors). These efforts will enhance our student's opportunities for achieving their goals both in school and in life.

REFERENCES

Bureau of the Census. 1965. *Population and Housing, Summary Tape File 3A.* Washington, DC: U.S. Department of Commerce, 1990.

Bell, Robert. "Lower Class Negro Mothers Aspirations for their Children." *Social Forces* 42: 493-500.

Chilman, Catherine. 1988. "Never-married, Single, Adolescent Parents." In *Variant Family Forms*, edited by C. Chilman, E. Nunally and F. Cos. London: Sage.

Clark, Reginald M. 1983. *Family Life and School Achievement: Why Poor Black Children Succeed or Fail.* Chicago: University of Chicago Press.

Cushner, Kenneth, McClelland, Averil, & Safford, Philip. 1996. *Human Diversity in Education: An Integrative Approach.* NY: McGraw-Hill Companies, Inc.

Della Fave, L. Richard. 1974. "Success Values: Are they Universal or Class-Differential?" *American Journal of Sociology* 80: 153-169.

Dole, Arthur. A. "Aspirations of Blacks and Whites for their Children." *Vocational Guidance Quarterly* 22 (1973): 24-31.

Davies, Don. 1988. *Poor Parents, Teachers and the School: Comments about Practice, Policy and Research.* ERIC Document No. ED 308 574.

Epstein, Joyce. 1988. "How do we Improve Programs for Parent Involvement?" *Educational Horizons* 66: 58-59.

Erickson, Frederick. 1973. "What Makes School Ethnography 'Ethnographic'?" *Council on Anthropology and Education Newsletter* 4: 10-19.

Fetterman, David. 1994. "Ethnography in Educational Research: The Dynamics of Diffusion." *Educational Research* 51: 509-541.

Finn, Jeremy and Owings, Maria. 1994. "Family Structure and School Performance in Eighth Grade." *Journal of Research and Development in Education* 27: 176-187.

Goldenberg, Claude and Gallimore, Ronald. 1991. "Local Knowledge, Research Knowledge, and Educational Change: A Case of Early Spanish Reading Improvements." *Educational Researcher* 20: 2-14.

Gomez, Mary. 1996. "Prospective Teachers' perspectives on Teaching Other People's Children." In *Currents of Reform in Preservice Teacher Education, Chapter 6*, edited by K. Zeichner, S. Mulnick, and M. Gomez. New York: Teachers College, Columbia University.

Guiang, Evelyn. 1980. *The Relationship between Home Environment and Reading Achievement among Filipino-American Grade Three and Grade Five Pupils.* Ph.D. diss., New York University.

Guttmann, Joseph, Geva, N., & Gefen. S. "Teachers' and School Children's Stereotypic Perceptions of the Child of Divorce." *American Educational Research Journal* 25 (1988): 555-571.

Haberman, Martin. 1994. "Preparing Teachers for the Real World of Urban Schools." *Educational Forum* 58: 162-168.

Hardy, Michael and Crow Graham. 1991. "Introduction." In *Lone Parenthood: Coping with Constraints and Making Opportunities,* edited by M. Hardey and G. Crow. NY: Harvester Wheatsheaf.

Hale-Benson, Janice. 1989. "The School Learning Environment and Academic Success." In *Black Students: Psychosocial Issues and Academic Achievement,* edited by G. L Berry and J. K. Asamen. Newbury Park, CA: Sage Publications, Inc.

Hare, Bruce. 1987. "Structural Inequality and the Endangered Status of Black Youth." *Journal of Negro Education* 56: 100-110.

Haskey, John. 1991. "Lone Parenthood and Demographic Change." *In Lone Parenthood: Coping with Constraints and Making Opportunities,* edited by M. Hardey and G. Crow. New York: Harvester Wheatsheaf.

Henderson, Anne. T. & Berla, Nancy. (Ed.). 1994. *A New Generation of Evidence: The Family is Critical to Student Achievement.* Washington, DC: National Committee for Citizens in Education.

Hetherington, E. Mavis, Cox, M., & Cox, R. 1978. "The Aftermath of Divorce." In *Mother-Child, Father-Child Relations*, edited by J. Stevens and M. Mathews. Washington, DC: National Association for Education of Young Children.

Holms, Gunilla, & Nations Johnson, Lynn. 1994. "Shaping Cultural Partnerships: The Readiness of Preservice Teachers to Teach in Culturally Diverse Classrooms. In *Partnerships in Education: Teacher Education Yearbook II, Chapter 4*, edited by M. O'Hair and S. Odell. Fort Worth, IN: Harcourt Brace College Publishers.

Keith, Timothy, Reimers, Thomas, Fehrman, P, Pottebaum, S., and Aubrey, L. 1986. "Parental Involvement, Homework, and T.V. Time: Direct and Indirect Effects on High School Achievement." *Journal of Educational Psychology* 78: 378-380.

Lalyre, Yvonne. 1989. *Home Environment and the Achievement of Hispanics in Mathematics: Six Urban Case Studies*. Ph.D. diss., Boston University.

Leahy, Alice. 1936. *The Measurement of Urban Home Environments*. Minneapolis, MN: University of Minnesota Press.

LeCompte, Margaret. & Goetz, Judith. 1982. "Problems of Reliability and Validity in Ethnographic Research." *Review of Educational Research* 52: 31-60.

Lee, Courtland. 1984. "An Investigation of Psychosocial Variables Related to Academic Success for Rural Black Adolescents." *Journal of Negro Education* 53: 424-434.

Lomotey, Kofi. 1989. *African American Principals: School Leadership and Success*. New York: Greenwood Press.

Macintyre, Sally. *Single and Pregnant*. 1997. London: Croom Helm.

Marjoribanks, Kevin. 1995. "Parents' Involvement in Learning as an Opportunity Structure: A Model for Evaluation. *Studies in Educational Evaluation* 21: 73-83.

Mark, Dianne L. H. 1993. *High Achieving African American Children in Low-Income Single Parent Families: The Home Learning Environment*. Ph.D. diss., State University of New York at Buffalo.

Marotz-Baden, Ramona. & Tallman, Irving. 1978. "Parental Aspirations and Expectations for Daughters and Sons: A Comparative Analysis." *Adolescence* 13: 251-268.

Matthew-Juarez, P. 1982. *The Effects of Family Backgrounds on the Educational Outcome of Black Teenagers in Worchester, Massachusetts.* University Microfilm International, Ann Arbor, Michigan.

McCormick, Theresa. 1990. "Collaboration Works! Preparing Teachers for Urban Realities." *Contemporary Education* 61: 129-134.

Morris, Delores. 1992. "African American Students and their Families." In *Contemporary Families: A Handbook for School Professionals*, edited by M. E. Procidano and C. B. Fisher. New York: Teachers College Press.

Nation's School Losing Ground, Reports Show: Youth Lagging Behind in Math, Reading and Science. *Buffalo News* (Sept. 1991): p. 1.

Norman-Jackson, Jacquelyn. 1982. "Family Interactions, Language Development and Primary Reading Achievement of Black Children in Families of Low Income." *Child Development* 53: 349-358.

Oakes, Jeannie. 1988. "Tracking: Can Schools Take a Different Route?" *NEA Today* 6: 41-47.

Ogbu, John. 1986. "The Consequences of the American Caste System." In *The School Achievement of Minority Children*, edited by U. Neisser. New Jersey: Lawrence Elbaum.

Ortiz, Vilma. 1986. "Reading Activities and Reading Proficiency among Hispanic, Black and White Students." *American Journal of Education* 95: 58-76.

Page, Robert. 1984. *Stigma.* London: Routledge and Kegan Paul.

Parham, William & Parham Thomas. 1989. "The Community and Academic Achievement." In *Black Students: Psychosocial Issues and Academic Achievement*, edited by G. L Berry and J. K. Asamen. Newbury Park, CA: Sage Publications, Inc.

Peters, M. and deFord, C. 1986. "The Solo Mother." In *The Black Family: Essays and Studies*, edited by R. Staples. Belmont, CA: Wadsworth Publishing.

Powell, Gloria. 1989. "Defining Self-Concept as a Dimension of Academic Achievement for Inner City Youth." In *Black Students: Psychosocial Issues and Academic Achievement*, edited by G. L. Berry and J. K. Asamen. Newbury Park, CA: Sage Publications.

Schultz, Eileen, Neyhart, T. Kelley, & Reck, U. Mae. 1996. "Swimming Against the Tide: A Study of Prospective Teachers' Attitudes Regarding Cultural Diversity and Urban Teaching." *The Western Journal of Black Studies* 20: 1-7.

Sell, Jane. 1973. *The Relationship between Black Mothers' Attitudes toward Sex Roles and their Educational Aspirations and Expectations for their Daughters.* (ERIC Document Reproduction Service No. ED 078 996).

Shields, Portia, Gordon, J., and Dupree, D. 1983 "Influence of Parent Practices upon Reading Achievement of Good and Poor Readers." *Journal of Negro Education* 52: 436-445.

Slaughter, Diana and Epps, Edgar. 1987. "The Environment and Academic Achievement of Blank American Children and Youth: An Overview." *The Journal of Negro Education* 56: 3-20.

Solorzano, Daniel. 1992. "An Exploratory Analysis of the Effects of Race, Class, and Gender on Student and Parent Mobility Aspirations." *The Journal of Negro Education* 61: 30-44.

Soto, Lourdes. 1992. *Hispanic Families as Learning Environment for Young Children.* (ERIC Document Reproduction Service No. ED 344 709).

Spradley, James. 1979. *The Ethnographic Interview.* New York: Holt, Rinehart & Winston.

Spindler, George. 1963. "The Transmission of American Culture." In *Education and Culture*, edited by G. Spindler. New York: Holt, Rinehart & Winston.

Stevens, Floraline. 1993. "Applying an Opportunity-to-Learn Conceptual Framework to the Investigation of the Effects of Teaching Practices via Secondary Analysis of Multiple-Case-Study Summary Data." *Journal of Negro Education* 62: 232-248.

Voelkl, Kristin. 1993. "Academic Achievement and Expectations among African American Students." *Journal of Research and Development in Education* 27: 42-55.

White, Karl. 1982. "The Relationship between Socioeconomic Status and Academic Achievement." *Psychological Bulletin* 91: 461-481.

Wolcott, Harry. 1975. "Criteria for an Ethnographic Approach to Research in School." *Human Organization* 34: 111-127.

Zimpher, Nancy.   1989. "The RATE Project: A Profile of Teacher
     Education Students." *Journal of Teacher Education* 40: 27-
     30.

2. Family Involvement: Learning from Secondary Schools in the Texas Borderland

Michelle D. Young

A growing body of evidence has emerged suggesting that involving parents involved in the educational process enhances school success. As a result, educators and educational policy makers have begun shifting and broadening the focus of their search for new ideas and resources to include family members. Educational researchers have also given increased emphasis to the role of the family in education. Thus far, however, family involvement research has not fully explored how race, ethnicity, and cultural factors influence the expression of parental involvement in different community contexts. Given the increasing number of Mexican-American families in such states as Texas, New Mexico, Arizona, and California, it is important that the interpretations, expectations, and involvement experiences of these families as well as those of the school staff who work with them are considered carefully. Doing so will contribute greatly to understanding the role of Mexican-American parents in the educational process. Similarly, while the involvement of parents at the elementary level is well documented, few have given careful consideration to the involvement of parents in secondary schools.

Secondary schools differ from elementary schools in a number of important ways, and one result of these differences is the dramatic change in the nature of parental involvement. This paper addresses both of these heretofore neglected areas and provides a portrait of the involvement of Mexican-American parents in secondary schools located along the Texas-Mexico border.

This study was conducted as part of the Effective Border Schools Research and Development Initiative (EBSRDI), a collaborative project between the University of Texas and the Region 1 Service Center and School Districts of Texas. The EBSRDI attempts to identify the best educational practices used in borderland schools that contribute to high achievement among students. This particular study is directed toward strengthening parental involvement in school communities where cultural and linguistic diversity, poverty, mobility, and lack of English proficiency present challenges to school staff and parents. It examines the ways in which successful schools--particularly those enrolling predominantly Mexican-American students from poor, limited English proficient, non-English speaking, and/or migrant backgrounds--develop and sustain meaningful parental involvement.

The principal assumption guiding this study is that effective border schools have developed contextually specific means for reaching out to families, for gaining their support and involvement, and in forming partnerships that support the education of children. The study proceeded through a number of steps. The first phase involved an extensive review of the literature. On the basis of this review and the intent of the study, a design for the field research was developed and research and interview questions were generated and revised. During this time, schools were selected to be included in the study and initial contact was made. Pilot studies were then undertaken in two of the selected schools, and based on the data collected through this effort, revisions were made to the interview protocols. Subsequently, each of the focus schools were visited to make observations and interview teachers, administrators, other school staff members, and parents. Following the field work stage, teams began the process of data analysis, interpretation, and writing.

Research Methods and Design

The study was primarily qualitative in nature. Quantitative research approaches are limited in their ability to cope with the complexities of relationships and interactions (Bogdan & Biklen, 1992; Lincoln & Guba, 1985; Patton, 1990). Consequently, researchers have suggested that qualitative methods be used to enhance and expand the existing knowledge base, particularly for meeting the needs of linguistically and culturally diverse populations (Anderson, 1993; Baker, 1983; Bogdan & Biklen, 1992; Marín & Marín, 1991). The process is cyclical in nature, juxtaposing personal observation and interviews combined with theory and reflection (Bogdan & Biklen, 1992; Patton, 1990).

Qualitative research methods enable the researcher to study a number of phenomena in order to understand individual actors' perceptions of events that take place in their school and community (Bogdan & Biklen, 1992). Relevant to the purpose of this study, researchers can (a) examine the activities and types of interactions that occur in naturally occurring and integrated community contexts; (b) describe the daily realities and experiences of parents in various areas of the school; (c) improve the validity of programs in the school; and (d) develop practices that foster the involvement of parents and the academic achievement of linguistically and culturally diverse students.

To ensure robustness in the results of the study, a variety of research methods and data sources were utilized. In addition to the extensive literature review, these included: 1) a survey component targeting best practices used by teachers to develop and sustain family involvement and family school partnerships; 2) campus site visits focusing on understanding the nature of parental involvement and the activities that support involvement; 3) developing an overall representation of school culture, operation and climate; and 4) review of school and district documents concerning parental involvement.

The Findings
Parent involvement, as a practice and a concept, is affect by a multitude of complex phenomena. These aspects include grade level, practices, belief systems, culture, feelings, relationships, resources, and values. Thus, each individual, each school, and each community is likely to have a distinct understanding of parental involvement, a unique way of encouraging involvement or being involved, and a diverse set of rationales that connote why they feel involvement is or is not important. Accordingly, findings reveal obvious commonalties, contradictions, and uniqueness' among the parents, school staff, and

parental involvement programs in the borderland schools. Through the data analysis process, answers to three basic questions emerged. These answers reflected how members of these school communities conceptualize and experience parental involvement, why they value it, and what it looks like in practice.

The remainder of this paper is divided into three sections. The first provides a description of the nature of parental involvement in the borderland schools included in the study. Specifically, how parental involvement is viewed and why it is valued. The second section describes the practices that facilitate parental involvement in these schools. The final section discusses how the findings from this study relate to the existing research on parental involvement.

Views of Parental Involvement

Parent involvement in borderland school communities often includes the participation of the extended family and sometimes even neighbors and friends who share a concern for the welfare for a particular student. Thus, this discussion uses concepts of parent and family interchangeably inclusive of all individuals within the family circle who advocate for the welfare of the student. Parental involvement is a rather complicated concept. There is no agreed upon definition that includes or excludes all the elements asserted by different actors. Similarly, there is a lack of agreement regarding the reasons for supporting and/or valuing involvement. These differences in perspective and opinion are most clearly represented by two groups: parents and teachers. For example, in this study, parents tend to emphasize more informal involvement activities. When formal activities are mentioned, the reasons given tend to differ from those provided by school staff. For instance, parent rationales are typically less tangible and focus primarily on relationship and environmental factors. In this section, we present the views of both parents and school staff concerning what they believe parental involvement is, and why they believe it is important.

Parental Views

Similar to the elementary level, there are two general domains into which participants categorize involvement: formal or informal. However, unlike the elementary level, informal activities are of greater concern. This focus on informal involvement is related to at least four pertinent factors. At the secondary level, fewer opportunities are available to parents to become meaningfully involved at the school. Similarly, as children grow older, mothers are more likely to seek employment and, thus, have difficulty attending meetings sponsored by the school, especially during the day. Further, in many of the communities that were visited, public transportation systems are nonexistent for parents to use to get to the school. Many of the families rely on a single automobile, and it is primarily used by the father. The majority of the mothers who do participate at the school either walk, or take taxicabs to get there. Therefore, participating in volunteer work at the school requires inordinate effort on the part of many parents. Finally, many parents limit the amount of contact they have with the school because they feel their children wish them to.

Interviews became animated when mothers began to talk about the informal things they did for their children. Parents described practices such as getting to know their children's friends, instilling cultural values, monitoring homework, obtaining tutorial assistance, and talking with children about school and their futures. Another prevalent activity that emerged from the interviews was the importance of teaching their children how to be responsible for themselves and their actions. For example, one mother talked of instilling the value of "owning up to mistakes" and "assuming responsibility for consequences." Another important component for mothers is the importance of maintaining a "home" for their families. It is important for these mothers to be at home when their children are dismissed from school. Safety is an issue, but more important is the value placed on care giving. Their roles as mothers and their everyday activities are viewed as important aspects in supporting school success.

Regardless of the barriers to formal involvement, the parents that were interviewed are all engaged in some volunteer capacity in the schools. They are responsible for a diverse array of activities, including monitoring the hall ways, volunteering in the special education classroom, making copies, decorations, or classroom materials in the parent centers, and holding various leadership positions. When asked why they are involved, parents listed a number of reasons. These include: supporting the development of their children, building and strengthening relationships with teachers and other parents, enhancing the school environment, maintaining relationships with their children, providing good role models for their children, and enriching their own lives.

Supporting the Development of their Children

All parents described their involvement as expressions of concern, love, or as a means for being watchful over their children. One mother shared a story of how she overcame her own fear of the school and teachers out of love for her children. She was intimidated by the professional nature of the school and her children's teachers but recognized the importance of being involved as a way to help her own children. With the support of the parent specialist, this mother has managed to overcome her fears.

About half of the parents said they are involved as school volunteers because they are concerned about their children's academic progress. They viewed involvement as a way to monitor their children's school progress and to establish a working relationship with teachers. For example, one parent, whose son is in special education, sees her involvement as a way to make sure that teachers read his file, know his capabilities, and understand that she will be watching out for his best interest.

> I could tell at home he was having a hard time with his homework, and I requested an ARD meeting to have him tested. . . . I have to say that years back, I met with a brick wall. They didn't want to let him be tested; I kept fighting it and finally got it done. That's how I became involved. I knew that he needed all the help he could get, so it meant me really being involved. I want him to learn as much as he possibly can. - *Parent at Porfirio Diaz High School.*

Parents feel it is important to understand what is going on at the school and in the classroom, as well as to understand how their children are faring academically. Another parent indicated that she became involved at her daughter's middle school when she recognized that certain things were not being done to her satisfaction.

> They call me the "Watchdog of Francisco Villa." . . . My concern was that if my child is having problems the first day, I want to know right away. If you let me know and I don't care then fine, you have done your job. But if I am, then I can turn that kid around and you wont have to deal with future grief and my

child will make a better grade.   - *Parent at*
Francisco Villa Middle School

Many of the parents stated that it is their responsibility to ensure the
school is doing everything possible for their children. Similarly,
parents feel obligated to do whatever they can for their children. In
fact, many parents first initiate involvement based on a realization that
something is wrong or might go wrong. Thus, in addition to
cooperating with the school and ensuring teachers are doing all that
they can, parents are also taking part in their children's development.
As mentioned above, some parents teach their children to respect
themselves and others and to take responsibility for their actions.
Others also ensure their adolescents know the value of a dollar and
how to behave in public. Further, some parents teach their children
about their cultural heritage. According to one group of mothers, the
annual Folklorico dancing exhibitions provided a perfect opportunity
for sharing their culture. Mothers are involved in sewing costumes,
making braids, and decorating. As they perform these activities, they
often find themselves telling stories about their family's history and
culture. Thus, both formal and informal activities are geared toward
the development of their children.

Building and Strengthening Relationships
The building of relationships with other parents and teachers as well
as the strengthening of these relationships once established was also
identified as an important part of parental involvement. By
establishing personal relationships with teachers and other school staff
members, such as the parent specialist, as well as by attending
meetings and becoming involved in committees, some parents are able
to stay "on top of things."

> I want them to call me up and let me know--don't be
> afraid to call me at home, don't be afraid to call me
> at work to tell me she [my daughter] is not doing
> what she should be doing. -Parent from Porfirio Diaz
> High School
> I want to know why she [my daughter] is not doing
> well so I get acquainted with the teachers. *-Parent*
> *from Porfirio Diaz High School*

The parents value relationships with teachers because they want to prevent problems from becoming major difficulties. Parents feel their presence is perceived by the teachers as caring. "The teachers know you care." Further, having working relationships with teachers provides opportunities for parents and teachers to interact as a team.

> Teachers are easier to work with when you give them positive feedback. - *Parent from Francisco Villa Middle School*

One parent indicated that she makes certain her child's teachers know they have her support.

> "I'm here to support you as a teacher" and if [I] do have any problems, or see that there might be a problem, get both sides of the story, not just your child's - *Parent from Porfirio Diaz High School*

Parents also felt that developing relationships with teachers provides them with an opportunity to demonstrate that they value education. The close working relationships facilitate their efforts to support the school and to stay informed about what activities are taking place at the school. Further, such relationships provide them access to information regarding what their children are learning and what is going on in their children's lives during the day. Being familiar with their children's social group and daily activities is particularly important to parents at the secondary level.

In an effort to describe how important relationships between the home and school are for her, one mother revealed a very personal story. Her daughter, a middle school student, had a traumatic experience at school. This young girl had become so afraid of going to school that she had fainted, gone into convulsions, and had an anxiety attack. The mother had no idea what to do. At first she let her daughter stay home, but she later sought help from the school when a judge threatened to jail her for not meeting the compulsory school laws. The mother has forged a strong partnership with school staff in an effort to help her daughter. She volunteers in the school daily and has made an arrangement with her daughter's teachers and the administration for dealing with the anxiety. When her daughter begins to experience anxiety, she finds her mother, touches her, and then returns to class. Since the crisis brought the mother into the school, she had gained a strong sense of belonging and felt that she made a great contribution to both her daughter's life and the life of the school.

Parents also establish relationships and information networks with other parents. Some of the parents who volunteer at the school use their involvement as opportunities not only to see their children and help the teachers, but also to exchange information and make friends. For example, while cutting out decorations for the school hall way, several mothers were also discussing issues concerning adolescent development and child rearing. For Spanish speaking parents, there is another advantage to having a parent network. These networks provide them with access to bilingual persons who can translate rather than simply relay information to them.

In sum, participation is seen as a means for nurturing relationships with the different people who parents perceived could help their children do well in school. Relationships with teachers improve communication and ensure that parents have access to information regarding their children, and relationships with other parents provide them with access to information about adolescent development, school and community events, and other important facts.

Enhancing the School Environment

Parents stressed the positive effects they can have on the school environment. For example, a group of middle school volunteers described their involvement as an important contribution to keeping the school halls orderly and safer for students because they are "extra eyes" for teachers. Their presence in the school halls and cafeteria also allowed them the opportunity to get to know the students enrolled in the school. These parents consider their involvement at the school as contributing to the creation of a safer learning environments for students.

The school environment is also an important factor in encouraging parental involvement. Parents mentioned that a key to creating a welcoming environment is having school personnel acknowledge parents' presence when they are on campus, walking down the halls, or monitoring the cafeteria. For example, parents spoke about how pleasant it feels to have school staff greet them and introduce them to others.

> They make time to greet you and it makes you feel so
> much better. - *Parent at Porfirio Diaz High School*

Schools that have developed effective relationships with parents acknowledge their presence and work, treat them respectfully, and make them feel at home.

Another important contribution of a welcoming and safe school environment involves the schools' sensitivity to the circumstances of non-English speakers. Several mothers described how the cultural environment changes for them at school when only English is spoken. The fear that "no one will understand them" was related to the larger context for these mothers. For example, a bureaucracy that they hardly understand, school buildings that sometimes house over a thousand children and are by necessity large physical structures, teachers that may or may not acknowledge or greet them, and school offices that often have an officious nature. In those schools where efforts to build relationships with parents are well developed, school staffs have attempted to create parent-friendly environments, and non-English speaking parents have supportive communication networks to exchange information and develop social relationships.

Overall, the parents spoke positively of schools and described feeling part of the staff, being greeted and acknowledged by everyone, having their concerns listened to, and communicating well with everyone. The schools are seen as places where they can seek support and assistance, where people are amiable and approachable with smiles on their faces, a sense of humor, and where an openness to their participation are appreciated. Parent involvement in the school seems to both support and depend upon this environment.

Maintaining relationships between parents and their children
Parental involvement decreases dramatically as students move from elementary through secondary school. Several factors contribute to this decline. For example, the number of teachers per child increases making it difficult for parents to stay abreast of each of their child's classes. Similarly, the number of students per teacher increases dramatically, making it difficult for teachers to reach out to each individual parent. Thus, opportunities for informal encounters decrease as students moved into the upper grades, due to both structural and social constraints. According to one teacher, "it becomes harder because each teacher has so many students to keep up with. It is harder to get to know the families."

Parents at the high school level often expressed disappointment in not being involved to the same degree and with equal enthusiasm at the high school as had been their experience at the elementary school. One of the reasons given for decreased levels of interaction between parents and teachers was the lack of opportunity available to parents of secondary students to become meaningful involved. They asserted that parental involvement activities should be designed that allowed increased interaction between the home and school. Parents also communicated a desire for a clearly defined purpose for coming to school. As one mother put it: "Parents want a mission." "Just tell us what we can do." They argued that a lack of purpose for organizations such as the Parent Teacher Association (PTA) and parental involvement in general contributes to low attendance and involvement.

> The PTA does not have a purpose. I am here a great
> deal. I have a reason to be here. I am a member of
> site-based, and I am a member of the gifted parents
> PTA. But I don't feel like it matters. It doesn't' feel
> meaningful. - *Mother from Madero Middle School*

Another mother agreed. She feels that she is at school a lot but does not feel as if her presence makes much difference. She knows her daughter's teachers and, thus, is able to keep up with her daughter's progress, but she often feels she should be doing more. The two women together argued that many parents do not come to school because they are uncomfortable being there without a purpose. These parents seemed to be saying that if teachers and school people could provide a mission or a reason for coming to school, more would come.

> You have to give them [parents] an idea of what they
> can do. They aren't just going to come to school.
> There has to be a purpose. This is especially true for
> working parents who have little free time. You can't
> just tell your boss "I'm just going to go up to the
> school." What are you going to do with them once
> they are here? If you don't know they are gonna ask
> "why are we here?" Parents don't know what to do.
> If you would give them a task, they would be here.
> Personally, I don't know how to help out. - *Mother
> from Madero Middle School*

Moreover, students spend more time with peers and less time with family members.   Some adolescents try to assert themselves as individuals, but social norms typically discourage students from involving parents in their social lives.   The parents we spoke to in the study are cognizant of these patterns.   They often complain that as children grow older they do not want their parents around.   Students tell them they are embarrassed by their parents' presence.   It was asserted that this was more of a problem for parents who were not very involved when their children were younger   One young man told his mother: "Don't come to the classroom. You'll embarrass me."   Thus, maintaining relationships is not always easy for parents.

> My daughter gets irritated with my involvement:
> Why do you have to ask so many questions? Why do
> you have to know what I am doing? Why do I have to
> show you my work? - *Mother from Porfirio Diaz HS*

Additionally, as students get older they often discourage their parents from having any contact with the school.   Teachers report that students often fail to give their parents notes that they have sent home and phone messages that they have left.

> A lot of parents complain that their kids tell them
> they don't have homework when they really do, but
> there is really no way to tell. - *Teacher at Francisco
> Villa Middle School*

According to one teacher, when parents are alienated from the school or have infrequent contact, students are more likely to manipulate the situation.

> The thing is that they don't want their parents to, in
> my opinion, come in until its something that they
> don't like--then they want the parents to come in and
> confront the teacher. . . if they feel that the teacher's
> riding them, [they will say] "oh, mom's going to be
> here tomorrow. I'm going to make her come and
> talk to so and so."

In other words, students use the adults to their advantage and the less information either group has of what is going on, the more easily information can become manipulated.   The teacher, quoted above, believes that relationships between parents and teachers serve as a check on student achievement and behavior. Interestingly, one group of parents and teachers indicated that this is more of a problem for boys than for girls. One mother from Madero Middle School made the following comment: "They have an image to keep up." Also, parent presence at the school is often associated with "being in trouble," providing adolescents with yet another reason to discourage parents from coming to school.

> "Mom, they told me you came to the school. What was the problem? Why did you come?" It had nothing to do with you, I would say. - *Mother from Porfirio Diaz High School*

This parent realized that her daughter was associating her presence with being in trouble. To combat this misconception, the parent talked to her daughter and now attempts to be at school and visible as much as possible.

Unlike many of the other parents, one parent stated that while her son protests verbally to her persistent presence at the school, that he actually likes having her around.

> My son sees me more at school and he's at the point where he is embarrassed to be seen around me. He wants to be independent. However, he likes to see me here and the other kids like to see me as well, and I think indirectly he likes that I am here because then I can see what he is doing. - *Mother from Francisco Villa Middle School*

The decrease in involvement at the secondary level is felt to be problematic by some. It was noted that the higher grades might be where involvement is most needed. Parents and teachers seem concerned about the multitude of adversities that many adolescents face. It was asserted that students who are supported by their family will be much better able to cope during this difficult time in their lives. Thus, many parents described struggling to find avenues for being present in the lives of their children. Some parents volunteer at the school, some are involved in community activities with their children (e.g., church), and others attend all of their children's extracurricular events. One mother explained: "When she sees me at her games, when she sees me going to open house, when I attend her

Interscholastic League contests, she knows I am interested in her activities. Plus, we have more to talk about. See?" Parents whose children are involved in school activities and organizations tend to be more involved than other parents. Their children's activities provide avenues for parents to maintain relationships with them--avenues they believe their teenagers feel are acceptable. Thus, encouraging students to become engaged and supporting their efforts were considered substantial aspects of parental involvement in these schools.

Being Good Role Models
Providing positive role models was also proffered as an important involvement activity. Several parents stated that teenagers have too few good role models and that it is their responsibility to be upstanding citizens and to show, through their actions, that education is important.

> I've tried to instill in my kids that education is very
> important. I want to see them go onto college. And
> you know, uh, that's the reason I'm here for them. -
> *Porfirio Diaz High School Parent*

They consider doing volunteer work and participating in organizations such as PTA and Booster clubs and committees such as Site-Based Decision Making (SBDM) teams and Parent Advisory Committees (PAC) because they are viewed as important ways to model the value of school, the value of being a lifelong learner, and the value of struggling. For example, not knowing English but working in a school is viewed by at least one mother as a way of modeling the importance of overcoming barriers for her children.

> I know my English is not so good--getting better--but
> I come up here and I work. Working is important. I
> want my son to be a hard worker too. - *Mother from*
> *Benito Juarez Middle School*

As indicated previously, modeling is often done in the face of teen resistance. Regardless, the parents felt that students benefited from their involvement in terms of motivation and realization--"opening their eyes" to the importance of education.

Benefits to Parents Personally

A final and highly relevant reason for being and staying involved concerns the benefits that parents themselves gain from the experience. All the participants related how much enjoyment they experience from their volunteer work. They meet friends, enjoy the camaraderie of the teachers, feel pleased about the help they provide their children. They also enjoy having access to information. Parents described the following benefits: developing new friendships, building teacher and parent relationships, gaining support from others, developing interpersonal skills, acquiring typing skills, increasing their self-confidence and self-respect, improving communication and English skills, and accessing information. In other words, parents experience tremendous personal growth.

Parents shared stories of learning to type, developing the ability and courage to answer the telephone in English, and developing supportive relationships with each other.

> Besides making friendships that I have here with teachers and parents. I reach out to parents who do not come to school frequently. . . . I try to build trust with the parents so that they will open up to us about personal issues so that we can help them. I help by listening and acting on the part of other parents. -
> *Parent from Porfirio Diaz High School*

Another mother told us that before she began volunteering at the school, she thought she had no talents. However, her free-hand drawings and posters earned her praise from parents and teachers. She revealed that this boosted her ego so much that she is less shy about other things as well. The new skills parents learn are often used to help their own children. For example, knowing the library or typing are skills they use to assist their children write better reports or turn in more polished products. Two of the parents spoke of buying used typewriters in order to practice their new typing skills at home.

Finding that other parents share their struggles regarding access to information, parenting, and personal growth was also mentioned. Parents discussed learning to recognize that children develop at different rates and to be more realistic with their own expectations. The information they learn about children's behavior and discipline management transfers to the home. They also reported being able to communicate more with their children because they could talk about things that had happened at school, and future events.

Involvement related to personal growth is also evident in their confidence and self-assurance. For example, one mother told us that prior to being involved at school, meetings were intimidating because she did not know the school building and was afraid of getting lost. Since she did not know any teachers or parents, attending a meeting was a major ordeal. Similarly, several mothers related the growth in confidence they have experienced since beginning to volunteer at the school. They come to meetings knowing the layout of the building, knowing some teachers and parents, and feeling secure. Thus, these parents not only have more access to information because they are at the school, but they are also more likely to attend a meeting.

The personal benefits that parents gain from being involved are important to the maintenance and growth of parental involvement programs. First, and perhaps foremost, they entice parents to sustain involvement. Second, the benefits are not entirely personal. The entire school community gains from their friendly and enthusiastic demeanors, from the work they do, and from the support they provide.

Involvement, from the parents point of view, encompassed a wide range of activities and is valued far beyond its potential effect on student achievement. Many parents saw their involvement as a partnership with school staff and other parents as opposed to seeing themselves as only supporting the cognitive and emotional development of their children. This enhanced the overall effectiveness of the parental involvement program and seemed to benefit all who were involved.

School Staff Views

Members of the school staff and specifically teachers agree with the parental views described above in a number of areas. For example, teachers also feel that communication fosters the development of relationships and that the presence of parents on campus improves the school atmosphere. However, the perspectives school staff hold also differ in some substantive areas. They focus on more formal activities in their descriptions of parental involvement. Many suggest that parent involvement is limited to activities such as volunteering in the office, library, or teacher work room, monitoring the school grounds, hall ways, and cafeteria, and supporting teachers when students are behaving inappropriately in the classroom. School staff interpreted parents attendance at functions such as open house, as demonstrating an "I care" attitude. One middle school teacher explained:

> Parental involvement means bringing the parents into the educational process. This could be in the form of participating at school, fundraising, or helping out teachers. Seeing parents in the school makes a big difference. - *Teacher from Francisco Villa Middle School*

Thus, for many teachers, the level of parental involvement at a school is defined in terms of the absence or presence of parents at formal, school initiated functions like PTA meetings or parent-teacher conferences, or serving in school volunteer capacities, as hall monitors, library support personnel, clerical assistants, or classroom assistants.

> It [parental involvement] includes having parents show up for teacher conferences, having them come up and sit in the classrooms and see what their children are learning, assisting teachers, teaching parents parenting skills. These would be the main components of a parental involvement program. - *Counselor at Madero Middle School*

Few teachers or administrators feel that parents can be of assistance in the classroom; it is generally believed that parents do not have enough education to assist at this level. The school staff members, who do believe that parents can be useful in all facets of the school, are either special programs teachers or non-teaching staff. For example, the school librarian at Porfirio Diaz Middle School indicated that she has many activities in which parents could be involved.

> I could really use some parent volunteers. They would help with routine things: checking in books, checking them out, shelving, pasting. . . . We will start word-processing soon, and we need some assistance. Also the accelerated reader program.

Similarly, one of the Special Education teachers at Benito Juarez High School listed numerous ways where parents can be involved both in and outside the classroom. She asserted:

> In my classroom they take students to the rest room;
> help with instructional reinforcement both academic
> and functional areas, they provide role models for
> them. I have a student who is very low functioning
> and this parent is there for him. Talks to him.... I
> can think of a thousand ways to involve parents. I
> know what my students need, and I figure out ways
> to have them help me.... Parents could be beneficial
> in all classrooms through not in the same ways; they
> could do so much.

Unlike regular classrooms, special programs teachers and non-teaching staff are able to articulate more clearly how parents can be involved and what roles they can play both within their work environment as well as in the school at large. Similarly, this group is also more likely to be familiar with the home life situations of more parents. Some feel this provides them with a better understanding of involvement patterns and a greater appreciation for informal involvement.

Such an appreciation, however, is not always fostered at the district level. Indeed, one district parent specialist is planning on giving "Campus of the Year" awards for the campus with the most parental involvement. Thus, she is basing parental involvement on the number of clock hours volunteers log at school. No attempt has been made to recognize informal activities. Such a failure may serve to reinforce the school's tendency to focus on formal activities. Regardless, the basic difference between the two definitions (i.e., the definition provided by the majority of parents versus that generally offered by school staff) is that teachers often thought of parents as being involved in the schools whereas parents often thought of it as being involved with their children and the school.

In addition to the different activities identified, teachers, administrators, and parent involvement specialists also perceived a multiplicity of purposes for engaging parents in educational processes. Educational staff considered parental involvement an important way to serve the needs of both the children and the school. Specifically, their rationales include: improving academic achievement, garnering support and assistance, reducing discipline problems, and providing parent and adult education.

Improving Academic Achievement

Parent involvement was also seen as having a positive impact on student achievement. The explanations given for this relationship suggest that the relationship between parental involvement and increased student achievement is indirect. For example, one teacher explained that parents, who attend parent-teacher conferences and keep in touch with the school, are in a better position to monitor their children's progress. Similarly, several teachers reported that communication with parents on a regular basis allows teachers to know where the child is coming from, when things are rocky at home, or if the child is having difficulty understanding something. Having parents around allows teachers to be familiar with the whole child. One teacher explained that knowing about the child and their activities beyond school provides teachers with useful information. Teachers are better able to use examples and activities with which the kids will connect, and s/he can attempt to capitalize on the students extra-curricular strengths. Likewise, several teachers mentioned that if they are familiar with their students' parents, then they are more likely to call them if their children start falling behind.

Several teachers made comments regarding the motivational effect that parental presence at the school has on their students.

I think having parents in the school has a positive effect on student behavior. They tend to act more like young adults. . . . When parents volunteer in the library, kids have an opportunity to interact with more adults. I think that kids need to interact more with adults. - Librarian at Francisco Villa Middle School.

It was also indicated that involvement is instrumental in keeping kids in school. "Some kids get to the point where they aren't interested in class or anything else. . . the parent can show they care." Although none of the participants in the study said parental involvement unambiguously prevented dropping out, many felt that students would be less likely to drop out if one or both of their parents were involved.

Several school sponsored activities are aimed at increasing student achievement and parental involvement. For example, one of the middle schools sponsors a Saturday academy where parents can participate in academic subjects with their children. In order for students to participate they must have a parent or guardian "learning partner." This particular program is highly successful. The academy is filled to capacity each weekend. Another parent-child learning program, the South Texas Engineering and Mathematics (STEM) program, provides opportunities for parents and students to visit NASA and other organizations that use math and science technologies. Madero Middle School's new Communities in Schools (CIS) program, which focuses on "at-risk" students, endeavors to involve parents in all areas of the lives of their children.

Garnering Support and Assistance
Getting to know parents and gaining their support is viewed as important for a number of reasons. Primary among these is the effect that such relationships have on communication. Communicating and sharing information are considered to be two crucial components of parental involvement. It was indicated that both information and expectations are more easily communicated when parents are part of the school-community. For example, teachers consider parent involvement as an avenue for dispensing information regarding school functions, meetings, classroom events, testing schedules, and individual student progress.

Further, these relationships facilitate two-way communication, an element that is important to mutual understanding. For example, one teacher at Porfirio Diaz High School commented:

> I have found that just having conferences with the parents, especially when you have a student having problems, and you call for a... parent-teacher conference. That's when you get to know the parent and what they're doing at home and why it's so hard. They didn't follow up on them to know what their child is doing in school.

Parent-teacher conferences were mentioned as effectual means for sharing information.

Second, it is critical in any school change effort to have parents involved, informed and supportive. An administrator at one middle school noted that the information that parents garner on school reform is typically shared more effectively with other parents, and their involvement in initiatives generally leads to support. Parental support is especially important during bond elections and at other times when fund raising is an issue.

While some schools do not have a PTA, in those schools that have them, teachers point to these organizations as good examples of support for the school. For example, at one school, the PTA is raising funds to buy a marquee for the school. The campus leadership requested the marquee to provide another avenue for communicating school information to parents and community members.

School staff members also feel that parental support and assistance are important in the daily operations of the school a well as in the success of special school sponsored activities. Teachers at one school indicated that parents can be relied upon to participate as chaperones on field trips, at athletic events, and at Interscholastic League activities. They also pointed out that parents often donate time, money, and other resources in order to help the school or to support an activity in which their children are involved (e.g., laminating, running off the school newsletter, fundraising, planning or hosting senior graduation celebrations, sewing and decorating for Folklorico dancing, and speaking on career day).

Reducing Discipline Problems
School staff, like many of the parents, are concerned about the drop in involvement as students move through secondary school. The librarian as Francisco Villa Middle School stated: "Parents tend to slack off by the time their children get to this age." She feels this is problematic given the increased amount of peer pressure with which adolescents are confronted. The parent coordinator at this school asserted that the schools were in part responsible for the decline. "District-wide we have a very strong parental involvement program, but it is geared more toward the elementary schools. . . . We are dropping the ball too soon." Regardless of who is responsible, most teachers and administrators feel that the decrease in parental involvement is associated with the increase in behavior problems as students grow older.

Similarly, it was asserted that by increasing parental involvement that behavior problems should be reduced. Both formal and informal activities were mentioned. For example, parents at one high school were asked to monitor the halls during the break between classes. At another school, parents have been asked to act as companions to their children when student behavior is inappropriate. Some teachers feel parents are being very supportive of school staff efforts to improve behavior in secondary schools.

> We have asked several parents to shadow kids so far and they have come. The kids of course don't act up with their parents following them around, but their parents know that isn't the point. *-Teacher at Madero Middle School*

Teachers also mentioned the benefit of having parents reinforce the discipline standards of the school at home. Similarly, they recognize the important role that imparting values such as "el respecto" plays when children come to school. It is felt that those children whose parents' stressed respect and who reinforced a sense of responsibility at home, were better behaved at school.

> I think they demand that their children are going to respect their elders which is what my parents brought me up with - *Teacher at Porfirio Diaz High School.*

Some forms of involvement automatically involve student behavioral elements. For example, annual Admission, Review, and Dismissal (ARD) meetings, for students in special education, require a discussion of student behavior. Similarly, at Madero Middle School parents attend conferences with team members, at which time, academic progress and behavior are discussed. The teams involve the parent, the student, and the teachers in developing behavior management programs, if such a program is necessary.

Providing Parent and Adult Education
A final area of parental involvement that was frequently mentioned by members of various school staffs was parent and /or adult education. Parent education includes lessons on parenting skills as well as seminars on new school programs. Alternately, adult education includes Graduation Equivalency Diploma (GED) courses, English as a Second Language (ESL) classes, computer training, typing or sewing classes, etc.

At one middle school, the assistant principal indicated that parent education is needed in order for parents to understand how schools have changed, what is expected from their children (e.g., behavior, dress, attitude, and work), as well as how to be school advocates. Similarly, several teachers mentioned the importance of parents understanding the school's curriculum, the importance of and reasons for standardized testing, and the way that standards in the different content areas have changed. For example, a math teacher at one middle school stated

> It might be good to have in-service for parents to look at curriculum so that they know that we are teaching. Parental involvement lets parents know what we do in math. Some parents are afraid of math and this rubs off. We want them to understand.

Many of the schools have PACs or other groups or programs that are required or supported by the federal government. Parent education is usually a required component of these programs. Several parent specialists work to adapt the lessons as much as possible to the needs of the parents. Two, in particular, mentioned sending out surveys to obtain parental advice on topics they wanted to have covered. "We don't want to waste their time."

A number of the schools and/or their districts offered adult education classes. Parent specialists considered the development of parents skills and self-confidence as an important aspect of involving parents. Typically classes like key-boarding, sewing and arts and crafts were offered. In some districts, parents also had access to GED courses, ESL classes, and driver education courses.

Overall, staff members viewed parent and adult education favorably. Some felt that increased parental knowledge would allow them to become better parents. Similarly, others indicated that it showed children that their parents valued education enough to be life-long learner.

Involvement, from the perspective of school staff, contains both formal and informal activities. Of which, the formal activities are valued more often and to a higher degree. Most school staff value involvement activities that facilitate their work (i.e., educating). Teachers, unlike parents, are less likely to describe parental involvement as a relationship and rarely mention any intrinsic benefits of involvement. However, most participants feel that parental involvement is important and that they do what they can to support it.

In the section that follows, the strategies that school staffs employ to sustain and develop parental involvement will be discussed.

Best Practices for Building Collaborative Relationships Between Parents and Schools

The primary purpose of this study was to identify those practices that participants feel are most effective in developing and sustaining meaningful parental involvement. It is difficult to make broad generalizations regarding what can be described as best practices. Each campus is situated in a distinctly different historical, political, economic, and educational context. And each is responding to localized needs, and interacts and responds to environmental and organizational changes differently. However, at each of the schools it is apparent that seven particular elements contribute substantially. These include: 1) fostering communication and information exchange, 2) teaming teachers, 3) maintaining a parent-friendly school environment, 4) establishing parent centers and providing parent coordinators, 5) engaging students and inviting parents, 6) providing more opportunities for parental involvement, and 7) building on Mexican-American culture, values and experiences.

Fostering Communication and Information Exchange

As mentioned previously, parents and teachers regard communication as critical to building relationships between parents and teachers, keeping track of student progress, and to exchanging information. All of the schools were continually attempting to find more effective means for improving communication. Phone calls are listed as the major means for communication. Teachers reported calling parents to inform them not only of academic progress and discipline issues, but to invite parents to school events or activities that might be of interest to them.

In addition to phone calling and sending notes home, certain schools are using less traditional routes to advertise activities and events and to provide information. Three are using local newspapers to announce upcoming events and have found this to be an effective strategy for increasing attendance. Several have also designed and now publish parent newsletters and monthly calendars that they mail home. The principal at one middle school was reported to carry around extra copies of their newsletter and hands them out randomly to parents, in an attempt to ensure that they all receive them. Two school districts are planning to install a service called the parent connection. This is a phone service through which parents or student can access information about tests, assignments, events, etc. One school has even begun using a local television channel to inform the public of upcoming events.

At the beginning of each school year, most of the secondary schools reported giving out parent-student handbooks. These handbooks contain information such as teachers' names, teams, classroom numbers, class schedules, as well as school and district rules and regulations. These books are provided in both Spanish and English. At one middle school, three days are set aside at the beginning of the year during which meetings are held in English and Spanish to explain the contents of the handbook and to answer parent questions. Open house, a traditional strategy for having parents come to the school to view their children's work and meet their teachers, are handled differently in some of the secondary schools. For example, Francisco Villa Middle School holds two open houses per year. During these events, report cards are given out by the homeroom teachers or the academic team.

Parents reported that the innovations schools have implemented are making a difference. The most effective strategies, however, are those that involve personal contact. One of the most effective ways to communicate information, nurture a caring environment, gain parents' trust, and overcome parental fears related to their limited English proficiency or less developed formal education is the use of personal communication and contact by school staff. This is a frequent practice of teachers and parent specialists, calling parents, visiting them, or speaking to them individually when they are on the campus. Parents spoke of being "invited" to join a committee, contribute a talent to the school, provide assistance during an event, or attend a meeting.

Given the importance parents place on personal contact, the role of body language must not be overlooked. Many parents shared that they would not feel comfortable working with teachers who exhibit *"una mala cara"* (an ugly face or disposition). Fortunately, in these schools, teachers communicated a welcoming and approachable demeanor with parents. Parents also reported that when the educational staff communicated respect and integrity, in the way they greet them and listen to their concerns, they tend to provide more information then they might have otherwise, and they are motivated to continue their involvement with the school. Knowing they can have their questions answered or their concerns heard by a teacher, parent specialists, or counselor makes parents feel they can trust the school.

At all the school sites, schools were extending their efforts to communicate and provide information to all parents, teachers, and the surrounding community. It is imperative that parents and school staff understand the importance that access to information and communication play in building collaborative relationships with borderland parents. For instance, it is important for teachers to know what parents perceive their responsibilities to be with respect to their involvement with their children's education and vice-versa. Two-way positive and proactive communication is necessary to the development of effective parental involvement programs.

Teaming Teachers
Academic teams are comprised of a group of teachers from different disciplines who all teach the same group of students. Teaming facilitates planning academic programs and activities for these students, but the benefits do not stop there. Another benefit is having a group of teachers teach and share information about the same child. This allows parents a cross-disciplinary overview of their child's academic progress and behavior. Teaming was highlighted by several teachers and parents as an important element in the home-school relationship. Teaming allows teachers to make contact with and get to know many more parents, and it allows them to develop a fuller understanding of their students. For parents, teaming meant fewer and more productive parent-teacher conferences. In addition to discussing academic progress, topics of study, examinations, and activities in which the child is or will be engaged, team meetings also provide an opportunity to discuss concerns and develop strategies.

Teaming also facilitates more frequent contact with parents. According to one teacher, teams schedule annual meetings with each parent, and if a parent wishes, other meetings can also be scheduled. One team member reported that two teachers in her team are in charge of making phone calls This allows the team to make sure that parents know when students are having difficulty as well as when they have done something outstanding. In short, these large secondary schools are finding ways to provide a closer and more communal environment by consolidating through academic teams. The results of this effort thus far have been positive in terms of parental involvement.

Maintaining a Parent-Friendly School Environment
School climate was considered to be a deciding factor in parental willingness to become and remain formally involved. At least two of the schools are perceived as going out of their way to make parents feel comfortable and part of the school community. Parents at these schools referred to being part of the school family, and described visiting the school as a pleasure.

The responsibility of creating this warm environment is assumed by everyone in the school. Several school staff members discussed how they attempt to make parents feel welcome and appreciated. The parent specialist at Francisco Villa Middle School makes certain that parents know their support is appreciated. She organizes award ceremonies and provides them with pins and vests that identify them as important "staff." Parents at this school are awarded for their involvement and diligence.

Other school staff described attempts to get to know parents as individuals. In an effort to make limited English proficient parents more comfortable, the staff at several schools have made certain that at least one of the office assistants are bilingual, that the Spanish language is used in some hallway displays, and that all school correspondence is printed in both Spanish and English. Others reported that some parent activities are scheduled at night and on the weekends in order that more parents can attend. For example, at Francisco Villa Middle School a Saturday Academy provides an opportunity for parents and students to work together on interesting academic activities. Team meetings and team parent conferences are also scheduled in the evenings at this school. Treating parents courteously, acknowledging their presence and thanking them for their hard work are all considered important in the development of parent-friendly school environments.

Establishing Parent Centers and Providing Parent Coordinators
At the secondary level, all but one of the focus schools have parenting centers. Parent centers provide a place for volunteers and visitors to feel at home. At Francisco Villa Middle School, the parent center is viewed as a supportive place for parents to meet and develop their

confidence. Parents are able to meet informally, have coffee, discuss their children, successes, and problems, work on projects, and help teachers with various tasks.   The only secondary school without a parent center, Porfirio Diaz High School, did have an efficacious Parent-Teacher Organization (PTO). Parents from this school feel the PTO provides them with many of the advantages that other parents attributed to parent centers.

For those schools with parent centers, its location is an important consideration.   The proximity of parent centers to other areas of the school affects the amount of personal contact taking place between parents and school staff. At Francisco Villa Middle School, the parenting center is located in an alcove outside the main flow of the school.   This makes chance encounters unlikely and lessens the visibility of parents at the school. This was demonstrated in several teacher interviews from this school. These teachers were unaware of the amount of time that the parent volunteers spend at the school and what they do while they are there.   The librarian at this school indicated that when the parent center was located in one of the library rooms, she knew more of them and had more volunteers in the library. Thus, location is an important factor.

The provision of parent coordinators also contributes to the effectiveness of parental involvement at these schools. These women are members of the local community, and serve as a liaison between the school and community for many families.   Their links to the community are particularly useful to school teachers and administrators in terms of communication.   Further, parent coordinators organize volunteers, plan activities and events, and run parental involvement programs.   These women also serve as informational resources for parents and oftentimes as friends as well.

Engaging Students and Inviting Parents
Parents whose students are engaged, whether in scholastic, artistic, musical, or athletic activities, seem to have higher levels of involvement than those parents whose children are un-engaged in school beyond attending class. Student engagement seems to facilitate both formal and informal involvement activities.   For example, at Madero Middle School two mothers were interviewed whose daughters are intensely engaged in school. Both are in the gifted and talented program, are members of school clubs, and one is a cheerleader. These parents are in contact with the school on a weekly basis, if not

more. One of them is a member of a number of school committees. Similarly, several teachers mentioned that the parents of athletes are often involved in the Booster club and attend their children's games and award ceremonies.

Several schools have responded to this connection by organizing student performances to precede meetings at which parents are the invited audience or participants. One act plays, choral or band performances and science fair displays are some of the attractions. It is felt that such activities provide avenues for students to show off their talents for their peers and parents, for parents to see what is going on at the school, and for school staff to provide information to or solicit information or ideas from their parent. These activities are supported or associated in some way with the school, and they provide opportunities for parents to demonstrate their interest in and concern for their children. Moreover, they allow parents an opportunity to connect with an age group that tends to reject parental attention.

However, it is difficult to ascertain the direction of this relationship. That is, which comes first, student engagement or parental involvement? Or is the relationship more dynamic? Does the engagement of students send a message to parents that the school is taking an interest in their child? Or do students become interested in school activities because their parents are involved? Can it work both ways? While these questions remain unanswered in this research, it does appear that when students are involved, parents have a reason to cross the school threshold and link into their children's social and academic activities.

Providing More Opportunities for Parent Involvement
Parental involvement does not have to decrease, nor should it, after the sixth grade. Although school structures change from child centered to subject matter orientation, the importance of parents in supporting the education of their children remains as before. Thus, efforts must be made to encourage parents to sustain informal involvement and to provide more opportunities for formal involvement. In the schools studied, parents expressed a wide range of interests and named a number of talents from which their school could benefit. Staff members at Madero Middle School recognized this untapped pool of talent and are attempting to capitalize on it. The teachers surveyed parents and then brainstormed ways in which parent interests and

abilities could be used in the school. Once designed, activities or "learning opportunities" were introduced to the parents for their thoughts, and objectives and roles were defined. Another strategy for combating the decline in involvement as students grow older has been developed by Porfirio Diaz's district office. They call their program "Volunteers in Place." It provides training to parents concerning involvement in the early grades and encourages participation throughout their child's education. The same district is entertaining the idea of providing staff development training to teachers in the upper grades regarding how to utilize parents.

Parents reported that activities that create shared experiences for them and their children are important ways of strengthening family communication. Francisco Villa Middle School has added a number of new activities that provided opportunities for shared family experiences. One example is their Saturday Academy, which engages students and their learning partners (typically parents or other family members) in academic activities. Another example is the STEM program activities, which include field trips and math and science projects. At Huerta Junior High, the school has invited a local University to run a mother-daughter program. This school has also developed an active parent center. The mothers who frequent the center volunteer in classrooms, the library, and the office, and provide the more traditional services such as copying, cutting and laminating. These women also design their own projects and involvement activities.

Among professional staff, however, there are differences in opinion regarding how to bring about meaningful parental involvement. Some staff tended to think of parent involvement as a parent responsibility to be initiated by parents, rather than as a collaborative responsibility of the entire school community.

> It would be nice if parents would initiate involvement more often rather than having the teachers always having to contact them. - *Teacher at Francisco Villa Middle School.*

> Parents should keep in touch with teachers and see what they might need. If they say there is nothing, push a little bit. - *Librarian at Francisco Villa Middle School*

Conversely, others feel that the school should advocate for parent involvement by providing parents with opportunities to become involved in activities they find interesting. In general, the parent coordinator is in charge of parent involvement. The more effective strategies, however, involve both parents and school staff working together for increased parental involvement.

Building on Mexican-American Culture, Values, and Experiences.
Mexican-American cultural values are dynamic and dependent on factors such as place of birth, regional differences, acculturation stages, social class, educational levels, and personal experiences in the mainstream culture. Understanding key cultural values and recognizing the diversity of experiences was identified as an important determining factor to fostering collaborative relationships between schools and parents. It is important to recall that although the majority of the parents interviewed for the study was composed of Spanish-speaking women, there was great diversity in their educational levels, length of time living in the community, socio-economic level, child-rearing philosophy, and English proficiency.

In developing collaborative relationships with parents, schools endeavor to build on the sense of extended family that many of the mothers talked about. A family oriented climate in some schools is achieved through extending personal invitations to parents, by providing parent centers where mothers can meet informally, and by planning infrequent morning breakfasts where the principal and/or teachers chat informally with parents over "cafe y pan dulce." Personal contact is valued in the Mexican-American culture. Therefore, teachers from several schools make efforts to personally greet parents and students. These and other teachers recognize that for the borderland parents a personal note, phone call, and/or personal invitation communicate respect, warmth, value and a sense of belonging.

Facilitating parent-child communication and interaction is another culturally relevant practice. Often, parents and children are struggling to find common ground in the painful process of acculturation and/or childhood maturation. Rather than the school setting acting as a catalyst for irreversible separation from home values and mores, it becomes a place for parents and children to interact and provides a basis for continued dialogue at home.

Conclusions
This study examined the nature of parental involvement at the
secondary level in borderland schools. It was found that parental
involvement is viewed differently by parents and school staff and that
the different views affected both definitions of and reasons for
involvement. In addition to describing these perspectives, this study
also provided seven practices, identified by parents and school staff,
that are believed to support parental involvement. While the study
was exploratory in nature, provides educators with a working model of
effective practices for increasing the involvement of Mexican-
American parents in their children's education at the secondary level.

The findings that emerged from the study contribute to the
literature in several significant ways. Some findings support or build
on the parental involvement research base and others provide new
insight. For example, the findings in this study support the literature
that argues that barriers exist that hinder parental involvement
(Cummins, 1986; Epstein & Becker, 1982), that information is
important (Calabrese, 1990; Epstein, 1986), that parental involvement
decreases as students grow older (Villanueva & Hubbard, 1994), and
that both formal and informal involvement activities are important and
should be supported (Lightfoot, 1978). In these areas, our report offers
further confirmation.

This study also makes seven important contributions to the
literature. The seven best practices can be thought of as general
recommendations for program development. The first of these is the
focus on secondary schools that serve primarily Mexican-American
students and families. Second, we attempted to provide concrete
examples of practices that are used by these schools in addition to
relaying participants' comments. An effort was made to provide not
only things to think about but also examples to learn from.

Third, while "El respecto" has been documented as an
important Mexican-American cultural value (Marín & Marín, 1991),
it has not been directly linked to social class in the parental
involvement literature. The findings in this study suggest that schools
which successfully engage parents in their children's educational
process, also link "respecto" with involvement. That is, staff members
from successful schools treat parents and students with respect, and
they support parental efforts to teach this value to their children.
Further, paying "respecto" to persons who are typically marginalized

and less socially visible is a powerful factor for encouraging involvement. The parental involvement literature has identified "respect" as important but has not linked it with the visibility it creates for marginalized parents.

Fourth, the literature stressed achievement as the key reason for increasing parental involvement (Henderson, 1987). However, borderland parents equally stressed (sometimes more so) the opportunity for forging relationships and developing personal efficacy. For example, some parents purposefully sought involvement in order to establish a relationship with their children's teachers and other parents. These relationships provide parents with important information with which they can better support their children, and contribute to the development of parental efficacy.

Fifth, the findings of this study illuminate the importance of personal contact. Teachers, parents, parent specialists, counselors, and administrators stressed the value of personal contact. Although the literature has identified helpful considerations, such as communicating in the parents' dominant language and providing newsletters, in the borderland context, personalized communication was identified as critical. Parents reported that it makes them feel valued and respected. Consequently, effective schools responded by making personal phone calls, making efforts to issue "personal invitations," and in some cases, conducting occasional home visits.

Sixth, a number of studies have shown the benefit of engaging students in school activities. Increased motivation, achievement, and trust have been linked to the engagement of students in "extracurricular" activities (Banks, 1988; Comer, 1988). However, our findings suggest that engagement in school activities may also be beneficial for increasing parental involvement. The research suggests that if one could capitalize and build on the less formal, more frequent involvement activities, one might be able to increase parental involvement with their children and the schools.

Finally, this study emphasizes that the cultural diversity of the school community cannot be ignored in efforts to develop parental involvement programs. The schools we studied recognized the importance of culture and included culturally sensitive practices in their parental involvement initiatives. Similarly, although this chapter did not discuss this earlier, the findings suggest that parental level of English proficiency and socio-economic level are also related to involvement. For example, depending on their socio-economic level and language ability, some parents have higher status and more meaningful roles than others. Our observations indicate that English dominant parents participate as PTA officers, club leaders, or on the site-based decision team, while limited English proficient parents are more likely to be found in the parent center making copies. The need to provide Spanish dominant speakers with avenues to formal decision making entities is evident. This current arrangement unintentionally supports the high status of English speakers and marginalizes parents who do not speak the dominant language.

Although this study was exploratory in nature, the findings will hopefully guide further research. More research is needed on the nature of parental involvement in secondary schools. The dynamics of the parent-school relationship are so different from elementary schools, that the abundance of research on elementary parental involvement is of little use to program planners and implementers at the secondary level. Furthermore, research is needed on non-majority populations. The characteristics and influence of culture and class on parental involvement should be further explored. Finally, the best practices provided herein also need to be examined in greater depth so that educators can understand them more fully and apply them in appropriate contexts.

Several general themes and issues have emerged during the research project. These themes have implications for program development. Broad generalizations regarding the best practices for involving Mexican-American parents in school have been made. However, program planners and implementers must take care in how these generalizations are used. Each must be applied differentially (or not at all depending on the unique characteristics of the school setting. As Miles and Huberman (1984) suggest, the best practices are useful foremost as general guidelines. They can assist practitioners in making sense out of their particular context. It is the context that should drive the design for educational change.

References

Anderson, M. 1993. Studying across difference: Race, class, and gender in qualitative research. In *Race and ethnicity in research methods*, ed. J. Stanfield and R. Dennis, 39-52. Newbury Park: SAGE.

Baker, C. D. 1983. A 'second look' at interviews with adolescents. *Journal of Youth and Adolescence* 12: 501-519.

Banks, J. A. 1988. *Multiethnic education.* Boston: Allyn and Bacon.

Bogdan, R., and S. K. Biklen 1992. *Qualitative research for education.* Boston: Allyn & Bacon.

Calabrese, R. 1990. The structure of schooling and minority drop-out rates. *The Clearing House* 61: 325-328.

Comer, J. P. 1988. Educating poor minority children. *Scientific American*, 259: 2-8.

Cummins, J. 1986. Empowering minority students: A framework for intervention. *Harvard Educational Review*, 56: 18-36.

Epstein, J. 1986. Parents' reactions to teacher practices of parent involvement. *The Elementary School Journal* 86: 277-293.

Epstein, J., and H. Becker 1982. Teacher reported practices of parent involvement: Problems and possibilities. *Elementary School Journal* 83: 103-113.

Henderson, A. 1987. *The evidence continues to grow: Parental involvement improves student achievement.* Columbia, M.D.: National Committee for Citizens in Education.

Lightfoot, S. 1978. *Worlds apart: Relationships between families and schools.* New York: Basic Books.

Lincoln, Y., and E. Guba 1985. *Naturalistic inquiry.* Newbury Park, C.A.: SAGE.

Marín, G., and B. V. Marín 1991. *Research with Hispanic populations.* Newbury Park, CA: SAGE.

Miles, M., and A. M. Huberman 1984. *Qualitative data analysis: A source book of new methods.* Thousand Oaks, C.A.: SAGE.

Patton, M. Q. 1990. *Qualitative evaluation and research methods.* Newbury Park, CA: SAGE.

Villanueva, I., and L. Hubbard 1994. *Toward redefining parental involvement: Making parents' invisible strategies and cultural practices visible.* Paper presented at the American Educational Research Association Annual Conference, New Orleans.

3. *A Cross-National Study: Children's Math Self-Concept and it's Relationship with Mathematics Achievement*

Deniz Senturk, Angela Whipple, Hsiu-Zo Ho, Jules Zimmer, Sou-Yung Chiu, and Chang-Pei Wang

Introduction

Constructs of the "self" have undergone considerable refinement and redefinition during the last two decades. Previous theories surrounding self-concept promoted a unidimensional and undifferentiated construct (Coopersmith, 1967; Marx & Winne, 1978). Further developments in statistics, such as factor analysis techniques, began to exert an influence on the study of self-concept (Marsh & Hattie, 1996). Taxonomic models were then developed, which supported the multidimensionality of self-concept (Soares & Soares, 1977). Multi-trait multimethod (MTMM) analyses were then applied to examinations of self-concept. Early MTMM analyses (Marx & Winne, 1978) indicated support for an underlying unified dimension of self-concept, however reanalysis indicated the presence of a global dimension as well as separate domains within a self-concept (Shavelson & Bolus, 1982). This led to the Marsh/Shavelson model where self-concept was viewed as multidimensional (Marsh & Shavelson, 1985). Further research to date confirms hierarchical and multi-faceted self-concept theoretical models (Bracken, 1992; Guilford, 1985).

Previous literature has used the terms "self-concept" and "self-esteem" interchangeably (Byrne, 1996; Marsh & Hattie, 1996). Overall, self-esteem uses an evaluative process to assess and compare the self against a standard of some kind. Yet, self-concept has been found to contain both evaluative and affective components (Byrne, 1996; Marsh & Hattie, 1996). Much like self-esteem, the evaluative component utilizes cognition to assess the self. Conversely, the affective component incorporates descriptives of the self that utilize emotion or affect.

Academic Self-Concept

One specific domain, that of academic self-concept, has become the focus of several researchers. This has resulted in modifications to the original Shavelson et al. (1976) model described earlier. Marsh & Shavelson (1985) further divided general self-concept into three second-order factors (nonacademic, verbal/academic, and mathematics/academic). Third-order factors have also been identified, with geography, history, English, and foreign language comprising the verbal/academic component, and mathematics, physical science, biological science, and economics business as factors for the mathematics/academic component. Marsh (1990a, 1990c, 1993a, 1994) has continued this research and has currently identified nine school subject self-concept areas (English language, English literature, foreign language, mathematics, science, history, geography, commerce, and computer studies), in addition to six non-core areas (physical education, health, music, art, industrial arts, and religion). Academic self-concept may also become increasingly differentiated with age (Harter, 1985; Marsh, & Craven, 1991). While some gender differences have been found, where girls tend to have higher verbal self-concepts and boys tend to have a higher self-concept for physical ability, equivalent factor structures of self-concept continue to be found for both boys and girls (Marsh, 1994; Marsh & Yeung, 1998; Marsh & Hattie, 1996).

Academic self-concept has been associated with many behavioral and cognitive constructs such as locus of control (Covington & Omelich, 1984; Watkins & Astilla, 1986), perceptions of control (Marsh & Gouvernet, 1989), self-efficacy (Pajares & Miller, 1994), self-esteem (Eccles, Wigfield, Flanagan, Miller, Reuman & Yee, 1989), ego orientations (Skaalvik, 1997), test anxiety (Bandalos, Yates &

Thorndike-Christ, 1995), and academic achievement (Marsh, 1984). Several studies have examined its relationship with academic achievement (Byrne, 1984; Hattie, 1992; Marsh, 1990c, 1993a; Marsh, Byrne & Shavelson, 1988; Marsh & Shavelson, 1985). There have been mixed findings regarding the causal relationship between academic achievement and self-concept. Support for the influence of achievement on self-concept has been found (Byrne & Carlson, 1982), whereas other research has reported effects of self-concept on achievement (Chapman, Cullen, Boersma & Maguire, 1981; Shavelson & Bolus, 1982).

It should be noted that, within self-concept research, academic achievement has been assessed in several fashions, including grades (Irwing, 1996; Marsh, 1990b; Marsh & Yeung, 1997), standardized test scores (Marsh, 1990b; Pajares & Miller, 1994), teacher ratings (Marsh & Yeung, 1997; Skaalvik & Hagtvet, 1990), and high school and college mathematics course completion (Pajares & Miller, 1994). A stronger relationship has been found between academic self-concept and academic achievement when achievement was operationalized with school grades rather than by standardized test scores (Marsh, 1987, 1990c, 1993a 1994; Wylie, 1979). In an extensive meta-analysis, Hansford and Hattie (1982) reported an approximate magnitude of 0.4 for the correlation between academic achievement and academic self-concept.

Mathematics Self-Concept
As with global self constructs, academic self-concept has been shown to be differentiated and domain-specific. Separate and measurable academic self-concepts have been found for mathematics, science, history, and English-reading (Eccles, Wigfield, Flanagan, Miller, Reuman, & Yee, 1989; Marsh & Yeung, 1997; Simpson, Licht, Wagner, & Stader, 1996). Higher correlations have been found between isomorphic dimensions of achievement and self-concept than non-isomorphic constructs such as mathematics achievement and math self-concept (Marsh & Yeung, 1997).

Moreover, specific academic self-concepts, such as math self-concept, have been theorized as having two components as well, with both an affective component and an evaluative component (Irwing, 1996; Marsh, 1990a; Simpson et al., 1996). It has been suggested that the affective component may be more strongly related to academic motivation (Marsh & Gouvernet, 1989) or to measures of satisfaction (Irwing, 1996); whereas the evaluative component may have a stronger relationship with performance (Irwing, 1996). "Mathematics confidence" and "mathematics self-concept" are another pair of terms that have been used interchangeably (Reyes, 1984). This blurring of terminology was due to the lack of a clear distinction between the affective and evaluative components within academic self-concept. Terms such as "self-esteem," "self-evaluation," "self-confidence," "perceived ability," and "perceived performance" have been used to refer to the evaluative component of academic self-concept (Byrne, 1996; Simpson et al., 1996; Strein, 1993). Whereas, terms such as "self-description," and "academic interest" have been used for the affective component (Byrne, 1996; Simpson et al., 1996; Strein, 1993).

Most research has focused on "mathematical self-confidence" (the evaluative math self-concept) in terms of its relationship to mathematics achievement (e.g., Kloosterman, 1991; Mullis, Martin, Beaton, Gonzalez, Kelly, & Smith, 1997; Stevenson & Lee, 1990; Stevenson, Lee, Chen, Stigler, Fan, & Ge, 1990). The magnitude of the correlation between mathematical self-confidence and mathematics achievement has ranged between 0.22 and 0.47 depending on gender and grade level (Kloosterman, 1991).

Cross-National Research
Several cross-cultural studies have used single items rather than scales to tap students' interest in mathematics or math self-concept (Beaton, Mullis, Martin, Gonzalez, Kelly, & Smith, 1996; Mullis et al., 1997; Stevenson & Lee, 1990). The Third International Mathematics and Science Study (TIMSS) included only two questions, one of which asked the student how well he or she was doing in mathematics and the other asked the student how much he or she liked mathematics (Beaton et al., 1996; Mullis et al., 1997). Each question was separately evaluated as tapping perceived level of performance in mathematics or math interest for both primary and middle school students. Stevenson & Lee (1990) evaluated perceived performance in mathematics by asking the children how good they were at mathematics. It has been found that primary school students in the United States reported liking mathematics, while also holding the belief that they were doing well in mathematics (Mullis et al., 1997; Stevenson & Lee, 1990; Stevenson et al., 1990). Moreover, the students in the United States reported more enthusiasm and confidence for mathematics than either the Japanese or Taiwanese students in the study (Stevenson & Lee, 1990). Additionally, high positive associations (.58 to .77) were found for mathematics interest and the student's perceived level of performance in mathematics (Stevenson & Lee, 1990). Similarly, both math interest

and math confidence were found to be positively related to mathematics achievement for Japan, Taiwan, and the United States (Beaton et al., 1996; Mullis et al., 1997; Stevenson & Lee, 1990). However, no gender differences were found with respect to the aforementioned constructs within Japan, Taiwan, or the United States (Stevenson & Lee, 1990).

Cross-cultural studies have made a unique contribution to educational research such as accounting for the influence of social context on constructs of interest (Brislin, 1993). For example, it has been hypothesized that self-concept within individualistic cultures may be more independent of the social context than in collectivist cultures (Markus & Kitayama, 1991). Varying levels of dependence on social context are expected to cause differences in the structure of self-concept of individuals from other cultures (Markus & Kitayama, 1991; Triandis, 1989). This may result in theoretical models that are more hierarchical and multi-faceted within collectivist cultures.

Vijver & Leung (1997) also argued that "cross-cultural research was essential in establishing the generalizability of theories and empirical results" (p. 145). However, several methodological issues should be examined in order for the results of the cross-cultural research to maintain validity and reliability (Vijver & Leung, 1997). These issues include the comparability of the construct under study, as well as ensuring the reliability of the instruments across the nations or groups of interest. If a single item must be used, item comparability should be accomplished before comparing the distributions or the means across the nations or groups of interest in order to ensure construct validity (Watkins & Cheung, 1995). The use of structural equation modeling techniques has allowed an increasing number of studies to provide evidence of the equivalence of measures across different groups (Vijver & Leung, 1997; Watkins & Cheung, 1995; Marsh & Yeung, 1997, 1998).

While self-concept instruments have become increasingly more sound, problematic issues remain (Keith & Bracken, 1996). Several instruments are now outdated and no longer reflect current theoretical thinking. Others have demonstrated low test-retest reliability, in addition to poor internal consistency (Brown & Alexander, 1991; Harter, 1985). The Perception of Ability Scale for Children (PASS) is one of the most psychometrically sound, however it is limited to only six subscales and utilizes "yes/no" forced answers rather than Likert-type scales (Boersma & Chapman, 1992). Overall, the Self-Description Questionnaire (SDQ) is more comprehensive and includes nine school subject subscales. It is also considered to be psychometrically sound and has been utilized in cross-cultural research (e.g., Keith & Bracken, 1996; Marsh, 1984, 1988, 1989, 1990b, 1990c).

The Self-Description Questionnaire (SDQ) was utilized for this study which includes a 10-item mathematics self-concept scale with good internal consistency and the capability to evaluate both the cognitive and affective aspects of academic self-concept (Abu-Hilal & Aal-Hussain, 1997; Keith & Bracken, 1996; Marsh, 1992). An item that taps evaluative math self-concept is "I'm good at mathematics," whereas an item that captures affective math self-concept is "I like mathematics" (Marsh, 1992). This instrument has been shown to be reliable both in measuring multiple dimensions of academic self-concept and for use within other nations cross-culturally (Boyle, 1994; Hattie, 1992; Wylie, 1989). In keeping with this, special attention will be focused on the comparability of math self-concept as measured across the studied nations. Also, while several cross-cultural studies have utilized the SDQ, a two-factor math self-concept has not been specifically studied (Abu-Hilal & Aal-Hussein, 1997; Marsh, 1993; Watkins & Cheung, 1995).

While an examination of gender differences is not a focus of this paper, it is important to note that other research utilizing the SDQ has indicated that the factor structure of academic self-concept has been found to be equivalent for both boys and girls (Abu-Hilal & Aal-Hussein, 1997; Marsh, 1994; Marsh & Yeung, 1997, 1998).

The current study seeks to examine mathematics self-concept across three nations: China (The People's Republic of China), Taiwan (The Republic of China), and the United States. The SDQ will be used to assess math self-concept for each sample of 6th grade boys and girls. The aim of this study was to address the following questions: (a) Is the construct of math self-concept comparable across the three nations? That is, will the factor structure of math self-concept support a two-factor model containing both evaluative and affective factors for each of the three nations? (b) Are there mean differences in the math self-concept factors across nations and genders? (c) If the two-factor model holds for math self-concept, are the two factors related to each other? Is the direction and the magnitude of the relationship between the factors comparable across the three nations? (d) Is there an association between the factors of the measurement model and the mathematics achievement test scores and are the direction and the magnitude of this association equivalent across the three nations?

METHODS

Sample

The data utilized in this study was part of a larger longitudinal project that sampled four nations: China, Japan, Taiwan, and the United States (U.S.). The data included student measures of mathematics achievement as well as self-report measures from their teachers and parents. Time 1 data was collected when the students were enrolled in the fourth grade and Time 2 data was collected when the students attended sixth grade. The respondents for this present study included sixth grade students from three nations: 215 (97 girls and 118 boys) from China, 226 (111 girls and 115 boys) from Taiwan, and 278 (123 girls and 155 boys) from the United States. Since the Japanese students did not complete the self-concept instrument (SDQ), this group was not included in the present study. After evaluating the missing data for the variables of interest, listwise deletion was used and the sample reduced to 661 respondents: 201 (93 girls and 108 boys) from China, 210 (104 girls and 106 boys) from Taiwan and 250 (108 girls and 142 boys) from the U.S.

      The participating schools in each nation were selected on the basis of educational, economic, institutional, and residential characteristics and recommendations of the respective educational authorities and researchers in each nation. The schools were located in Beijing and Men Tou Gou, China; Taipei, Miao-Li, and Yang Ming Shan, Taiwan; and Claremont, Cuyama, and Santa Ynez California, United States. Over 95% of the sixth grade students in each randomly selected classroom participated in the study. The mean ages of the respondents were 12.80 ($\underline{SD}$ = .65), 12.11 ($\underline{SD}$ = .42), and 11.95 ($\underline{SD}$ = .47), for China, Taiwan, and theU.S., respectively.

Measures

The measures of mathematics achievement and self-concept were group-administered by researchers and teachers in each nation as part of a large battery of tests. Standardized instructions were given by the test administrators. All instruments were translated into the languages of the participating nations by native speakers and then translated back into English for verification of the translation. This process was iterated until comparability was achieved in the "back-translated" English version.

The Self-Description Questionnaire for Preadolescence (SDQ)

Marsh (l988) developed a 76-item Self-Description Questionnaire (SDQ) that taps eight domains of self-concept (physical ability, physical appearance, peer relations, parent relations, reading, mathematics, general school, and general self). In the current study, only the 10 items evaluating mathematics self-concept are utilized. Marsh (1989) has described "Math SDQ" as the subjects' perceptions of their mathematical skills, mathematical reasoning ability, and interest in mathematics. Respondents were asked to rate the degree of relevance of each item on a five-point scale (1=false, 2=mostly false, 3=sometimes false sometimes true, 4=mostly true, and 5=true). Table 1 presents the ten items for the math self-concept. The reliability coefficients for these ten items, utilizing Cronbach's alphas, were .89, .95, .93 for China, Taiwan, and the U.S., respectively.

Table 1 – Self-Description Questionnaire (SDQ)

Affective Component

Item Name	Question
A1	I hate mathematics.
A2	I look forward to mathematics.
A3	I am interested in mathematics.
A4	I like mathematics.
A5	I enjoy doing work in mathematics.

Evaluative Component

Item Name	Question
E1	I am dumb at mathematics.
E2	Work in mathematics is easy for me.
E3	I get good marks in mathematics.
E4	I learn things quickly in mathematics.
E5	I'm good at mathematics.

Mathematics Achievement Tests

All sixth grade respondents were administered a test of mathematics achievement consisting of two parallel forms developed for this study. The two forms combined were comprised of thirty-five items derived from three sources. Approximately one-third of the items were adapted from a test used by Stevenson, Lee, and Stigler (1986) from a cross-national study that included Asian nations. Another third of the items were selected from sixth-grade textbooks used in each of the participating nations. The remaining one-third of the items were developed by the project researchers to assess processing skills involved in mathematics problem-solving. The two parallel forms were administered within an average interval of four to six weeks, with a reliability coefficient of .82, and with a Cronbach's alpha of .88, .89, .82 for China, Taiwan and U.S., respectively. The measure of mathematics achievement utilized in the present study was a weighted average score of the two parallel forms.

Statistical Analyses

Confirmatory factor analyses (CFA's) for mathematics self-concept were conducted to test the measurement model for each nation. In addition, structural equation models (SEM's) were conducted to test the relationships between the factors of mathematics self-concept and mathematics achievement. Two-way analyses of variance were conducted to examine nation and gender effects for each component of mathematics self-concept. Correlation analyses were also conducted for the components of mathematics self-concept and mathematics achievement to complement the CFA and SEM results.

AMOS, a structural equation modeling software, companion to SPSS, was utilized for the CFA and SEM analyses. Raw data with listwise deletion of missing variables were imported from the statistical program SPSS for the analyses.

A model was accepted or rejected as having a good or bad fit to the data based on several goodness-of-fit indices: a) the chi-square statistic; b) goodness-of fit index (GFI); c) comparative fit index (CFI); and d) root-mean-square-error-of-approximation (RMSEA). The GFI is a ratio that adjusts for scale, while the CFI measures the improvement of fit within nested models. Values for GFI and CFI range from 0 to 1.0, with .9 indicating a good fit of the data to the proposed model (Schumacker & Lomax, 1996). On the other hand, for RMSEA, a value of .08 or less would indicate a reasonable fit (Browne & Cudeck, 1993). Among these goodness-of-fit indices, the chi-square

Figure 1 – The Two-Factor Model with Correlated Affective and
Components of Mathematics Self-Concept

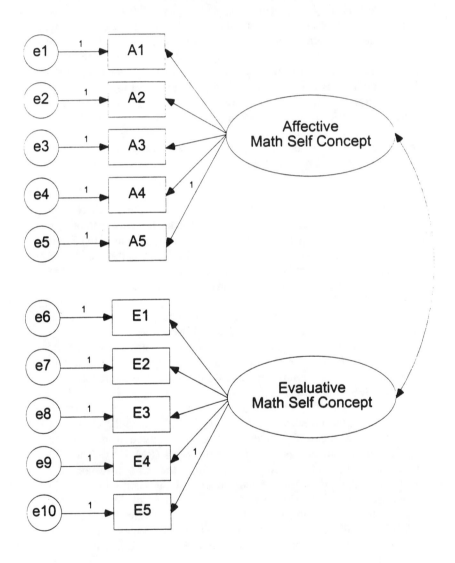

criterion was the only statistical test procedure. A non-significant chi-square statistic indicates a good model fit. One of the disadvantages of evaluating the fit of a model with respect to the chi-square test statistic was it's sensitivity to sample size. "As sample size increases (generally above 200), the chi-square test has a tendency to indicate a significant probability level" (Shumacker & Lomax, 1996, p.125). It is known that GFI, CFI, and RMSEA are less sensitive to sample size (Shumacker & Lomax, 1996). Another procedure used in the analysis, was constraining some or all of the parameter estimates to be equal across groups. This procedure tests for invariance of the constrained parameter for different groups (Joreskog & Sorbom, 1989; Marsh & Hocevar, 1985). These tests of invariance were used to assess comparable measurement and structural models across the three nations.

RESULTS

It was hypothesized that a two-factor model (see Figure1) with correlated affective and evaluative components of math self-concept would provide a better fit to the data than a one-factor model of math self-concept across the three nations. The one factor-model was obtained by constraining the correlation between the two components to one (Joreskog & Sorbom, 1986; Long, 1983). Shown in Table 2, the goodness-of-fit indices indicated that for each nation the two-factor model provided a significantly better fit than the one-factor model. The chi-square difference test results [for China, Taiwan, and the U.S. respectively, ΔX^2 (3)=79.52; ΔX^2 (3)=53.41; ΔX^2 (3)=410.50] were significant at an alpha-level of .05, indicating a better fit for the two factor model.

The two factors were interpreted as math interest (affective component) and math self-confidence (evaluative component). Moreover, the results of the invariance tests for the constant factor loadings and error variances across the three nations provided further support for the construct validity of the factors for China, Taiwan, and the U.S. A series of nested models were tested for the invariance of the two-factor structure across the three nations. Model 1 and 2 constrained all factor loadings to be equal across the three nations for the affective and the evaluative components, respectively. Parallel with the results obtained from these two models, model 3 constrained both the factor loadings and the error variances to be equal across the nations for the affective mathematics self-concept only. In contrast, model 4 constrained the loadings and the error variances for the evaluative mathematics self-concept only. Finally, model 5 constrained the covariance between two factors to be equal across the nations.

Table 2 - Goodness-of-Fit Indices for the Two-Factor and
the One-Factor Measurement Models

Model	China N=201	Taiwan N=210	U.S. N=250
Two-Factor Model			
X^2(df), p-value	36.07(34), $p > .05$	60.89(34), $p < .05$	75.97(34), $p < .05$
GFI	0.97	0.95	0.94
CFI	1.00	0.98	0.98
RMSEA	0.02	0.06	0.07
One-Factor Model			
X^2(df), p-value	115.6(37), $p < .05$	114.3(37), $p < .05$	486.5(37), $p < .05$
GFI	0.87	0.90	0.63
CFI	0.91	0.96	0.78
RMSEA	0.10	0.10	0.22
X^2 difference between two-factor and one-factor models	79.52(3) sig. at $\alpha = .05$	53.41(3) sig. at $\alpha = .05$	410.5(3) sig. at $\alpha = .05$

Each nested model was tested against the "multiple-groups" model with unconstrained parameters. Table 4 presents the goodness-of-fit indices (GFI, CFI, and RMSEA) for the nested models. These tests of invariance via the goodness-of-fit indices (GFI, CFI, and RMSEA) provided evidence for the comparability of the evaluative and affective components of math self-concept across the studied nations. This conclusion is supported by the high goodness-of-fit indices for the constrained nested models. Altogether, the results revealed that the constructs of math interest and math self-confidence were equally well defined and in a similar fashion for all three nations, with large and significant factor loadings.

Unit weights were used in computing the composite scores for the two factors of math interest and math self-confidence. Two-way analyses of variance (ANOVA's) with Nation and Gender as factors were conducted for each composite score as the dependent variable. The results for the construct of math interest indicated a main effect for Nation {$\underline{F}$ (2, 654)=59.64, $\underline{p}$<.05}. However, there was no significant Gender main effect or Gender X Nation interaction effect on math interest. Post-hoc Scheffe analyses with a .05 family significance level indicated mean differences in the math interest composite score among the three nations (China > U.S .> Taiwan). The same pattern of results was obtained for the construct of math self-confidence. Further analyses revealed main effects for Nation [$\underline{F}$ (2,654)=22.93, $\underline{p}$<.05 (U.S.> China> Taiwan, Scheffe contrasts, $\underline{p}$<.05)]; yet no significant Gender main effect or Gender X Nation interaction effect was found.

For each nation, the correlations of each component (math interest and math self-confidence) with mathematics achievement, presented in Table 5, were positive and significant at an alpha-level of .05. Within each nation, the correlation between the math self-confidence and mathematics achievement was greater than the one between the math interest and mathematics achievement. Moreover, the difference between the two correlations was more marked for China and the U.S.

The structural equation model in Figure 2 (illustrating the correlated "affective" and "evaluative" components of mathematics self-concept in predicting mathematics achievement) indicated a good fit for each of the three nations. Table 6 indicated the goodness-of-fit indices. Predicting mathematics achievement from either one of the two math attitudes revealed an emerging picture. For all three nations, math self-confidence significantly predicted mathematics achievement in a

Table 3 - The Goodness-of-Fit Indices for "Multiple-Groups" Model and for the Five Nested Models

	X^2(df), p-value	GFI	CFI	RMSEA
"Multiple-Groups" Model (No Constraint)	72.92(102), $p<.05$	0.95	0.98	0.03
Nested Model 1 (Factor loading for affective math SDQ invariant across groups)	211.58(110), $p<.05$	0.94	0.98	0.04
Nested Model 2 (Factor loading for evaluative math SDQ invariant across groups)	180.94(110), $p<.05$	0.95	0.98	0.03
Nested Model 3 (Factor loading & error variances for affective math SDQ invariant across groups)	268.5(120), $p<.05$	0.94	0.97	0.04
Nested Model 4 (Factor loading & error variances for evaluative math SDQ invariant across groups)	216.3(120), $p<.05$	0.94	0.98	0.03
Nested Model 5 (Covariance between factors of math SDQ invariant across groups)	184.37(104), $p<.05$	0.95	0.98	0.03

Table 4 - Factor Loadings for the Two-Factor Model

Model Path	China	Taiwan	U.S.
A1→Affective	.55	.83	.77
A2→ Affective	.59	.74	.84
A3→ Affective	.85	.93	.85
A4→ Affective	.76	.92	.96
A5→ Affective	.86	.88	.89
E1→ Evaluative	.71	.78	.83
E2→ Evaluative	.76	.85	.80
E3→ Evaluative	.67	.77	.84
E4→ Evaluative	.75	.87	.87
E5→ Evaluative	.60	.66	.71

Table 5 – Correlation Coefficients among the Components of
Math Self-Concept and Mathematics Achievement

	China N=201	Taiwan N=210	U.S. N=250
Pearson correlation p-value <.000 (2-tailed)			
Affective & Evaluative factors of math SDQ	0.67	0.85	0.63
Evaluative Factor & Mathematics Achievement	0.42	0.59	0.53
Affective Factor & Mathematics Achievement	0.28	0.49	0.29

positive direction when math interest was held constant (β_{China} = .45, β_{Taiwan} = 1.12, $\beta_{U.S.}$ = .69). However, for all three nations, math interest (affective component) did not significantly predict mathematics achievement when math self-confidence was held constant.

Figure 2 – SEM Model with Correlated Affective and Evaluative Components of Mathematics Self-Concept Predicting Mathematics Achievement

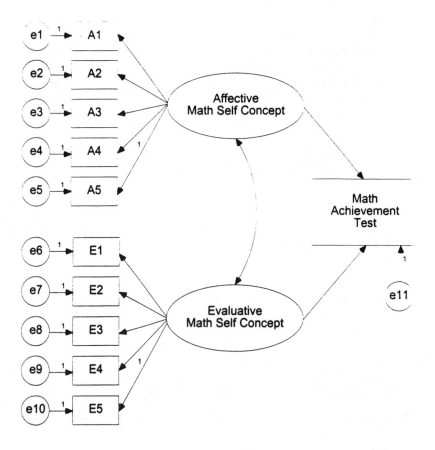

Table 6 - Goodness-of-Fit Indices for the SEM with Components of Mathematics Self-Concept Predicting Mathematics Achievement

	China N=201	Taiwan N=210	U.S. N=250
X^2(df), p-value	58.57(42), p <.05	66.53(42), p <.05	84.29(42), p <.05
GFI	0.95	0.95	0.94
CFI	0.98	0.99	0.98
RMSEA	0.04	0.05	0.06

DISCUSSION

The current study examined the dimensionality of mathematics self-concept and its relationship with mathematics achievement in sixth-grade students across three nations: China, Taiwan, and the United States. Several questions were examined in the paper with respect to the structure of self-concept and the relationship between math attitudes and mathematics achievement. In sum, the results indicated that (a) the pattern of mathematics achievement prediction from math attitudes was comparable for all three nations, (b) math self-confidence (evaluative component) predicted mathematics achievement significantly and positively when math interest was held constant, and (c) in contrast, math interest (affective component) did not significantly predict mathematics achievement when math self-confidence was held constant.

A parallel line of self-concept study operated within a "network" frame. Byrne (1984, 1996) categorized the research on the structure of self-concept as "within-network" and "between-network" studies. Within network research designs view the multidimensionality of self-concept with an emphasis on consistent and distinct components; whereas between-network studies focus on the relationship of measures of self-concept to criterion measures and depict a consistent and logical pattern of relationships (Irwing, 1996). Similar to within-network studies, the results of the current confirmatory factor analyses supported the distinct "affective" and "evaluative" components of math self-concept as well as provided consistency in interpretation across the studied nations.

Within the present study, the results of the invariance tests for the two-factor measurement model indicated the validity of math self-confidence, or the evaluative component, both with respect to the chi-square difference test and the goodness-of-fit indices for China, Taiwan, and the United States. The validity of math interest, or the affective component, and the equivalence of the reliabilities for both components were confirmed with respect to the goodness-of-fit indices across the three nations. In sum, this illustrated construct comparability via factor structure comparability across the three nations. Therefore the mathematics sub-scale of the Self-Description Questionnaire (Marsh, 1992) was found to be valid and reliable for our sample. This was a strength of the present study as the assurance of construct validity and the reliability of the measurement of math attitudes is essential when undertaking cross-national research.

A particular focus within general cross-cultural research, and within this study specifically, is the relationship between the affective and evaluative components of math self-concept and mathematics achievement. Stevenson et al. (1990) found positive relationships of mathematics achievement with math interest (affective math self-concept), ranging from .15 to .46 and mathematics achievement with math self-evaluations of performance (evaluative math self-concept), ranging from .41 to .49 across Taiwan, Japan and the United States. Within the present study, the correlations between math self-evaluations of performance and math interest were also positive ranging from .58 to .77 across Taiwan, Japan and the U.S. These results support similar findings from several other cross-cultural studies (e.g., Beaton et al., 1996; Hansford & Hattie, 1982; Mullis et al., 1997; Stevenson, Lummis, Lee & Stigler, 1990).

Previous research found strong relationships between academic self-concept and academic achievement when achievement was operationalized with school grades or teacher ratings rather than by standardized test scores (Marsh, 1987, 1990c, 1993a, 1994; Wylie, 1979). The current study measured academic achievement using mathematics tests, which are less subjective and can be evaluated for validity and reliability.

Most of the previous studies, focusing on different domains of academic self-concept, ignored the two-dimensional structure of domain specific academic self-concept (Irwing, 1996). As Irwing (1996) noted, ignoring this two-dimensional structure in mathematics self-concept has resulted in the underestimation of the relationship between self-concept and other constructs. Consistent with this argument, the current study found higher associations between self-concept and achievement when the evaluative component of self-concept was acknowledged.

Using structural equation modeling (SEM), two questions of special importance to the between-network studies were addressed in the present study: (1) what is the effect of evaluative math self-concept on mathematics achievement after controlling for the affective math self-concept?; and (2) conversely, what is the effect of the affective math self-concept on mathematics achievement after controlling for the evaluative math self-concept? The SEM results indicated a positive effect of evaluative self-concept on achievement after controlling for the affective component and no effect of the affective self-concept on achievement after controlling for the evaluative component for all three nations. Moreover, the tests of invariance results indicated no difference among the magnitudes of these effects across China, Taiwan, and the U.S. In other words, following the pattern of between-network studies (Irwing, 1996; Marsh, 1990a), it was found that evaluative component of math self-concept predicted mathematics achievement better than the affective component across the three nations.

Additionally, within cross-cultural research, the relationship between the different components of math self-concept and mathematics achievement has been studied mainly within a correlational analysis research design (Mullis et al., 1997; Stevenson & Lee, 1990; Stevenson, Lee, Chen, Stigler, Fan, & Ge, 1990). Therefore, the effect of math interest on mathematics achievement after controlling for math confidence has not been compared nor questioned across various cultures. However, this was specifically addressed within the current study. After controlling for students' perceptions of performance in mathematics or their math self-confidence, math interest was not able to predict mathematics achievement for the Chinese, Taiwanese, and the U.S. sixth graders. This offers a new insight to the relationship between math interest and mathematics achievement across the three different nations.

While evidence for the distinction between the affective and evaluative components of self-concept has been found for our samples of Chinese, Taiwanese, and U.S. sixth graders, future studies should seek to cross-validate the two-factor structure of mathematics self-concept across age levels, various cultures and by gender. It should be noted that an examination of gender differences was not a focus of this paper. While no mean gender differences were found for the different components of math self-concept in this study, the factor structure and construct comparability was not specifically tested for each gender. Additionally, it is important for future research to validate the affective component of math self-concept by seeking a construct that may be related to the affective component versus the evaluative component.

In sum, this study compared the nature and the level of math self-concept across samples of Chinese, Taiwanese, and U.S. sixth graders. The research reported herein clearly indicates that there is a distinction between the affective and evaluative components of mathematics self-concept which is applicable to these cross-national samples. The findings also generalize the positive effect of evaluative math self-concept on mathematics achievement to the three nations under study. Moreover, the findings show that affective math self-concept does not predict mathematics achievement when keeping the evaluative math self-concept constant. However, while the purpose of this study was to evaluate constructs cross-nationally, a natural progression would be to further evaluate academic self-concepts by gender, socio-economic status, and student ability. While the U.S.

sample was considered to be representative within this study, further research is needed within the United States in particular in order to explore the impact of ethnic diversity, social class, and gender. Additional comparisons could be made between similar ability student samples, such that high, middle, and low achievers in order to determine if the constructs hold across ability levels as well.

Several possible prescriptive actions can be posed. This study found variability in the motivation in 6th grade pre-adolescent students, therefore interventions or educational programs aimed at changing this should target children at earlier ages. Parents, teachers, and school administrators should be made aware of these findings in order to monitor the academic achievement of the children, while taking into consideration the role that self-confidence may play. While parents can be reached through newsletters and conferences, teachers and administrators would benefit from more extensive training programs and in-service sessions that address the incorporation of motivational methods into the curriculum. When additional research has been completed, those results may also give further direction in targeting specific school subjects for self-confidence strategies, with the possible necessity of attending to the gender, achievement level, social class, or ethnic background of students.

In the end, given the results of this study, what children are thinking may be more important than how they feel. In other words, a child's cognitive processes regarding academic subjects, in particular mathematics, may be more influential for their achievement than affective processes. Keeping this in mind, it is important that studies of this kind are replicated within the various academic disciplines in order to determine if there are similar patterns across school subjects. If this trend continues to hold true both within the United States and cross-nationally, it is important that those who formulate public policy are made aware of these findings. The multi-layered constructs that have been found within academic self-concepts should be given due consideration, particularly with the current movement toward legislative and curriculum reform underway within the schools in the United States. This has several implications for the nations under study and for the United States in particular. In the U.S., there has been a shift away from the consideration of self-confidence as an academic goal, with a return to the "basics," such as reading and writing. Rather than an "either/or" approach, it may be prudent to incorporate school subject self-confidence strategies with a "back-to-the-basics" approach to learning. Ultimately, the findings of this study, which are built upon those of others, can be used to further our understanding of academic achievement and lead to the facilitation of achievement for all students.

REFERENCES

Abu-Hilal, M., & Aal-Hussain, A. (1997). Dimensionality and hierarchy of the SDQ in a non-Western milieu: A test of self-concept invariance across gender. *Journal of Cross-Cultural Psychology, 28,* 535-553.

Bandalos, D.L., Yates, K., & Thorndike-Christ, T. (1995). Effects of math self-concept, perceived self-efficacy, and attributions for failure and success on test anxiety. *Journal of Educational Psychology, 87,* 611-623.

Beaton, A., Mullis, I., Martin, M., Gonzalez, E., Kelly, D., & Smith, T. (1996). *Mathematics achievement in the middle school years: IEA's third international mathematics and science study (TIMSS).* Chestnut Hill, MA: Center for the Study of Testing, Evaluation, and Educational Policy, Boston College.

Boersma, F.J., & Chapman, J.W. (1992). *Perceptions of Ability Scale for Students.* Los Angeles: Western Psychological Services.

Boyle, G. (1994). Self-description questionnaire II: A review. *Test Critiques, 10,* 632-643.

Bracken, B.A. (1992). *Multidimensional Self-Concept Scale.* Austin, TX: Pro-Ed.

Brislin, R. (1993). *Handbook of self-concept: Developmental, social, and clinical considerations.* Orlando: Harcourt Brace Jovanovich.

Brown, L., & Alexander, J. (1991). *Self-Esteem Index.* Austin, TX: Pro-Ed.

Byrne, B. (1984). The general/ academic self-concept nomological network: A review of construct validation research. *Review of Educational Research, 54,* 427-456.

Byrne, B. (1996). Academic self-concept: Its structure, measurement, and relation to academic achievement. In B.A. Bracken (Ed.), *Handbook of self-concept* (pp. 287-316). New York: Wiley.

Byrne, B., & Carlson, J.E. (1982, March). *Self-concept and academic achievement: A causal modeling approach to construct validation using a multiple-indicator structural equation model.* Paper presented at Annual Meeting of American Educational Research Association, New York.

Chapman, J.W., Cullen, J.L., Boersma, F.J., & Maguire, T.D. (1981). Affective variables and school achievement: A study of possible causal influences. *Canadian Journal of Behavioural Science*, 13, 181-192.

Coopersmith, S. (1967). *The antecedents of self-esteem.* San Francisco, CA: Freeman.

Covington, M.V., & Omelich, C.L. (1984). An empirical examination of Weiner's critique of attribution research. *Journal of Educational Psychology*, 76, 1214-1225.

Eccles, J., Wigfield, A., Flanagan, C., Miller, C., Reuman, D., & Yee, D. (1989). Self-concepts, domain values, and self-esteem: Relations and changes at early adolescence. *Journal of Personality*, 57, 283-310.

Guilford, J.P. (1985). The structure-of-intellect model. In B. B. Wolman (Ed.), *Handbook on intelligence: Theory, measurement and applications.* New York: Wiley.

Hansford, B.D., & Hattie, J.A. (1982). The relationship between self and achievement/ performance measures. *Review of Educational Research*, 52, 123-142.

Harter, S. (1985). *Manual for the Self-perception Profile for Children.* Denver, CO: University of Denver.

Hattie, J. (1992). *Self-concept.* Hillsdale, NJ: Erlbaum.

Irwing, P. (1996). Evaluative and affective dimensions of self-concept: A test of construct validity using structural equations modeling. *Psychological Reports*, 79, 1127-1138.

Joreskog, K.G., & Sorbom, D. (1986). *LISREL VI user's guide: Analysis of linear structural relationships by maximum likelihood, instrumental variables, and least squares methods.* Mooresville, IN: Scientific Software, Inc.

Joreskog, K.G., & Sorbom, D. (1989). *LISREL 7: A guide to the program and applications.* Chicago: SPSS, Inc.

Keith, L., & Bracken, B. (1996). Self-concept instrumentation: A historical and evaluative review. In B. Bracken (Ed.), *Handbook of self-concept: Developmental, social, and clinical considerations* (pp. 91-170). New York: John Wiley & Sons, Inc.

Kloosterman, P. (1991). Beliefs and achievement in seventh-grade mathematics. *Focus on Learning Problems in Mathematics*, 13, 3-15.

Long, J.S. (1983). *Confirmatory factor analysis.* Beverly Hills, CA: Sage.

Markus, H.R. & Kitayama, S. (1991). Culture and the self: Implications for cognition, emotion, and motivation. *Psychological Review*, 98, 224-253.

Marsh, H. (1984). Relations among dimensions of self-attribution, dimensions of self-concept, and academic achievements. *Journal of Educational Psychology*, 76, 1291-1308.

Marsh, H. (1987). The hierarchical structure of self-concept and the application of hierarchical confirmatory factor analysis. *Journal of Educational Measurement*, 24, 17-19.

Marsh, H. (1988). *Self-Description Questionnaire, I.* San Antonio, TX: The Psychological Corporation.

Marsh, H. (1989). Age and sex effects in multiple dimensions of self-concept: Preadolescence to early adulthood. *Journal of Educational Psychology*, 81, 417-430.

Marsh, H. (1990a). The structure of academic self-concept: The Marsh/Shavelson model. *Journal of Educational Psychology*, 82, 623-636.

Marsh, H. (1990b). The causal ordering of academic self-concept and academic achievement: A multiwave, longitudinal path analysis. *Journal of Educational Psychology*, 82, 646-656.

Marsh, H. (1990c). A multidimensional, hierarchical model of self-concept: Theoretical and empirical justification. *Educational Psychology Review*, 2, 77-172.

Marsh, H. (1992). *Self-Description Questionnaire I: Manual.* Macarthur, Australia: Publication Unit, Faculty of Education, University of Western Sydney.

Marsh, H. (1993a). Academic self-concept: Theory measurement and research. In J. Suls (Ed.), *Psychological perspectives on the self* (Vol. 4, pp. 59-98). Hillsdale, NJ: Erlbaum.

Marsh, H. (1994). Confirmatory factory analysis models of factorial invariance: A multifaceted approach. *Structural Equation Modeling*, 1, 5-34.

Marsh, H.W., Byrne, M.B., & Shavelson, R.J. (1988). A multifaceted academic self-concept: its relation to academic achievement. *Journal of Educational Psychology*, 80, 366-380.

Marsh, H.W., & Craven, R.G. (1991). Self-other agreement on multiple dimensions of preadolescent self-concept: Inferences by teachers, mothers, and fathers. *Journal of Educational Psychology*, 83, 393-404.

Marsh, H., & Gouvernet, P. (1989). Multidimensional self-concepts and perceptions of control: construct validation of responses by children. *Journal of Educational Psychology*, 81, 57-69.

Marsh, H., & Hattie, J. (1996). Theoretical perspectives on the structure of self-concept. In B. Bracken (Ed.), *Handbook of self-concept: Developmental, social, and clinical considerations* (pp. 38-89). New York: John Wiley & Sons, Inc.

Marsh, H., & Hocevar, D. (1985). Application of confirmatory factor analysis to the study of self-concept: First- and higher order factor models and their invariance across groups. *Psychological Bulletin, 97,* 562-582.

Marsh, H., & Shavelson, R.J. (1985). Self-concept: Its multifaceted, hierarchical structure. *Educational Psychologist, 20,* 107-125.

Marsh, H., & Yeung, A. (1997). Causal effects of academic self-concept on academic achievement: Structural equation models of longitudinal data. *Journal of Educational Psychology, 89,* 41-54.

Marsh, H., & Yeung, A. (1998). Longitudinal structural equation models of academic self-concept and achievement: Gender differences in the development of math and English constructs. *American Educational Research Journal, 35*(4), 705-738.

Marx, R.W., & Winne, P.H. (1978). Construct interpretations of three self-concept inventories. *American Educational Research Journal,* 15, 99-109.

Mullis, I., Martin, M., Beaton, A., Gonzalez, E., Kelly, D., & Smith, T. (1997). *Mathematics achievement in the primary school years: IEA's third international mathematics and science study (TIMSS).* Chestnut Hill, MA: Center for the Study of Testing, Evaluation, and Educational Policy, Boston College.

Pajares, F., & Miller, M. (1994). Role of self-efficacy and self-concept beliefs in mathematical problem solving: A path analysis. *Journal of Educational Psychology, 86,* 193-203.

Revicki, D.A. (1982, March). *The relationship between self-concept and achievement: An investigation of reciprocal effects.* Paper presented at the Annual Meeting of the American Educational Research Association, New York, NY.

Reyes, L.H. (1984). Affective variables and mathematics education. *Elementary School Journal, 84,* 558-581.

Schumacker, R., & Lomax, R. (1996*). A beginner's guide to structural equation modeling.* Mahwah, NJ: Lawrence Erlbaum Associates.

Shavelson, J.R., Bolus, R. (1982). Self-concept: The interplay of theory and methods. *Journal of Educational Psychology*, 74, 3-17.

Shavelson, J.R., Hubner, J.J., & Stanton, G.C. (1976). Validation of construct interpretations. *Review of Educational Research*, 46, 407-441.

Simpson, S., Licht, B., Wagner, R., & Stader, S. (1996). Organization of children's academic ability-related self-perceptions. *Journal of Educational Psychology*, 88, 387-396.

Skaalvik, E., (1997). Self-enhancing and self-defeating ego orientation: Relations with task and avoidance orientation, achievement, self-perceptions, and anxiety. *Journal of Educational Psychology*, 89, 71-81.

Skaalvik, E., & Hagtvet, K. (1990). Academic achievement and self-concept: An analysis of causal predominance in a developmental perspective. *Journal of Personality and Social Psychology*, 58, 292-307.

Soares, L.M., & Soares, A.T. (1977, April). *The self-concept: Mini, maxi, multi.* Paper presented at the annual meetingof the American Educational Research Association, New York.

Stevenson, H., & Lee, S. (1990). Contexts of achievement. *Monographs of the Society for Research in Child Development*, 55, 49-58.

Stevenson, H.W., Lee, S-Y, & Stigler, J.W. (1986). Mathematics achievement of Chinese, Japanese, and American children. *Science*, 231, 593-699.

Stevenson, H.W., Lee, S-Y, Chen, C., Stigler, J.W., Fan, L., & Ge, F. (1990). Mathematics achievement of children in China and the United States. *Child Development*, 61, 1053-1066.

Stevenson, H., Lummis, M., Lee, S & Stigler, J.W. (1990*). Making the grade in mathematics.* Reston, Virginia: The National Council of Teachers of Mathematics, Inc.

Strein, W. (1993). Advances in research on academic self-concept: Implications for school psychology. *School Psychology Review*, 22, 273-284.

Triandis, H.C. (1989). The self and social behavior in differing cultural context. *Psychological Review*, 96, 506-520.

Vijver, F.van de, & Leung, K. (1997). *Methods and data analysis for cross-cultural research.* Thousand Oaks, CA: Sage Publications.

Watkins, D., & Astilla, E. (1986). Causal dominance among self-concept, locus of causality, and academic achievement. *The Journal of Psychology*, 120, 627-633.

Watkins, D., & Cheung, S. (1995). Culture, gender, and response bias: An analysis of responses to the Self-Description Questionnaire. *Journal of Cross-Cultural Psychology*, 26, 490-504.

Wylie, R. (1979*). The self-concept (Vol. 1).* Lincoln, NE: University of Nebraska Press.

Wylie, R. (1989). *Measures of self-concept.* Lincoln, NE: University of Nebraska Press.

Correspondence concerning this study should be addressed to Deniz Senturk, Graduate School of Education, University of California, Santa Barbara, California 93106. Electronic mail may be sent via Internet to dsenturk@education.ucsb.edu. The home mailing address is 770-K Cypress Walk, Goleta, California 93117, with a home telephone number of (805) 971-6924.

ACKNOWLEDGEMENTS
We would like to acknowledge the contribution of the principals, teachers, and the students of the schools that participated in the study. Appreciation is extended to the school officials and ministries of education in the respective nations for their support of the project. This research was supported in part by grants to Drs. Ho and Zimmer from the Pacific Rim Research Program, University of California, Office of the President, Berkeley, CA 94720.

4. *Student Hopes Transcend Fears: School Transition in an Urban School Cluster System*

Donna P. Towns and Hakim Rashid

Many reasons have been given for the disproportionate failure of students of color in the nation's schools. While transition from one school level to another has been cited as a factor affecting the general population of students, the objective of our study was to discover whether or not the issues surrounding school transition were the same for low-income, minority children in an inner-city feeder system as they are for other children. The answer that emerged from our study of third, fifth and eighth grade students in the system was that in some significant ways the issues are different. In this paper, we propose (1) to present data from both teachers and students in a predominantly African American school feeder system which reveal a polarity between teacher and student expectations surrounding moving up the school ladder, (2) to show ways in which these perspectives compare and contrast with those found in the literature, and (3) to suggest implications for school reform.

Most of our inner-city schools are located in communities that no longer have the resources--financial or emotional--to provide the kinds of support that children need for optimal performance in school. Further, neighborhood stress has brought about an alienation and disconnectedness among formerly closely-knit institutions, such as the family, the school, the church and the business community. The complexity of the problem has brought educators and policymakers to the realization that piecemeal efforts to address this problem are not adequate and that a more systemic approach is required. While what constitutes a systemic reform is still a debatable issue, initiatives in that direction have taken the form of the re-creation of collaboratives both between the community and the school and among schools within a neighborhood feeder-school system (Butler 1994, Colorado Department of Education 1983, Unseem 1994). Among the manifestations of the former is the formation of university/school partnerships and of the latter a "cluster" school system.

This paper will address the processes and outcomes involved in a university/cluster-school collaboration with a focus on one aspect of such a collaboration: a school-to-school transition study. The purpose of the paper is not only to provide insights that may be beneficial to others anticipating such collaboration, but to add to the data on school transition for minority children who have been placed at risk for failure.

A multi-disciplinary team of university-based researchers in a research center located in an inner-city, minority community in the Mid-Atlantic Region of the United States, set out in September, 1995 to examine the impact of an intensive collaboration of university educators, researchers, district and school personnel, parents and community participants on the achievement, motivation, and success of school-age children that matriculate through an urban public school feeder system. Utilizing both quantitative and qualitative research methods, efforts were directed toward gathering base-line data on demographics of the schools involved, teacher-and student-attitudes and perceptions of school life and the inter-personal dynamics among principals, teachers, central administrative personnel, parents and community representatives.

The literature on collaborative, feeder systems indicates that problems challenging the successful implementation of the concept rest largely in strained interpersonal relationships, sustaining a high level of "buy in" by all the parties (Brown 1994, Walker 1992) and school transition issues (Fenzel 1989, Pettit 1994, Simmons 1991, Taylor 1991).

THE CASE STUDY - *The Five-School Academy*
This inner-city feeder-system cluster (we shall call "the Academy") began in the 1991-92 School Year, when central administration, in response to community outcry for stemming the disintegration of its schools in a major restructuring initiative, designed a two-phased plan based on the feeder-system, collaborative school cluster concept. The first phase (School Year 1991-1992) involved one lower-elementary school (headstart through grade

3), one upper elementary school (grades 4 and 5) and one middle school (grades 6 through 8). The second phase (1992-1993 School Year) included another lower elementary school and a high school (grades 9 through 12). Underlying the design was the premise that student success may be predicted through collaborative efforts that yielded effective educational programs. The mission statement articulated by central educational administration office was "to provide a continuous learning experience for urban, culturally diverse students, headstart through adult education, on five specialized campuses spanning three instructional levels: early childhood, intermediate, and secondary." In targeting this particular group of schools, the community was described by some as the city's most culturally diverse, but troubled section. The goals were aimed at improving family and community involvement through a family learning center, offering English as a Second Language classes and cultural and ethnic enrichment programs. A university/school cluster partnership was recommended at the outset.

Since the philosophy of the Research Center was strongly centered in the co-construction of reform efforts in collaborating with schools, one of the first questions raised was how could the university be of assistance to the schools. The principals articulated that their major concerns were quality of school life for the students and improved academic performance. These were completely in sync with those of the research center and the areas identified for immediate collaboration were: (1) tutoring of students; (2) professional development for the teaching staff; and (3) facilitating transition for students as they moved through the system from lower elementary to upper elementary, from upper elementary to middle school and from middle school to high school.

Before launching an intervention program in response to the transition issue, several questions required preliminary investigation: (1) What existing programs did the cluster have to ease transition for the students?; (2) What were the students' and teachers' perceptions of the need or existing efforts to facilitate transition?; and (3) What did the literature say about the issue of transition for students in general and for minority students in particular?

Review of the Literature on Transition Issues
Moving from one school to another, whether it be a transfer or a natural progression in grade level, has been the subject of many studies in the field (Hargreaves, 1990, 1993). The transition issue in the literature evolves around children's developmental issues as well as the schools' structural and pedagogical issues (Fenzel 1989, Pettit, 1994; Seidman, 1994; Simmons,

1991; Taylor, 1991). The fact that such transitions can be a stressful event in the life of a school child has been documented (Smith, 1991; Odegaard, 1992). Some studies point out the anxiety experienced in moving abruptly to new surroundings (Marlett, 1993; Weldy, 1991). Others pinpoint the new academic challenges that the students face (Feldlaufer & Eccles, 1988) positing that a major change in the classroom environment occurs in the elementary to junior high school transition. Students are given few opportunities to make suggestions about the context of instruction, there is an increase in whole class organization, and there is a decrease in cooperative interaction.

In addition, post transition teachers are characterized as less caring, less warm, less friendly and less supportive than pre-transition teachers. Developmental issues are the focus of other studies (Fenzel, 1989; (Nottelmann, 1982; Seidman 1994). These refer to physical development (Nottelman 1982) as well as behavioral repertoire. Some scholars have suggested that trauma related to school transition that begins as early as the home or preschool to kindergarten transition, can have lasting effects throughout the school career of a student. Taylor (1991) has identified it as a problem in "goodness of fit" for many African American children. According to Taylor, "goodness of fit" matches occur when there is congruence between teacher expectations and the behavioral repertoire the child brings to the classroom. When kindergarten teachers expect a particular kind of academic competence (e.g. knowing the alphabet) or a particular kind of social competence (e.g. sitting still while a story is being read), and the competence is not forthcoming over time, the resulting label is likely to follow a child as he or she makes the transition to first grade. From Ebaugh's (1988) role-exit perspective, children for whom the transition into first grade is problematic are likely to experience doubts as they exit the role of kindergartners and assume the role of students who are about the business of getting an education. This process may lead young children to search for alternate roles such as "high achiever," "most popular," or "class clown" roles that may have implications for achievement in later school years.

According to Entwisle and Alexander (1989), the transition into first grade can be viewed as a "critical period" for a young child's academic development. Just as the nature of the child's thinking is undergoing a critical transition, so also is the nature of the schooling process itself. First grade represents a transition from the more social and affective orientated kindergarten to a classroom context that is organized around skill acquisition, particularly in the area of reading and math. First grade is where formal grading often makes its first appearance in a young children' life.

The next major transition is from third to fourth grade, a transition that can be characterized as moving from early childhood to primary education. O'Brien (1991) has contrasted the goals of early childhood programs with the goals of primary school classrooms. This shift in goals is directly related to the changes in teacher roles in early childhood compared with primary classrooms.

The fourth major transition encountered in the K-12 system is the middle/junior high to high school transition, typically from eighth to ninth grade. Many high schools are characterized by a large impersonal environment that places under achievement students at further risk. In many urban districts, the high drop out rate is related to the alienation felt by students during their ninth grade year. The reform efforts of many high schools are now including ninth grade academies designed to create smaller learning communities that are more responsive to students as they make their critical transition (LaPoint 1996; Roderick 1993).

Differences between black and white students in making the adjustment to a new school environment have been noted (Entwisle &Alexander 1988; Simmons, Black & Zhou 1991; Taylor, 1991). Davis and Jordan (1995) examined contextual and structural factors affecting the success of African American male students in the transition to high school. They pointed out the deleterious effects on these students with an over-emphasis on disciplinary activities.

Interventions suggested by some scholars include peer helpers (Pettit, 1994) and shadowing (Ferguson, 1994) designed to help the incoming students not only in social adjustment, but academically as well. Adult mentoring has also been recommended (McPartland, 1991) along with parental involvement (Pohl, 1995).

In keeping with findings in our study, Graham (1994) disputed the theory that poor performance on the part of African American students was attributable to low expectations and motivation on the part of those students. Our study suggests that African American students in an urban system often move into a new school environment with high expectations. Their disproportionate rate of failure as reported in national studies may be due to the failure of the new school to nurture and sustain such enthusiasm. The impact of abrupt change, more rigorous academic challenges, and developmental changes may be secondary in importance to that one factor.

Categories for exploration in school transition
Based on a review of the literature and our own observations, we decided that the issues we wanted to explore in relation to transition were: (1)

differences at the various school levels in inter-personal relationships between the teacher and the students and among students; (2) differences in curriculum and teaching techniques; (3) what was being offered by both the receiving and the departure schools to ease the transition for students; (4) teachers' perceptions of the transition issues; and (5) the students' perceptions. In this article, we will focus on the last two categories: teachers' and students' perceptions of the issues involved in school transition and the effectiveness of existing programs.

Methodology
We decided to begin the transition study with the "departure" classes. In this cluster, that meant grades three, five and eight. A variety of research methods were utilized: surveys, participant/observation, structured interviews and open-ended interviews with both students and teachers. Participant observation of overall school climate began at the beginning of the school year. The surveys were administered in the middle of the year and the classroom observations and interviews were carried out at the end of the school year.

The research was carried out by a team of researchers from the university center. The team of researchers consisted of a principal investigator, who was also a professor of human development in the School of Education, a research associate, who was an anthropologist with a specialty in classroom ethnography and eight graduate assistants from the School of Education and Department of Psychology at the University.

To gather data in these three areas, researchers: (1) sat in on joint meetings of principals of the five schools in the cluster and the central administration "project coordinator;" (2) participated in once a month "Academy Collaborative Meetings" which involved principals, teachers, support staff, parents, the project coordinator, and a representative from the Local School Restructuring Team of each school; (3) attended special assemblies and activity days at the cluster schools; (4) observed beginning of school activities to note transition issues; (5) observed transition classrooms at the end of the school year for a two-week period; (6) held structured interviews with teachers of transition classes; and (7) interviewed students in the departure classes.

Although a "Letter of Understanding" had been negotiated between the school district and the university center, letters were sent to the principals of the schools explaining the purpose of the study and seeking their permission to observe classes and to interview teachers and students. After many follow-up telephone calls and visits to the school, permission was obtained.

Teacher Interviews

Interviews with the teachers whose classrooms had been observed, were conducted by the principal investigator and the research associate on the project working together. Some of the interviews were conducted during school hours and others after school. Both researchers took notes in each session and later analyzed the data in terms of both grade and gender differences. Twelve teachers in the feeder system were interviewed. The teachers represented the departure grades from lower elementary to upper elementary, from upper elementary to middle school, and from middle to high school. Some were interviewed individually and some in groups, based on exigencies of their schools at the time. In addition, teachers were asked to fill out a form indicating their opinion as to the ease of transition on the part of each student in their class. Six questions were put to the teachers during the interviews. The research questions that related to the issues presented in this paper were as follows:

(1)   Are there any teaching methods that will change for
      them next year?
(2)   Do you have activities specifically designed for school
      transition?
(3)   What are some of the issues that you feel we should
      consider in studying school transition?
(4)   Do you anticipate any gender differences in making
      the transition?

While the researchers were careful to see that all the above questions were asked, a rigid format was not followed. When the teachers' responses led to other questions, these were pursued and conversation was allowed to flow freely. Whereas some of the teachers had been reluctant to allow their classes to be observed by the observers, all who participated in the interviews appeared to do so without hesitation, which is not to say that rescheduling was not often the case.

Teaching Methods

In response to the first research question, all the teachers felt that things would change in significant ways for the students after they made the transition to their new schools in the fall. Some of the changes anticipated were social in nature, while others related to school structure and pedagogy. Social changes noted by third grade teachers involved the opinion that students would be moving from an atmosphere that allowed the development of self-discipline, to a more externally-imposed disciplinary system: "I let students think for themselves... I don't tell them things," said one male third-grade teacher. The same teacher added, however, "we have the "Responsive Classroom Model" that they won't have at the fourth grade level, but I have my own method of interpreting it. I don't allow students to walk around when they want to. They are not from an environment that fosters that kind of freedom." Some felt choice period needed to be controlled and rules established at the beginning of the year.

Another female third-grade teacher saw the greatest difference between third and fourth-grade teachers as a philosophical one: "Our way of dealing with children is based on the premise that children develop differently. The fourth grade is not as concerned with developmental issues. The management technique will change. We merely remind them of the rules that they have established. We don't holler at them."

The third grade teachers were in agreement that their students would be moving from a student-oriented classroom to a teacher-oriented one. Associated with this was the belief that the third graders would no longer be allowed to settle disputes through peer mediation. The third-grade teachers felt that cooperative work and play that they had encouraged would be discouraged, by fourth-grade teachers.

One of the fifth-grade teachers who said that she, too, used the "Responsive Classroom Model" indicated that she did not like choice time. "It might work better if they were different, yes smarter, kids. Maybe then they could handle choice time. When they have finished doing their work, I assign something for them to do until the others are ready."

Some of the fifth-grade teachers worried about their students' ability to adjust to the single-gender classrooms of the middle school. Middle school teachers, on the other hand, feared that the girls especially, might not be able to "handle" the freedom to interact with boys in classes at the high school level, since "girls tend to get distracted by the boys."

All teachers at every grade level in the study felt certain that the teachers in the receiving schools would not be as nurturing and as tolerant of student misconduct and shortcomings as they had been.

With regard to pedagogy, the teachers anticipated the most dramatic changes between grade three and four, rather than from elementary to middle or middle to high school. In relation to language arts, the third grade teachers thought the whole language approach would change to a more skills-based approach in the fourth grade. They felt that teachers at the upper elementary school did not have the resources to supplement teaching aids and reading materials that they had provided for their students, sometimes out of their personal funds. The eighth grade teachers expressed the same sentiment, saying that they often "bought their own school supplies and they doubted that the high school teachers would do that." The third grade teachers feared their students' ability to adjust to a new assessment program that took them from a "continuous progress" program to possible retention after the fourth grade; from proficiency grades to absolute letter grades. They also anticipated a move for their students from "community-based instruction to a textbook orientation." One of the third-grade male teachers was adamant in his feeling that the move would be detrimental to the students, unless he could move up with them. This strategy, called "looping" had worked for him in the past. The following are his words:

> "I read to the students a lot and they write a lot. More than they will next year. I have five shelves of books that the students have to select from. They type a lot on the computer. They actually created their own literary magazine. (He shows us a copy.) I have been with the same students since they were in the second grade. I would like to go to the fourth grade with them. I'm afraid that they will change. I have some geniuses in here. Some have scored at the 8th grade level in reading and math on the CTBS. Moving with the students helped me to learn how to teach and to communicate and to change with the students. I could actually see where I had prepared them well for the third grade and where I had not."

The fifth grade teachers described the transition to middle school for their students as a movement from a more "hands-on approach to a more abstract approach to learning in the sixth grade." The fifth grade teachers were also concerned about their students' adjustment to moving as individuals from one subject teacher to another in the middle school without the whole class moving as a unit, as was the case in the upper elementary school.

The teachers at each level anticipated that teachers at the next level up would place more stress on individualistic learning and not encourage cooperative learning to the extent that they had done. A third grade teacher emphasized that, "We have cooperative learning and interactive learning here." A fifth-grade teacher said, "I use a cooperative learning method. The students like it." An eighth-grade teacher said, "we have cooperative learning and interdisciplinary units." At each of these levels, the teachers were certain that students would not be exposed to the same techniques in their new schools.

Designed Activities for School Transition

When teachers were asked whether they had activities especially designed for school transition, reference was usually made to what had been done in the past. For example, a female third grade teacher said, "We used to go over to H school (which contained the fourth grade) to actually see what the school would be like, but this year there has been such confusion with the change in administration, they haven't done any of that." A third-grade male teacher said, "We have talked and collaborated with the fourth-grade teachers. The problem is that they do not prepare for the kind of students they get." Another third-grade teacher said of fourth- grade teacher visitations, "Visiting our school for a day is not going to prepare them to understand the kids. They should try to find out as much as possible about each student before the student enters the school." The eighth-grade teachers said that although the guidance counselor usually accompanied students to various high schools in the area, only one such school had been visited that year.

On the positive side, one third-grade teacher said that she gave demonstration lessons about "choice time" and group reading to the fourth grade teachers. Another male third-grade teacher said, "I try to combine the whole language method with the skills-based to get them ready for the fourth grade." Two female third-grade teachers said their students, "Read a book called Amber Brown, about going to the fourth grade. They indicated that their students were in the process of writing a "Memory Book" about the third grade. "They write it themselves," one of the teachers said, "and in the sharing time, they will be sharing things about going into the fourth grade with the class." At the fifth grade level, the teachers said that the school's guidance counselor worked with students on transition issues, "She takes every fifth grader to visit G School (the middle school in the feeder-system). The eighth-grade teachers said that they had a project that indirectly had an impact on transition from middle school to high school. It was a project called "Moods and Masks" that allows students to identify different moods and emotions that they experience and to learn how these moods and emotions may affect their high school behavior.

School Transition Issues

The teachers' response to issues that they considered most salient in studying transition were social adjustment (stressed by both third and eighth grade teachers) and the receiving teachers' awareness of the skills and knowledge the incoming students were bringing with them.

Gender Difference

The teachers had two opportunities to indicate whether or not they felt there were difference between the ease with which boys and girls made the transition from one school to another. The question was put to them first in the interview session. Later, they were asked to fill out a form rating anticipated ease of transition for each student in their class on a scale from one to five (1= a very difficult transition to 5= a very easy transition.) A total of 108 children were rated (31 third- graders, 20 fifth-graders and 57 eighth-graders.) No mention was made of a possible analysis on the basis of gender.

The results of the teacher rating scale showed significant differences in teacher expectations and the ease of school transition by both gender and grade level. Forty-one percent (41%) of the male students (13 out of 32) and 11% of the female students (8 out of 75) were expected to have "somewhat difficult," or "very difficult" transitions. Seventy-six (76%) of the females (57 out of 75) and 59% of the males (19 out of 32) were expected to have "somewhat easy," or "very easy" transitions (X = 17.76, D = 5,p.<.005). The teachers were uncertain about 13% of the females (10 out of 75). In terms of grade level, 26% of third-graders (8 out of 31), 5% of fifth graders (1 out of 19) and 21% of eighth-graders (12 out of 75) were expected to have somewhat difficult or very difficult transitions. Sixty one percent of third graders (19 out of 31), 95% of fifth- graders (18 out of 19) and 68% of eighth graders (39 out of 57) were expected to have somewhat easy or very easy transition. Teachers were not sure about 13% of third-graders (4 out of 31) and 11% of eighth-graders. Clearly, the fifth grade teachers were more optimistic about their students' ability to make the transition with ease than the third or eighth-grade teachers.

To the explicit question in the interview sessions, three of the twelve teachers stated that they saw no differences of gender in ability the to make the transition. Most teachers felt that girls would make the transition more easily than boys: A third-grade male teacher stated his reason for this belief," "Girls are more mature and flexible in their thinking." Two third-grade teachers gave academic reasons, "The girls are more eager and conscientious about learning activities," and "The girls are more capable in language arts, but the boys are good in math." Another third-grade teacher disagreed by saying, "Boys are the good readers in my room. The girls are the ones who will have trouble because they are very grown. They will get caught up in the crowd." Reasons given for the belief that boys' find it more difficult to make the transition were as follows: "The boys show more aggression and anger. Therefore, I think the boys will have more difficulty in making the transition. The teacher will have to break through the hardness to reach them. Many are bright, but need attention." This was the opinion of a third grade female teacher. An eighth-grade teacher stated, "Boys are more immature academically."

Student Interviews
By the time students were interviewed, central administration had decided to restructure the configuration of schools in the cluster; the upper elementary school was closed and third-grade students ordinarily moving up from the lower elementary school remained in the same school for grade four, while the upper elementary school's fourth grade students moved on to fifth grade in the middle school. Fifth and eighth-graders then became the focus of the study.

Fifth-graders from the upper elementary school in the system (that housed only fourth and fifth graders, and eighth graders from the middle school) that contained grades six through eight were interviewed in the penultimate week of the school year. Two teams of two interviewers conducted the interviews with groups of four to five students at a time. The graduate assistants were allowed to conduct the interviews with the rationale that the closer proximity in age to the students might ease the tension that could exist in such circumstances. All but one group of students contained both boys and girls. The children were randomly selected by the interviewers. Handwritten notes were taken by one of the interviewers in each session and each session was tape-recorded and later transcribed. The interviews lasted approximately forty minutes each.

Twelve questions revolving around transition issues were put to the students. No suggestions for answers were made by the interviewers. The questions were as follows:

1. What are some of the things you like about this school?
2. What are some of the things you dislike about this school?
3. Which school will you be attending next year?
4. Have you visited that school yet?
5. How do you think things will be different at the new school?
6. How do you think things will be the same?
7. How do you feel about moving to the new school?
8. Will any of your friends be moving to the new school along with you?
9. What will you miss most about this school?
10. Do you have brothers or sisters at the new school? (If not, do you have any family members who have gone to the new school?)

11. Tell me about the ways your teacher teaches math, science,
     reading, language arts, social studies or describe some of
     the learning activities in your classroom.
12. Would you like your teachers next year to teach in the same
     way?

Results from Student Interviews

Since the focus of this part of the study was on teacher and student attitudes,
the answers to questions 5, 6 and 7 were most relevant. It provided some
context for those responses, however, we briefly discussed some of the
answers to the other questions posed during the sessions.

In analyzing questions 1 and 2 above, the references to what
students liked and disliked were put into five categories: (1) building or
physical objects; (2) people; (3) core lessons; (4) extra-curricular activities;
or (5) attitudes and behavior. Overall, it was clear that their likes and
dislikes revolved mainly around the people in their respective schools.
Liking a particular core subject did not appear to feature into one's feelings
about school. The fifth graders had a new principal; the former principal
having been summarily dismissed toward the end of the school year. In five
of the seven groups of fifth graders, the students spoke of disliking their new
principal. In contrast, only one student among the eighth graders spoke of
disliking his principal. The teachers who fared most highly in the students'
opinions were music and physical education teachers and the guidance
counselor (fifth graders.)   Field trips and sports featured highly in the things
students at both grade levels liked about school. A fifth grade girl said she
liked the school because "It's big. It's got a lot of rooms in it." About the
same school, however, one boy said he disliked the fact that "It's old. I'm
sorry it's so old." "It's falling down," another boy chimed in. One eighth
grade boy said "I like this school because I've been here for three years and
I kinda got used to it," thus making a case for the comfort of familiarity. The
eighth graders unanimously agreed that they did not like wearing uniforms.
Not having to wear uniforms in high school was one of the factors that took
part in their joyful anticipation of changing schools next year.

In response to the third question, we were surprised to find that,
contrary to the intentions of this feeder school system, only 50% of the fifth
graders indicated that they would be going to the middle school in the system
the following year and only 65% of the eighth graders said that they would
be going to the high school. This raised questions about the effectiveness of
a feeder-school-system and its presumed effectiveness in easing transition
for its students.

Most of the students said that they had, in fact, visited the schools to which they would be transferring, not as a result of planned activities on the part of the schools, but because of family ties. "I've been to G school before when I went to pick up my brother," said a fifth grade girl. "I went there a year ago when my cousin graduated and she was going there," another fifth grader added.

Some of the most significant responses as they related to students' attitudes about transition, were revealed in response to question five. They not only believed that things would be different in the new school, but they believed that they would be better.

The fifth graders made the following comments in anticipation of their move to middle school:

"It will be cleaner."
"Teachers will be nicer."
"There are a lot more teachers."
"The school is bigger."
"There are more children that I know."
"Lunch will be better; we'll get to pick our own lunch."
"We'll be able to get ice cream and jello."
"I'll have a new principal."
"We'll have a basketball team."
"There will be less hard-headed people there."

The eighth graders reiterated their pleasure over not having to wear school uniforms, but were also thoughtful about other matters they would find in high school:

"Courses will be more relevant to life after school."
"The teachers will let you work on your own without staying on you."
"We'll have more responsibility for ourselves."
"You don't stay with the same group of students all day."
"You get to choose your own classes."

These students expressed excitement over the prospect of having new experiences, new teachers, new friends and better equipment. This is not to say that there were no responses that reflected some anxiety over the transition. "You'll have to worry about bigger kids taking your stuff," one eighth grade boy lamented. "You'll have to be more mature," a girl in the same group added. Fifth graders had more concerns than eighth graders: "The work will be harder," a girl said, and "The teachers will be stricter," another added. Other remarks revealed a fear held mainly by the boys of being "picked on" by bigger boys: "The kids are bigger," "I might get beaten up," "The big boys will pick on me," were words that they used to express this fear.

In comparing positive to negative responses regarding how the children felt things would be different for them in their new school, we found that sixty-four percent (64%) of the fifth graders and eighty-nine percent (89%) of eighth graders expressed belief that the change would be for the better. This trend was repeated in response to the question "How do you feel about moving to the new school?" "Better, happy, glad, very excited, excellent, and good" were the adjectives used by most. One eighth grader was philosophical, "I will have to adjust to their ways and they to mine," he said with a sigh. "Nervous, a little sad, a little nervous, scared, terrified, mad, bad," and "not that good," were adjectives used by a minority. A further probe to the "mad" response elicited the explanation, "A boy I know will beat me up." One fifth grader said, "I don't feel nothing, but I'd rather go where my friends are." (He was moving to a new district.)

The latter two responses lead into our questions 8 and 10 regarding whether or not friends or relatives would be with them in the new school. All students had relatives, friends or acquaintances who would be with them in the new school. However, as indicated by the boy above, not all those familiar faces would be welcomed ones.

The questions relating to the teachers' methods of teaching and whether or not students wanted their teachers to teach in the same way at the new school were seeking information that would or would not support the teachers contentions about the way teaching methods would change for the students and our researchers classroom observations of these methods. The responses are less relevant to the focus of this report and so we will only reported the remarks that showed the students' attitudes or perceptions about the ways in which their teachers taught.

Most of the fifth graders said that they would like the teachers to teach in the same way. When they expressed displeasure with their teachers, their comments revealed, that it was the teachers' attitudes that they would like to change, not their teaching methods. The following remarks were indications of this as expressed by three members of one class: "Not like the math teacher, because he yells too much and kicks the desk." "He tries to kick the chair and make us fall down."

In one group a boy said, "I like the women but I don't like the men....The men give too much homework." "Some teachers just don't like you," a boy added, "Like Mr. H. He don't like nobody." One fifth grade boy said that he liked the way his teacher taught, but "I want it to be more learning-centered."

A group of fifth graders were unanimous in extolling the way their teacher taught and looked forward to having a teacher who taught the same way the following year. The following were the reasons given:

"She does not tell us to take out all this work, and if we don't do it, we just don't do it."

"She doesn't like giving out bad grades."

"It is fun when she is teaching."

"She'll do something that is not good for us, if your parents come and you have been bad, she'll say you have been good."

"If you're good, she'll give you lolly-pops."

The eighth graders were not as satisfied as fifth graders with the ways their teachers taught.

"I would like a better math teacher," one girl replied.

"I want none of them to be my teachers next year," a boy said emphatically.

" I would like to have some of my teachers again next year," replied one girl, slightly changing the question, "because sometimes in high school, teachers are mean and bitter."

Another group of eighth graders felt positively toward the way in which their teachers had taught them saying, "They teach in a fun way," and "They try to get the best out of you."

CONCLUSIONS

The students' belief that things would, indeed, be different at the new schools and that the difference would be better, came through very clearly in their interviews. They anticipated better and kinder teachers, a more caring and "in touch" principal, a well-maintained building, better food and a more relevant curriculum. Most felt "good" and "happy" about going to a new school, but there were mixed responses regarding whether or not they wanted their new teachers to teach them as their old teachers. In the minority were the fears reported in the literature concerning harder work, new teachers and a bigger building. A few students expressed apprehension about making new friends, but most had relatives or friends already attending the school. The greatest apprehension, which was expressed more by boys than by girls, was of being "beaten up" by older and bigger boys at the new school.

Their teachers, on the other hand, tended to express fear that the students would not make the transition well for both social and academic reasons. At each "departure" grade level, teachers felt that teachers at the "receiving" grade level would not be as nurturing or sensitive to individual differences as they had been. They tended to feel that teaching methods at the next level would not be as child-centered and that subject matter would not be shown as relevant to the child's life. More teachers felt that girls would make the transition between schools easier than boys, but there was no consensus as to whether this was due to social reasons (greater maturity on the girls' part) or academic ability. It was also apparent that the teachers expected at least 26% of their students to have school transition problems as early as third grade. Since the third to fourth-grade transition is so critical to a child's success, special attention needs to be paid to this level.

Contrary to results reported in most of the literature on anxiety associated with school transitions, we have come to the conclusion that the majority of students in this inner-city feeder system did not fear the prospect of moving up to another school in the future. Their anxieties lay mostly in maintaining the status quo. Despite low expectations on the part of their teachers, warnings from teachers about the difficulties of adjusting to less-caring teachers, a larger school building and harder work, the majority of these boys and girls held high expectations for their new experience and held onto hopes that life in the new school would be better.

EDUCATIONAL IMPLICATIONS
The implications of these findings for educators are many. As studies cited above have shown, the academic performance and social adjustment of a great many African American students, after making the transition from one school to another, have not been good. When you juxtapose those statistics to the findings in our study, (i.e. that many African American children feel positive about making the transition), you have to ask yourself, what happens? Are the low expectations of their teachers transferred to them? Why do their own high expectations and motivation not translate into high performance and good adjustment? While an easy answer may be that the students' expectations were unrealistic based on former academic performance and achievement level, a great deal of the answer must come from the way the students are treated once they reach the new school.

Ensuring that students' expectations of finding kind, caring teachers and principals, palatable food, a well-maintained building, and a relevant curriculum in their new schools means giving serious consideration to some of the earlier proposed interventions for easing the transition for students, such as the "buddy" system; peer-tutoring (Petit, 1994) and shadowing (Ferguson, 1994); parent and student school visitations (Pohl 1995); and ninth-grade academies that ease the tensions for those entering high school (LaPoint, 1996). All these are steps in the right direction, but the problem is much bigger. It is a systemic one that involves making the whole system better in every way that affects student learning and the quality of school life.

As stated in a previous forum (Rashid, 1998), we need to develop programs that target children's developmental needs at each of the four major transition points. Having regard to the teachers' expressed concerns in this study about the transition from third to fourth grade, more attention needs to be paid to both academic and personal differences between these two grade levels and efforts exerted toward ease of articulation. The literature on school transitions must be thoroughly infused into teacher training programs at both the pre-service and in-service levels. An understanding of the culture that inner-city minority children bring into the school can minimize the over-emphasis on disciplinary measures (Davis and Jordan, 1995). Finally, principals of inner-city feeder schools must capitalize on the familial and friendly ties among inner-city children and their enthusiasm about moving up the school ladder. They must coordinate professional development, social and community activities to ensure that the high hopes of these students in making their transition from school to school are fulfilled.

REFERENCES

Butler, E.D. (1994). *Strategic planning for urban school reform.* Memphis: Memphis State University.

Camoni, G. (1996). Crossing the bridge to middle school. *Principal,* 76,no.1:48-49.

Colorado State Department of Education (1983) *The school improvement cluster.* Colorado State Department of Education.

Davis, J. and Jordan, W. (1995). The effects of school context, structure and experiences on African American males in middle and high school. Special Issue: Pedagogical and contextual issues affecting African American males in school and society. *Journal of Negro Education, 63(4),* 570-587.

Entwisle, D. and Alexander K. (1989). *Beginning school with competence: Minority and majority comparisons.* Baltimore: Center for Research on Elementary and Middle Schools.

Feldlaufer, H. & Eccles, M. (1988). Student, teacher, and observer perceptions of the classroom environment before and after the transition to junior high school. *Journal of early adolescence. 8,* n.2,133-156.

Fenzel, L. (1989). Role strains and the transition to middle school: Longitudinal trends and sex differences. *Journal of early adolescence.* 9,211-226.

Ferguson, J. (1994). The effect of the shadow transition program on the social adjustment of Whitewater Middle School students. Carrollton, GA: West Georgia College. (ERIC Document Reproduction Service No. ED380878).

Graham, Sandra (1994). Motivation in African Americans. *Review of educational research* 64, n.1,55-117.

Hargreaves, A. (1990). *Rights of passage: A review of selected research about schooling in the transition years.*

Hargreaves, A. (1993). Years of transition: Times for change. *A review and analysis of pilot projects investigating issues in the transition years. v 3: The realities of restructuring: case studies of transition.* Toronto: Ontario Ministry Education and Training.

Marlett, D. (1993). *Causes of anxiety for transfer students: Implications for teachers.* University of Virginia. (ERIC Document Reproduction Service No. ED359162).

McPartland, J. and S. Nettles (1991). Using community adults as advocates or mentors for at-risk middle school students: A two-year evaluation of Project RAISE. *American journal of education.*

LaPoint, V, W. Jordan, J. McPartland, and D. Towns. (1996). *The Talent Development High School.* Washington & Baltimore: The Center for Research on the Education of Students Placed at Risk.

Nottelmann, E. (1982) *Children's adjustment in school: The interaction of physical maturity and school transition.* Paper presented at the Annual Meeting of the American Educational Research Association. New York. March 19023,1982.

O'Brien, M. (1991). *Promoting successful transition into school: A review of current intervention practices.* Kansas City: Kansas Early Childhood Research Institute.

Odegaard, S. & Heath, J. (1992). Assisting the elementary school student in the transition to a middle level school. *Middle school journal* 24, n2,21-25.

Pettit, N. (1994). *Improving the transition of students moving into sixth-grade through middle school orientation and peer helper program.* A Dissertation. Nova University.

Pohl, J. (1995). Coming and going: Helping students succeed. *Schools in the middle,* 4, n.3,19-20.

Rashid, H. (1998). Educational Transitions: A Review and Examination of the Role of Transition on the lives of Students Placed at Risk. Washington, DC: Unpublished paper from the Center for Reseatch on the Education of Students Placed at Risk.

Roderick, M. (1993). *The path to dropping out. Evidence for intervention.* Westport, CT: Auburn House.

Rounds, T., Ward, B. et al (1982). Junior high school transition study. *Ecological perspectives for successful schooling practice.* San Francisco: Far West laboratory for Educational Research and Development

Seidman, E. (1994). The impact of school transitions in early adolescence on the self-esteem and perceived social context of poor urban youth. *Child development* 65,507-522.

Simmons, R., Black and Zhou. (1991) African-American versus white children and the transition into junior high school. *American journal of education.*99, n.4, 481-520.

Smith, K. (1991). Easing the transition between elementary and middle school. *Schools in the middle, Fall 1991:*29-31.

Stennett. R., Isaacs, L. (1979). The elementary to secondary transition: A follow-up of high risk students. *Research report n 79-03.* London, Ontario: Educational Research Services.

Taylor, A. (1991). Social competence and the early school transition: Risk factors and protective factors for African-American children. *Education and urban society,* vol.24 No. 1, :15-26.

Unseem, E. (1994). *Renewing schools: A report on the cluster initiative in Philadelphia.* Philadelphia: Philadelphia Public Schools.

Weldy, G. (1991). Stronger school transitions improve student achievement: A final report on a three-year demonstration project "Strengthening school transitions for students K-13." *National Association of Secondary School Principals.*

5. A Cross-National Study of Children's Perceived Control: Its Dimensionality and Relationship with Math Achievement

Hsiu-Zo Ho, Jules Zimmer, Deniz Senturk, Jill Fisher, Ruby Peralta, Sou-Yung Chiu, and Chang-Pei Wang

Introduction

Perceived control has been shown to play a central role in motivational and cognitive accounts of behavior. Of particular concern regarding perceptions of control is how these perceptions affect the outcomes (successes or failures) of the events with which they are associated (Little, 1987). Perceived control has commonly been studied for its relation to achievement in the academic domain. Most of these studies have found that certain types of causal perceptions (e.g. an internal locus of control) are positively correlated with academic achievement (Findley & Cooper, 1983). These findings have extensive implications for psychological and educational research as well as practical implications for our schools.

Early research on perceived control focused on the locus of control dimension and primarily grew out of Rotter's (1954) social learning theory. The theory states that people with an internal locus of control believe that they are personally responsible for what happens to them. In contrast, people with an external locus of control believe that forces beyond their control have power over the outcomes in their lives (Findley & Cooper, 1983). Rotter developed the first measure of locus of control in what is now known as the Rotter I-E (Internal-External) Scale. However, the Rotter I-E Scale has been criticized because it fails to systematically vary the situations and domains in assessing perceived control over events (Munro, 1979, Dweck, 1986). Findley and Cooper (1983) reported that the locus of control measures that target specific and varied domains tended to be more accurate and associated with larger effects.

Weiner later developed a theory of perceived control which expands on Rotter's theory (Weiner, Heckhausen, Meyer & Cook, 1972; Weiner, 1986). This more recent theory classifies causal attributions not only according to locus of control (internal/external), but also according to the dimensions of stability (stable/unstable) and controllability (controllable/uncontrollable). Stability refers to how likely the perceived cause of a success or failure outcome is to change when the event recurs and controllability refers to how able the subject of that event is to personally change the agent of causality. For example, the construct of ability is internal, stable, and uncontrollable while the construct of effort is internal, unstable, and controllable.

The measure of perceived control used in the current study (i.e., the Multidimensional Measure of Children's Perceptions of Control, MMCPC) was developed by Connell (1985) to conceptually differentiate three sources of perceived control: internal, powerful others, and unknown. According to Connell, the internal and powerful others sources of control differentiate whether the cause of a particular event or outcome rests within the actor or within other people, respectively. The unknown source of control, however, indicates a lack of knowledge regarding the cause of that event or outcome. This unknown source of control is important, particularly in regard to young children, because it interferes more than any other source of control with engagement for children of this age (Skinner, 1995).

Connell's scale improves upon previous measures of perceived control by utilizing a domain-specific approach which centers its questions around certain specific domains, such as the social, the cognitive and the physical. The new unknown source of control is particularly important for this type of domain-specific measure, in that children often report that they "know" the causes of academic success and failure while outcomes in the social domain are often attributed to unknown or to multiple causes (Skinner, 1995). The current study concentrates on both the social and academic spheres, while emphasizing the role of perceived causality in academic performance.

Connell's test is one of the first aimed expressly for investigation of the causal beliefs of children, the subjects of the present study, and it has proven both reliable and valid for each domain and source of control (Connell, 1985). Moreover, this measure has been hailed on many accounts, most notably by Herbert M. Lefcourt, a leading researcher in the field of perceived control. Lefcourt states, "The contribution unique to this scale is the advancing of the 'unknown control' variable. Findings by [many researchers] have attested to the value of this variable in the MMCPC...this scale may prove to be one of the best for assessing a variety of control beliefs among children because of the meaningful components contained within it" (p. 450).

Culture has been found to be a greater determinant on one's ratings of perceived control than most other variables, including age, and social class (Jensen, Olsen, & Hughes, 1990). Unfortunately, most of the literature to date that has investigated perceived causality and its relation to academic achievement has focused on white, middle-class, Western subjects (Duda & Allison, 1989). In addition, many of the relatively few studies that have been conducted cross-nationally have failed to take many important cultural problems into account; for example, how the different value systems of each culture may play a part in determinations of locus of control (Duda & Allison, 1989). In a study examining the validity of the Weiner's model for children from Sri Lanka and England, Little (1987) supported Weiner's model, but suggested categorical modifications. Weiner acknowledges that achievement judgments "are influenced by the culture of the evaluator. Specific culture-based learning experiences are likely to produce differences in values that are evidenced in evaluations" (Weiner, 1976, p. 189).

The present study evaluates the Connell measure of children's perceptions of control in regards to its validity and reliability across cultures. We have chosen to compare American and Asian nations due to the vast discrepancies in academic achievement, especially mathematics achievement, between Asian and American students (e.g., Husen, 1967; LaPointe, Mead & Phillips, 1989; Stevenson, Lee & Stigler, 1986; Tuss, Zimmer, & Ho, 1995) in order to assess whether these differences are reflected in measures of perceived control.

The bulk of the literature has found that individuals generally attribute successful achievement to internal causes, while more often attributing their failures to external causes (e.g. Findley & Cooper, 1983; Chandler et al., 1981). This trend has been labeled as one of "self enhancement," sometimes called a "self-serving bias" (Crittenden & Bae, 1994). However, some researchers have found an opposite pattern with regard to Asian countries: students in Asian countries tend to attribute their failures more often than their successes to internal causes, a trend of "self-effacement" (Chandler et al., 1981; Crittenden & Bae, 1994; Yan & Gaier, 1994). Furthermore, the fact that Asian students tend to outperform their American peers on achievement tests suggest that self-enhancement may not benefit students from other countries as much as the term suggests (Tuss, Zimmer, & Ho, 1995).

Discrepancies in academic achievement, again particularly mathematics achievement, have also been noted in relation to gender (Dweck, 1986). Gender differences also exist in measures of perceived control (McGinnies et al., 1974), although these differences are rather inconsistent. For example, Rotter (1966) found females to have a more external locus of control than males. Many other researchers have also found that females tend to attribute a more external locus of control such as luck or task difficulty to their achievement outcomes, while males invoke a more internal locus of control such as effort or ability (Weiner, 1976; Cellini & Kantorowski, 1982; Doherty, 1983; Sadowski, Woodward, Davis, & Elsburg, 1982; Lee & Dengerick, 1992). But the greater external locus of control for women is not found in all studies (e.g Strickland, 1977).

The few studies on gender differences in Asian populations yielded inconsistent results. Hung (1974), using Rotter's I-E Scale, found no gender differences in locus of control among Taiwanese college students. Using Levenson's (1974) IPC Scale, Lao, Chuang, and Yang found female Taiwanese college students to score more externally than their male counterparts on two subscales, but more internal on another. While there is evidence that the patterns of perceptions vary with either the gender or the culture of the perceiver, less is known about the interaction of both culture and gender on students' perceptions of control.

The present study utilized a version of Connell's Multidimensional Measure of Children's Perceptions of Control (MMCPC) that conceptually differentiates among internal, powerful others, and unknown control perceptions. In the present investigation of cultural variation of children's perceived control, we addressed the following questions: (a) Does a three-factor model (internal, powerful others, and unknown sources of control) replicate across our samples of six-grade students from China, Taiwan, and the United States? (b) How do the associations among sources of perceived control vary across nation and gender? (c) What is the relationship between the sources of perceived control in the cognitive domain and mathematics achievement and how do they vary across nation and gender?

METHOD

Subjects
The data included in this study is part of a large four-nation longitudinal project on mathematics achievement in which data were collected from students (tested at fourth and sixth grade) as well as their teachers and parents. The subjects for this present study included 719 sixth-grade students from three nations: 215 (97 girls and 118 boys) from the People's Republic of China; 226 (111 girls and 115 boys) from Taiwan; and 278 (123 girls and 155 boys) from the U.S. The Japanese students did not complete the instrument on perceptions of control and thus were not included in the present study.

The participating schools in each nation were selected on the basis of educational, economic, institutional, and residential characteristics, and recommendations of the respective educational authorities and researchers in each nation. The schools were located in Beijing and Men Tou Gou, China; Taipei, Miao-Li and Yang Ming Shan, Taiwan; and Claremont, Cuyama and Santa Ynez California, United States. Over 95% of the sixth-grade students in each selected classroom participated in the study. The mean ages of the students were 12.85 (SD = .69), 12.11 (SD = .42), and 11.96 (SD = .49), for China, Taiwan, and the U.S., respectively.

Measures
Perceptions of Control. The present study utilized Connell's (1985) Multidimensional Measure of Children's Perceptions of Control

(MMCPC). The MMCPC consists of 48 items with 12 items tapping each of four domains, cognitive, social, physical, and general. Because the present project focused on factors that influence academic achievement, items tapping the physical domain (e.g., "I can be good at any sport if I try hard enough") were not included in our study. Hence our modified version of the MMCPC consists of thirty-six items. Table 1 presents a list of the thirty-six items and identifies each item's respective domain (cognitive, social, or general) and source of control (internal, powerful others, or unknown) as reported by Connell (1985).

Table 1 – Perception of Control Questionnaire Items

Cognitive Domain:
  Internal Control:
  CI1)   If I want to do well in school, it's up to me to do it.
  CI2)   If I don't do well in school, it's my own fault.
  CI3)   If I want to get good grades in school, it's up to me to do it.
  CI4)   If I get bad grades, it's my own fault.
  Powerful Others Control:
  CO1)   The best way for me to get good grades is to get the teacher to like me.
  CO2)   If I have a bad teacher, I won't do well in school.
  CO3)   When I do well in school, it's because the teacher likes me.
  CO4)   If I don't have a good teacher, I won't do well in school.
  Unknown Control:
  CU1)   When I do well in school, I usually can't figure out why.
  CU2)   If I get a bad grade in school, I usually don't understand why I got it.
  CU3)   When I get a good grade in school, I usually don't known why I did so well.

  CU4)   When I don't do well in school, I usually can't figure out why.

Social Domain:
  Internal Control:
  SI1)   If somebody doesn't like me, it's usually because of something I did.
  SI2)   If somebody likes me, it is usually because of the way I treat them.
  SI3)   If someone is mean to me, it's usually because of something I did.
  SI4)   If somebody is my friend, it is usually because of the way I treat him or her.

Powerful Others Control:

SO1)   If I want to be important, I have to get the popular kids to like me.

SO2)   If my teacher doesn't like me, I probably won't be very popular.

SO3)   If the teacher doesn't like me, I won't have many friends in that class.

SO4)   If I want kids to think I'm important, I have to be friends with the popular kids.

Unknown Control:

SU1)   If somebody doesn't like me, I usually can't figure out why.

SU2)   A lot of times I don't know why people like me.

SU3)   When another kid doesn't like me, I usually don't know why.

SU4)   A lot of times there doesn't seem to be any reason why someone likes me.

General Domain:

Internal Control:

GI1)   When I am unsuccessful, it is usually my own fault.

GI2)   I can pretty much control what will happen in my life.

GI3)   When I don't do well at something, it is usually my own fault.

GI4)   I can pretty much decide what will happen in my life.

Powerful Others Control:

GO1)   If an adult doesn't want me to do something I want to do, I won't do it.

GO2)   If there is something I want, I have to please the people in charge to get it.

GO3)   I don't have much chance of doing what I want if adults don't want me to do it.

GO4)   To get what I want, I have to please the people in charge.

Unknown Control:

GU1)   When something goes wrong for me, I usually can't figure out why.

GU2)   Many times I can't figure out why good things happen to me.

GU3)   A lot of times I don't know why something goes wrong for me.

GU4)   When good things happen to me, there doesn't seem to be any reason why.

For purposes of the present study, the English version of the questionnaire was translated into the languages of the participating nations and then back-translated into English for verification of the translation. Subjects were asked to rate the degree of relevance of each item on a four-point scale (i.e., "1" = "not at all true," "2" = "not very true," and "3" = "sort of true," and "4" = "very true"). Reliability coefficients of our modified version of the MMCPC utilizing Cronbach's alpha are .74, .80, and .76 for the China, Taiwan, and U.S. samples, respectively.

Mathematics Achievement Tests. All subjects were administered a test of mathematics achievement consisting of two parallel forms developed for this study. The two forms combined were comprised of thirty-five items derived from three sources. Approximately one-third of the items were adapted from the test used by Stevenson, Lee, and Stigler (1986) in their cross-national study. Another third of the items were selected from the sixth-grade textbooks used in each of the participating nations. The remaining one-third of the items were developed by the project researchers to assess processing skills involved in mathematics problem solving. The two parallel forms were administered within an average interval of four to six weeks, with a reliability coefficient of .82. The measure of mathematics achievement utilized in the present study is a weighted average score of the two parts.

RESULTS

Factor Structure of Children's Perceived Control in Each Domain
Given the results of previous work demonstrating the domain-specificity of children's self-perceptions (Harter, 1982; Connell, 1985) as well as the complex subscale structure of the instrument (i.e. 18 possible subscales: 3 domains x 3 sources of control x 2 outcomes), factor analyses were conducted separately on the 12 items within each domain (cognitive, social, and general). Principal-components analyses with varimax rotations were conducted on data for each of the three nations separately as well as for the three nations combined. Tables 2a, 2b, and 2c present results of the factor loadings of each of the items tapping the cognitive, social, and general domains.

Table 2a: Factor Loadings on Children's Perception of Control for the Cognitive Domain: Internal, Powerful Others, and Unknown

Items	All Nations			China			Taiwan			U.S.		
	I	O	U	I	O	U	I	O	U	I	O	U
CI3	.72	-.07	-.04	.70	.00	.09	.73	.00	-.15	.66	-.22	-.26
CI4	.65	.04	-.07	.61	.14	-.17	.46	-.10	.01	.57	-.07	.00
CI1	.63	-.08	-.02	.68	-.10	.06	.46	.15	-.22	.65	-.04	.01
CI2	.66	-.06	.02	.53	-.06	.00	.58	-.06	.18	.64	.07	-.08
CO2	-.03	.81	-.04	-.05	.83	.06	-.05	.73	.03	-.16	.82	-.08
CO4	.11	.78	.10	.24	.77	-.04	.06	.44	.21	-.04	.82	.13
CO1	-.14	.51	.13	-.22	.38	-.04	.03	.58	.10	-.30	.43	.21
CO3	-.20	.43	.34	-.09	.25	.44	-.08	.64	.05	-.48	.25	.39
CU1	-.07	-.05	.69	.05	-.07	.69	-.03	-.03	.78	-.26	-.09	.48
CU4	-.03	.10	.69	-.09	-.02	.65	.07	.38	.56	-.02	.00	.78
CU3	-.02	.14	.69	.13	-.03	.61	-.02	.21	.71	-.02	.13	.62
CU2	.03	.12	.62	-.01	.09	.76	-.12	.10	.69	.28	.26	.58

Table 2b   Factor Loadings on Children's Perception of Control for the Social Domain: Internal, Powerful Others, and Unknown

Items	All Nations			China			Taiwan			U.S.		
	I	O	U	I	O	U	I	O	U	I	O	U
SI2	.72	.00	-.11	.63	.08	-.03	.74	-.01	.12	.54	-.11	-.18
SI4	.62	.01	.01	.55	.13	.13	.53	.15	-.13	.48	-.19	.15
SI3	.58	.19	.09	.61	.12	-.02	.45	.21	.13	.73	.18	.09
SI1	.54	.04	.12	.52	-.09	.07	.49	-.10	.40	.71	.09	-.04
SO3	-.06	.76	.01	-.09	.83	-.11	.06	.70	.09	-.25	.62	.17
SO2	-.06	.74	.08	.03	.74	.00	-.01	.73	.15	-.24	.66	.09
SO4	.24	.67	.08	.38	.49	.06	.21	.71	-.09	.20	.72	.03
SO1	.29	.60	.13	.30	.45	.21	.42	.49	-.08	.18	.71	.05
SU3	.06	.04	.73	.12	.00	.65	-.18	.21	.74	.14	.06	.75
SU2	.03	.14	.66	-.02	.05	.75	.27	-.06	.56	.01	.19	.61
SU4	-.17	.27	.61	-.10	.04	.70	.02	.50	.25	-.02	.33	.62
SU1	.17	-.09	.57	.32	-.07	.55	.05	.14	.52	-.13	-.16	.63

Table 2c: Factor Loadings on Children's Perception of Control for the General Domain: Internal, Powerful Others, and Unknown

Items	All Nations			China			Taiwan			U.S.		
	I	O	U	I	O	U	I	O	U	I	O	U
GI4	.64	.09	-.09	.70	.03	.02	.16	.45	-.43	.61	.05	-.28
GI2	.67	-.01	-.10	.65	-.24	.14	.02	.23	-.07	.36	.05	-.49
GI1	.22	-.19	.43	-.44	-.20	.30	.53	-.14	.00	.70	-.13	.13
GI3	.44	-.05	.47	-.12	-.23	.35	.68	.07	.01	.77	.06	.12
GO2	.00	.86	.03	.06	.86	.20	-.16	.78	.22	.01	.43	.52
GO4	.00	.85	.05	.03	.86	.12	-.09	.73	.32	.06	.47	.47
GO1	.55	-.05	-.06	.27	-.46	.13	-.10	.25	.11	.26	.35	-.46
GO3	.32	.33	.17	.24	.01	.41	-.15	-.11	.56	.06	.62	-.02
GU3	.03	.04	.56	.11	.08	.64	.68	.13	.14	-.06	.52	-.01
GU4	-.16	.32	.50	.16	.07	.57	.22	.20	.54	.03	.12	.72
GU2	-.19	.10	.62	-.24	.08	.56	.13	-.09	.66	.14	-.06	.69
GU1	-.13	.08	.52	-.34	.04	.50	.27	.29	.42	-.04	.62	.04

For the cognitive and social domains, the results of analyses (for the three nations combined) support a three-factor model comparable to those extracted by Connell (1985) that can be interpreted as "internal," "powerful others," and "unknown" sources of control. With minor exceptions, the separate factor structures for each nation also support Connell's three-factor model. Specifically, one exception is with respect to the cognitive domain variable CO3 ("When I do well in school, it's because the teacher likes me") which is hypothesized to load on the "powerful others" factor for the cognitive domain. This item, however, for the Chinese sample loads more highly on the "unknown" factor; and, for the American sample, loads more highly on the "internal" factor. The second exception is with respect to social domain variable SU4 ("A lot of times there doesn't seem to be any reason why someone likes me") which is hypothesized to load on the "Unknown" factor for the social domain, but instead loads more highly on the "Powerful others" factor in the Taiwan sample.

As can be seen in Table 2c, the factor analytic results for the "general" domain items were not comparable across nations. Because of the lack of comparability across nations with respect to generalized expectancies of control, only the domain-specific (i.e., cognitive and social) perceptions of control were examined in subsequent analyses.

Because of the comparability across nations with respect to the three sources of control for each of the cognitive and social domains, scores representing the six subscales were computed for each subject by using unit weights for those items (with the exception of CO3 and SU4) with factor loadings above .40 (i.e., for the data on all three nations combined). The variables CO3 and SU4 were omitted in computing the subscales due to the above noted discrepancies in the factor structures for each nation. It may be noted that the present study did not distinguish between success and failure outcomes because for the instrument employed with only two items for both success and failure in the same source of control and domain, results separating success and failure would not be reliable or generalizable.

Intercorrelations Among Subscales by Nation and Gender
Intercorrelations among internal, powerful others, and unknown control subscales between and within the cognitive and social domains are shown in Table 3. Note first that, with the exception of the boys from China, significant positive correlations were found between the social and cognitive domains for each of the three sources of control. Within the cognitive domain, significant negative correlations were

found between internal and powerful others as well as internal and unknown sources of control for U.S. boys only.

Table 3: Intercorrelations of Children's Perception of Control Between and Within the Cognitive and Social Domains*

	China		Taiwan		U.S.	
Between Domains						
CogI and SocI	NS	(NS, .24)	.37	(.26, .48)	.28	(.27, .28)
CogO and SocO	.36	(.38, .33)	.35	(.24, .46)	.32	(.31, .28)
CogU and SocU	.45	(.42, .50)	.44	(.30, .56)	.40	(.41, .44)
Within Cognitive Domain						
CogI and CogO	NS	(NS, NS)	NS	(NS, NS)	-.30	(-.32, NS)
CogI and CogU	NS	(NS, NS)	NS	(NS, NS)	-.22	(-.25, NS)
Within Social Domain						
SocI and SocO	.28	(NS, .39)	.28	(NS, .37)	NS	(NS, NS)
SocI and SocU	.20	(NS, NS)	.20	(NS, NS)	NS	(NS, NS)

* Correlations shown are significant at $p < .05$; correlations in parentheses correspond to those for boys and girls, respectively; NS = non-significant.

Within the social domain, however, significant positive correlations were found between internal and others sources of control for girls in both Asian nations. No significant correlations between internal and unknown sources of control within the social domain were found for either boys or girls across the three nations.

Correlations of Subscales with Math Achievement

The correlations between internal, powerful others, and unknown subscales within the cognitive domain and math achievement scores are presented for each nation and gender in Table 4. Results indicate that both the internal and powerful others sources of control in the cognitive domain correlated significantly with math achievement in the U. S. sample, but only for the U. S. boys. Specifically in this sample, a significant positive correlation was found between the internal source of control and mathematics achievement; and a significant negative correlation was found between the powerful others source of control and achievement. These associations found for the sample of U.S. boys were consistent with Connell's findings (1985), although for Connell's analysis boys and girls were pooled. Unlike Connell's findings, the unknown source of control was not correlated significantly with math achievement for the U. S. sample. However, for both Asian nations, unknown source of control correlated negatively with mathematics achievement for both boys and girls.

DISCUSSION

The present study was able to replicate comparable factors of perceived control across samples of sixth-grade students from China, Taiwan, and the U.S. The results supported both the discriminability of the three sources of control within the cognitive and social domains as well as the domain specificity of the internal, powerful others, and unknown dimensions. The pattern of intercorrelations among the perceived control dimensions, however, varied across nations as well as genders with similarities between the two Asian samples. One major factor affecting nation differences for perceived control contructs focuses on the difference between independent and interdependent cultures (Markus & Kitayama, 1991). As a rule, people in Asian cultures have an interdependent construal of the self in which fitting in with others and having harmonious interpersonal relationships is of primary importance. In contrast, American culture is based on independence in which self-assertion and individualism are most highly valued. These divergent self-views can have profound effects on aspects of cognition and motivation.

Table 4: Correlations of Cognitive Perceptions of Control with Achievement*

	China		Taiwan		U.S.	
Math Achievement						
CogI	NS	(NS, NS)	NS	(NS, NS)	.26	(.32, NS)
CogO	NS	(NS, NS)	NS	(NS, NS)	-.20	(-.22, NS)
CogU	-.32	(-.34, -.29)	-.30	(-.25, -.34)	NS	(NS, NS)

* Correlations shown are significant at $p < .05$; correlations in parentheses correspond to those for boys and girls, respectively; NS = non-significant.

Results of the present study showed that the U.S. sample followed the predicted pattern of a negative relationship between internal and powerful others source of control in the cognitive domain. Interestingly, however, for the Asian nations, these two sources were positively correlated in the social domain. This finding may be interpreted to the Eastern cultural view of the self as part of an encompassing social relationship where the individual is not seen as separate and distinct from others but as connected and dependent on them (Markus & Kitayama, 1991).

For the U.S. sample, internal control correlated positively with math achievement while powerful others had a negative relationship. Many explanations have been offered regarding similar findings in other Western studies. According to Cortez & Bugental (1995), children with higher internal control respond better in stressful situations because they believe that success is controllable and therefore have a "mastery orientation" (Diener & Dweck, 1978). This type of orientation causes them to be attentionally mobilized to deal with the challenge. On the other hand, children with low perceived control believe that any effort on their part is useless and thus exhibit "learned helplessness" (Diener & Dweck, 1978). Learned helplessness leads to avoidant strategies for stressful situations that in turn lead to poorer processing of these events.

In both of the Asian nations, a pattern different from the U.S. sample was again seen in that neither internal nor powerful others control had a significant relationship with mathematics achievement. However, for both Asian nations, unknown control was negatively correlated with the performance outcome. One possible explanation for the non-significant relationships is that in interdependent cultures, internal attributes are seen as situation specific, and therefore unreliable (Markus & Kitayama, 1991). They are therefore seen as unlikely to regulate overt behavior. Another plausible explanation for the absence of the expected relationships among internal, powerful others, and mathematics achievement is that interdependent subjects are more likely to attribute their success to external causes and their failure to internal ones (Smith & Bond, 1994). If the distinction between success and failure outcomes could have been made in this study, this non-significant relationship of internal and powerful others with mathematics achievement may have revealed the above mentioned pattern for our Asian subjects. Still, it may be that "internal" and "powerful others" are not see as separate and distinct but that some other construct that encompasses these sources of perceived control are in play for the Asian boys and girls. It appears that the only significant association with mathematics achievement for both boys and girls in the Asian samples is when the source is "unknown" implying that lower achievers tended to have little awareness of the cause of their academic successes and failures. On the other hand, while higher achievers tended to be more aware of the perceived sources of control, it appears that the attributions made for our Asian participants were not along the "internal" and "powerful others" constructs as measured by Connell's MMCPC. Our results suggest that the Western classification of "internal" vs. "powerful others" may not be relevant or distinct sources of perceived control for Asian students.

The results in the relationship of perceived control and achievement for Asian cultures may also be reflected in Moghaddam's new classification scheme for attribution in interdependent cultures (Moghaddam, Taylor, & Wright, 1993). In this new classification, "person's group" is treated as a potential unit of attribution that is linked to "self." Consequently, internal and powerful others sources of control come closer to one another in the continuum of perceived control with internal versus external sources of control as extremes. This unification of "person's group" and "self" for interdependent cultures may lead to a lack of linear relationships between internal (or powerful others) and achievement.

It is important to note that had the present study focused solely on nation differences without also considering gender variations, the results would have been misleading. The examination of the correlational patterns for both genders within each nation yielded a particularly interesting picture. For the cognitive domain in the United States, the positive correlations between internality and achievement and the negative correlations between both internal and powerful others control and powerful others and achievement appeared in the U.S. boys only. The U.S. girls followed the same pattern with the Asian boys and girls in terms of the relationship between internal and powerful others as well as the relationship between these sources of control and mathematics achievement.

In the social domain, the positive correlations between internal and powerful others source of control were seen in the Asian samples for girls only. Interestingly, in the social domain, the Asian boys appear to follow the pattern of U.S. boys and girls with respect to the relationship between internal and powerful others. While no gender differences are seen among both Asian samples in the cognitive domain (with respect to relationships among sources of control and between sources of control and mathematics achievement), gender differences do exist in the social domain with respect to the relationship between internal and powerful others. On the other hand, for the U.S. sample the pattern is reversed. That is, there are no gender differences in the social domain; whereas gender differences do exist in the cognitive domain (with respect to relationships among internal, powerful others, and powerful others).

Our results suggest that for U.S. boys, the self was seen as both different from others and as having control over achievement outcomes. These traits are consistent with the proposed Western independent cultural idea, as mentioned above. However, for girls in both Asian samples, the self was seen as related to others in the social domain. These traits are consistent with the proposed Eastern interdependent cultural idea. In fact, Sampson (1988) states that interdependence, emphasizing "relationality, interdependence, and connection", corresponds to the female qualities conceptualized by Chodorow (1978), Gilligan (1982), and others. Independence, emphasizing "separation, independence, individuation, and self-creation" corresponds to the male qualities conceptualized by these researchers. Greenfield (1994) has suggested that we examine the relationship between societal culture and gender culture.

As discussed previously, American students tend to exhibit self-enhancement (attributing success to internal sources of control and failure to external sources of control) while Asian students tend to exhibit self-effacement (attributing success to external sources of control and failure to internal sources of control). Unfortunately, the distinction between success and failure outcomes could not be tested in the current study because of the scarcity of items corresponding to either success or failure in the same locus of control in the same domain (there are only two for each locus and domain) hence limiting the reliability. Further studies could expand on the current measure in order to obtain a more accurate measure of cultural differences in self-enhancement versus self-effacement.

Finally, it has been argued that most comparative research in the area of perceived control has typically ignored cultural differences in the meanings and implications of different sources of control (Duda & Allison, 1989). Furthermore, theories of perceived control almost never predict a direct relationship between beliefs and actual performance; rather, the theories hypothesize that perceived control influences children's motivated behavior (Skinner et al., 1990). It is therefore important for educators and researchers to realize that children's active & motivated engagement in activities is considered to be the mediator between perceived control and actual achievement (Skinner et al., 1990).

Based on these implications and findings from the current study, some suggestions for achievement enhancement are tentatively prescribed. First, in formulating strategies for academic improvement, educators must take into account the combination of cultural and gender differences in perceived control. While past studies have not typically addressed both cultural and gender variations, the present study found the patterns of intercorrelations among the sources of perceptions of control to be similar for U.S. girls and Asian boys and girls with respect to the cognitive domain, and for Asian boys and U.S. boys and girls with respect to the social domain. Educators and researchers must understand the viewpoint of various cultures regarding perceived control and the profound effects that divergent self views can have on aspects of cognition and motivation. Second, teacher contingency and teacher involvement should foster positive perceptions of control for students, since they both play a role in supporting children's engagement in learning activities (Skinner et al, 1990). Teacher contingency provides students with the knowledge of what is required to achieve in school; teacher involvement is associated with children's beliefs about effort as effective learning strategies. The investigation of children's perceptions of control and their role in motivation and achievement within gender and cultural contexts certainly has important practical implications for our classrooms.

REFERENCES

Bond, M. H. (1986) *The Psychology of the Chinese People.* New York: Oxford University Press.

Brabander, B. & Boone, C. (1990). Sex differences in perceived locus of control. *Journal of Social Psychology, 130*(2), 271-272.

Cellini, J.V. & Kantorowski, L.A. (1982). Internal-external locus of control: New normative data *Psychological Reports, 51*, 231-235.

Chan, C. (1981). *A study of acculturative stress and internal-external control on Hong Kong foreign students at the University of Waterloo.* Unpublished bachelor's honors theses, University of Waterloo, Ontario, Canada.

Chandler, T.A., Shama, D.D., Wolf, F.M., & Planchard, S.K. (1981). Multiattributional causality: A five cross-national samples study. *Journal of Cross-Cultural Psychology, 12*(2), 207-221.

Chodorow, N. (1978). *The Reproduction of Mothering.* Berkeley: University of California Press.

Cortez, V. L. & Bugental, D.B. (1995). Priming of perceived control in young children as a buffer against fear-inducing events. *Child Development, 66,* 687-696.

Crittenden, K. S. (1989). *Attributional styles of Asian and American students: A four-country study.* Paper presented at the annual meeting of the Midwest Sociological Society, St. Louis.

Crittenden, Kathleen S. (1991). Asian self-effacement or feminine modesty? Attributional patterns of women university students in Taiwan. *Gender & Society, 5*(1), 98-117.

Crittenden, Kathleen S. & Bae, Hyunjung (1994). Self effacement and social responsibility - Attribution as impression management in Asian cultures. *American Behavioral Scientist, 37*(5), 653-671.

Connell, J.P. (1985). A new multidimensional measure of children's perceptions of control. *Child Development, 56,* 1018-1041.

Diener, C. I. & Dweck, C. S. (1978). An analysis of learned helplessness: Continuous changes in performance, strategy, and achievement cognitions following failure. *Journal of Personality and Social Psychology, 36,* 451-462.

Doherty, W.J. (1983). The impact of divorce on locus of control orientation in adult women: a longitudinal study. *Journal of Personality and Social Psychology, 4,* 834-40.

Duda, J.L. & Allison, M.T. (1989). The attributional theory of achievement motivation: Cross-cultural considerations. *International Journal of Intercultural Relations, 13,* 37-55.

Dweck, C.S. (1986). Motivational processes affecting learning. *American Psychologist, 41*(10), 1040-1048.

Findley, M.J. & Cooper, H.M. (1983). Locus of control and academic achievement: A literature review. *Journal of Personality and Social Psychology, 44*(2), 419-427.

Frieze, I.H., Whitley, B.E., Hanusa, B.H., & McHugh, M.C. (1982). Assessing the theoretical models for sex differences in causal attributions for success and failure. *Sex Roles, 8,* 333-43.

Fry, P.S. & Ghosh, R. (1980). Attributions of success and failure - comparison of cultural differences between Asian and Caucasian children. *Journal of Cross-Cultural Psychology, 11*(3), 343-363.

Gilligan, C. (1982). *In a Different Voice: Psychological Theory and Women's Development.* Cambridge, MA: Harvard University Press.

Greenfield, P. M. (1994). Independence and interdependence as developmental scripts. In P. M. Greenfield & R. R. Cocking (Eds.), *Cross-cultural roots of minority child development,* (pp. 1-37). Mahwah: Lawrence Erlbaum Associates

Harter, S. (1982). The perceived competence scale for children. *Child Development, 53,* 87-97.

Hau, K-T. & Salili, F. (1991). Structure and semantic differential placement of specific causes: Academic causal attributions by Chinese students in Hong Kong. *International Journal of Psychology, 26*(2), 175-193.

Hung, Y.Y. (1974). Socio-cultural environment and locus of control. *Acta Psychologica Tawainica, 16,* 187-89.

Husen, T. (1967). *International Study of Achievement in Mathematics: A Comparison of Twelve Countries.* New York: Wiley.

Jensen, L., Olsen, J., & Hughes, C. (1990). Association of country, sex, social class, and life cycle to locus of control in Western European countries. *Psychological Reports, 67*(1), 199-205.

Jones, E. E. & Wortman, C. (1973). *Ingratiation: An Attributional Approach.* Morristown, NJ: General Learning Press.

Lao, R.C., Chuang, C.J., & Yang, K.S. (1977). Locus of control and Chinese College students. *Journal of Cross-Cultural Psychology, 8,* 299-313.

LaPointe, A.E., Mead, N.A., & Phillips, G.W., (1989). *A World of Differences: An International Assessment of Mathematics and Science.* Princeton, N.J.: Educational Testing Service.

Lee, V. K. & Dengerink, H. A. (1992). Locus of control in relation to sex and nationality. *Journal of Cross-Cultural Psychology, 23*(4), 488-497.

Levenson, H. (1974). Activism and powerful others: Distinctions within the concept of internal-external control. *Journal of Personality Assessment, 38,* 377-83.

Little, A. (1987). Attributions in a cross-cultural context. *Genetic, Social, & General Psychology Monographs, 113,* 63-79.

Little, C.B. (1979). Stability of internal-external control as measured by the Rotter scale. *Journal of Social Psychology, 108,* 127-128.

Malikiosi, M.X. & Ryckman, R. M. (1977). Differences in perceived locus of control among men and women adults and university students in America and Greece. *Journal of Social Psychology, 103,* 177-183.

Markus, H. R. & Kitayama, S. (1991). Culture and the self: Implications for cognition, emotion, and motivation. *Psychological Review, 98*(2), 224-253.

McGinnies, E., Nordholm, L.A., Ward, C.D., & Bhanthumnavin, D.L. (1974). Sex and cultural differences in perceived locus of control among students in five countries. *Journal of Consulting and Clinical Psychology, 42*, 451-455.

Moghaddam, F. M., Taylor, D. M., Wright, S. C. (1993). *Social Psychology in Cross-cultural perspective*. New York: W. H. Freeman. (pp. 43,44 & Chapter 3).

Munro, D. (1979). Locus of control attribution: Factors among Blacks and Whites in Africa. *Journal of Cross Cultural Psychology, 10*, 157-172.

Rotter, J.B. (1954). *Social Learning and Clinical Psychology*. Englewood Cliffs, NJ: Prentice-Hall.

Rotter, J.B. (1966). Generalized expectancies for internal versus external control of reinforcement. *Psychological Monographs, 80*, 1-28.

Sadowski, C.J., Woodward, H.R., Davis, S.F., & Elsburg, D.L. (1982). Adjustment correlates of locus of Control. *Journal of Personality Assessment, 47*, 627-31.

Sampson, E. E. (1988). The debate on individualism: Indigenous psychologies of the individual and their   role in personal and societal functioning. *American Psychologist, 43*, 15-22.

Sherif, M. & Cantril, H. (1947). *The Psychology of Ego-Involvements, Social Attitudes and Identifications*. New York: John Wiley.

Smith, P. B. and Bond, M. H. (1994). *Social psychology across cultures*. Needham Heights, MA: Simon and Schuster Inc. (Chapter 3: Culture: the neglected concept; Chapter 6: Social cognition; Chapter 7: The individual and the group: pathways to harmony)

Skinner, E.A. (1995).*Perceived Control, Motivation, & Coping*. Thousand Oaks, CA: SAGE Publication, Inc.

Skinner, E.A., Wellborn, J.G., Connell, J.P. (1990). What it takes to do well in school and whether I've got it: A process model of perceived control and children's engagement and achievement in school. *Journal of Educational Psychology, 82*(1), 22-32.

Strickland, B.R. (1977). Internal-external control of reinforcement. In T. Blass (Ed.), *Personality Variables in Social Behavior*. New York: Halstead Press-Wiley: 219-74.

Stevenson, H.W., Lee, S-Y, & Stigler, J.W. (1986). Mathematics achievement of Chinese, Japanese, and American children. *Science, 231,* 593-699.

Tuss, P., Zimmer, J., & Ho, H. (1995), Causal attributions of underachieving fourth-grade students in China, Japan, and the United States. *Journal of Cross-Cultural Psychology, 26*(4), 408-425.

Wan, K. C., & Bond, M. H. (1982). Chinese attributions for success and failure under public and anonymous conditions of rating. *Acta Psychologica Taiwanica, 24,* 23-31.

Weiner, B. (1976). An attributional approach for educational psychology. In L. Shulman (Ed.), *Review of Research in Education, 4,* 179-208. Itasca, IL: Peacock.

Weiner, B. (1986). *An Attributional Theory of Motivation and Emotion.* New York: Springer-Verlag.

Weiner, B., Heckhausen, H., Meyer, W.U., & Cook, R.E. (1972). Causal ascriptions and achievement motivation: A conceptual analysis of and reanalysis of locus of control. *Journal of Personality and Social Psychology, 21,* 239-248.

Yan, W. & Gaier, E.L. (1994). Causal attributions for college success and failure: An Asian-American comparison. *Journal of Cross-Cultural Psychology, 25*(1), 146-158.

Yang, K. S. (1986). Chinese personality and its change. In M. H. Bond (Ed.), *The Psychology of the Chinese People,* pp. 106-170. Hong Kong: Oxford.

Acknowledgements

This research was supported by grants to Hsiu-Zu Ho and Jules Zimmer from the University of California Pacific Rim Research Program. We are grateful to the principals, teachers, and students of the schools that participated in the study. Appreciation is extended to the school officials and ministries of education in the respective nations for their support of the project. Please address any correspondence related to this article to Hsiu-Zu Ho, Graduate School of Education, University of California, Santa Barbara, CA 93106 (telephone: 805-893-3893). Electronic mail may be sent to ho@education.ucsb.edu.

6. *ABCs for Effective Schools: Creating a Nurturing Environment to Enhance Learning*

Reginald L. Green

Many school districts are participating in reform efforts to improve their effectiveness. However, most of these efforts focus on establishing standards, redesigning the school curriculum, and administering proficiency tests. These changes may have merit, but they all tend to suggest that the student is the cause of diminished academic progress in schools. Thus, the reform efforts fail to address the developmental needs of students and the structure and environment of the school and classroom. Such omissions leave a huge void. While it is necessary for reform efforts to be concentrated in these academic areas, consideration should also be given to the environment and structure of the school and classroom where many of the practices that reinforce the student's problems occur (Pierce, 1994).

Reform programs tend to fail because they do not adequately address the developmental needs of students and there is a potential for conflict in the relationship between home and school, among school staff, and among staff and students (Comer, 1993). Little attention is given to: the nature of the individual who attends school; the structure of the school environment; the way students feel about the school; and the professionalism among the administration, faculty and staff members--all forces that strongly influence what happens to students in the schoolhouse (Bosworth, 1995).

While academic standards are important, schools must also simultaneously attend to students' social and ethical development and the environment and structure of the school and classroom (Pierce, 1994; Lewis, Schaps, and Watson, 1995). These changes should foster the creation of a climate in which effective learning conditions exist for every student, particularly those who are not succeeding in school.

The challenges faced by students are multifaceted and exist as a result of the social interactions that occur in the climate of the school. These challenges are reflected in their attendance, achievement, behavior, rate of graduation, and in a number of other areas. In order for schools to be effective, students must experience a degree of compatibility with the environment of the school (Sinclair & Ghory, 1994). The critical issue that educators must address is the extent to which the school environment is responding productively to the needs of students. "Attending to students for whom schools are not satisfying and productive places is a largely unheeded but an absolutely central place for creating meaning and lasting school reform that will make our schools more responsive to all children and youth." (Sinclair & Ghory, 1994, p. 127).

CHANGING THE ODDS
Students bring to school a set of experiences and talents that must be addressed. Teachers must know what to teach and how to teach. "There is more to life and learning than the academic proficiency demonstrated by test scores," states Noddings (1995, p. 27). Lewis, Schaps, and Watson (1995) argue that while schools are focusing on the intellectual development of students, the social and ethical development of students are going unattended. The learning environment of the school and the ideology of the teacher contribute greatly to student development and the teaching and learning process. If this environment and ideology are not supportive, providing the motivational factors that stimulate student engagement in the teaching and learning process, the reform efforts or changes in educational practices are not likely to be effective (Deal, 1993; Sashkin & Walberg, 1993). Both the environment and the ideology of school personnel must reflect what is best for the student and not in terms of satisfying the teacher's needs or the preferences of the school. The primary concern of school personnel is connecting with students in a manner that will interest them and influence them to participate in the teaching and learning process (Haberman, 1995).

Educators are taking steps to change the odds by better preparing young people for schools, but we must also better prepare schools for young people. Schools and classrooms are often dull and uninteresting places for students who are unable to cope with the standards set by school leaders or the structure of the school environment. School personnel are becoming preoccupied with a narrow standardization of the curriculum, often to the total exclusion of recognition of differences in children's experiences (Soder, 1996). In order for the odds to change, so that all students, regardless of variations in their interests, capabilities, or learning styles will be educated, teaching methods, content, and function must be combined with the human qualities and potential of students (Goodlad, 1984).

In creating an effective learning climate, school personnel should seek to make schools nurturing places by focusing on 13 characteristics (Green, 1997). When schools are nurturing places with effective learning climates:

1. Students feel a sense of self-worth and acceptance.
2. Students feel safe and involved in their education.
3. There is mutual trust and positive interaction between teachers and students.
4. A sense of community, family, and collaboration exists in the school.
5. Everyone values individual differences, and the self one brings into the environment is respected and nurtured.
6. There is a sense of caring among individuals and a collective sense of responsibility for student success.
7. The need for self-actualization is respected.
8. There is recognition of a wide range of talents and the need for empowering all individuals.
9. Teachers have an in-depth knowledge of students.
10. The school models the values of the community and involves the community in the education of students.
11. Teachers model caring attitudes for students.
12. Teachers demonstrate a love for their subject matter and continuously search for competence.
13. Students value themselves and others.

These characteristics cluster into four themes:
➢ Students' feeling about themselves
➢ The environment of the school and classroom

➤ Effective teacher/student relationships
➤ Professionalism among administration, faculty, and staff.

A SEARCH FOR CAUSE AND EFFECT
Over the past six years, my research in the area of nurturing characteristics in schools has consisted of two formal studies and a variety of individual interviews and observations. The first study was conducted during my tenure as Professor of Educational Leadership at Wright State University and associate to John Goodlad at the Institute for Educational Inquiry. The second study was conducted to address questions raised as a result of the first study. Since the completion of the second study, inventories have been conducted at over 60 schools and followed up by individual interviews and on-site observations. These activities have contributed greatly to the identification of strategies that can be offered to enhance the academic performance of all students, especially students who are not achieving up to their potential.

Several reform organizations, including the Institute for Educational Inquiry and the Coalition for Essential Schools, advocate nurturing characteristics in schools. The Institute for Educational Inquiry, founded by John Goodlad, fosters the concept of nurturing schools through a national network of partner schools based on nineteen postulates which advocate schools as communities. The Coalition of Essential Schools, founded by Theodore Sizer, also fosters the concept through a national network of partner schools. His partner schools are based on nine common principles, of which principle seven specifically addresses nurturing (Cushman, 1991). Given that these organizations advocated nurturing, it was deemed appropriate to survey affiliated schools, as well as schools not participating in either program.

STUDY 1
In study 1, three groups of schools were formed to participate in the study: Group 1 selected Coalition of Essential Schools (CES) n = 6; Group 2 selected Wright State University Partner Schools (WSUPS) n = 7, and Group 3 selected schools not participating in either program (NPS) n = 9.

In the first study, the 13 characteristics of nurturing schools previously mentioned were used to construct a 31-item student questionnaire (Student Nurturing School Inventory) and a 45-item teacher questionnaire (Teacher Nurturing School Inventory). Both questionnaires were later refined to 26 and 41 questions respectfully. Initially the inventories were distributed by mail and administered to 20 students and 20 teachers in each of 22 schools. Teachers and students rated the characteristics on a four-point Likert-type scale. Within this range, a 4 indicated the highest degree of importance and existence, while a 1 represented the belief that the characteristic lacked any degree of importance or was nonexistent. A total of 365 teachers and 325 students responded to the survey.

The research was guided by the following questions:
1. To what extent do teachers and students perceive identified characteristics of nurturing to be important, and to what extent do they perceive these characteristics to exist in their schools?
2. Is there a difference between the perceived importance and existence of nurturing characteristics as reported by three groups of schools?
3. Are there themes of nurturing characteristics and, if so, to what extent do teachers and students perceive these themes to be important in the academic achievement of students, and to what extent do they exist in their schools?

Survey Responses
Students rated the characteristics an average of 3.50 in importance, as compared to an average of 2.73 rating on the existence variable. An analysis of the means on the two variables showed a statistical difference between the degree to which students viewed these characteristics as important and the degree to which they perceived them to exist in their school.

Teachers rated the characteristics an average of 3.67 in importance, as compared to an average of 2.71 in existence. An analysis of the means on the two variables also showed a statistical difference between the degree to which teachers viewed these characteristics as important and the degree to which they perceived them to exist in their school.

A paired t-test was conducted to test for significant differences between the mean responses of teachers and students on both the importance and existence variable. In each case, the mean responses for importance were statistically higher than the existence responses at the 0.05 level of significance.

Most students and teachers in the study considered nurturing characteristics important to the academic success of students and felt that nurturing is of value in schools. It was equally clear that these characteristics did not exist to the extent desired in any of the schools analyzed. In addition, teachers and students in the study agreed that most of the characteristics were important, but teachers perceived them to be more important than students.

Teachers of Group 1 schools perceived the characteristics to be significantly more important than teachers of Group 2 schools. Coalition of Essential Schools (Group 1) had the nurturing concept embedded in one of its guiding principles, but Wright State University Partner Schools (Group 2) also had a focus on nurturing characteristics as its program is based on the 19 postulates of John Goodlad. One might have expected teachers of Groups 1 and 2 to report that nurturing characteristics were important, but it was interesting to find that teachers not participating in either program (Group 3) also stressed the importance of nurturing characteristics by teachers.

Students in all three groups perceived nurturing characteristics to exist in their schools. However, in none of the schools did students perceive them to be in existence to the extent of their importance.

Students in the study expressed an interest in self and being involved in their education. This finding supports the assertion of Good and Weinstein (1986) when they reported that schools are a place where children develop or fail to develop a variety of competencies and build the self-esteem which are a critical underpinning of success in academic learning. One might conclude that until the self student's bring to school are nurtured, it is likely to be difficult to get students to shift their focus to aspects of the academic program.

A difference was also observed in the perception of teachers and students regarding teacher/student relations. Teachers reported a better relationship existed than students perceived, and teachers also felt better about the environment than students. These findings suggests there were unequal expectations existing in schools, and when unequal expectations existed, there was the potential for confusion, disappointment, and ineffective program planning. The data from Study 1 raised several questions that motivated additional analysis. To that end, Study 2 was conducted.

Table 1   Comparison Between Teacher Mean Scores by School Group means for Existence Rating

Comparisons	Significant	Mean Diff.	F	Prob.
Group 1 vs. Group 3	*	0.24		
Group 1 vs. Group 2	*	0.22		
Group 2 vs. Group 3	N S	0.02	7.69	0.00

• significant < 0.01

Table 2 Comparison Between Teacher Mean Scores by School Group means for Existence Rating

Comparisons	Significant	Mean Diff.	F	Prob.
Group 1 vs. Group 3	N S	0.02		
Group 1 vs. Group 2	N S	0.00		
Group 2 vs. Group 3	N S	0.02	0.07	0.93

STUDY 2

In the second study, using the state of Ohio directory of schools, three categories of schools were identified: urban, rural, and suburban. There were ten randomly selected schools in each of these categories, and twenty teachers randomly selected from each school completed the Teacher Nurturing School Inventory. The 3rd, 6th, 9th, 12th, and 15th student on the roll of each teacher's homeroom in the selected schools were identified on a rotating basis and asked to complete the Student Nurturing School Inventory.

The Nurturing School Teacher Inventory and The Nurturing School Student Inventory designed in Study 1 were sent to each of the schools (N=30) via US Mail (Green, 1997). Principals of participating schools were asked to administer the Nurturing School Inventories to the selected random sample of (20) teachers and (20) students in each of the schools. In addition, average daily attendance data, number of suspensions for the first semester of the 1996-97 school year, and first time eighth grade proficiency test (pass percentage) scores for current eighth graders were also collected from each of the schools. Survey data sufficient to use in the study were received from 21 of the 30 schools (N=21). Analysis was based upon 20 teachers and 20 students from each of the 21 schools.

In this study, a nurturing school was defined as a school where there is trust and caring among all individuals and where supportive relations existed in a positive environment. There was a sense of community where all individuals were valued and participated in the decision-making process and the self one brought into the environment was respected and nurtured, with everyone accepting responsibility for student success.

Using the characteristics embedded in this conceptual definition, a nurturing school was predefined in two ways. First, a primary definition of nurturing was selected. According to the primary definition, a school was considered to be nurturing when the mean of students and the mean of teachers on the existence variable of all four themes were 3.0 or above.

The primary definition was selected because there appeared to be a need to have all four themes perceived to be in existence by teachers and students in order for that school to truly be nurturing. The themes worked in conjunction with each other. The nurturing effect in a school appeared to be greatest when all four themes were in existence at the level of 3.0 or above.

The secondary definition of nurturing was used to identify schools where individual teachers and/or students may not have perceived the characteristics in the conceptual definition to be in existence in their school at the level of 3.0 or above on the Likert-type scale, but the average of the teachers' mean and students' mean indicated broad existence of the characteristics. This definition was formulated by first calculating a single number using the average of the teachers' mean and students' mean on the existence variable. The single number (Overall Nurturing Mean ONM) provided a single measure of nurturing on the Likert-type scale as was used in the teacher and student nurturing school inventories. Alternatively, a school was considered to be a nurturing school if it received a score of 3.0 or above.

In this study, using two different definitions, only four of twenty-one schools could be classified as nurturing, and in only one of the four was it found that teachers and students perceived their schools to be nurturing at or above 3.0. In most of the schools studied, neither teachers, students, nor a combination of "both," perceived their schools to be nurturing consistent with the definitions. These data suggest that nurturing characteristics are perceived to be important by both teachers and students but are not in existence in their schools to the extent of their importance.

The school with the greatest magnitude of nurturing had the highest attendance of all the schools in the study. Of particular interest was the observation that the greater the perception of nurturing by teachers, the higher the proficiency test scores. It was also revealed that when teachers perceived the environment of the school and classroom to be positive, proficiency scores were higher. When the environment of the school was perceived to be positive by both teachers and students, attendance was high, fewer student suspensions existed, and proficiency test scores were higher.

Of the four nurturing themes in this study, the theme, "students' feelings about themselves" was perceived to be least existent in 15 of the 21 schools. Yet the data from both teachers and students revealed that when students' feelings about themselves are positive, student attendance increased and so did proficiency test scores. The data also revealed that when students reported feeling positive about themselves, there were fewer suspensions.

The theme "professionalism among administration, faculty, and staff" was most existent in 15 schools. When teachers perceived professionalism among administration, faculty and staff to be in existence, fewer student suspensions existed and proficiency test scores were higher.

Table 3: Existence Rating of the Four Themes in Schools

Nurturing

School Code	Teachers (# of themes)	Students (# of themes)	Both Teachers & Students	Average of Student mean & Teacher mean
03	(4) *	(4) *	(4) (4) *	X (3.35) **
12	(3)	(3)		X (3.09) **
13	(1)	(4) *		X (3.03) **
19	(4) *	(3)		X (3.24) **

• represents a rating of 3.0 and above on all four themes.
** represents 3.0 or above for the average of all four themes.

BUILDING A BETTER CLIMATE

After conducting two studies, independently implementing the inventories in a variety of schools, conducting on-site interviews, and making observations in schools were the inventories were administered, several conclusions have been reached regarding the four themes and strategies that can be used in building a better climate in schools. The following section addresses those conclusions and strategies.

Students' Feelings About Themselves
Students in all three groups in Study 1 perceived nurturing characteristics to exist in their schools. Yet, in none of the schools did students perceive them to be in existence to the extent of their importance. These results offer an area for consideration by school personnel, especially personnel in schools where nurturing is advocated. The concept of nurturing may philosophically be a part of the program, but the programmatic aspect is questionable.

        Students do not come to school perceiving the world in exactly the same way; teachers must know, understand, and develop an appreciation and respect for students as individuals. If a student is not respected as an individual, or if his or her experiences are deemed unimportant in the school, the academic progress of that student could be negatively impacted (Pierce, 1994). Every student is unique; it is this uniqueness that must be nurtured in the school.

        The experiences of students must be recognized, acknowledged, and respected if they are to fully embrace the instructional process (Soder, 1996). One could be keenly interested in the academics, but if the self is not nurtured, the individual might be subject to all types of distractions that are disruptive to the educational process and hard to overcome. Placing pressure to achieve rigorous standards in this instance would seem counterproductive as students may elect to preserve their self-esteem by reducing their efforts. Rather than placing pressure to achieve rigorous standards, school personnel could consider providing planned educational experiences that instill positive feelings in students and assist them in acquiring the attributes that provide them with the strength and fortitude to confront the challenges they face in and outside of school. Perhaps attention to nurturing in a planned and consistent manner would enhance the importance of nurturing for students and the extent to which teachers and students work to make it a reality in their schools.

Table 4   Spearman Correlation Between the Variables

Nurturing	Spearman Correlation		
	Attendance	Suspension	Proficiency
All Themes			
Average	.34	- .39*	.41*
Student	.25	- .32	.19
Teacher	.29	- .29	.47**
Theme 1			
Average	.21	- .31	.09
Student	.18	- .40*	.13
Teacher	.25	- .18	.27
Theme 2			
Average	.26	- .32	.34
Student	- .13	- .14	-.03
Teacher	.25	- .37*	.42*
Theme 3			
Average	.38 *	- .41*	.38*
Student	.31	- .34	.24
Teacher	.26	- .24	.42*
Theme 4			
Average	.38*	- .35	.45**
Student	.24	- .38*	.27
Teacher	.44 **	- .37*	.57***

*   p < .1
** p < .05
*** p <.01

Building Resiliency in Students

It is extremely difficult for anyone to reach his/her full potential without a feeling of self-worth. Every student requires a support system of some sort. Few can thrive, or even survive, in a meaningful way without one. Henderson and Milstein (1996) offer evidence that schools can provide this support through resiliency building. Having a variety of peak experiences contributes to a student's support system and builds resiliency in that student. A peak experience is the satisfaction and fulfillment an individual receives from participating in an event or activity. These experiences build on the self-confidence of students, providing them with a feeling of importance and acceptance.

A peak experience varies and is determined by the student but is more often than not controlled by school personnel. For some students, making the basketball team is a peak experience. For others, it may be making the football team, or the cheering squad, or the drama club, or being in the band. Acquiring peak experiences builds relationships, draws out the personal beauty inside students and enhances them as individuals.

A growing body of resiliency research suggests that students have to believe and hope they have the strengths and the abilities to make a positive difference (Henderson & Milstein, 1996). Perhaps this belief system can be developed through the occurrences of peak experiences. The more peak experiences a student has, the stronger his support base becomes and the more likely he is to succeed in school (Green, 1998). However, "the most critical resiliency builder for every student is a basic trusting relationship with adults, even with just one adult" (Henderson & Milstein, 1996, p. 18). Based on this premise, there has been an increase in mentoring programs in schools. Creating mentoring programs and providing opportunities for students to have peak experiences are two strategies that could become a part of the nurture that teachers profoundly affect to create a better climate for effective schools.

ENVIRONMENT OF THE SCHOOL AND CLASSROOM

As well as recognizing students as individuals, the school environment must respond productively to the differences among them. Our current school and classroom structure does not produce the type of nurturing environment that allow all students to reach their full potential. The structure of the school must have meaning for students. "It is through consistent respect for and recognition of the particular child's particular experiences that the child develops a self who, in turn, can recognize, respect, and trust others" (Soder, 1996, p. 51).

Data from Study 2 supports the notion that students will be more interested in attending school, actively participate in the instructional process, receive fewer suspensions, and have better test scores if the environment of the school and classroom is nurturing. When students believe that what is occurring in school is meaningful to them, and their teachers' behaviors demonstrate a sense of caring and a belief in their ability to achieve, they have a greater interest in learning. Similarly, other studies have shown that when children feel they are respected and cared about, they care about one another, and when they care about one another and are motivated by important, challenging work, they are more likely to care about learning (Lewis, Schaps, and Watson, 1996; Quint, 1994; Comer, 1993). When students feel cared about and respected, they maintain an open relationship with teachers, maintain free and open communication, and all parties share a deep sense of trust (Rossi and Stringfield, 1995).

A Convergence of Effort

Schools, to a large extent, do not plan and set aside time for students to be nurtured. Nurturing in schools is a chance happening, occurring mostly outside the classroom in hallways and other unstructured places (Goodlad, 1984). The way schools are structured, students are led to believe that what is important is implemented. The absence of nurturing characteristics in a structured manner may be saying to students that nurturing is not important. It appears that the focus of teachers is on structure and conformity in the environment of the school, whereas students tend to focus on self and being involved in their education. Teachers appear to want to teach and seek an environment in which teaching can occur. This was also an observation made by Goodlad (1984).

Often we hold students responsible for their shortcomings and do not stop to realize the factors which are influencing their behavior. In one school, there was a student (let's call him Robert) who was labeled as being very disruptive. In fact, the reports about his behavior were such that they reached the office of the superintendent of schools. He wanted to observe Robert in a classroom setting. Therefore, one morning he paid a visit to Robert's classroom. The day was just beginning, and all students were assembling in their classes. Robert was present and preparing for the day. His behavior was not out of the ordinary. In fact, it was commendable. Robert seemed to be happy and pleased to be in school. Just as the bell sounded to begin the day, the special education teacher entered the room and made a request of

Robert to accompany her to a special area of the building. She stated, "Come with me, Robert. We have some very special things planned for you today." Robert became irate. He stated, "Why do I always have to leave? Why can't I remain in this class? Why do I always have to be treated differently?"

The school personnel had very good intentions for Robert, but the intentions were not addressing the self that Robert brought into the classroom. The school perceived Robert to need special attention that would be provided in a separate setting by specific personnel when what Robert wanted most was to have the self he brought into the classroom nurtured and to be treated, not differently, but as an individual who was different. The disruption Robert was causing was actually precipitated by the lack of nurturing of the self he brought with him to school. This example illustrates that there must be a convergence of effort. Teachers must recognize the differences of background between their students and themselves, and they must help students understand and accept individual differences and realize the importance of giving feedback and taking responsibility for their behavior. Also, teachers and counselors functioning as a team can help make the structure of the school compatible with the needs of students.

The importance of nurturing must be emphasized and demonstrated. In the absence of nurturing characteristics, many students such as Robert, simply stop coming to school or become a disruptive force in school. To prevent such occurrences, teachers must make sure that students know that they have confidence in them and their ability to learn. When students feel that teachers listen to their concerns, they are more expressive, allowing the teachers to adequately assess the challenges that impact their learning.

Observations at Caldwell

Some schools have recognized this need and are implementing programs that will raise the awareness level of teachers regarding the characteristics of nurturing. One such school is Caldwell Elementary School in the Memphis, Tennessee City School System. Principal Sabir is implementing "The Work Sampling System" at Caldwell. The Work Sampling System (a comprehensive approach of assessing student development) recognizes the importance of developing the child personally and socially and demonstrates how the lack of this development can negatively impact academic achievement. One of the seven areas assessed using this program is the personal and social development of students. Teachers specifically assess student development in the areas of: (1) self-concept; (2) self control; (3)

ches to learning; (4) interaction with others, and (5) conflict
on. All of these characteristics are identified in the nurturing
esearch as factors that have an effect on the academic
nt of students.

at Riverview

Elementary School, another Memphis City School, the
environments of the school and classrooms are very conducive to
teaching and learning. When the principal was asked how the faculty
and staff were able to develop such a conducive environment, his
response was, "We praise our teachers for the outstanding manner in
which they perform. Each teacher receives some type award or gift
each year. The history of the school is displayed to create a sense of
pride in where we have been and to create a vision of where we need to
go. Student work is displayed, indicating to our students that we are
pleased with their efforts and encouraging them to achieve greater
heights. We teach all our students to respect themselves, their fellow
students, school, teachers, parents, community, and the city. Our
students understand there is a time to work and a time to play, and they
know how to separate the two. Our program is about building a
community of learners and respecting one another in the process."

The environment of the school and the classroom influences
the manner in which individuals think and behave; if this behavior is
not nurturing, it can produce barriers to student success (Duncan,
1989). The challenge for school leaders is to create effective learning
conditions for all students who attend schools. The environment must
be safe, indicating respect for diversity and acknowledging the
proposition that all students can learn. In fact, student learning must be
viewed as the fundamental purpose of the school's existence (ISLLC,
1996).

EFFECTIVE TEACHER/STUDENT RELATIONS

It was not surprising to find in Study 2 that when students perceived
that a positive relationship existed between them and their teachers,
student suspensions were fewer. Students needed to establish a caring
relationship with adults as much as they needed books (O'Neil, 1997).
When positive performance was affirmed, both teachers and students
strived to do their best. (Rossi and Stringfield, 1997). Students learned
a great deal from the behavior of their teachers. Relationship building
was a prerequisite to a positive classroom climate, and a positive
classroom climate was a prerequisite to effective instruction.

Currently, little if any time during the school day is planned and devoted to nurturing the self the student brings to school (Goodlad, 1984). At best, such efforts have been left exclusively to the counselor. A growing body of literature supports the notion that the self the child brings to school must be understood and nurtured by all school personnel. Knowledge of the student often provides the teacher with an understanding of the challenges that confront the student (Pierce, 1994; Theobald & Nachtigle, 1995; and Soder, 1996). When this understanding exists, the teacher develops a sense of appreciation for the student, respects the student as an individual, and teaching takes on new meaning. There is a sense of acceptance that penetrates the student's world; trust is established between the teacher and student and, learning becomes meaningful.

In a nurturing school, when effective teachers/student relationships exist, teachers arrange classrooms to make it easier for students to work and to learn:

➢ Students know exactly what is expected of them.
➢ Teachers prepare material that reaches the different strengths of each student.
➢ There is adequate material and time to accomplish the task of the day.
➢ There is no wasted time.
➢ The environment supports learning.
➢ The teacher has control of the room without being in control.

Teachers explore the community in which students live and see the world from their students' perspectives. They envision exciting and interesting ways of doing things and helping their students reach their full potential. "The teacher is not so much a purveyor of knowledge as an architect and catalyst who helps students persistently engage in important concepts" (Lewis, Schaps, and Watson, 1995, p. 550). Without a positive relationship with the teacher, students have little reason to commit to the instructional activities of the curriculum, and teachers must rely on discipline and classroom management techniques to facilitate teaching and learning (Noblit, Rogers, and McCadden, 1995, p. 681).

Every individual can likely remember at least one person who has been influential in his/her life. In many instances, that individual is a teacher who likely had a major impact and who at some point helped that individual overcome a barrier that stood between him/her and a particular goal. If this type relationship existed between all teachers and students, then the school environment would contain the nurturing necessary to foster success for all students.

Many stories exist to confirm the benefits that students derive from such relationships. One such story involves Leon and Mrs. Ramey. Leon was a ninth grader who paid little attention to the academic side of school. He was very active, often attracting attention through humorous antics. Few teachers, if any, believed that he had the potential, desire, or academic capability to complete high school.

One day following his English class, he approached Mrs. Ramey who was in charge of the annual ninth grade theatrical performance. He made a request to participate in that performance. To Leon's amazement, Mrs. Ramey's reply was "I will give it some thought." Two days later, not only did Mrs. Ramey give him a part in the performance, "Love Hits Wilbur," but she gave him the leading role! When other teachers and students became aware of this decision, they responded in amazement, and predicted failure for the performance. However, with each rehearsal, the performance got better and better, and when the curtains were drawn the final time that night, not only was "Love Hits Wilbur" awarded best performance, but Leon was awarded best actor. This event became a turning point in his life, and he went on to graduate from high school and complete college.

Teachers must accept students as they are and realize that although the experiences that children have had may not be the ones society would wish for them, never-the-less, they are their own, are a part of them, and their teachers can build upon those experiences. Teachers must eliminate the negative labels must be eliminated and teachers must come to realize the benefit of diversity. When teachers deny the value of their students' differences, they deny the value of their students.

PROFESSIONALISM AMONG ADMINISTRATION, FACULTY, AND STAFF

In a nurturing school, every student becomes the responsibility of every member of the staff. A sense of belonging is fostered for all students, and all school personnel work to build bonds between students and teachers and between home and school (Comer, 1980). Teachers are empowered, participate in the decision-making process, and consistently seek better ways to educate children. The school reflects the values of the community, and parents become partners in the educational process. In essence, professionalism exists among administration, faculty, and staff, and when professionalism exists among administration, faculty, and staff:

> Teachers are empowered and participate in the decision-making process;
> Teachers demonstrate a genuine love for their subject matter;
> There is collaboration among the faculty;
> Everyone is a part of the school family, the faculty, staff, students, parents, and the community;
> Teachers consistently seek better ways to educate children;
> The school draws in the values of the community;
> The curriculum is child centered;
> Parents are considered partners in the educational process;
> There is a continuous search for competence;
> There is respect among the faculty for the full range of talent;
> All teachers are prepared to respond to student needs;
> The faculty and staff can respond to student and neighborhood needs spontaneously;
> The school faculty serves the individual's greatest need for self-actualization
> Everyone has the capacity for creativity;
> The faculty and staff aid student nurturing by not allowing "non nurturing behavior;" and
> Teachers model caring attitudes for students and other teachers.

In a numbers of districts, changes in practice are being made to enable these characteristics to become a reality. Leadership, commitment, focus, district culture, inclusivity, and professional development comprise the practices commonly changed in districts where professionalism between administrators, faculty, and staff is of primary importance. The following changes have been observed:

Leadership
> The leadership has changed to a more persuasive and inclusive style with all individuals being included in decisions that govern the school or district.

Commitment
> There is strong commitment by the community, board of education, central administration, and association leadership to improving student success.

➤ Money is not the driving force behind decisions; student data drives decisions.

Focus
➤ A single focus is established either by district leaders or through a collaborative discussion and decision-making process.
➤ Decisions are made based on the district's vision, mission, and goals.

District Culture
➤ A non-threatening culture where disagreements can occur without threat of punitive action is established in the district and in each school.
➤ There is consistency between the vision/philosophy espoused by the district superintendent and the action taken to implement change.
➤ Risk taking is encouraged.

Inclusivity
➤ There is a changed view of the roles played by various groups, and these new roles are accepted as appropriate.
➤ A collaborative decision-making model is used where everyone has an opportunity to be a decision-maker and leader.
➤ Curriculum is revamped based on identified learning standards.
➤ Five groups are active in facilitating change: district administrators, school board, local association leaders, parents, and community leaders.

Professional Development
➤ Professional development is considered necessary and is provided for all levels from the building staff through central office.
➤ Professional development integrates application with problem solving and skill development rather than lecture and demonstration (Etheridge and Green, 1998).

As the search continues for answers to the complex problem of educating students in an age of accountability, all stakeholders are coming to the realization that establishing and maintaining a professional relationship is advantageous to the educational process. As a result, individuals are working together to enhance student success and improve the quality of education in schools and school districts.

SUMMARY

Schools must become communities within themselves, accepting people as individuals and respecting the value of their contribution. We must stop blaming the victim for needing assistance. "There is no question that those predisposed to blame the victim will fail as teachers, while those whose natural inclination is constantly to seek more effective teaching strategies, regardless of youngsters' background or the obstacles youngsters face, have a fighting chance of becoming effective teachers of children" (Haberman, 1995, p. 53). Teachers and administrators must be willing to risk establishing relationships with each other, teachers and with students.

Teachers must promote nurturing, for nurturing forms the underpinning for the development of relationships that make a difference in students' academic achievement. Currently, students do not feel that nurturing characteristics (identified through this work) are as important as teachers feel they are and are not likely to promote the type of relationships that make a difference in these characteristics until they perceive them to be important. Programs and services are needed to reduce the variance between the importance of nurturing characteristics in schools and the extent to which they exist.

The goal of schools should be to educate youngsters, and the focus should remain on them. Administrators and teachers must resist maintaining the structure of the school as it now exists. Maintaining structure and holding fast to strict academic standards must give way to seeking continuous renewal and finding ways to address all the needs of all the children. If academic achievement is to be improved, schools will have to become more effective, and to become more effective, schools need a better climate.

REFERENCES

Bosworth, Kris (1995). Caring for others and being cared for. *Phi Delta Kappan*, 76(9), 686-693.

Comer, James P. (1993). *School power: implications of an intervention project*. New York: The Free Press.

Cushman, Kathleen (1991). Behavior in a thoughtful school: The principal of decency. *The Coalition of Essential Schools*, 7(4), 1-8.

Deal, T.E. (1993). The culture of schools. In M. Saskin & H.J. Walberg (Eds.), *Educational leadership and school culture*. Berkeley, CA: McCutchan Publishing Cooperation.

Duncan, W. J. (1989). Organizational culture: "Getting a fix" on an elusive concept. *Academy of Management Executive*, 3, 229-236.

Good, T., & Weinstein, R. (1986). Schools make a difference: Evidence, criticisms, and new directions. *American Psychologist*, 41(8), 1090-1097.

Goodlad, John I. (1984). *A place called school: prospects for the future.* New York: McGraw-Hill.

Green, Reginald L. (1994). Who is in charge of the schoolhouse? *Education, 114(4), 557-559.*

Green, Reginald L. (1997). In search of nurturing schools: Creating effective learning conditions. *NASSP Bulletin* 81, (589), 17-26.

Green, Reginald L. (1998). Nurturing characteristics in schools related to discipline, attendance, and eighth grade proficiency test scores. *American Secondary Education*, 26, (4), 7-14.

Haberman, Martin. (1995). Star teachers of children in poverty. *Kappa Delta Pi*: West Lafayette, Indiana.

Henderson, N., & Milstein, M.m. (1996). *Resiliency in schools: Making it happen for students and educators.* California: Corwin Press, Inc.

Interstate school leaders licensure consortium: Standards for school leaders. (1996). *Council of Chief State School Officials.* Washington DC.

Kerr, Donna H. (1993). Beyond education: In search of nurture. Seattle: Institute for Educational Inquiry, (Work In Progress No. 2).

Lewis, Catherine C., Schaps, Eric, and Watson, Marilyn. (1995). Beyond the pendulum: Creating challenging and caring schools. *Phi Delta Kappan,* 547-554.

Noblit, George W., Rodgers, Dwight L., and McCadden, Brian M., (1995). In the meantime the possibilities of caring. *Phi Delta Kappan 680-685.*

Noddings, Nel. (1995). Teaching themes of caring. *The Education Digest,* 25-28.

O'Neil, John. (1997). Building schools as communities: A conversation with James Comer. *Educational Leadership,* 54, (8), 6-10.

Pierce, Cecilia. (1994). *Importance of classroom climate for at-risk learners. Journal of Educational Research,* 37-42.

Quint, Sharron. (1994). *Schooling homeless children: A working model for America's public schools.* New York: Teachers College Press.

Rossi, Robert J., and Stringfield, Samuel C. (1995).What we must do for students placed at risk. *Phi Delta Kappan,* 77, (1), 73-76.

Sashkin, M. & Walberg, h. (1993). *Educational leadership and culture.* San Francisco:McCutchan.

Sinclair Robert L., & Ghory Ward J. (1994). Last things first: Realizing quality by improving conditions for marginal students. In John I Goodlad & Pamela Keating (Eds.), *Access to knowledge: The continuing agenda for our nation's schools* (125-144). New York: The College Board.

Soder, Roger, (ed.). (1996). *Democracy, education, and the schools,* San Francisco: Jossey-Bass.

Theobald, P. and Nachtigal, P. (1995). Culture, community, and the promise of rural education. *Phi Delta Kppan,* 77, 132-135.

7. Perspectives of African American Parents of High-Achieving Students Regarding the Home-School Relationship

Donna Mahler and Stanley J. Zehm

> "I'm having my say, giving my opinion. Lord, ain't it good to be an American..... Truth is, I never thought I'd see the day when people would be interested in hearing what two old Negro women have to say."
>
> *Bessie Delany*

INTRODUCTION

The proud, strong voices of America's persons of color, such as Bessie Delany, are frequently muffled by racists, yet have added enriching perspectives of our country's socio-political fabric. These perspectives, in turn, have been responsible for assisting in the initiation of numerous societal reforms that have brought more hope and access to millions of minority citizens. The voices of minority parents, however, have seldom been heard by educational reformers seeking to improve the academic performance of students in American public schools. While the benefits of active parent involvement in the improvement of the academic performance of students has been well documented in the literature (Coleman et al., 1966; Walberg, 1984; Henderson, 1987; Epstein, 1990; Swap, 1993), few studies have sought to collect and study the perspectives of minorities regarding their involvement in the academic success of their children. The results of the study described in this chapter begin to fill the gap in the literature of parent involvement which has neglected the voices of minority parents (Mahler, 1997).

After a brief review of the benefits of genuine parent involvement, an examination of the preparation of teachers for supporting parent involvement, and an analysis of what current demographics reveals about the need for more parent involvement, this chapter will focus on the perceptions of African American parents of high-achieving students. More specifically, it will share the voices and views of twelve African American parents of varying socio-economic levels regarding their perceptions of parental roles and responsibilities in supporting the academic success of their children. It will also describe their beliefs about the roles and responsibilities of the school in ensuring the academic success of minority students. Finally, we will examine the recommendations these parents offer for improving the home-school relationship to make these overlapping spheres of influence more effective for supporting the academic and social successes of minority children in America's elementary schools.

The Benefits of Parent Involvement
Students of all ethnic groups and socio-economic levels will benefit from genuine parent involvement. This is not the "cookies and juice" type of parent involvement of previous times. Parents of today do not have time for superficial kinds of involvement with their children's schools. They want what little time they have to be involved with their children's schools to be of a substantive nature. They want a say in the school's philosophy and goals; they want their voices heard about school discipline and safety. When parents are regularly informed and consulted about important school issues, they will begin to feel genuinely involved. When they are asked to participate in the decision making process about important school policies and procedures, they will more readily answer the call to be involved.

The more roles parent's play in their children's education, at home and school, the better will be the academic and social outcomes for their children. It must be noted that these benefits will not just be recognized and appreciated by parents and students, elementary teachers will also benefit from genuine parent involvement. Teachers report more positive feelings about their teaching and schools when there is a greater degree of parent involvement (Leitch & Tangri, 1988; Epstein & Dauber, 1991). Teachers who regularly involve the parents of their students, regardless of the level of parent education, rate parents more positively. Moreover, they stereotype parents less frequently than do other teachers (Epstein, 1996).

Teacher Preparation For Meaningful Parent Involvement
While we have long understood the benefits of involving all parents in meaningful home-school partnerships, teachers remain ill-prepared for involving parents, particularly those who are parents of minority children (Ost, 1988; Comer, 1988). Teacher preparation programs often neglect parent involvement practices, producing teachers who lack appropriate strategies for involving parents in the educational process. One result of this lack of teacher preparation can be seen in the drop in teacher efforts to involve parents which begins as early as the second or third grade (Barndt, 1989).

Although the simultaneous influence of schools and families on a student's academic and social growth is undeniable, the overlapping influence is too often ignored in research and in practice (Ost, 1988; Epstein, 1990). Epstein (1990) states, "Most family textbooks and courses ignore the school, and most education courses ignore the family" (p. 118). Teachers are also not prepared to understand the broader kinds of involvement parents seek of their schools today. Teachers and administrators maintain a very limited definition of parent involvement and define a narrow range of parent behaviors as legitimate and helpful (Lareau, 1993). Comer (1986), one of the most active supporters of minority parent involvement for improved student achievement, states that "Many schools simply don't want parents present, and many parents are reluctant to become involved, as well" (p. 444). It is a fact that involving parents more results in a more complex instructional environment for teachers. In order to deal with this complexity more effectively, pre-service and in-service teachers will require additional training and support before they can initiate and maintain programs of genuine parent involvement.

Parent Involvement and Demographic Trends
One reason often cited as a factor contributing to the low levels of parental involvement is the demographic changes in our school populations. Present demographic trends predict that by the year 2000, one-third of the nation's school children will be those of color (Grant &

Secada, 1990). In many of today's urban schools, minority students are already in the numerical majority. Moreover, a higher proportion of America's children, twenty-five percent, is below the poverty line today than at any time in the past thirty years (Hodgkinson, 1995). A decade ago, nearly half of our nation's African American children were burdened with poverty (Eshleman, 1998). This percentage has alarmingly continued to increase during this decade. The correlation between poverty and unacceptable school performance has been amply demonstrated (Grant & Secada, 1990; Knapp & Woolverton, 1995). Poor and minority children are disproportionately represented in special education programs. They are scoring lower on achievement tests and are dropping out of school at an alarming rate.

Another demographic trend has arisen during this decade that forebodes even greater problems for children of color in our nation's schools. While our student population is becoming increasingly diverse, our teaching force is becoming more White and female (Grant & Secada, 1990). At the present time, only 12 to 14 percent of the current teaching force is nonwhite; approximately 68 percent of teachers in our nation's public schools are female. If present trends continue, the discontinuity between teacher and student demographics is likely to become even greater. This cultural mismatch can result in a mutual distrust between parents and teachers and the loss of hope on the part of minority parents that schools will provide equal access to educational opportunities for their children.

In line with these demographic trends, there is increasing evidence that teachers are most able to understand and support students who are like themselves in culture, race, ethnicity, and socio-economic levels. Several studies indicate that when teachers differ culturally from their students, they are less likely to get to know the parents of their students and more likely to believe that parents are disinterested in their children's schooling (Epstein & Dauber, 1991; Cochran-Smith, 1995). Other studies, however, that have focused on teachers who regularly engage parents in a high level of involvement in their children's education at home and school, have found the teacher less inclined to stereotype poor and minority parents as uncaring and uninterested in their children's education (Comer, 1985; Epstein, 1990). Today, more than ever, the challenges of parent involvement include the need for schools to respond with sensitivity and understanding to the social and cultural differences found among families.

The Importance of Family Environments
It is important to recognize that student's from poor and minority

family backgrounds are finding social and academic successes even though they may be designated as "at-risk" students. While many previous studies have focused on why students fail, more researchers are now turning their attention toward examining the stories of these successful poor and minority students. One theme that has emerged from this research is the importance of family environment.

The literature has begun to suggest that family environment is a critical factor influencing the school achievement of students (Walberg, 1984; Epstein, 1990; Davies, 1991). These studies have found that the more families are involved in their children's education, the less parent behavior or student success can be explained by status variables such as race or social class.

Walberg (1984) reports that studies focusing specifically on the effects of home conditions on learning suggests that "the curriculum of the home" (p. 400) predicts academic learning twice as well as the socioeconomic status of families. This curriculum includes, Walberg maintains, leisure reading and discussions about the reading, informed parent/child conversations about current events, the monitoring and discussions about television viewing, deferral of immediate gratifications in favor of long-term goals, and expressions of interest and pride in children's personal and academic growth. Walberg concludes that given the relationship between home conditions and student learning as well as the amount of time children spend at home, school programs that aim at improving the academic curriculum of the home should promote student achievement at school. We believe that this research demonstrates that families can compensate for the lack of material or economic resources when they marshal their determination to support and guide their children's education.

African American Parents Have Their Say About Their Roles

The knowledge base about home-school partnerships for families of diverse backgrounds continues to grow. Many questions, however, remain. How do families with different racial, socioeconomic, and cultural backgrounds support the education of their children? What do minority families teach their children? What forms of educational resources do minority families provide for their children? What do parents and schools expect of each other? What can be done to improve the relationships between minority families and schools to create conditions that are more beneficial for children's personal, social, and academic growth? In the section that follows, the African American parents of high achieving elementary students who participated in this study give voice to their beliefs, ideas, and convictions about these crucial questions. Their voices are genuine and convincing.

Families, Schools, and Shared Responsibilities
The first question the study described in this chapter attempted to answer was how do African American parents of high achieving students perceive their role in the education of their children. We believe that their responses can suggest to teachers, principals, and school counselor's specific strategies and family practices that can be shared with other minority parents whose school performance may not be satisfactory.

In having their say about home-school relationships, these parents made clear distinctions between the responsibilities of parents and of schools. They were unanimous that the education of children is the joint responsibility of teachers and parents who must work closely together to insure student's academic success and social growth. They were not tolerant of parents who failed to become actively involved in their children's schooling.

> I don't think so much blame should be put on teachers. I think it is the parent's responsibility to make sure that your child is educated. Put the blame where the blame is due, and that's on those parents that are sitting back and just accepting anything because they're not involved.

The African American parents who participated in this study identified two major responsibilities of parents in the education of their children: 1) to teach core values, especially the importance of having an education and a strong work ethic, and 2) To actively support learning at home.

The Importance of Having an Education
Nearly every parent interviewed in this study reported that his or her parents emphasized the importance of getting an education. They all described their efforts to instill this same value in their children. Those parent participants with little formal education themselves were as adamant about the importance of education for their children as were the parent participants who were highly educated. One father who learned about the importance of an education by earning his education the hard way in a life of military service, described the importance of education for his children this way:

> I know how important education is. It is the backbone to
> the future. If you don't have an education, you can go more
> or less astray.

Some of the participants, including several who were raised in poverty, credited their parents with the high value they placed on education. One parent recalled how her mother fought hard for "those little Black children" at school. She recalled that one day during testing at school her mother learned that Black children were being tested separately and described how she stormed into the school to find out why:

> My mother was always at school making sure those little
> Black children got their rights. She had a reputation. My
> mother was only four foot eleven, but she packed a mean
> punch! She did the best she could with the knowledge she
> had. I know more. I hope it's getting better.

The African American parents in this study also recognized the positive influence that extended family members can have in influencing their grandchildren and siblings about the importance of education. Parents, if there are two and if they both are required to work, can value education, but can't always be there to help their children with school work even if they wanted to be involved. Thus, having extended family members who are willing to step in and help can compensate for a parent's inability to get as involved as he or she would like. One parent described how, since both of her parents worked, she received help from her siblings:

> There were six of us and it was kind of hard. I had a sister
> who was older. When we had problems, we tried to work
> things out together. If we had problems, we went to the one
> who had more knowledge.

The research on family environment has demonstrated that effective families, regardless of race or socioeconomic levels, have historically valued and supported their children's education (Hidalgo et al., 1995). This study supports this finding and demonstrates that the emphasis on education that African American parents experienced growing up is reflected in their own parenting practice today. This intergenerational effect can especially be seen in the participant's perceptions about the value of work.

The Work Ethic

The African American parents of academically successful students who participated in this study frequently spoke of the importance of instilling a strong work ethic in their children. They encouraged their children to take pride in their academic work and accomplishments. One parent remarked:

> A lot may be modeled by a work ethic that may be translated with just seeing your parents go to work everyday and then making you accountable for what you do or don't do and the way your classroom work is. You know, it was always told to me, my (her parents) job is to go to work; your job is to go to school. My reward for going to work is a paycheck. Your reward for going to school is good grades.

Another parent's comment about her child's grades also reflected a strong work ethic:

> A "hard C" I'll take over a "soft A." If I know that my child has worked to get that "C." That type of a "C," I can accept.

This same parent expressed her perception of what the work ethic meant to her by sharing the "work first, then play" philosophy she used with her children.

> My philosophy is, if you do what you have to do, then you can do the things that you want to do!

While all of the parents in this study emphasized the values of getting a good education and working hard with their children, several parents voiced the belief that these values are even more important for African American children. They recognized that, as a minority, their children may have to work even harder to prove themselves in a predominantly white society where stereotypes, especially about Black males, are common. Parents shared these thoughts about why the work ethic is especially important for African American students.

> Education is the key. I know that with him, being a Black male with a single mother, that it's going to be hard.

> I was always told that I couldn't do as good as White students. I had to be better if I were going to be considered

for anything. She (her mother) never said that's not fair.
She never said that it shouldn't be that way. She said that's
the way it is and if you're gonna play, be a player. Then
you need to know that's one of the rules, and you accept
that rule and decide to play or you don't accept that rule
and not win.

I want him (the son) to know who he is and where he
comes from and how hard that he has to study in order to
succeed. He's always going to have to stay a step or two
ahead because we have to work harder to be successful and
to get ourselves established.

Supporting Learning at Home
As we pointed out earlier in this chapter, the literature suggests that the
"curriculum of the home" (Walberg, 1984), is twice as predictive of
student achievement as factors such as gender, race, or socioeconomic
status. In this study, every African American parent interviewed voiced
the high importance they gave to supporting the learning of their
children at home. They all were careful to monitor the homework of
their children. One parent expressed this view about the importance of
monitoring her daughter's homework:

We're definitely on her about her homework. We don't let
her do anything, watch TV, until that homework is done.
It's the main thing.

These parents also reported that involvement with their children's
learning at home was not limited to checking homework assignments.
When their children did not grasp the concepts and skills presented in
the classroom, the parents tried to help them by filling in the gaps in
their children's understanding. Many of their comments reflected this
kind of parent responsibility they believed they needed to fulfill:

I'm very much into education, and with my daughter, I
believe that my idea is for her to master each subject. I do
not like skipping. And that's why when my daughter comes
home, we go through another time of school. I think it
helps a lot at home when you work with your child.

It's better to teach your kid at home just as well as it is at
school. Just don't think it is the teacher's job to teach your
child, because it's 50/50. It's just as well the parent's job as

> it is the teacher's. You send them to school to get an
> education. But the teacher cannot educate him on all things.
> At home, that's when you need to, you know, educate him
> better on everything.

While some families may use the lack of money as an excuse for not helping their children at home, one mother commented that economic resources should not prevent parents from being fully involved in their children's education:

> You don' t always have to have money to buy things. If
> parents would just sit down and help the kid, I think
> together with the teacher, that would be, I mean, the kids
> would be successful.

Not only did these African American parents find the lack of money as an invalid excuse for not supporting their children's learning at home, they also voiced their opinions that not knowing the most up-to-date methods of learning was also an insufficient argument for excusing parents from active involvement in their child's learning at home. One mother recalled the frustration she felt when practicing subtraction with her son. She soon discovered that the method she was using was not the approach used in her son's classroom. She visited her son' teacher and quickly learned the "new way" which enabled her to continue to support her son's school learning at home. Another parent expressed her view on this issue in these words:

> I work real hard with my daughter and if I don't understand
> something because of where I'm from, I go to the teacher
> and say, "You are teaching this subject this way. Now can
> you show me how to teach my daughter the way you are
> teaching her so we can be the same?"

Social Learning
While teaching and supporting learning at home were by far the most frequently identified parental responsibilities, several of the African American participants in this study identified behavior as being the parent's responsibility. The sense of responsibility for a child's social behavior may have accounted for the fact that none of the children of the parents participating in this study exhibited major behavioral problems at school. Their children were not only accustomed to academic success, they enjoyed the benefits that come to children who, because of the high expectations of their parents, learn to be

responsible for their own personal and social behavior. One mother explained that she maintains high standards for her daughter's behavior and described how she has followed her own parents in that respect:

> If she (her daughter) gets out of line, you let me know. You won't have a problem with that. The school stuff you're gonna have to teach her, but the discipline stuff, I will handle.

Another parent had this to say about a parent's responsibility for student behavior:

> Regarding behavior, I feel that it is our responsibility to make sure our son behaves in the classroom. It takes too much time away from teaching if the teacher has to correct behavioral problems. I don't expect the teacher to be constantly disciplining our son. She is going to have to stop disruptive behavior if it arises, but I'm not expecting her to raise our child. That's our job as parents. The teachers are supposed to be educating him with our assistance.

The parents in this study were of one mind; teachers need to maintain strict discipline in their classrooms, but parents must take ultimate responsibility for their children's behavior.

African American Parents Have Their Say About School Roles

The African American parents of academically successful elementary students were not only conscious about their roles and responsibilities for being involved in their children's schooling, they also expressed strong convictions regarding the roles and responsibilities of schools. While most of the parents made attempts to fill the gaps in their children's learning, they were clear in their beliefs that the school's primary responsibility was to provide competent instruction in each of the major curriculum areas and to teach them concepts and skills appropriate for their grade levels. Additionally, these parents expected teachers to make the daily effort to reach every student in the classroom by using a variety of instructional methods. Because they were involved with schools in the education of their children, they were more informed and more insistent that teachers provide for their children the most up-to-date curriculum and instructional methods.

Curriculum

Parents in this study expected their children's teachers to be astute practitioners who were informed about current curricular developments and kept parents informed about the content of any new curriculum shared with their children. Parents also voiced the desire to know what the curriculum expectations were at each grade level and what the corresponding learning expectancies for their children included. One father was very enthusiastic in describing how his daughter's teacher sent home a "syllabus" every week which included: subject-specific topics of study and skills the students were working on in class, descriptions of assignments, and their due dates and testing dates. Another parent simply stated, "I want to know what's required for this grade and what books are to be used. Another parent voiced this concern regarding the curriculum:

> We're parents not teachers. We do not always know what is
> expected of our son at this particular grade level. We ask
> his teachers to send us notes home letting us know where
> our son is relative to where he should be and where we
> would like him to be. He may bring home homework that
> we as parents are not familiar with. It is imperative that the
> teacher sends home instructions that clearly relate both
> what is expected of our son and us as parents.

In addition to keeping informed about the school's curriculum, parents wanted to be informed in a timely manner when their children were experiencing any difficulty learning the curriculum.   One mother became upset when she recalled how on a particular occasion she did not know her son was experiencing difficulty mastering the school curriculum until the report card came home at the end of the term. She stated that to avoid such problem of students falling behind in their learning of the school curriculum, teachers should let their parents know how their children are doing on a frequent basis.

Instructional Methods

The parents participating in this study were well aware that children learn in different ways and at different rates. However, they expressed their expectations that teachers would make the effort to find out what their students know, what backgrounds they come from, and how they best learn. One mother explained how she has taught her children to ask questions until they fully understand what is being taught:

> I say to my kids, you always ask questions until you
> understand exactly what the person is telling you. Ask 1001
> questions. If he (the son) gets on her (the teacher), that's
> her job (laughs), that's what I tell them. Cuz that's her job,
> to explain it to you until you under-stand.

Other parents made similar comments about the teacher's instructional
methods:

> They (teachers) should be able to teach, come down enough
> on their (the students') level to make sure they get it.

> And the teacher should be more open to change. If it means
> for a teacher to change her strategy, she should be willing
> to do that because we are teaching a child and that's where
> it goes wrong sometimes.

One parent's compelling voice shared a common concern of the
African American parents involved in this study; the frustration that
their children often experience coming from a different cultural
background. She expressed her concern regarding the impact that could
result from teachers who were unwilling or unable to adjust their
teaching methods to accommodate the cultural backgrounds of their
students:

> I think teachers do have a very, very strong responsibility
> towards the kids in the sense that when they're teaching,
> they have to make sure that because of the different back-
> grounds, and because of the different environment that we
> do live in, there are things that they should explain in
> maybe a different way. And they have to honor the kids and
> make sure that all the kids understand.

Shared Responsibilities

The parents in this study were able to make clear distinctions between
the major responsibilities of families and schools. Virtually all the
participating African American parents recognized that these
responsibilities overlap and that families and schools need to work
together to insure student's academic success. The perceptions of these
parents regarding the home-school relationship supported Epstein's
(1986) theoretical model of schools and family connections (See Figure
1). They recognized how their own actions as well as the actions of
their children's teachers affect the home-school relationship.

FIGURE 1

Epstein's Model of Overlapping Spheres of Influence
in Families and Schools

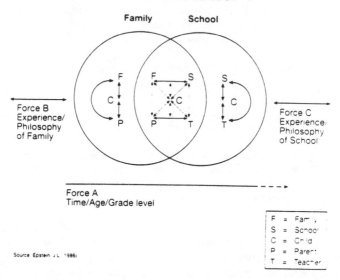

Force B
Experience/
Philosophy
of Family

Force C
Experience/
Philosophy
of School

Force A
Time/Age/Grade level

F = Family
S = School
C = Child
P = Parent
T = Teacher

Source Epstein J L 1986

Parental perceptions of the responsibilities of families and schools also suggested that parents embraced a partnership model (Swap, 1993) of the home-school relationship which emphasizes active collaboration, two-way communication, building on parental strengths, and problem solving that involves both parents and educators. Examples of the parent's voices about the home-school relationship included the following:

> My tax dollars run that organization (the public schools) and therefore, they're providing me with something, a service of some kind. The service they're providing me within this particular venue is an education for my children. However, that cannot be successful without me participating in it to a great degree.

> When you have a child, and you don't think about this before you have one, you eventually have to commit yourself and go back to school. Okay, we're going back to elementary school. I am back in the third grade and then the fourth grade and that's where I'll be until we graduate (laughs).

Parent Involvement Practices

The African American parents of academically successful elementary students who participated in this study shared the specific ways they got involved in their children's schooling. The parent responses were grouped according to Epstein's (1995) typology of six kinds of parent involvement: (1) parenting; (2) communicating; (3) volunteering and/or attending school events; (4) learning at home; (5) decision making; and (6) collaborating with the community. While there were parent responses that demonstrated a degree of involvement in all of these six types of parent involvement, the most frequently reported types were communicating, learning at home, and volunteering and/or participating in events at school.

Communicating

Communication was the most common type of parent involvement practice reported by parents in this study. Parents described their practices of frequent communication with their children's teachers on matters related to curriculum, homework assignments, grades, and behavior. Phone calls, notes, conferences, classroom visits, and daily or weekly progress reports were the most common forms of communication reported. Parents shared these descriptions of how they communicated with teachers in solving problems together:

> I write the teacher a note and have her call me and go over what I have a problem with. And if we can solve it that way, then we can get it solved and we keep going on with the thing. He'll (son) learn better, that's what I think.

> I talk to the teacher any time there is a problem. At one point this year, she (daughter) was not finishing her homework and she was talking to another little kid all the time. So I started getting daily notices. It there was a problem, I'd know every day instead of at the end of the week. And then once she got back on track, I told the teacher it was no longer needed. But anytime, I'd call the teacher and she'd let me know.

Realizing that emotional upsets at home can affect a child's learning and behavior at school, one African American mother explained how she keeps her children's teachers informed about their home life:

> I said look, there are some things going on at home, (parents separating). If you notice anything, any change, with the kids in their attitudes, let me know so that I can help you. And then I let them know what was going on so that they can look for some things and provide some support.

Parents in this study voiced strong opinions that they expected two-way communication with teachers. One parent shared the following story that forcefully demonstrated her powerful voice:

> Last year when he (son) was in the second grade, he had two teachers in one classroom and we ran into a problem. He had forgot to turn in some homework Friday so I had him complete it over the weekend and bring it in on Monday. And I asked him to have the teacher send a note home saying that he had received all of his homework. Well, she told him that wasn't her job. Well, (laughs) I blew. I was furious! So I called the principal and said I'm calling you because I hope this will be taken care of!

Needless to say, this mother's voice was heard by the principal and the problem of the lack of genuine two-way communication was taken care of! All of the African American students in this study were insistent on the need for on-going two-way communication as a critical part of a positive home-school relationship.

Volunteering and Attending School Events

The parent participants in this study identified four kinds of school support activities in which they frequently volunteered to participate: (1) helping prepare the PTA newsletter; (2) working in booths at the school carnival; (3) serving as chaperones for class field trips; (4) assisting in the preparation and conducting of fundraisers to obtain money for special school needs; and (5) tutoring students in classroom programs like "Read Across America." One mother described her involvement with a PTA fundraiser when recognized how excited her son became about her involvement in the project:

> No, I just never have time to join the PTA. But when they do the fundraisers and stuff like that, I volunteer. Like before Halloween, they were having a fundraiser for the American Hear t Association. I brought it to work and collected over $200 for him to jump rope. I gave 100% of my time because I felt it was important stuff for him. He

> was very excited over that. Most parents don't try to
> fundraise. They have their kids out there trying to get
> money instead of the parents saying, 'Hey, I'll help you.
> We can go door to door together.'

Several African American parents also described how they make it a
regular practice to visit their children's classrooms throughout their
schooling to learn more about their children's academic and social
development. One parent described her motivation for visiting her
son's classroom with this observation:

> Last year, I sat in his class twice so I could observe what's
> going on. Hopefully, before the end of this year, I'll be able
> to sit in on this class he's in right now. To see how the
> program is, what they're learning, and what they're getting
> out of it. And also, to see what he's doing, you know, how
> he's acting in school.

Parents participating in this study reported that they routinely attend
school-sponsored events such as Back-to-School Night and special
student performances, especially those connected with holiday
presentations. Several parents, however, acknowledged that work
schedules sometimes limited their participation in school events. One
mother explained that when she wants to participate in such school
events, her employer will release her from work to attend; but admitted
this was an unusual practice that most parents would not have available
to them. Another mother, employed in an executive position, had this to
say about how she tries to balance work demands and participation in
her children's school events:

> One of the things is that, even though I have a white collar
> position as opposed to my parents' blue collar position, I
> think it affords me some flexibility in my work day which
> they didn't have. So, although I can't make it to PTA
> meetings. I pay my PTA dues and I volunteer in my
> daughter's classroom.

Learning At Home

As described earlier, parents in this study were unanimous that it was
their responsibility to support the learning of their children at home.
Helping their children with school-related activities at home was by far
the most frequently reported type of parent involvement practice. There
were differences in the amounts of time they were able to devote to this

kind of participation depending on their work requirements. Nevertheless, all the parents described a variety of ways in which they supported the learning of their children at home. The most common involvement identified was assisting their children with homework. These parents described how they regularly monitored their children's homework, checking assignments for completeness, accuracy, and neatness. The following description was typical of how these parents described their home involvement:

> And pretty much at home, I basically stay on him to get his work done. Most of the time he doesn't need help, so he'll come to me and I'll look it over. Or if I feel it's not neat enough, I say, 'well, you need to rewrite this'.

One parent also described how she helps her son at home with reading:

> Well, we had parent-teacher conferences about a week ago. She (the teacher) told me his weaknesses. So, what we do now is we read a book 20 minutes a day, and he has to write about what we read. And then I will correct it and make changes. If he spells a word wrong, I have him look it up in the dictionary and have him write it over again. If I can't tell him how to spell the word, he'll never learn.

Some of the parents described other ways they participated in supporting their children's learning at home. They acquired games, books, and other educational materials. Some purchased these educational materials from commercial stores; others acquired the materials they used with their children at places like Goodwill Industries and thrift shops. Another mother described how she used home-based experiences like preparing shopping lists, food budgets, and cooking as opportunities for her to work with her daughter in reinforcing reading and math skills such as measurement and estimations.

Several other parents described how they try to create home environments conducive to learning or the "school-like families" concept (Epstein, 1995). They set up in their homes special places for their child to study in and complete their school assignments. These places were outfitted with desks, pencils, and other necessary learning tools. One mother described such a space she had arranged in her daughter's bedroom:

> We encourage her (our daughter) at all times to write. In
> her room she has her own desk where she sits. And she has
> her own dictionary. She has a thesaurus she uses. She has
> all the tools she needs.

Another parent explained the different ways she and her husband work
with their daughter to support her learning at home:

> We're very involved. We have different roles. Like I'm
> more into the educational roles, and he (my husband) backs
> her up with physical education. Different things, like when
> she wants to go for a bike ride. Actually, he fills the gaps
> where I lack, and that's how we work it.

Although the parents involved in this study did report that their
involvement at school activities was influenced by their work
schedules, they all expressed a strong sense of obligation to participate
regularly in supporting the learning of their children at home.

African American Parents Express Their Concerns
This study also sought to find out what obstacles to involvement were
experienced by the participating parents of high-achieving African
American elementary students. Parents in this study perceived
themselves as being very involved in their children's education and,
therefore, did not report major obstacles to their involvement.
Moreover, they considered families as equally responsible as schools in
establishing and maintaining effective home-school relationships. For
example, when asked how schools could do a better job of involving
minority parents in their children's education, parents made these
statements:

> It's really hard to say. I don't know what would help bring
> everyone together. If their parents really want their kids to
> succeed, they're going to do whatever they can.

> You can't keep on blaming one system where every-body
> has to work together.

When they were asked, however, to share any concerns they might
have about their children's education, these parents identified two areas
of concern: the racial identity development of their children and current
teacher placement practices.

Racial Identity Development

As African Americans, the parents participating in this study recognized the need for their children to develop positive self-images and skills for coping in a racist society. This parental concern reveals the emphasis on the development of the whole child, socially, emotionally, physically, and academically, that is consistent with current definitions of genuine parent involvement (Davies, 1991). In giving voice to their concerns about their children's racial identity development, these parents identified three issues they believed were related to this need: self-esteem enhancement, the importance of Black history in the curriculum, and the beneficial effects that minority teachers can have as positive role models for their children.

Self-Esteem

When asked about the obstacles African American parents face in helping their children succeed in school, parents expressed a general concern they shared for the development of their children's self-esteem both at home and at school. One parent related the following story:

> We have a very positive home in terms of who we are as a people and my daughter told me, 'My teacher told me that I was very pretty.' And I said, 'Well, we tell you that all the time. Should we widen the doorways now so that your head can get through?' And she said, 'No, mommy.' So we laughed about that, but then she said, 'But you know, I would be even prettier if I were lighter like you and him (her brother).' So, even in an environment that is Afrocentric as ours, meaning that we really pride being who and what we are, I cannot compete with the television, what it reinforces, where Barbie always comes out looking like Barbie with everything. Which tells you, if you look like Barbie, you can have everything (laughs). With the cartoons, the cultures that students are bringing from their households, I mean, all you can do is to continue to challenge them, continue to get them to think through the processes.

Another parent explained how hurtful remarks about being African American don't always come from non-Blacks. She suggested that African Americans can be just as cruel to each other:

> It seems like someone is always trying to rip your child's and your self-esteem. Even between races. You know, my

> daughter is very dark skinned and I have to always tell her,
> always just show her. I do care if who-who-who calls you
> Black, you just tell them, 'I come from kings and queens.'
> You know, you just tell them straight up, you're just
> jealous! (laughs). It comes from every single place. It's
> everywhere. And like I said, it's between races also,
> because we're fair-skinned to a dark-skinned Black.

These parents valued teachers who treated all of their students with
respect regardless of their race, gender, or socioeconomic status. One
mother described how pleased she was with her daughter's relationship
with a White teacher, calling her classroom another "home" for her
daughter:

> We don't have to worry about our daughter's feelings (in
> school). She never comes home and says, 'Oh, Mom, this
> teacher does not like me. This teacher is prejudiced against
> me.' But if a child is having that feeling, it's sad, and I can
> imagine what that child is having to go through. And I'm
> happy we don't have to feel that way. She goes to the
> teacher, she goes to another home. That's how she looks at
> it. She's going to another mother.

This same parent further suggested that teachers, who develop positive
relationships with all of their students and work to boost their self-
esteems, open the door to improved home-school relations with
minority parents:

> I think that if a child expresses that, 'Oh, my teacher likes
> me, I feel comfortable,' I think that also encourages the
> parent to get with the school because they know the
> teacher really cares about the child. It encourages the
> parent to go and get involved.

Another parent recognized that there could be negative effects of what
teachers say to students, both on the children and the parent-teacher
relationship. "Be careful of what you say to these kids," this parent
advised teachers, "because they will go back home and repeat it." She
explained that when kids come home and repeat negative things the
teacher has done or said about her children, the relationship between
the parent and teacher can become negative and problematic.

Black History and the Curriculum

A curricular issue that parents viewed as being related to their children's racial identity development, was how schools teach history and the extent to which the histories of ethnic minorities were included in the curriculum. Virtually all the parents interviewed in this study expressed the viewpoint that it is important for their children to learn about the contributions of African Americans to the world as well as to America. One mother described how she teaches her children to respond to people who question the contributions of African Americans to our country by saying, "Hey, we're (African Americans) the same. Anyone who says (a derogatory remark) is stupid. We're a part of history. Everyone made America!"

Parents also believed that Black history should be integrated into the curriculum throughout the school year, not just during the month of February during 'Black History Month'. One parent remarked:

> Black history should be a part of history, period! Black or
> Hispanic, it should be taught throughout the school year.

Integrating ethnic content into the curriculum throughout the school year would, as one parent believed, ensure that the learning is purposeful as opposed to becoming an add-on subject or just teaching ethnic content in a superficial way. She explained her position:

> There's a lot of things that I think we could clear up or
> eliminate in a child's development just by embracing that
> we have some ethical responsibilities early on in the
> educational process. And I think that is more important
> than a Black History Month, Native American Week, Asian
> Day, or Latino Month. I mean, because we're learning very
> early to respect each other, not just tolerate, because I'm
> not something to be tolerated. And I think it's essential that
> that is included in the curriculum, which is why
> multiculturalism has been non-successful at the elementary
> and secondary levels. The learning isn't purposeful; it's not
> integrated into the curriculum.

These parents, however, did not expect schools to teach an Afrocentric curriculum. They emphasized instead that the histories and contributions of all peoples should be included where they had been previously left out. The voice of the following parent demonstrates the strong views held by most of these African American parents':

> In terms of students' curriculum, I'd like to see more
> representation across the board. It's been real difficult for
> me because my son's in the fourth grade and they're really
> getting into American history. And it's not so much what's
> said that bothers me, it's what's not said. And knowing that
> these students don't have the critical thinking skills to ask
> the right questions to fill those gaps of what is not being
> answered.

While all the parents suggested that the history of African Americans
and other ethnic groups be integrated into the regular curriculum and
taught throughout the school year to all students, they also recognized
that it was parents responsibility for teaching their children about their
own heritage and history at home.

Role Models for Minority Students
All of the African American parents who shared their perceptions in
this study were very favorable to school hiring practices that sought to
recruit more minority teachers into the teaching profession. Although
they all felt that there should be more minority teachers serving as role
models in our nation's elementary schools, they did not, however,
identify the race of a teacher as being the major factor in insuring
students' academic successes. Instead, parents expressed their desire
for teachers to be "open-minded" and sensitive to the needs of
culturally diverse children. In describing how irrelevant she felt the
race of a teacher can be, one parent shared her grandmother's wisdom
on the subject:

> My grandmother had a saying that not everybody Black
> you meet is Black. (Laughs). You know, I guess you gotta
> be Black to really understand. (Laughs again). And she also
> said that every White person you meet ain't got a sheet in
> the back of their truck. There are a lot of people who want
> to help people, who realize that we all should be afforded
> the same opportunities simply because we're people. I
> found that prejudice exists within one's own ethnic group.
> So it's more important to have someone committed to the
> philosophy of access for all people. And it doesn't matter
> what ethnicity that person is.

Several parents in the group identified a special need that they felt
required more minority teachers in the classroom. They felt that there

was a special need for more Black males in today's elementary schools to serve as role models. One parent stated: "What I would like to see are more Black male teachers. I haven't seen many." Another parent expressed her hope for more Black administrators in schools:

> Especially with this school, with having a Black principal, that right there is a big plus. It's some-thing, you know, as far as status or something for a kid to look up to. It's a very high position and how you portray yourself..... It's gonna rub off on other people.

All of the parents in this study wanted the school district to be more proactive in recruiting more qualified minority teachers to serve in their schools.

Teacher Placement Issues

Finally, there was one additional issue that caused a major concern to the African American parents participating in this study that relates directly to the issue of attracting more minority parents to be partners with the schools in their children's education. That issue was directly related to the age of the teacher. These parents were concerned that placement of young, inexperienced teachers or old, weary teaching veterans waiting desperately for retirement. They felt that in their experience, too many of these teachers were being placed in schools with large populations of minority students. The two parents views that follow share this concern:

> I've noticed that the school district, they tend to hire new teachers from out of state. And the new teachers, they tend to send them to they call 'at-risk' schools. It's hard for a new teacher coming into the state to do that because they get terrified. Especially, when they talk to other teachers and they say, 'Oh, you know, you're on the bad side of town. Be careful, watch your back!' You know, and that's not good. When a problem is not being resolved and this person is like, 'I'm getting ready to retire and I just really don't care,' I've gotta get him (son) out of there!

Another teacher placement practice these parents expressed concern about was the use of money as a motivating factor for making teaching positions in low-income areas more attractive to new teachers. Several parents voiced their dismay regarding the practice of allowing teachers to work off their student loans or receive "combat pay" by teaching in schools designated "at risk." These parents remarked:

> This area maybe gets some good teachers, but only for a year because you can work off a student loan in this area.

> That's why she (the teacher) came here. She didn't care about those kids! She came here to get combat pay. And she had a brain. She had a lot to give those kids.

Despite these concerns with teacher placement practices, parents in this study held their own children's teachers in high esteem and made few negative comments about them. Because they were more involved as participants in the home-school partnership with their children's teachers, they expected they could solve any disagreement or difference through ongoing two-way communication with their children's teachers. One African American parent was particularly adamant in her belief that most teachers care about their students, no matter where they teach, and wanted them to be successful in school:

> They (teachers) want to help kids or they wouldn't go into education. You know, you don't go into education, even White women, going, 'Well I'm just gonna go out and educate all the White kids.' That's ludicrous! They go in saying, 'I want to get a kid excited about learning.' I'm sure there's some that are probably racist or prejudiced because there's just some of those types of individuals in everything we do. But I really don't think that the majority of teachers go into education going, 'Now I'm going to go into the suburbs and teach at the best schools and turn out the next Nobel prize winner.' I don't think that's in the back of their minds.

We are confident that when educational reformers listen to the hopeful, compelling voices of minority parents like those presented in this chapter, more effective home-school partnerships will be cultivated that will insure successful learning for all students in our nation's schools.

REFERENCES

Brandt, R. (1989). On parents and schools: A conversation with Joyce Epstein. *Educational Leadership*, 47 (2): 24-27.

Cochran-Smith, M. (1995). Uncertain allies: Understanding the boundaries of race and teaching. *Harvard Educational Review*, 65 (4): 541-570.

Coleman, J.S., Campbell, E.Q., Hobson,C.J., McPartland, J., Mood, A.M., Weinfield, F.C., & York, R.l. (1966). *Equality of educational opportunity.* Washington, D.C.: Government Printing Office.

Comer, J.P. (1985). Empowering Black children's educational environments. In H.P. McAdoo & J.L. McAdoo (Eds.), *Black Children: Social, Educational, and Parental Environments* (pp. 123-138). Beverly Hills, CA: Sage.

Comer, J.P. (1986, February). Parent participation in the schools. *Phi Delta Kappan,* 442-446.

Comer, J.P. (1988). Educating poor minority children. *Scientific American,* 259 (5): 42-48.

Davies, D. (1991). Schools reaching out: Family, shool and community partnerships for students' success. *Phi Delta Kappan,* 72 (3): 376-382.

Delany, B. (1993). *Having their say: The Delany sisters' first 100 years.* New York: Kodansha International.

Epstein, J. L. (1986). Parents' reactions to teacher practices of parent involvement. *The Elementary School Journal,* 86: 277-294.

Epstein, J. L (1990). School and family connections: Theory, research, and implications for integrating sociologies of education and family. In D.G. Unber & M.B. Sussman (Eds.) (pp. 99-126), *Families in Community Settings: Interdisciplinary Perspectives.* New York: Haworth Press.

Epstein, J. L. (1995). School/family/community partnerships: Caring for the children we share. *Phi Delta Kappan,* 76 (9): 701-712.

Epstein, J. L. (1996). In Booth, A., & Dunn, J.F. (Ed.), *Family-School Links: How Do They Affect Educational outcomes?,* pp. 209-246. Mahwah, New Jersey: Lawrence Erlbaum Associates.

Epstein, J. L. & Dauber, S.L. (1991). School programs and teacher practices of parent involvement in inner-city elementary and middle schools. *Elementary School Journal,* 91 (3): 289-305.

Eshleman, J.R. (1988). *The Family: An Introduction* (5th ed.). Boston: Allyn and Bacon.

Grant, C.A. & Secada, W.G. (1990). Preparing teachers for diversity. In W.R. Houston (Ed.), *Handbook of Research on Teacher Education* (pp.403-422). New York: Macmillan.

Hidalgo, N.M., Siu, S., Bright, J., Swap, S., & Epstein, J.L. (1995). Research in families, schools and communities: A multicultural perspective. In J.A. Banks (Ed.), *Handbook of Research on Multicultural Education* (pp.498-524). New York: Macmillan.

Henderson, A. (1987). *The evidence continues to grow: Parent involvement improves student achievement*. Columbia MD: National Committee for Concerned Citizens in Education.

Hodgkinson, H.L. (1995). What should we call people? Race, class, and the census for 2000. *Phi Delta Kappan*, 77 (2): 173-179.

Knapp, M.S., & Woolverton, S. (1995). Social class and schooling. In Banks, J.A., & Banks, C.M. (Eds.), *Handbook of Research on Multicultural Education* (pp. 548-569). New York: Macmillan.

Lareau, A. (1987). Social class differences in family-school relationships: The importance of cultural capital. *Sociology of Education*, 60: 73-85.

Leitch, M. & Tangri, S. (1988). Barriers to home-school collaboration. *Educational Horizons*, 66: 70-74.

Mahler, D. (1997). *Having their say: Parents of high-achieving African American elementary students talk about the home-school relationship*. Unpublished Doctoral Dissertation, University of Nevada, Las Vegas.

Ost, D.H. (1988). Teacher-parent interactions: An effective school-community environment. *The Educational Forum*, 52 (52): 165-176.

Swap, S. M. (1993). *Developing home-school partnerships: From concepts to practice*. New York: Teachers College Press.

Walberg, H.J. (1984, February). Families as partners in educational productivity. *Phi Delta Kappan*, 397-400.

II.

Perspectives on
High School
Academic Performance

8. Cultural Differences in Self-Esteem: Ethnic and Gender Variations in the Adaptation of Recent Immigrant Asian Adolescents

Madelon F. Zady and Pedro R. Portes

Introduction

Psychological and sociological traits expressed by individuals are influenced by interactions among various levels of culture and self. The contexts in which group members find themselves at a given time during the process of cultural adaptation would seem to provide useful insights into the development of self-esteem as well as other psychological and social traits. Such a view would be consistent with an ecological (Bronfenbrenner, 1979), and a cultural-historical (CH) perspective (Portes, 1996; Valsiner and Cairns, 1992; Vygotsky, 1978). Self-esteem, a particularly important trait that reflects how a person feels about the self being constructed socially and reveals the picture of a person's developing consciousness about self, can be used to index individual and group adaptation in terms of mental health, schooling and related areas. These adaptive processes, when examined in the case of immigrant adolescents, was of particular value and interest to the field. This chapter examined the extent to which differences in self-esteem existed among various Asian groups at a time of collective transition or adaptation during adolescence. The study employed a cultural historical (CH) perspective on development, mediated experience and the activity, setting construct and some of its features including motivations, purposes, goals, beliefs and values of the personnel involved (Gallimore, Goldenberg and Weisner, 1992; Weisner, Gallimore and Jordan, 1988; Tharp and Gallimore, 1988). This perspective was used to focus on the context of various conditions associated with a group's reception and a number of psychosocial predictors.

Adolescence appeared as a fruitful choice for comparative developmental research (Tudge, Shanahan and Valsiner, 1997). This wss particularly true in that there was a metamorphic quality in the development of self at this age that was compounded by the cultural adaptation tasks for immigrant youth.   Although relatively little is known about the latter situation, the development of self-esteem tended to become stable in middle adolescence for mainstream groups (Rice, 1998). As self-esteem developed from the individual's self-concept and others' concept of that self, it became a mirror of self-regard that was constantly mediated by others' regard. Self-esteem was an "index of the survival of the soul" (Rice, 1998).   The fashioning of positive self-esteem was pivotal in the quest for identity which was multifaceted and the resolution of subsequent psychological and social crises (Adams, Gullotta, and Montemayor, 1992; Erickson, 1968).   Indeed, many see self-esteem as the driving force behind all behaviors, that is, positive self-regard must be maintained and enhanced at any expense.   Self-esteem touches many domains, including sexual, social, ideological and vocational.   It was central to issues concerning ego identity development, the study of cultural and individual adaptation, school achievement and vocational choices.

The development of self-concept and its affective index, self-esteem, appeared to be related to the mechanics behind the development of identity.   Identity was theorized to be largely influenced, if not constructed, by the social experience and history found in a particular context (Vygotsky, 1978).   Were the topic not adolescence, one would conclude that a health identity was mediated by good self-regard.   Adolescence, however, was characterized by the emergence of formal or symbolic operations that allowed for greater awareness of self and others.   It was also a time of changes in perspective and instability of one's own assessments were common.

The fluctuating nature of the adolescent has been termed the "barometric self" by Rosenberg (1986) and yet these were important times. From these testing grounds, social identities and competencies were formulated through social experience and context. Indeed, these could even include mental health propensities that were generally masked by society's acceptance of a "psychosocial moratorium" (Erickson, 1968) in adolescents. Self-esteem is a global self-evaluation of the self that is based on how one feels about the various domains that constitute one's self-concept. The effects of certain social and psychological factors on this evaluation of self-worth was the main concern of the chapter.

Problems in Assessing Cultural Differences in Self-Esteem

Various aspects of adaptation have been considered in the sociological and psychological literature related to studies of children of immigrants (Portes and McLeod, 1996; Rumbaut, 1994; Suarez-Orozco, 1991). Established minority groups have been the usual topic of this research (Dukes and Martinez, 1994; Wade, Thompson, Tashakkori and Valente. 1989). While such cross-cultural research offers unique opportunities for observing how socio-genetic changes influences individual development, studying newer immigrant groups may provide useful insights into the adaptive processes in development. Some groups may be considered similar in terms of factors that affect development, while others may show distinct differences. It is true that the literature on cultural differences on a variety of traits has increased, however, the literature tends to portray fossilized trait-context snapshots such as the different self-esteem, school achievement relations between African Americans and non-Hispanic Whites in the U.S. (Goldenberg and Gallimore, 1989) and other groups as well. Immigrant groups vary in terms of consistent cultural patterns that undergo adaptation, which in turn, influence developmental processes at the individual level. Just as importantly, groups that emigrate to other contexts may be treated and supported differentially by the hosts and each responds with various types and levels of agency to different circumstances (Portes, 1996). The relative standing of each community, with respect to other groups, would seem to impact on the development of individuals in those groups undergoing acculturation. Based on analyses of different cultural histories and contexts of a variety of immigrant groups, adaptation at the social level may be linked to the individual level in ways that go beyond research conducted in national cultures, or at least in rather monocultural conditions.

Portes (in press) described a cultural context approach in accounting for the adaptation of immigrants. Membership in an immigrant group, particularly during this early stage of acculturation, did not ensure an advantage over impoverished domestic minorities. Developmental differences among immigrant groups appeared to be mainly a function of four types of interacting factors: a) the cultural history and traits of the immigrant group; b) the degree to which the latter were compatible with or conducive towarded adaptation into either domestic minorities' cycle of poverty, or compatible with the mainstream; c) the host/mainstream's reception to the immigrant group, inclusive of its reaction to ethnic markers (phenotypic and cultural) in a particular historical moment; and d) the political and social capital developed by the immigrant group in the host culture that supports its members' agency in the community.

Based on the above model, a closer approximation may be possible in accounting for the data now available. For example, Asian immigrant groups' "a" factor (cultural history and traits) did not generally lend itself toward a "b" type path. As a result, Asian groups may had to cut their own path. Some were supported from ethnic enclaves (the "d" factor) which were neutralized or overcome, to some extent, the discriminatory reactions on the part of the mainstream's "c" factor. Filipinos may have been regarded essentially as similar to the above group. Take Cubans in private school, for another example. These students had factor "a" compatibility with the mainstream's ("b" factor), and counted on the protective factors inherent in their "d" factor. Also, the reaction by the host culture to the latter had been relatively benevolent due in part, to compatibility in markers which facilitated adaptation, to compatibility in views regarding political history, and to possession of available means. Unlike the Cubans, Mexican and Haitian immigrants faced a double risk because of their "b" factor compatibility with disparaged domestic minorities (Ogbu, 1991) and the prevailing negative reaction by the dominant majority (factor "c"). Their enclaves' social and political capital ("d" factor) was not yet developed sufficiently enough to protect their members in relative terms. It may take several generations to achieve conditions comparable with those of other groups.

This model was consistent with a segmented assimilation view (Portes and Zhou, 1993). While more work was necessary to support the model, finding answers to what had become a "cultural difference" riddle is important in addressing fundamental issues in educational research and policy. Those issues concerned not only ethnic but also majority students. Differences in adaptation are relevant to equity and excellence in education.

Factors Affecting Self-esteem

Physical appearance and peer social acceptance were most highly associated with adolescent's global self-esteem (Harter, 1989, 1990). During this period, peer judgements and relations increasde in influence, and the support of classmates seemed to be more important than even that of close friends (Harter, 1987). Still parental influences were important and included expression of affection, concern about the adolescents' problems, and conflict and related factors.

There was some indication that, besides the family relationship in the development of self-esteem, the family's social class also exerted an influence. Depression, delinquency, eating and other conduct disorders were the consequences of low self-esteem during adolescence. These were confounded when there were stressful events, and school or family life transitions (Vega and Rumbaut, 1991). Factors that improved self-esteem generally concerned the causes of low self-esteem such as competence in desired areas, social and emotional support, dealing directly with problems (in contrast to avoidance or denial), and achievement (Bednar, Wells and Peterson, 1989). In fact, significant and reciprocal relationships existed between self-esteem and academic achievement (Markstrom, Adams and Adams, 1995). This relationship was more positive for boys than girls, and the relationship improved over time. In the case of immigrant youth, English proficiency seemed to be of utmost importance. Perhaps the mastering of the host language provided a critical cultural "gateway" tool that allowed access to self-validating experiences in the host culture. Its influence was not well established with regard to self-esteem research.

The literature contrasting the self-esteem of immigrant and mainstream, or immigrant with non-immigrant minority adolescents was sparse. A better comparative understanding of the development of self-esteem between these groups may be gained by using standard instruments and controlling for many of the factors associated with this construct in the literature.

As the prior model (Portes, 1999) indicated, environmental influenced in cultural adaptation were varied and inter-connected. In the case of self-esteem, two of these influences were prominent: 1) The extent to which the person's culture was similar to that represented in the standard literature; and 2) the relations among the native and host cultures. The first concern was relevant to the degree of assimilation presented for both the individual and the group in which she was "nested." For example, in Southeast Asian cultures, humility (as a cultural value) may have influenced the way that self-esteem was viewed. Secondly, self-esteem and identity development may have also been influenced by the relations among native and host cultures. Rarely had the relative status and political power of a group been related to psychological development, except in rather broad contexts such as SES. Other relative factors, such as prior family status and parental educational levels, may have made these groups different from non-immigrant minorities and acculturated mainstream groups. How similar the experience of immigrant youth from different groups may have been and the influence of these experiences on the development of self-esteem were unknowns.

Background of the Study
With some exceptions from other cross-national studies, research on how different types of structural and psychological predictors were related to the development of self-esteem have been rare. One such study (Rumbaut, 1994), a parallel study of the data employed in this chapter, found that self-esteem was highly associated with parent-child conflict, depressive symptoms, English proficiency and gender in a large sample of immigrant adolescent students from various Asian, Latin American and Caribbean countries. This report also noted that teens born in the U.S. tended to have lower self-esteem than those born abroad.   Poor school performance and high perceptions of discrimination were also associated with low self-esteem. Black self-identity was predictive of higher self-esteem while Vietnamese and Filipino students scored significantly lower on the Rosenberg Self-Esteem Scale. In a subsequent study of these data, Portes and MacLeod (1996) found lower self-esteem when immigrant adolescents assumed the ethnic identity imposed by the dominant society.

This chapter drew on the above data set and aimed to examine the relation of self-esteem to culture in a more process-oriented fashion. The focus was the extent to which some Asian groups varied in self-esteem across demographic and psychosocial variables. While some of the psychosocial variables from the prior studies remained important including SES, gender family conflict, and others, inter-group relations, history and gender roles within cultures may shed some light on the development of self-esteem.

Research on Self-Esteem of Asian Groups
It should be noted first that the use of the Asian pan-label as a broad grouping of various cultures was problematic and has received increased attention in education. Some of the concern relates to socio-

psychological constructs extending from mental health and school achievement to self-esteem, discrimination and family variables (Aldwin and Greenberger, 1987; Kelly, 1986; Treuba, Cheng and Ima, 1993). A number of studies have shown differences among Asian and other pan-ethnic groups as well as within some of these (Beiser, 1988; Cheng, 1989; Pang, 1991; Rumbaut and Ima, 1988; Santos, 1983; Treuba and colleagues, 1993). The literature of the self-concept and self-esteem of Asian groups have produced a number of hypotheses concerning findings of lower self-esteem relative to other groups (Huang, 1993; Pang, 1991; Uba, 1994). Personality differences attributable to cultural norms, such as abasement and conformity, raise questions about the suitability and appropriateness of Western-based measures of self-components. The literature suggests that Asian adolescents have a lower self-concept than Euro-Americans when it comes to physical appearance (Arkoff and Weaver, 1988; Chang, 1975; White and Chan, 1983) however, other components may impact upon the overall level of self-esteem. The extent to which Japanese-origin students varied from Korean-origin and Chinese-origin students differed depending on context, what other groups were present, as well as the measures used (Uba, 1994, p.84). Since cultural norms vary, particularly between Asian and non-Asian groups, gender appeared to be an extremely important variable in making inferences in this area. It should be noted that the literature was limited with respect to gender differences within Asian and other groups. Finally, the degree of assimilation into a new country's culture warrants attention as a mediating factor.

     In an effort to comprehend these complex issues, it appeared useful to first distinguish among the different social histories of the groups being compared, i.e., their status and demographic characteristics. The construct of status was multifaceted with many competing and interrelated aspects that needed to be delineated. The first cut concerns minority versus majority status. Groups in the former category could be further subdivided according to whether they belong to established "involuntary" minorities (Ogbu, 1991) or more autonomous minorities. Additionally, there were the new minorities or those representing recent immigrant populations. The development of self-esteem under these various social conditions, such as those found in the United States and other developed countries, can provide theoretically useful information. Although prior work suggests some ethnic variation in self-esteem (Rumbaut, 1994), the scope of that literature was beyond this report. This study examineed predictors of self-esteem across various immigrant Asian adolescent groups in order to inform some of the explanations proposed in the findings and discussion of the reviewed literature.

There are four questions addressed in the study. What heterogeneity exists in Asian groups when it comes to self-esteem? What constitutes the most important psychosocial determinants? How similar are these Asian groups on these traits? Are gender differences negligible?

Rationale of the Study

For developmental researchers, the study of social and psychological phenomena was particularly attractive in periods of change and transition (Vygotsky, 1978). Observing samples in flux or in periods of collective adaptation using comparative design, may help to reveal the role of structural and other factors in the development of "traits." The window on the particular beliefs, values, and activities (Gallimore and Goldenberg and Weisner, 1992; Tharp and Gallimore, 1988) as they cross from the social to the psychological plane, and vice versa, may help in the understanding of the development of self. Since with immigrant youth, development emerged often in a dialectical and intercultural context, an opportunity existed to uncover (or to make somewhat clearer) the ways that social and familial factors contributed to the formation of self-esteem. That is, examining the role of various elements predictive of self-esteem for distinct cultural groups can provide a useful baseline that, in turn, may eventually contribute toward a cultural and developmental, unified theory of human development. This examination may also serve to test some of the assumptions about Asians reflected in the literature.

Method

The data for this study stemmed from the Youth Adaptation and Growth Questionnaire developed for the Second Generation Project in Miami and San Diego (Portes and McLeod, 1996). In Rumbaut (1994), a full description of the design of the study, sampling, and procedures can be found. A total of 5,267 second-generation students from various groups were interviewed. According to the author, second generation status for children was defined as living in this country (U.S.) for at least five years or being the child of at least one immigrant parent. By limiting the sample to eighth and ninth graders, the bias created by school dropouts in the higher school years was reduced. This was a time when most children were still in school. One-half of the sample participants were born outside the U.S. before age 12. The other half were U.S. born. The sample was also evenly distributed by grade and gender.

Children from 77 different nationalities and 42 different schools in Dade County (Miami), Broward County (Ft. Lauderdale) (n>2800) and the San Diego metropolitan area (n>2400) were interviewed using the survey tool. The total participants in the study were 5,264. The study accessed school records thus allowing researchers to match the characteristics of the respondents (nationality, sex, age, parental education, length of U.S. residency and aspirations) with their school performance.

Sample Selection

Students were foreign-born or had at least one foreign-born parent. A brief initial survey of all eighth and ninth graders in the school districts indicated above were conducted in order to locate participants. Parental consent were obtained for all eligible participants. The return rate was 67% of the South Florida group and 75% for the San Diego group (Rumbaut, 1994). About 1600 participants from various Asian nationalities were included in the current study. The nationalities represented included: Filipino, Vietnamese, Laotian, Cambodian, Hmong, Thai, Chinese, Japanese, Korean, Indian, Asian/Middle Eastern, and other Asian. Only the first four groups had numbers that were sufficient to allow for the multivariate analyses that follows.

General Measures

Data on the respondents' demographic characteristics were provided by the survey: nativity and citizenship of respondents and parents; family size and structure; socioeconomic status including parents' education level and occupation; and home ownership. Students from the over 11 Asian cultural groups were initially grouped together and analyses were performed. This was done to examine the relation of the psychosocial variables, culture, and achievement to self-esteem in the overall or "pan-Asian" participants.

Control variables included grade, age, gender, English language proficiency (EPI), inner city school, and parental SES. Since those in the earlier grade were more recent immigrants and generally were less bilingual, grade could be seen to index cultural adaptation indirectly.

Psychosocial Measures
A collection of attitudinal and other psychosocial variables were analyzed and subjected to data reduction schemes. As defined in an earlier study (Rumbout, 1994), measures of parent-child conflict, depression, familism and self-esteem were included. A familism scale assessed the strength of family bonds (FAMSCA, alpha=.56). Parent-child conflict (PCC, alpha=.56), self-esteem from a ten-item Rosenberg scale (Rosenberg, 1979) (ROSEN, alpha=.81), and depressive symptoms from a four-item subscale from the Center for Epidemiological Studies-Depression (CES-D, alpha=.74) were used and have been found in the past to be predictive of major depression among adolescents (Vega and Rumbaut, 1991).

Measures Based on Factor Analysis
From selected interview items, several measures were developed through factor analyses. One analysis yielded a scale measuring perceived discrimination (alpha=.54). Another indexed felt discrimination (alpha.98) and a third factor analysis represented an achievement motivation scale (alpha=.69).

Variables dealing with adaptation to the American culture and to the ethnic culture were evaluated. A student's cultural development, for example, could be revealed through choice of language in daily routines, his/her parent's own cultural identification and attitudes and perceptions concerning American culture. To examine these constructs of cultural identity, a factor analysis of twelve such variables was conducted. A bipolar factor was hypothesized that would range from preferences for American to native ways. A two-factor solution was found to be more tenable, accounting for 49% of the variance. The first factor served to index the respondent's ethnic identification and adaptation. It was related to the "Pull" of the native culture on the individual and the extent to which the respondent's native language was maintained. The factor also served to measure the respondent's native language proficiency and the parents' use of the native language. The second factor contained variables related to adaptation to the American culture. This factor served to examine the parents' cultural adaptions and the respondent's assimilation into the mainstream of America. The first factor was dubbed "Ethnic Pull" (alpha=.80), and the second factor, "American Pull" (alpha=.66), was so named to reflect adaptation to the American way of life. These factor scores were used in subsequent statistical analyses.

Other Predictor Variables

Other variables were considered. These included a variable called SES that reflected the family's socioeconomic status at present compared to five years prior. The number of hours spent daily on homework was divided by hour's spent watching television, and the resulting variable was dubbed time management. Respondent's peer relationships were examined as to the total number of friends and the number of friends of similar ethnic background. Other variables were included in the subsequent analyses: limited English proficiency (LEP), grade point average (GPA), performance on standardized achievement tests (ACHTOT), father absence, mother absence, and span of time living in the U.S.

Results

To provide a fuller context for this particular study of four Asian groups' self-esteem and it specific predictors, two other samples were first considered. The results of an initial regression analysis with the full sample of immigrant children (nine broad cultural backgrounds) are presented in Table 1. Overall, the net effect of ethnicity entered as a block of dummied variables was not significant above and beyond the demographic and psychosocial predictors, which accounted for 8% and 23% of the variance in Rosenberg scores respectively. However, two broad Asian groups were found to differ significantly from the contrast group (Cubans in private school). The main predictors of self-esteem for this large group of immigrant children after controlling for English Proficiency, gender, age, grade, inner city school status and social class, were parent-child conflict, depression scores (CESD), familism, achievement total, and achievement motivation. These latter psychosocial variables appeared to mediate the effects of social class to a considerable extent since SES was not significant when the psychosocial variables were entered in the model. Membership in a Southeast Asian or other Asian groups was also significant. The Southeast Asian group consisted of Vietnamese, Laotians, Cambodians and Hmong. The other Asian group was more heterogeneous, and subgroups were too small for follow up comparisons.

Table 1: Significant Predictors of Self-esteem from Regressions Using
        Entire Youth Adaptation Sample

<u>Variable</u>	<u>Beta</u>	<u>Sig.</u>
English Proficiency Index	.132	.000
Gender	.048	.003
Parent-Child Conflict Scale	-.219	.000
Depression Scale	-.257	.000
Familism Scale	.090	.000
Total Achievement	.144	.000
Achievement Motivation	.144	.000
Southeast Asians	-.045	.027
Other Asians	-.045	.011

Note: Cubans in private school serves as the reference group.
        Southeast Asians include Vietnamese, Laotians,
        Cambodians, and Hmong

To examine more closely the role of the prior predictors, a sample consisting of the four Asian groups with large enough numbers were subjected to a regression analysis.   The groups that constituted this Asian sample were Filipinos (N=819), Vietnamese (N=372), Laotian (N=155) and Cambodian (N=96). The model again accounted for about a third of the variance in self-esteem, with some differences in the set of predictor variables (Table 2). After controlling for gender and the English Proficiency Index, predictors similar to the ones in the prior regressions surfaced as significant. Although group differences were not found by ethnicity, gender differences appeared to be of somewhat greater importance as compared to the prior, total sample analysis. In order to examine the relative importance of gender and other predictors in each sample further, a new set of regression analyses were performed separately for the Filipino, Vietnamese, Laotian and Cambodian groups.

Table 2: Significant Predictors of Self-esteem from Regression Using
Four Asian Groups

Variable	Beta	Sig.
English Proficiency Index	.165	.000
Gender	.089	.002
Parent-Child Conflict Scale	-.218	.000
Depression Scale	-.250	.000
Familism Scale	-.081	.003
Total Achievement	.172	.000
Achievement Motivation	.115	.000

None of the predictors for self-esteem were significant for the Laotian and Cambodian samples. Parent-child conflict, depression index and English proficiency continued to show significance for the Filipino and Vietnamese samples (see Table 3). Filipino students' self-esteem were distinguished by three other predictors: economic situation five years prior; achievement motivation; and total achievement, while gender and limited English proficiency attained only marginal significance. For the Vietnamese sample, familism appeared an important predictor but gender effects were not found.

Gender differences neared significance in the Filipino sample and appeared to be of practical significance in a number of the predictors concerning school achievement and motivation for the other groups. In an effort to tease out the gender effects, additional two-way ANOVAS were performed using each of the most significant predictors as the dependent variables. Table 4 showed the two-way interaction effects of ethnicity/gender on the important predictor variables. There was a significant two-way interaction effect of Filipino/gender on self-esteem and interaction effect of Vietnamese/gender on depression and English proficiency. While there was only a marginal two-way interaction effect of Filipino/gender and Vietnamese/gender with achievement on standardized tests, there was a significant effect when grade-point average was used as the dependent measure.

Table 3: Significant Predictors of Self-Esteem from Regression Using Distinct Ethnic Groupings.

Significant Predictors of Self-esteem from Regressions Using Distinct Ethnic Groupings

Group	Variable	Beta	Sig
Filipino	English Proficiency Index	104	006
	Gender	063	094
	Family's Economic Situation 5 Yrs. Prior	077	025
	Parent-Child Conflict Scale	- 201	000
	Depression Index	- 336	000
	Total Achievement	190	000
	Achievement Motivation	148	000
	Limited English Proficiency	- 060	092
	R^2 = 367		
Vietnamese	English Proficiency Index	274	002
	Parent-Child Conflict Scale	- 255	001
	Depression Index	- 146	050
	Familism	- 156	028
	R^2 = 289		

*No significant predictors of self-estem found for Laotian and Cambodian groupings

Table 4: Two-Way ANOVA Interactions of Four Asian Groups and Gender Using Selected Predictor Variables as Dependents

Relative Importance of Predictors

Variable	Total	Filipino Mean N SD	Vietnamese Mean N SD	Laotian Mean N SD	Cambodian Mean N SD	Mean SD
Self-Esteem	Female	31 7 411 5 18	30 7 175 5 22	30 6 80 5 28	29 8 54 4 45	32 5 5 53
	Male	33 0 403 5 06	30 6 192 5 59	30 4 75 5 35	31 7 41 5 50	33 0 5 38
	Total	32 4 814 5 16	30 6 367 5 41	30 5 155 5 30	30 6 95 5 00	32 7 5 46
Parent-Child Conflict	Female	5 4 408 1 98	5 4 174 1 75	5 2 79 1 66	5 9 54 1 97	5 2 1 90
	Male	5 2 402 1 87	5 7 189 1 97	5 6 75 1 83	5 7 40 1 80	5 1 1 81
	Total	5 3 810 1 93	5 6 363 1 87	5 4 154 1 75	5 8 94 1 89	5 1 1 86
Depression	Female	7 3 411 2 76	7 0 176 2 75	6 5 80 2 24	6 9 54 2 74	7 1 2 71
	Male	6 1 405 2 15	6 5 193 2 41	6 1 75 2 17	6 3 41 2 29	6 0 2 24
	Total	6 7 816 2 54	6 7 369 2 58	6 3 155 2 21	6 6 95 2 56	6 6 2 55
English Proficiency	Female	15 4 411 1 24	13 7 177 2 75	13 2 80 2 59	13 4 54 1 98	14 9 1 93
	Male	15 3 402 1 36	13 1 194 2 76	12 9 75 2 46	13 6 42 2 06	14 7 1 97
	Total	15 3 813 1 30	13 4 371 2 77	13 1 155 2 52	13 5 96 2 00	14 8 1 95
Grade Point Average	Female	3 2 412 70	3 3 175 65	3 0 80 70	2 9 53 72	2 7 89
	Male	2 7 405 74	2 8 194 80	2 7 75 76	2 5 41 78	2 4 91
	Total	2 9 817 75	3 0 169 78	2 9 155 76	2 7 94 78	2 5 91
Achievement Motivation	Female	15 401 83	00 163 90	-54 79 115	-26 50 103	-14 96
	Male	-13 388 84	-38 181 101	-102 67 108	-63 35 121	-14 101
	Total	00 789 85	-19 344 98	-76 146 114	-41 85 111	00 100
Total Achievement	Female	35 398 60	25 155 65	-15 70 60	-48 50 41	00 61
	Male	26 383 56	11 165 65	-27 68 50	-39 39 48	00 63
	Total	31 781 58	18 320 65	-21 138 55	-44 89 44	00 62

Discussion

The study suggests that the self-esteem of children of Asian immigrants were different from that of the overall immigrant population, given a number of important mediating factors. It also suggested that self-esteem was significantly associated with parent-child conflict and depression in Asian as well as other groups as expected. This was not surprising and actually confirmed the co-existence of all three factors in determining variations in socio-psychological adaptation, in general. Doing well in school and being motivated towards achievement helped such adaptation. However, maintaining close family links appeared to counter adaptation with the mainstream norm that may have explained the negative, modest influence of familism. In a related study (Portes, in press), familism, identification with the native, as well as the host culture, were negatively associated with school adaptation.

Another finding from these analyses was while the Asian samples appeared homogeneous on the surface, subtle differences existed even within the limited range of samples considered here. Gender differences appeared to be of greater importance in some groups than in others, which was relevant to the work of Dukes and Martinez (1994) work on ethnicity and gender.

Perhaps the results can be expressed best in terms of the model (Portes, 1999 in press) described earlier in the Introduction section of this paper. The model examined four facets of adaptation related to immigrant groups: a) the cultural history and traits of the immigrant group; b) the degree to which the group was compatible with or conducive toward adaptation into either domestic minorities' cycle of poverty or compatibility with the mainstream; c) the host culture's reception including reactions to ethnic markers (both phenotypic and cultural) in a particular historical moment; and d) the political and social capital developed by the immigrant group in the host culture that supports its members' agency in the community.

For example, since recent Filipino immigrants were joining a more established cultural group, and since the first wave of Vietnamese immigrants came to this country in 1975, the community-based or "d" factor was somewhat more in place for these two groups. This was especially true when compared with the Laotian and Cambodian samples who had more recent migrations with less established communities. This "d" factor may help to insulate to some extent, the discriminatory reactions on the part of the mainstream's "c" factor above that may result in lower self-esteem.

The "a" or the cultural history of all four groups differed. While most Asian groups had a higher proportion of two-parent households, father absence among Cambodians due to "death of the father prior to arrival in U.S. was a reflection of the extraordinary harsh contexts of exit" (Nidorf, 1985, Rumbaut, 1994, Rumbaut and Ima, 1988). These conditions of exit may be reflected in lower self-esteem related to Cambodian adolescents. Additionally, Rumbaut, (1995) found that Laotian and Cambodian adolescents had parents with the lowest levels of education, parents who were usually out of work, the highest rates of poverty and welfare dependency, and they were more likely to attend inner-city schools. These students faced a double risk because of their "b" factor compatibility with domestic minorities' cycle of poverty and the subsequent negative reaction by the dominant groups "c" leading to a sense of powerlessness and lowered self-regard.

Filipinos and Vietnamese youths had predictors of self-esteem that were somewhat closer to those of the entire sample and very different from those of the Laotians and Cambodians who were more recent immigrants. In this respect, we may actually be seeing a snapshot of the process of rapid assimilation to the more established groups and influenced by their "d" factor (social capital, etc). There is yet another issue associated with the rate of assimilation. First-generation Asian students have often been considered the "model minority." As such, they are commonly thought to have a more serious outlook on schooling, to spend more time on homework and less time on television, and to have higher GPA's. The performance of these model students were often contrasted with that of the mainstream middle- and lower-SES whites, who generally showed high educational aspirations, mediocre grades, low effort on homework and more time watching television. Additionally, they demonstrated more individualism, low depression, and high self-esteem (Rumbaut, 1994). The low effort and high self-regard may be related to the mainstream's social and political capital (although there were similar findings among other groups). What seemed particularly troubling is that the success of these individuals or their "immigrant edge" contrasted to that of true second generation members of even the same communities. Depending upon the circumstances of those communities, the youth may have figured out that discrimination trumps immigrant folk theories of success (Rumbaut, 1994) leading to declines in self-esteem.

A more micro-level analysis, particularly one related to values, beliefs, motivations, purposes, goals as well as personnel, may help in distinguishing factors related to self-esteem (Tharp and Gallimore, 1988). For example, Filipinos adolescent's parents were more often college graduates, while Laotians and Cambodians parents had the least education. Some of the adolescents, such as the rural Laotians, were not even exposed to a writing system prior to immigration (Treuba, et al., 1993). Most of the Indochinese immigrants were from rural villages or were urban poor. These parents were less likely to be the main source of help on homework that may or may not be compensated by peer-help.

Compared to the overall sample, Laotian and Cambodian adolescents had the highest scores on being embarrassed by parents (Rumbaut, 1994) and high scores on the Parent-Child Conflict Scale. These results most likely were related to the above situation and perhaps also reflected the difference in values between the generations. Adolescence constituted a period of stress when the child uses a more superficial examination of the self. What was attractive was of utmost importance and value. Additionally, in the mainstream American culture, the adolescent was allowed to switch freely between states of identity moratorium and diffusion (Erickson, 1968; Marcia, 1987) showing a lack of commitment or motivation. During this period of adjustment, adolescents may have had parental support and develop introspection or self-reflection (Marcia, 1987). The youth in this study may have faced a dual crisis--that of adolescent development and adjustment in two cultural settings simultaneously. Cultural adaptation here took on added difficulty, because this period of developmental transition was tied to a difference in ideological, linguistic and physical attributes from that of the mainstream. The Asian adolescent tried on the external culture first (Goldstein, 1985; Peters, 1988), but ethnic identity was strong (Rumbaut and Ima, 1988). Taking on the trappings of the host culture may cause the parent-child conflict (Yao, 1985). Nidorf (1985) has stated that these adolescents were operating out of four identity systems: Southeast Asian; American; refugee; and adolescent. These identities were often in conflict with each other.

Language itself may serve to divide parent and child with parents insisting on using the native tongue and children insisting on English. The use of English was particularly problematic in some cultures, because the pronouns did not show proper deference to parents (Rumbaut, 1995). In some cases, the child served as interpreter for parents, thus putting him or her in an unwelcome position of equality or even authority (Power, 1990). While in this study language proficiency in English was neatly controlled, it may require much deeper consideration.

Beliefs played an important role in achievement and self-esteem. Generally, Laotian and Cambodians were of lower SES and possessed more fatalistic beliefs and showed rigidity in thinking

(Treuba, 1993) that was in turn reflected in their self-esteem scores.

Even apparent compatibility in values and beliefs between Asians and mainstream Americans can obscure real differences that will affect children (Huang, 1993). Achieving in school brings honor to the family. Not achieving brings disgrace (Shen and Mo, 1990; Lee, 1989). Pressure on children to succeed may lead to psychological difficulties. Psychological difficulties, such as depression, have their own costs. To be depressed may be interpreted as lacking in motivation and considered shameful (Kleinman and Good, 1985).

Another important consideration was the issue of gender. Self-esteem may fit one gender better than the other. The females in this study generally worked harder in school. Their GPA's were higher than their standardized test scores would have predicted. These girls generally showed low self-esteem and high depression coupled with their higher educational achievement and higher- achievement motivation. The link between low self-esteem and high achievement appeared even with mainstream females. Doing well in school may be a protective factor in the maintenance of positive self-regard.

One could conclude that the validity of the self-esteem construct itself could be problematic. It was commonly accepted that Asian groups were socialized to have humility or not to promote themselves openly. They were polite and even submissive in social encounters (Hall, 1977). The self-esteem construct may be an outgrowth of the western ideology of individualism often characterized by self-assertion. Perhaps due to different meanings associated with self-worth in the native culture, the validity of the Rosenberg instrument can be called into question (Rogoff and Charajay, 1995). The construct may be more appropriate for Filipinos and Vietnamese than for Laotians and Cambodians. Perhaps the Laotian and Cambodian students were not as affected by American culture. There was another important culturally determined factor related to the self-esteem construct. Due to past political constraints, there was a general avoidance of self-disclosure among some Asian groups (Huang, 1993) calling into question the self-esteem instrument itself.

In sum, the study found differences in the self-esteem among Asian groups. In two groups, the more typical predictors of depression and parent-child conflict were shown to be significant. Self-esteem in the other two groups was largely open to conjecture. Academic achievement and achievement motivation appeared to be important in some groups dependent upon gender. While forging a causal link between achievement and self-esteem was difficult, it seems reasonable to expect that poor school performance could reinforce a low self-regard and vice versa. Girls in the study appeared to modify their low self-esteem with good grades and higher educational aspirations. To be sure, these conclusions were played out on a background of stormy adolescent development but just as important, was the consideration of cultural differences such as the group's history, host's reception, strength of community, values and beliefs. It was important to try to understand that self-esteem was socially constructed by different parties in different contexts, rather than generalize. More research is needed to establish the cultural validity of self-esteem measures with various groups before its relation to gender, achievement and other factors can be established.

REFERENCES

Adams, G. R., Gullotta, T. P., and Montemayor, R. (Eds.) (1992). Adolescent identity formation. Newbury Park, CA: Sage Publications.

Aldwin, C. and Greenberger, E. . (1987). Cultural differences in the predictors of depression. American Journal of Community Psychology, 15, 789-813.

Arkoff, A and Weaver, H. (1966) Body image and body dissatisfaction in Japanese Americans. Journal of Social Psychology, 68, 323-330

Bednar, R. L., Wells, M. G. and Peterson, S. R. (1989). Self-Esteem. Washington, DC: American Psychological Association.

Beiser, M. (1988). Influences of time, ethnicity and attachment on depression in Southeast Asian refugees. American Journal of Psychiatry, 145, 46-51.

Bronfrenbrenner, U. (1979). The ecology of human development. Cambridge, MA: Harvard University Press.

Chang, Theresa S. (1975). The self-concept of children in ethnic groups: Black Americans and Asian Americans. Elementary School Journal, 76, 52-58.

Cheng, L. L. (1989). Service delivery to Asian/Pacific LEP children: A cross-cultural framework. Topics in Language Disorders, 9(3), 54-77.

Dukes, R.L., and Martinez, R. (1994). The impact of gender on self-esteem among adolescents. Adolescence, 29(113), 105-115.

Erickson, E. H. (1968). Identity and youth crisis. NY: W.W. Norton.

Gallimore, R., Goldenberg, C. N., and Weisner, T. S. (1992). The social construction of subjective reality of activity settings: Implications for community psychology. American Journal of Community Psychology, 21(44), 537-559.

Goldenberg C. N. and Gallimore, R. (1995). Immigrant Latino parents' values and beliefs about their children's education: Continuities and discontinuities across cultures and generations. In P. R. Pintrich and M. Maehy (Eds.) Advances in motivation and achievement: Culture, ethnicity, and motivation, Vol. 9, 183-228.

Goldstein, B. L. (1985). Schooling for cultural transitions: Hmong girls and boys in American high schools. Doctoral dissertation, University of Wisconsin, Madison, WI.

Hall, E. T (1977). Beyond culture. Garden City, NY: Anchor Press.

Harter, S. (1987). The determinants and mediatorial role of global self-worth in children. In N. Eisenberg (Ed), Contemporary issues in developmental psychology. New York: Wiley.

Harter, S. (1989). Causes, correlates, and the functional role of global self-worth: A life-span perspective. In J. Kolligian and R. Sternberg (Eds.), Perceptions of competence and incompetence across the life-span. New Haven, CT: Yale University Press.

Harter, S. (1990). Self and identity development. In S. S. Feldman and G. R. Elliott (Eds.), At the threshold: The developing adolescent. Cambridge, M.A.: Harvard University Press.

Huang, G. (1993). Beyond culture: Communicating with Asian American children and families. ERIC Digest, 94 (EDO-UD-93-8).

Kelly, G. (1986). Coping with American refugees from Vietnam, Cambodia, and Laos in the 1970s and 1980s. Annals of the American Academy of Political and Social Science, 489, 138-149.

Kleinman, A. and Good, B. J. (1985). Culture and depression. Berkeley: University of California Press.

Lee, A. (1989). A socio-cultural framework for the assessment of Chinese children with special needs. Topics in Language Disorders, 9(3), 38-44.

Marcia, J. E. (1987). The identity status approach to the study of ego identity development. In T. Honess and K. Yardley (Eds.), Self and identity: Perspectives across the lifespan. London: Routledge and Kegan Paul.

Markstrom-Adams, C. and Adams, G. R. (1995). Gender, ethnic group, and grade differences in psychosocial functioning during middle adolescence? Journal of Youth and Adolescence, 24, 397-417.

Mizokawa, D. and Ryckman, D. (1990). Attributions of academic success and failure: A comparison of six Asian-American ethnic groups. Journal of Cross-Cultural Psychology, 21, 434-451.

Nguyen, L.T., and Henkin, A. B.. (1983). Perceived sociocultural change among Indochinese refugees: Implications for education. In R. J. Samada and S. L. Woods (Eds.), Perspectives in immigrant and minority education (pp. 156-171). New York: University Press of America.

Nidorff, J. F. (1985). Mental health and refugee youths: A model for diagnostic training. In T. Owan and E. Choken (Eds.) Southeast Asian mental health, treatment, prevention, services, training and research. Washington, D. C.: Department of Health and Human Services, Offic of Refugee Resettlement. ERIC Document ED266199.

Ogbu, J.U. (1991). Immigrant and involuntary minorities in comparative perspective. In M.A. Gibson and J.U. Ogbu (Eds.) Minority status and schooling: A comparative study of immigrant and involuntary minorities (pp. 3-33). New York: Garland.

Pang, V. O. (1991). The relationship of test anxiety and math achievement to parental values in Asian-American and European-American middle school students. Journal of Research and Development, 24(4), 1-10.

Peters, H. (1988, January). A study of Southeast Asian youth in Philadelphia. Final report to the U. S. Department of Health and Human Services, Office of Refugee Resettlement. Wahington, D. C.: U.S. Government Printing Office. (ERIC Document ED299371)

Portes, A. E. and MacLeod, D. (1996). What shall I call myself? Hispanic identity formation in the second generation. Ethnic and Racial Studies, 19(3): 141.

Portes, A. E. and Zhou, M. (1993). The New Second Generation: Segmented Assimilation and Its Variants. The Annals of the American Academy of Political and Social Science 520: 7.

Portes, P. R. (1996). Ethnicity in Education and Psychology, In D. Berliner and R. Calfee, (Eds.), The Handbook of Educational Psychology. New York, NY: McMillan Publishing.

Portes, P. R. (in press). Socio-Psychological factors in the academic achievement of children of immigrants: Examining the cultural history puzzle. American Educational Research Journal.

Power, M. (1990). The acquisition of English and ethnic language attrition: Implications for research. In R. Endo, V. Chattergy, S. Chou * N. Tsuchida (Eds.), Contemporary perspectives on Asian and Pacific American education. South El Monte, CA: Pacific Asia Press.

Rice, P. (1998) The adolescent (8th Edition). NY: Allyn and Bacon.

Rogoff, B. and P. Chavajay. 1995. What's become of research on the cultural basis of cognitive development?. American Psychologist 50 (10): 859-877.

Rosenberg, M. (1979). Conceiving the self. New York : Basic Books.

Rosenberg, M. (1986). Self-concept from middle childhood through adolescence. In J. Suls and A. G. Greenwald (Eds.) Psychological perspective on the self (Vol. 3). Hillsdale, NJ: Erlbaum.

Rumbaut, R. (1994). The crucible within: Ethnic identity, self-esteem and segmented assimilation among children of immigrants. International Migration Review, 28, 748-795.

Rumbaut, R. G. and Ima, K. (1988). The adaptation of Southwest Asian refugee youth: A comparative study. Washington, DC: U.S. Office of Refugee Resettlement. ERIC Accession Number: ED299372.

Santos, R. (1983). The social and emotional development of Filipino-American children. In G. Powell (Ed.), The psychosocial development of minority group children (pp.131-146). NY: Brunner/Mazel.

Shen, W. and Mo, W. (1990). Reaching out to their cultures: building communication with Asian American families. (ERIC document ED351435).

Suarez-Orozco, M. M. (1991). Immigrant adaptation to schooling: a Hispanic case. In M.A. Gibson and J. U. Ogbu (Eds.) Minority status and schooling: A comparative study of immigrant and involuntary minorities (pp. 37-61). NY: Garland.

Tharp, R. G. and Gallimore, R. (1988). Rousing minds to life: Teaching, learning and schooling in social context. Cambridge: Cambridge University Press.

Treuba, H. T., Cheng, L. L. and Ima, K. (1993). Myth or reality: Adaptive strategies of Asian Americans in California. Washington, DC: Falmer.

Tudge, J., Shanahan M. and Valsiner, J. (1997). Comparisons in human development: Understanding time and context. MA: Cambridge University Press.

Uba, L. (1994). Asian Americans: Personality patterns, identity and mental health. NY: Guilford Press.

Valsiner, J. and Cairns, R. (1992). Theoretical perspectives on conflict and development. In Shantz and W.W. Hartup (Eds.) Conflict in child and adolescent development (pp.15-35). MA: Cambridge University Press.

Vega, William A. And Ruben G. Rumbaut (1991). Ethnic minorities and mental health. Annual Review of Sociology 17: 351-383.

Vygotsky L. (1978). Mind in society. MA: Harvard University Press

Wade, T. J., Thompson, V. D., Tashakkori, A., and Valente, E. (1989). A longitudinal analysis of sex by race differences in predictors of adolescent self-esteem. Personality and Individual differences, 10(7), 717-729.

Weisner, T. S., Gallimore, R., and Jordan, C. (1988). Unpackaging cultural effects on classroom learning: Hawaiian peer assistance and child-generated activity. Anthropology and Education Quarterly, 19, 327-353.

White, W. G. and Chan, E. (1983). A comparison of self-concept scores of Chinese and White graduate students and professionals. Journal of Non-White Concerns, 19, 138-141.

Williams, C. and Westermeyer, J. (1983). Psychiatric problems among adolescent Southeast Asian refugees. Journal of Nervous and Mental Disease, 171, 79-85.

Yao, E. L. (1985). Adjustment needs of Asian immigrant children. Elementary School Buidance and Counseling, 19, 222-227.

*   This study was made possible through the data provided by the principal investigator of the Children of Immigrants: The Adaptation of the Second Generation (A. Portes and R. Rumbaut) with the support of the Spencer, Russell Sage and National Science Foundations. However, the authors are solely responsible for the content of the report.

9. Engineering Academic Success Through Institutional Support

Ricardo D. Stanton-Salazar, Olga A. Vásquez, and Hugh Mehan

Introduction

We have recently seen an increasing amount of research on educational interventions and restructured schools that appear to be quite successful in promoting academic success among minority children, even in the face of growing poverty-related conditions in our urban centers (e.g., Ansen, et al., 1991; Natriello, G. et al., 1990).

The educational research literature has also provided a wealth of information on different facets of the teacher-student relationship in various instructional contexts. Yet, only a few educational researchers have firmly addressed how access to various forms of institutional knowledge and support depend on the nature of daily interactions and relations with teachers, counselors, and other institutional agents (Erickson & Shultz, 1982; Oakes, 1986; Cicourel & Mehan, 1983; Mehan, 1992; Stanton-Salazar & Dornbusch, 1995; Vásquez et al., 1994).

A number of studies, outside the mainstream educational research arena, have provided evidence demonstrating the tremendous and positive impact institutional agents and community mentors can have on the social development and schooling experiences of youth from economically marginalized communities (McLaughlin et al., 1994; Villanueva, 1990; Williams & Kornblum, 1985). However, a framework that emphasizes the instrumental relations between children and adolescents and those working within different institutional settings has yet to fully surface in sociological and educational research circles. The precise role of agents and mentors in the schooling of minority students has been difficult to articulate, mainly because there has been a conspicuous lack of research geared toward isolating and understanding those fundamental social processes that function to engineer the academic success of minority children and youth. Such processes usually underlie special programmatic attempts to foster school success, and often operate alongside, and in spite of, conventional institutional arrangements.

Exactly what kinds of social processes or mechanisms operate within the most successful programs and interventions, and can they be understood in a sociologically meaningful way? These questions provided the impetus for us to come together to share the findings of our respective research projects, and to highlight examples from our data of Latino and other minority students who were experiencing success 'in spite of the odds.' By advancing our theoretical understanding of those micro-processes responsible for determining success under adverse and varied social conditions (within the family, neighborhood, larger school environment), we also call attention to ways in which current school restructuring designs throughout the country can be altered or refined so that they, too, can function to reconstitute these vital, success-producing processes.

Conceptual Framework
We present here a number of concepts we believe are quite useful for discussing ways to engineer the success of ethnic minority students. These concepts include institutional support, social capital, social scaffolding and social networking. Although these concepts have been appropriated from various and distinctive disciplines, we feel they point to basic processes that facilitate success. Under the proper conditions, these support processes can mediate many of the negative social forces associated with low socioeconomic status.

Institutional Agents and Access to Institutional Support
The concept of institutional support conveys our most basic understanding of these success-producing processes. We will develop this idea more fully within this paper, but for now, let us offer a preliminary definition. By institutional support, we refer to key forms of social support which function in powerful ways to facilitate a student's progress through the educational system and which enable the student to exercise considerable control or power over their lives and their futures. These forms of institutional support are most often seen being transferred between institutionally well-placed adults and socio-economically advantaged children and adolescents (Ianni, 1989).

Access to institutional support usually depends on embeddedness in social networks that provide supportive attachments to individuals we call "institutional agents." Institutional agents are those individuals who have both the capacity and commitment to either directly provide or negotiate the provision of institutional resources, support, and opportunities for others (Stanton-Salazar & Dornbusch, 1995). These individuals for the most part - - but not exclusively - - derive their status by way of their privileged position within a formal institutional context (e. g., schools, government bureaucracies and agencies, federally sponsored programs, colleges and universities, churches, voluntary civic and political associations, and small-scale institutions of the neighborhood). Due to their privileged positions in social networks, institutional agents have the power to access, in multiple ways, various resources and opportunities under the control of either their own institution or neighboring institutions. Their status as agents is activated when they access resources on behalf of others, or in the cases we are considering, on behalf of children and adolescents.

For children and youth from working-class and ethnically segregated communities, the support of institutional agents may come in a variety of forms. Sennett and Cobb (1972: 227) state that the power of institutional agents lies in their ability to give or withhold knowledge. We would add that their power also comes from their ability to situate youth within resource-rich social networks by actively manipulating the social and institutional forces that determine who shall "make it" and who shall not. Thus, from the point of view of the student, gaining access to institutional funds of knowledge and educational opportunity essentially entails gaining access to social networks. Although access to institutional knowledge can occur through a variety of channels (i. e., media, curriculum materials), based on our analysis of two innovative programs, we conclude that direct, personal social relationships are the most important channel.

Social Capital

Social capital refers to the social relationships and networks from which an individual is potentially able to derive institutional support (Bourdieu & Passeron, 1977; Bourdieu, 1977, 1986; Stanton-Salazar & Dornbusch, 1995). This concept allows us one meaningful way to distinguish rich and poor, upwardly mobile and not, academically successful and academically at-risk students. It also alerts us to *how* and *why* one group is able to attain power and privilege while another group can not. When a student is situated within a relationship with a teacher who is committed and determined to send him/her to college, and who actively transmits the necessary resources and support, we can say that the student possesses social capital.

Bourdieu (1986) has argued that the laws governing the exchange of economic capital are applicable to human social relations in all their various forms. Thus, social capital is (1) cumulative, (2) possesses the capacity to produce profits or benefits in the social world, (3), is convertible into other forms of capital and (4) possesses the capacity to reproduce itself in identical or in expanded form. Just as a twenty-dollar bill represents a form of capital that can be converted into a desired service or product, a social relationship (or social tie) also represents a form of capital that can be converted into valued institutional support previously not at the disposal of the individual, for example, assistance with getting into college. Lin (1990) calls this conversion process successful instrumental action, which serves to highlight the notion that attaining goals such as going to college is often contingent on knowing key people.

Social Scaffolding

In the cognitive development literature "interactional scaffolding" (Wood et al., 1976) or "zone of proximal development" (Vygotsky, 1978; Cole & Griffin, 1987) generally refers to the support that a learner receives from a more capable peer while engaged in an academic task. The idea is to provide extensive guidance to a learner at the beginning of the learning experience and slowly remove it as the learner internalizes the help and is able to carry out the task alone. In other words, the aim is to get the learner to accomplish alone tomorrow what today he or she can accomplish in collaboration with others. As used here, social scaffolding focuses on the engineering of instructional tasks so as to produce this powerful learning process. The role of the expert or more capable peer in social scaffolding is indirect by design, although the support that is provided typically requires planning and installing structured activities and projects without making them appear to be structured, as exemplified by the way that parents teach their young children to read (Ninio & Bruner, 1978). The overall goal is to use the power of collaborative learning to insure individual advancement through the system.

An example of an early learning activity is a parent sharing a book with a child. Initially, the child knows very little about reading and the parent must do much of the work. As the child gains knowledge, as attention shifts from pictures to words, the child begins to recite well-learned pieces of the story. This skill becomes more and more flexible as the support provided by the book and the parent recedes and the child becomes an independent reader. The activity -- parent and child sitting together reading the book -- remains constant throughout the whole process. What has changed is the degree of the child's participation in the activity.

Re-examining Research Findings with New Conceptual Tools
The next section describes two educational interventions that show substantial evidence of facilitating educational success and advancement. Although taking place in two distinct settings--one out-of-school and the other in-school --*La Clase Mágica* [The Magical Class] and A.V.I.D, exemplify the institutional processes at work in facilitating access to support and educational resources. We examined these two interventions using the conceptual tools we have introduced above and using the following questions as guidelines:

(1) What was the nature of the institutional support provided to learners?

(2) Did instances of institutional support occur within the context of particular kinds of relationships? If so, what was the nature of these social relationships?

(3) How were the respective contexts organized to facilitate the formation of supportive relationships between the students or learners and agents?

We conclude this paper by outlining the kinds of institutional support that might be key in any intervention directed at low-income minority students. We also discuss the kinds of social relationships that appear to engender academic success and mobility.

Case 1: *Strategically Implicit Socialization and The Intellectual and Academic Development of Latino Elementary School Children*

La Clase Mágica is an after-school educational activity specially designed to address the educational needs of Spanish-English bilingual elementary-school age children. It draws on the resources of the University of California, San Diego (UCSD) and a local community institution, St. Leo's Mission, in a complex multi-level structure of vertical and horizontal integration. The partner institutions interact in a mutual relationship that benefits the community, the university, and the mission. At each point of contact, the university and community institutions generate new opportunities for learning. Researchers, educators, students, parents, and elementary school-aged children have the opportunity to exchange material and intellectual resources at all levels of the system (see Vásquez, this volume).

Housed on the grounds of a small Catholic Mission, *La Clase Mágica* is held after school three times a week for two hours and children attend voluntarily. Adults, mostly undergraduate students taking classes at UCSD, participate as part of a course on Child Development offered jointly by the Departments of Psychology and Communication at UCSD. Over the last 15 academic quarters of operation, approximately 150 children and 116 undergraduate students have participated in *La Clase Mágica*.

The findings reported in this section are garnered from analyses of fieldnotes written by students and research staff, field-developed measures, and audio and video recordings. Through telecommunications, the professor/project director and a research assistant work closely to monitor the students' writing of fieldnotes, pointing out occasional questionable interpretations and asking for additional detail.

During their visits, adults and children collaborate on any number of the 70 computer games and telecommunication activities available at site. Many of the games reinforce a variety of cognitive and academic skills such as examining assumptions, using a model, identifying multiple solutions, and estimating, predicting and projecting. The literacy-based side-tasks that accompany the games encourage bilingualism and biculturalism by building on the knowledge base and skills that children encounter in the multiple learning environments in which they participate. For example, Spanish and Mexican cultural knowledge is woven into the written materials that guide children through the activities.

A 20-room maze is used to organize the activities and to create a fantasy world that mixes play and educational activity. While the maze is used to symbolically represent movement through the project activities, it also allows children to envision themselves as characters exploring a fantasy world, in much the same way as players do in the popular game of Dungeons and Dragons. Children and adults work together to construct the virtual environment with the assistance of an electronic overseer, *El Maga* (a neologism combining male and female morphemes). Serving as the genial and poly-genderized patron of this hybrid world, *El Maga* reinforces a new system of rules and behaviors as s/he monitors the children's progress through the maze.

Strategically Implicit Socialization into the Academic Culture: The Culture of Collaborative Learning
The theoretical foundations of mixing play and educational activity make it possible to engineer a warm, supportive environment and non-hierarchical relationships among the participants. Children and adults interact as equal partners in joint activity around games or telecommunication. The imaginary world on which *La Clase Mágica* is based, the leading figure of *El Maga*, and the role of *Amigos/as* [Friends] assumed by the adults, together generate a culture of collaborative learning in which new sets of relationships and expectations are made possible. The culture of collaborative learning lays the foundation for children to engage in activities beyond their ability to do alone, as more expert participants support their development (Vygotsky, 1978).

The *Amigos/as* and *El Maga* lend a helping hand in deciphering the difficult language and concepts embedded in the games and accompanying materials in a supportive rather than authoritarian role. Through e-mail and electronic dialogues, *El Maga* helps children reflect on their learning, develop both languages, and make connections between what they learn at home, at school, and in the community. In sharing their activities of the day with *El Maga*, children also have an opportunity to negotiate points of relevance, writing conventions, and possible responses to his/her queries with their collaborating adults.

Within the special domain of *La Clase Mágica,* institutional support takes multiple forms; these include exchanging funds of knowledge, building bridges to other institutional agents and/or experiences, and intervening in the participants' identity formation and conceptualization of self. It is important to note that in this context, the provision and acquisition of institutional support assumes an indirect role in the interactions between children and adults. The emphasis remains on meaningful interactions based on real and immediate situations rather than on didactic dialogues. Although agent as well as learner derive benefit from these interactions, the emphasis below will be on the impact it has on the child participants.

Validating Multiple Knowledge Sources
Through meaningful interactions around everyday activities, participants at *La Clase Mágica,* both adults and children, exchange funds of knowledge on sociolinguistic conventions, problem-solving techniques, and norms and expectations of the multiple worlds outside their own community. The participants exchange visions of their worlds, one that paints the possibilities of student-life at the university, and the other that describes an ethnic community beyond the image portrayed by the media. In the fieldnotes written by undergraduate students, we find that children and adults have many opportunities to re-examine their perceptions of each other's cultures. For example, in a clip from a longer field note describing a telecommunication session with *El Maga*, KJ, an undergraduate student, and ten-year old Nina, learn much more than to use the technology to write letters and engage in an electronic dialogue. Both child and adult exchange linguistic and cultural knowledge:

> ...*El Maga* interrupted and let us know he/she wanted to converse (engage in an electronic dialogue). He/She asked Nina if she knew what *La Malinche* is (name of one of the rooms in the maze). Neither of us knew what it was so Nina sort of just wanted to push it aside and go on to pursue what was more important to her, the photo. But *El Maga* said something like, "Hey, you didn't

> answer my question. Ask a teacher to tell you about *La
> Malinche,* send me the answer, and I'll send you a prize."
> She said good-bye to *El Maga* and asked Olga about *La
> Malinche.* Olga explained to her in Spanish that it is a
> name of a traitor, sort of like Benedict Arnold is in
> American culture. *La Malinche* was a woman who spoke
> both Spanish and the language of the indigenous groups
> in Mexico, enabling her to help Cortez and the
> conquistadors. [KJ, 04/29/92]

KJ and Nina not only learn telecommunication functions but also
learn to seek assistance from multiple knowledge sources. Many
activities such as this encourage the acquisition of Mexicano cultural
knowledge and Spanish language for both adults and children. In
other interactions, life in mainstream America is made more
apparent. In one such situation, AD, an undergraduate student
becomes cognizant of the influence adults like herself have on the
children's formulation of life goals:

> Out of the blue, Norma asked me if you need a computer
> to do your work on at college. I thought to myself what
> an impact college students have on these children, they
> are already thinking about college! I told her that some
> people have computers to do papers on but others use
> typewriters just as well. I also told her about computers
> that you can use on campus. She asked me if I had a
> computer and I said yes. Then she asked me what I
> wanted to be, " like a doctor or something?" I told her
> that I wanted to be psychologist. She asked me what that
> was and I told her that I wanted to help people who have
> troubles. [AD, 10/22/93]

In the natural process of collaborating with the children,
undergraduates such as AD are in a prime position to share cultural
and social knowledge of mainstream society, academia, and
technology. Not only can they share what another setting is like but
they can also point out its norms and expectations. Undergraduates
transmit problem-solving techniques and sociolinguistic conventions
when they suggest and mediate the use of reference materials such as
maps, dictionaries, and encyclopedias to help the children understand
the tasks required by the games. By building on the multiple

learning domains in which the children participate, the activities of *La Clase Mágica* validate the funds of knowledge of the home, school and community.   Whenever possible, Spanish language and Mexicano culture is deliberately integrated into the activities to supplement the limited resources in bilingual and Spanish-language software and personnel available at site. Each of the interactional and print-based tasks that accompany the games is carefully constructed to draw on and build upon the children's background experiences. *El Maga*, for example, prompts children to relate their experiences on the computer games to knowledge and skills they have acquired in the home and community.   In the following clip from a field note, IT, an undergraduate student, sets the stage for children to use their previous experiences as building blocks to comprehend and integrate the new vocabulary and cultural knowledge of the commercially designed game of Botanical Gardens:

> ...I first asked them if they ever planted any plants at home or maybe at school. Maria said, "Yeah in school we planted."   I then turned to Lisa who answered, *"¿Sabes que? Yo le ayudo a mi mama hecharle agua a las plantas en veces en mi casa* (You know what? I help my mother water the plants sometimes at my house)." I told them that I like plants and flowers a lot except every time I try to make them grow, the plants die instead. I emphasized that I don't have a green thumb--they thought my comment was funny and laughed.   Any how I continued by letting them know that this game would give them the opportunity to grow plants. [IT, 03/06/90]

Field-developed materials that accompany games like Botanical Gardens are designed bilingually and biculturally to give children an opportunity to situate themselves in a familiar context while experiencing the language and knowledge of school and an information-based society. The goal is to pose either language or culture as a viable resource to accomplish a task.

Engineering Optimal Learning Environments
The organizational structure and interactional dynamics at *La Clase Mágica* encourage children to problem solve, form goals, and make decisions; in essence, to become independent thinkers and doers. As they moved through the rooms of the maze, they were encouraged to

make important decisions. They choose which room to enter, which of the three available games to play and what level of difficulty to play. They make decisions about which language to use, with whom, and for what purpose (Vásquez, 1992). Tacitly, they also make decisions about which culture to operate in: the culture of *La Clase Mágica*, their home culture, or of that mainstream society. Even when communicating with *El Maga,* who is a fluent bilingual, they have options as to which language to use. These practices, and their reflections on them, suggest an image of themselves as active agents in their own learning.

In creating the opportunity for children and adults to interact on equal terms, the activities at *La Clase Mágica* also validate the children's role in the problem-solving process. Children are often placed in the role of experts, having to share accumulated knowledge and skills as they plot through the games and activities. Long-term participant children are often more knowledgeable about the games and the culture of the imaginary world than the transient 10-week undergraduate students. These experienced children are frequently called upon to resolve problems with the games or the technology by adults who find themselves in the position of novices. Seeing themselves as possessors of knowledge and having the opportunity to exercise this knowledge, reinforce a positive image children have of themselves at *La Clase Mágica*. This situation makes it possible for adults to contribute, within a more equitable relationship, their general knowledge of the world and their more developed problem-solving skills.

Children have many opportunities to put into practice what they have learned in collaboration with others. They perpetuate the culture of collaborative learning at *La Clase Mágica* by sharing with others what they have learned. For example, the following interaction among an undergraduate student, GF, a long-term child participant, Nora, and a newer child, Oscar, demonstrates the ways in which helping behavior becomes a fundamental characteristic of interactions between long-term participants and children or adults who have less knowledge of the games and technology. In the following clip from a longer field note written in 1991, Nora not only mediates oral expression in Spanish for GF but also mediates the game for Oscar who had recently joined *La Clase Mágica*.

...[I] began to explain that '*El plante necesita luz y agua y dirt. . .*' and finally Nora interacted with 'tierra' and quickly explained everything to Oscar who had evidently been taught the game before by a Spanish speaker. (GF, 11/8/1991)

Self-confidence and self-pride grow out of repeated experiences of validation of one's own knowledge base and experiences. Too often minority children look into the proverbial mirror of the curriculum and do not see themselves (Rosaldo, 1989). The accomplishments reached through her assistance are not lost on Nora. It is obvious that she assists GF complete her expression in Spanish when she contributes the word "*tierra.*" Nora also assumes the role of expert when she scaffolds Oscar's understanding of the game by explaining it in Spanish. Implicitly, she has mediated his participation in the activities but has also contributed to the collaborative culture of *La Clase Mágica.* One year and several months later, as a long-term participant, Oscar was using the same strategies that helped him transition into *La Clase Mágica,* using Spanish to facilitate comprehension and prompting first-level children to express their understanding. These meaningful interactions around real and immediate situations teach children to articulate their desires, needs, and opinions with self-confidence and ease, a characteristic not evident in their earlier participation in site activities (Vásquez, 1994). As they voice their opinions, decide on the activity for the day, and trouble-shoot for adults on the technical glitches in the system, they learn to see themselves as valid and contributing members of the problem-solving process. They learn to think of themselves as active agents in their own learning, as possible undergraduate students, and as movers and shakers in the multiple worlds outside their own community.

The Role of Institutional Linkages: Bridging to Other Resources
As the foregoing description makes plain, *La Clase Mágica* provides institutional support in various ways, including the linking of participants to experiences and institutional agents who can provide additional resources outside of the children's repertoire. *La Clase Mágica* facilitates a two-way exchange for undergraduates and participating community representatives. The undergraduates themselves are institutional agents representing the university and all its possibilities. They have the capacity and commitment to provide

children with new and exciting knowledge. Periodically, they have incorporated their interests in such areas as photography, dance, film, television, and fitness into *La Clase Mágica* activities. Children have learned about cameras, videotaping, balloon sculpture, and drama scripts as a result of an undergraduate's interest. At times, students have left indelible imprints in *La Clase Mágica*'s organizational structure. For example, it was at the urging of undergraduate students that the "Wizard Assistant Club" was formed for long-term participants who had traveled throughout the entire maze. These students assumed the role of club managers and organized special outings for these children -- i. e., a visit to UCSD, the library, and another site especially designed for English-speaking children at a local Boys and Girls Club.

On numerous occasions, students have interceded between the children and their parents in ways that helped parents learn about the cultural world in which their children participate. For example, after studying the behavioral patterns of Jake, a seven year old boy, for several quarters, BP, an undergraduate male, assured Jake's mother that her son was not behaviorally disordered but had difficulty working with undergraduates who teased him or who were too lenient. Parents often watch their children and undergraduates play on the computer and learn new ways of assisting children with problem-solving activities.

The literacy practices on the computer and telecommunication technology also connect participants to an information society they might not have access to in other settings. Children, their parents, and even some undergraduates learn to use information technology in ways that are becoming ubiquitous in educational settings--word processing, graphics, and distance-learning. In one quarter, several students developed and implemented a computer literacy class in which eight members of the community learned to use computers for writing and drawings.

Summary: Engineering Access to Institutional Knowledge Via Implicit Socialization
Gaining access to higher education is a life-long project, and children at *La Clase Mágica* are implicitly introduced to that possibility at the elementary school-age level. The interactions around everyday activities between university students and children from working class

minority background sets the foundation to consider university training as a future option.   Meeting and collaborating with undergraduate students makes the possibility ever more real.   When little Norma asks if students use computers in college, she is "already thinking about college!" as AD so aptly concurs.   When Nina walks across the university campus and she asks her mother if "this is the college I will attend," she expresses the goal she has formed through her interactions with over 100 undergraduates who have participated in *La Clase Mágica* over the last five years.

Thus, a great deal of implicit socialization goes on at *La Clase Magica* beyond the academic content of the project.   Children learn to become effective and productive border crossers.   They learn the strategies of problem-solving and decision-making that are the core of academic life.   They learn to use language and literacy in ways that are validated in multiple learning domains and importantly in the school setting.   An important lesson that we learn from *La Clase Mágica* is the strength of self and academic foundations that are gained when social relations and environments foster this kind of learning.   *La Clase Mágica* offers us a glimpse into the kinds of institutional support that can occur in educational settings that target minority children.

As part of nine-team consortium that focuses on creating innovative educational activities for local children, *La Clase Mágica* represents an example of how instructional activities can be shaped to address the needs of Latino children.   The theoretical framework of mixing play and education to create a warm supportive environment that fosters non-hierarchical relationships is the foundation on which the nine sites have developed, each with its own identity reflecting the target population and institutional constraints.   For example, the new site recently developed at University of California, Santa Barbara builds on this foundation to create Proteus Club, an educational activity that will try to merge in-school and out-of-school learning. Although our generalizability remains in community settings, we hope that Proteus Club will provide insights into how projects like *La Clase Mágica* can be situated in the school.

Case 2: *Explicit Socialization, Advocacy, and Bridging In The Success of High School Latino Students*
Schools in San Diego have established an "untracking" program. High school students who have demonstrated academic potential

(based on their high scores on 8th grade standardized tests) but mediocre academic performance (based on their low grades in 7th and 8th grade) are placed into college prep classes along with their high achieving contemporaries. These previously low achieving students are not left to sink or swim in this new, academically demanding environment. They are provided social supports in the form of tutors and a special class by the sponsoring program the "Advancement Via Individual Determination" program, which is better known by its acronym "AVID."

This untracking program has been successful in preparing its students for college. From 1990 to 1992, 1,053 students who had participated in the AVID untracking experiment for 3 years graduated from 14 high schools in the San Diego City Schools (SDCS) system. In those same years an additional 288 students started the program but left after completing one year or less. We (Mehan et al., 1994) interviewed 248 of the 3 Year AVID students and 146 of the 1 Year AVID students and observed in AVID classes and "academic" courses in 8 high schools in San Diego during the 1990-1993 school years.

Of the 248 students who "graduated" from AVID, 120 (48%) reported attending four year colleges, 99 (40%) reported attending two year or junior colleges and the remaining 29 students (12%) said they are working or doing other things. The 48% four year college enrollment rate for students who have been "untracked" compares favorably with the San Diego City Schools' average of 37% and the national average of 39%. It also compares favorably with the college enrollment rate of students who started, but did not complete the untracking program; 34% of them enrolled in 4 year colleges within a year of graduating from high school.

Furthermore, the untracking experiment assists students who are from low-income families and the two major ethnic groups that are underrepresented in college. African Americans and Latinos from AVID enroll in college in numbers that exceed local and national averages. Of the Latino students who have participated in AVID for 3 years, 43% enroll in four year colleges. This figure compares favorably to the San Diego City Schools average of 25% and the national average of 29%. African American students who participate in AVID for three years also enroll in college at rates higher than the local and national averages; 55% of Black students from AVID enroll in four year colleges, compared to 35% from the SDCS and the national average of 33%.

AVID students who come from the lowest income strata (parents' median income below $19,999) enroll in four year colleges in equal or higher proportion to students who come from higher income strata (parents' median income between $20,000 and $65,000). AVID students who come from families in which their parents have less than a college education enroll in 4-year colleges more than students who come from families who have a college education (Mehan et al., 1994).

AVID students persist in college once they enroll. Of 168 students we were able to interview after they had been out of high school for one year, 54 (or 32%) were enrolled in four year colleges, 74 (or 44%) were enrolled in two year colleges and 40 (or 24%) were working or "doing other things" (such as church missionary work). All the students enrolled in four year colleges had been in college the year before; that is there were no students who moved up from two year colleges to four year colleges. Of the 74 students in two year colleges after one year of high school, 54 had started in two year colleges and continue there, 12 began in four year colleges but are now enrolled in two year colleges and 8 who had begun their career after high school by working, now attend two year colleges. In short, there was little upward mobility; only 5% (8 of 168 students) went from work to two year colleges and some downward mobility in this cohort; 7% (12 of 168) left four year colleges to attend two year colleges.

As a means to achieve its main goal of preparing previously low achieving students for college, AVID works hard to place its students in college prep courses. Students are enrolled as early as their freshman year, usually in an advanced history class, an advanced English class or an advanced math class. If AVID students are successful in these classes, then the course load of academic courses is supposed to be increased in each successive year so that students have the requisite "a - f" courses upon graduation that enable them to apply to and be accepted into the California State University, the University of California or other colleges and universities that demand extensive liberal arts preparation.

AVID coordinators bring college recruiters to their high school, obtain college application and scholarship forms and assist students in filling them out and filing them on time. The net result of this effort is that AVID students receive explicit socialization into the often hidden curriculum of the school, benefit from teacher mediators who intervene on their behalf within the high school and serve as bridges between the high school and colleges.

Explicit Socialization into Implicit Academic Culture
An explicit socialization process takes place in the AVID classroom. Students who have been selected into this program devote one academic period a day, five days a week for the 180 day school year to a specially designed course, often in lieu of an extra-curricular activity or an other elective course.

Teaching Study Skills
AVID students are given explicit instruction in a special method of note taking which stresses specific techniques for compiling main ideas, abstracting key concepts and identifying questions that guide analysis. They are required to apply these techniques in notebooks which they keep for their academic courses. Tutors collect and check these notebooks once a week or once every two weeks. Students are graded on the completeness and quality of their notes. When asked what helps them the most, the 8 Pimlico students we interviewed singled out the importance of learning to organize and manage their time and "learning to take good notes."

At a minimum, students were given practice on vocabulary items likely to be found on the SAT. When a more extensive approach to test preparation was taken, students were provided explicit instruction in ways to eliminate distracting answers on multiple choice questions, strategies for approximating answers and probabilities about the success of guessing. One AVID teacher devoted two successive weeks to SAT preparation, reviewing vocabulary, analogies and comprehension questions. This teacher also sent her students to an expert math teacher for assistance on math test items. She told her students that she was teaching them the same test-taking techniques found in the expensive Princeton Review SAT preparation class.

Teaching the College Application Process
While note taking, test taking and vocabulary building strategies were taught routinely in the eight AVID classes we studied from 1991 to 1993, by far the most intriguing activity revolved around the college application process. Procedures for filing applications, meeting deadlines for SAT tests, requesting financial aid and scholarships

dominated discussion. In one high school, for instance, seniors must complete an AVID assignment each week in which they perform writing and/or reading tasks directly related to the college application process. The junior class at another high school we studied was given a handout, "Choosing Your College," containing a checklist of information typically found in college catalogs. Students were instructed to fill in the information for a particular college according to the assigned checklist. This task presumably made them more familiar with college catalogs and would help them choose an appropriate college.

Teaching Conflict Resolution Strategies
In addition to scaffolding the college application process, AVID coordinators explicitly teach conflict resolution strategies as part of their curriculum. Working class students, both "minority" and white, often have different codes for resolving conflict than their middle income white teachers. One of the four AVID coordinators at "Keeneland" High School extends her coaching to the organization of the phrases which students should employ when talking to their teachers. "Don't ask *if* you can make up an exam," she says, "ask politely *when* the next make up is. If you miss a class, don't say 'I'll get an excuse,' go to the attendance office, get a copy of the teacher's roll sheet and say 'I'm sorry I missed your class, but here's my excuse.' " The conversational prompts which this coordinator gives her students emphasize the importance of polite conversation, not putting teachers on the defensive and assuming teachers are agreeable people who make honest mistakes.

Using students to coach students in conflict resolution has the added benefit of encouraging students to be autonomous from, instead of dependent upon, adults when identifying ways to solve problems. In this way, students learn interactive skills that not only work within the high school, but may be helpful in other arenas of their life when they are separated from their AVID teachers.

The Power of 'Connections': Teacher Advocacy
Another role AVID teachers adopt is that of student advocate. When interviewed, students, at the eight schools we studied, consistently reported that AVID teachers intervene in the academic maze on behalf of their students. If students are absent, AVID teachers check in with their colleagues to insure that their students get missing assignments,

catch up on their work, and are not penalized for their absence. AVID teachers call their students in the evening to check on them, relay information on assignments, and inquire about their return to school.

Advocacy on behalf of students is not limited to the strictly academic realm; it extends into the personal realm as well. Coordinators told us they have intervened in suicide attempts, visited sick students, and called parents if they felt that a student was employed too many hours outside of school or was having difficulty in school.

Clearly, these teachers' interventions were instrumental in keeping students on the college track. Although students, especially those from low-income families, continue to labor under heavy academic and social pressure, they receive encouragement and support from dedicated AVID teachers. But not all interventions are successful. The resources that an innovative school program such as AVID can muster are limited and sometimes are not sufficient to overcome the constraints imposed by the overwhelming practical circumstances that AVID students face in their every day lives.

The existing social resources invested by AVID -- a special class that meets once a day for 180 days, a dedicated teacher who serves as an advocate, college tutors -- are not sufficient to propel all students down the college track. To reach students with less impressive academic records, even more extensive resources are necessary. To be sure, if AVID deployed more extensive social support resources, then the program could help more under achieving students. But we have to realize that school reform efforts such as untracking are not a panacea. Without significant change in the organization of the occupational structure, changes in the organization of schooling such as this untracking program will not be able to make a significant difference.

Bridging Between Institutions

AVID teachers mediate the college-going process in other ways; that is, they act as, or facilitate, other vital 'connections.' They take their students on trips to colleges and universities, usually in the local area. Some coordinators took their students on trips to universities that are some distance away, UCLA and USC, for example. Of particular note, the AVID coordinator at "Pimlico" High School takes her students to Northern California schools and also arranges a two-week trip to

Traditionally Black Colleges and Universities every other year. For many students, these field trips provided their first opportunity to see a college campus. While on college campuses, students visit classes and dorms and talk to college students:

> Field trips were great. I didn't even know what a college looked like until Mrs. Lincoln took us. Its like eating a cookie. It really tempts us to eat another one. You've smelled it and seen it and you want to buy it really bad.

"Career days" are another mediating mechanism occurring regularly in AVID programs. AVID coordinators invite guest speakers to their classes to discuss their professions or occupations. Career talks are always geared to those occupations that require a four year college degree.

In the pages above, we described the elaborate socialization process the AVID coordinator implemented at Golden Gate High School. His personal involvement in the application process does not end when students complete college application forms. He personally mails the applications, sometimes affixing his own stamps if students have forgotten them. He personally delivers the applications to one of the local colleges and goes through each application with the Equal Opportunity Program (EOP) admissions officer there.

Summary: Institutional Support and the Success of Untracking
The placement of low achieving students in rigorous academic courses is a fundamentally important ingredient in the success of this untracking project. It is a simple fact: kids can't go to college if they don't take college prep classes. And AVID is diligent in placing its students in college-prep classes: 70% of all students attempt the full complement of college eligibility courses, and 40% complete this arduous sequence.

While it is necessary to place students in college prep classes to prepare them for college, academic placement in and of itself is not sufficient. AVID is working with students who have not had previous experience with college prep classes. Social scaffolds must be erected in order to insure that students who have not had previous experience with academically oriented classes succeed in them. The social scaffolding supporting student placement in college prep courses is as important as the academic placement itself.

Among the most visible social supports in AVID classrooms

are test taking, note taking and study strategies. By dispensing these academic techniques, AVID is giving students explicit instruction in the hidden curriculum of the school. That is, AVID teaches explicitly in school what middle income students learn implicitly at home. In Bourdieu's (1986) terms, AVID gives low income students some of the cultural capital at school which is similar to the cultural capital that more economically advantaged parents give to their children at home.

Teacher advocacy (which is what an AVID teacher does to help a student within the high school) and bridging (which is what an AVID teacher does to assist a student move between the high school and the college) complement this explicit socialization process. AVID coordinators who form a bridge between high school and college help insure that their students will get to the college door.

The success of the San Diego untracking experiment is due in large part to the fact that the academic life of AVID students in school is supported by dedicated teachers who enter the lives of their students and serve as mediators between them, the school and the college system. By expanding the definition of their teaching role to include the sponsorship of students, AVID coordinators encourage success and help remove impediments to students' academic achievement.

Discussion and Conclusion
Our principal objective in this collaborative paper has been to identify some of the underlying institutional processes or mechanisms that may be operating within successful intervention programs. We understood that to successfully meet our objective, we needed to utilize an analytical framework that would allow us to see things others have tended to overlook. Ongoing research in the fields of social networks, social support, and sociocultural contexts of learning and child development provided us the tools for this endeavor. Ultimately, our concern has to do with knowing how to restructure urban public schools so that they function to engineer success rather than facilitate failure.

Traditional educational reform strategies have focused their efforts on compensating for the perceived deficits in working class and minority students' academic and intellectual foundations. As a consequence, instructional approaches based on deficit models have tended to be remedial and stigmatizing in nature. We suggest here a radically different approach to closing the achievement gap between "majority" and "minority" students, one that has yet to be considered, despite current reform efforts to "restructure" urban schools.

Our strategy calls attention to the ways in which middle-class and other privileged youth are *implicitly* and *explicitly socialized* in ways that equip them with various strategies and funds of knowledge that serve to strengthen and insure their position within the school system and society. Middle-class youth may or may not be aware of how critical certain socialization practices are to their success, yet many middle-class and more privileged parents regularly deploy practices that function to insure the competitive advantage of their children (Lareau, 1989; Cookson & Persell, 1985; McDonough, 1994).

Institutionalizing 'Institutional Support' and Strategic Socialization
One way that working-class and minority youth can enjoy the same advantages as their more privileged peers is for schools and their agents to collectively act in a deliberate, intensive and strategic fashion to generate a socialization process that produces the same sorts of learning found in privileged homes and institutions. In making this recommendation, we must be cautious and explicit. We are not asking schools, nor minority families, to merely imitate or duplicate the child rearing, socialization and education practices of middle-class parents. We know that any such strategic intervention must build upon the intellectual resources that students from diverse cultural and linguistic backgrounds bring to school (Heath, 1986; Moll et al., 1992; Tharp & Gallimore, 1988; Vásquez et al., 1994). We are not asking working-class and minority students to *subtract* their family-and community-based cultural knowledge, nor are we giving license to schools to continue this old destructive practice; we are suggesting that students can *add* to their repertoire the institutionally-based cultural knowledge that seems to be so essential for climbing the steps of success in US society.

Our collective efforts have led us to believe that educational interventions serving minority students can achieve success when certain institutional processes or mechanisms are operating. First, certain key forms of institutional support are engineered in an intensive, strategic and systematic way. These forms of institutional support include cultivating native funds of knowledge, implicit and explicit socialization in institutional knowledge, bridging, and mentorship. Second, success occurs in the context of relations of trust and [emotional] support between students and teachers (as well as other institutional agents). This is to say that institutional support cannot be delivered in a mechanical or technical manner. The provision of institutional support, including the delivery of key funds of knowledge, must occur in the context of genuinely supportive and nurturing relations (Stanton-Salazar, et al., 1995; Stanton-Salazar, 1995a). The two interventions featured in this paper, as well as some of the earlier "restructuring" experiments (Boysen, 1992; Comer, 1980; Levin, 1988), may have been successful because they incorporated these processes or mechanisms, however implicitly.

At the core, we are suggesting that educational interventions begin to engineer success when they employ a comprehensive and multifaceted approach that assumes that academic achievement and school success are inextricably tied to the students' accumulation and expenditure of institutionally-based cultural and social capital. That is, in order to be successful, students need to establish social relationships with those people who are not only technically capable of providing support, but who are also committed to doing so (social capital). It is through such relationships that students not only gain access to important types of resources and support, but also learn how to actively and strategically mobilize their network resources when necessary. Thus, institutional support is much more than giving students the fish they need to survive; it is teaching them how to fish, whatever waters they are in.

Establishing Authentically Supportive Relationships with Institutional Agents

The critical role of supportive relationships in the educational process cannot be overstated. A wealth of research has shown that optimal cognitive growth and the development of social competency occurs in the context of trusting and committed social relationships with caring adults (Brofenbrenner, 1979; Nestmann & Hurrelmann, 1994; Werner & Smith, 1982; Erickson & Shultz, 1982; Cole & Griffin, 1987). More recent research has shown that children can often overcome the worst of stressful and problem-plagued environments when they are connected to at least a few supportive and resourceful adults (Garbarino et al., 1992; Werner & Smith, 1982; Zweigenhaft & Domhoff, 1991).

Establishing supportive social relationships is not an easy task, however, especially given the traditional role of the teacher designated by compensatory models of education and the cultural/class differences between minority children and many institutional agents. Although such differences do not necessarily preclude the development of trusting and nurturing relations, they do seem to place undue burdens on the children involved, particularly in terms of the stress and strain of cultural accommodation (Padilla, 1980; Pearlin, 1989)

More problematic still is a point that is rarely discussed in educational circles. Social distance, distrust and latent antagonisms rooted in our stratified society often manifest themselves in subtle ways in the interpersonal relationships between people who occupy dominant and subordinate positions in the social system (Stanton-Salazar, 1995a, 1995b). It is therefore quite reasonable to expect that these tensions often interfere with the trust and rapport between school personnel and youth -- particularly during adolescence -- as the work of McDermott and collaborators (1977) to Willis (1977) shows.

In the two interventions reviewed in this paper the learners and adults did, in fact, appear to exhibit a trust that the other would enter into binding relations in such a way that the relations would serve the interests of both. We speak here, on the one hand, about students' trust that the teacher or adult "cared" and was "invested" in both the intervention and in the learners themselves and, on the other hand, about the adult's trust that the students would be receptive to his or her efforts and that the students would likewise be invested in the intervention. That is, the trust was mutual; each party conveyed an implicit commitment to honor the trust of the other.

Gaining Access to Institutional Support

Although establishing supportive social relationships between students and institutional agents is fundamental for engineering success, the nature and the quality of institutional support must also be emphasized. As the results of Jaime Escalante's heroic efforts with low-achieving Latinos show, caring and commitment on the part of institutional agents and *ganas* on the part of students are vitally important. Yet the full story is that Mr. Escalante also provided expert math instruction and professional monitoring of his students' learning; that is, his mentorship went far beyond emotional and moral support. We must remember that privileged youth gain their advantage by their consistent and systematic access to high quality instruction and curriculum, as well as by their access to multiple forms of institutional support. Yet, what exactly are these forms of institutional support and how do young people gain access to them?

Cultivating Funds of Knowledge
One fundamentally important form of institutional support entails the exchange of "funds of knowledge" (Moll et al., 1992; Greenberg, 1989). On the one hand, children bring to school the cultural knowledge and information that exists in households and neighborhoods, and that are used by members of the community for successfully negotiating everyday life. Community-based funds of knowledge can be mobilized by teachers for instructional purposes. Since this knowledge is derived from low-income, low-status and culturally diverse families, its instructional use validates its importance in the lives of children from diverse backgrounds and builds respect and appreciation for diversity among all students--those most disparaged and those from groups that have done the disparaging. Additionally, cognitive skills that are critical to performing academic tasks are built upon the foundations of community-based knowledge (Freire, 1973; Moll et al., 1994; Vásquez et al., 1994). On the other hand, schools and their agents reciprocate by providing institutionally-based funds of knowledge, including knowing how to operate successfully within bureaucracies. This institutionally-based knowledge is transmitted through a process of strategic socialization that is at times quite explicit as illustrated in the in AVID project, and at other times, implicit in the kinds of activities and interactions that are made available.

Strategic Socialization in Institutional Knowledge
Strategic socialization practices intended to transmit and cultivate both community-based knowledge and institutionally-based cultural capital represents a key form of institutional support. Socialization can occur in two ways, as shown in our two case studies. First, explicit socialization occurs when key problem-solving and learning strategies are called attention to as part of the content of instruction. This process was most evident in our study of AVID where teachers made clear what kinds of study skills and institutional knowledge students needed in order to succeed in academia. These skills and knowledge can also be tacitly transmitted in the kinds of adult-child interactions

that emerge out of problem-solving activities. This is what we call implicit socialization. At *La Clase Mágica,* for example, children learned the kinds of learning strategies and knowledge that are valued in school through meaningful interactions based on real-life situations. To fully appreciate the uniqueness of this latter process, it is critically important that we distinguish between the kind of socialization occurring in interventions such as *La Clase Mágica* and that often found in middle-class homes; in the former, the provision of tacit knowledge is strategically built into activities designed to empower low-status children, while in the latter, such knowledge is usually transmitted in the course of routine affairs that are part and parcel of a privileged lifestyle.

Our emphasis on role of strategic socialization in transmitting institutionally-based knowledge is based on two sociological premises: The first premise is that success within school (or other mainstream institutions) has never been simply a matter of tested subject knowledge and performance of technical skills, but rather and more fundamentally, it has been a matter of learning how to *decode the system* (Stanton-Salazar, 1995b). Such decoding requires either an explicit or implicit understanding that the rules governing advancement have much to do with mainstream cultural rules governing social interaction, or more fundamentally, with the modes of presentation, and schemes of perception and appreciation which appear as the universal standards for proper thinking and comportment (e.g., "common sense; " "normal," good and competent behavior; etc.). What this means is not only that the ways of institutional life are encoded in the cultural capital and ethos of the dominant group, but that dominant group children begin learning the rules of institutional life in the context of early socialization experiences within the home and community (Bourdieu & Passeron, 1977; Bourdieu, 1986; Bernstein, 1973). For outsiders to fully access this knowledge and to use it productively, for instrumental purposes, they must somehow "make sense" of the cultural logic of the dominant group.

One major reason why advancement within the school system requires learning mainstream codes is because advancement is still largely contingent upon the regular display of behavior which is recognized and officially sanctioned as "social competence" or which is labeled as intellectual or scholastic "ability" (Simpson & Rosenholtz, 1986). Another reason has to do with the fact that learning 'the ways of institutional life' has much to do with learning how to engage "powerful" adults in ways that will lead them to act as agent, for example as co-parent, advocate, and informal mentor (Erickson & Schultz, 1982; Stanton-Salazar & Dornbusch, 1995).

The second premise is that working class and minority children arrive at school rich in cultural resources, competent, perhaps masterful decoders in any number of cultural domains, but not in mainstream institutions, including the school. Their cultural and social resources are set within a different cultural context. Unless they are provided strategic forms of social support and training necessary for effective decoding with mainstream domains, such children will be systematically denied opportunities for success.

Such strategic support and training, however, are not routine components in conventional curriculum and classrooms. Yet, as the cases presented here illustrate, strategic socialization set within carefully planned educational interventions can equip children with strategies to decode the system, thereby teaching them that the system can be manipulated in ways that will engineer their success.

Mentoring

Mentoring is another form of institutional support for engineering the success of Latino students in school. We saw evidence of mentoring in the experiences of AVID students when their teachers arranged meetings between a student and other gatekeepers and defended a student's position when institutional norms were inadvertently violated. Mentoring also entails altering students' social status within the classroom and the school, and then conferring legitimacy on this new status. Even when students are untracked, the emergence or persistence of status distinctions among students on the basis of gender, ethnicity and language can undermine the potential benefits of these innovations (Cohen, 1983; Simpson & Rosenholz, 1986).

Solving this problem requires reversing the order of the process. The dominant rationality of the school states that students first exhibit intellectual talent and social competence, then are accorded legitimacy and high status. We propose changing (equalizing) and legitimating students' social status first, then following-through with a strategic socialization process that teaches them how to demonstrate competencies in conformity with dominant standards. In the AVID untracking project, we saw that students' status changed when they were placed in prestigious college-prep classes, and their new status legitimized through emblems and special privileges and by recognizing their success in public gatherings. In *La Clase Mágica*, we saw a complete reorganization of the traditional learning environment. This reorganization enabled participants to enter a culture of collaboration and within it, to demonstrate multiple competencies and to become active learners. In sum, changes in students' social status must correspond to organizational rearrangements that insure their success and to instances of public recognition that validate and legitimate their new social identity among their peers and other agents. In the two cases presented here, this status-manipulation process worked to engineer a dramatic change in students' academic performance. No matter how status differences are altered or equalized, the process changes the social distribution of opportunities, opening the doors to enriching experiences to students who would otherwise be locked out.

Bridging
Granovetter (1982) has argued that weak ties (i. e., relationships characterized by more formality, shorter duration, and less reciprocated assistance) rather than strong ties (i. e., relationships characterized by more intimacy, longer duration and more reciprocal assistance) increase the possibility that adults will gain access to institutional resources and opportunities. Granovetter (1982) has argued further that those ties that act as "bridges" to other networks and gatekeepers are typically the most consequential. We apply this insight to the supportive relations we have observed between institutional agents and students in these two successful educational interventions.

We found that institutional agents can act as "bridges" to agents in other institutions, as for example, when AVID coordinators sponsor AVID students' college applications to college admissions and financial aid officers. AVID and *La Clase Mágica* personnel also serve as bridges between institutions when they take their students to museums, universities, libraries, and cultural centers and provide them access to technological innovations such as computers and computer networks, which they use either for their enjoyment or educational advancement.

Like many others, we believe that encouragement and moral support are important ingredients for engineering the school success of working-class and minority students, but emotionally supportive social relationships are only truly effective when they are accompanied by systematic access to network-oriented forms of institutional support. Conversely, social relationships which act as conduits for the provision of institutional supports increase significantly their overall influence and effectiveness when they embody genuine emotional and moral support.

Although encouragement and personal relations of confidence and rapport with institutional agents may initially convey to working-class and minority youth that other forms of institutional support are potentially available, the actual provision of network-oriented resources may never occur. Although the initial perception that certain relationships are supportive may be sufficient to encourage some youth to continue to engage in the schooling process, across time, trusting relations that do not, in fact, provide institutional resources and support may eventually lead to resentment and disengagement from the schooling process.

As shown in our two studies, the ideal situation can be engineered. Institutional support becomes truly empowering when adults, teachers and informal mentors use personal relationships to make available institutional funds of knowledge, to engage in mentoring and social scaffolding, and to serve as bridges to gatekeepers in neighboring institutional domains. To do so consciously and strategically entails what we have termed strategic socialization and, following Bourdieu (1986) seems to account for the workings of social capital, although strategic socialization has a different institutional base. In Bourdieu's framework, social capital is rooted in the institution of the family, and the elite family at that. Elite families associate with other elite families to form networks that can be employed to benefit their sons and daughters. Job opportunities and college placement are only two of the benefits that accrue to the children of the elite because their parents are embedded in a rich set of interlocking directorates, "old boy" networks, professional associations, school ties and political connections. Mentoring, teacher advocacy and institutional bridging, as we have described here, look like the workings of elite social capital. Yet they have the school, not the family, as their base. If schools, not just well-to-do families, can deploy social capital to form productive social networks, then it means that schools serving low-status communities can cease being reproductive institutions, and become instead, transformative ones. Following this new logic, the sons and daughters of less privileged families *can* gain access to the often invisible networks of relationships and institutional funds of knowledge that are usually reserved for the sons and daughters of the more privileged.

Implications for Policy and Practice

We believe our analytical framework offers strong implications for how urban schools can be restructured to engineer the success of all minority students.   Thus, our next logical step would be to move to develop a set of carefully crafted guidelines for restructuring curriculum and teaching in minority-dominant schools and classrooms.   For now, we offer the following conclusions and suggestions:

1) *Minority students rise to the most rigorous of academic standards when educational environments are strategically engineered in ways that insure their success.*

2) *Current and future restructuring efforts should include plans for instituting into the school's curriculum and social structure proven methods of student social support and mentorship.* Such strategic support would include high expectations, embeddedness in a network of committed agents and mentors, and the implementation of multiple instructional methods for transmitting "institutional funds of knowledge" (e.g., *how to* collaboratively approach intellectual tasks; *how to* problem-solve and accomplish goals within formal bureaucracies).   The full development of a restructuring plan for teaching, based on our framework, would necessarily entail many stages and levels of execution. We suggest that one fruitful place to begin is a training plan for teachers, counselors, other staff, parents, and community members which focuses on which learning environments and socialization practices heighten motivation, accelerate learning, and facilitate success.

3) *School-engineered social support systems have their greatest impact on minority students when such systems are fundamentally bicultural in design.* Plans for instituting methods of social support and mentorship must also foster among both students and school personnel a real appreciation for and the critical utilization of community-based resources and *funds of knowledge*, particularly in the areas of curriculum and pedagogy, classroom social structure, and school governance. The work involved in mastering new knowledge forms can be both empowering and enriching, but only when students' own cultural knowledge is validated and refined.

REFERENCES

Ansen, A. R. , Cook, T. D., Habib, F., Grady, M. K., Hayes, N. & Comer, J. P. (1991). The Comer school developmental program: A theoretical analysis. *Urban Education,* 26 (1), 56-82.

Bernstein, B. (1973). *Class, codes, and control,* Vol. 3. London, Routledge & Kegan Paul.

Bourdieu, P. (1977). Cultural reproduction and social reproduction. In J. Karabel & A. H. Halsey (Eds.), *Power and ideology in education* (pp. 487-511). New York: Oxford University Press.

Bourdieu, P. (1986). The forms of capital. In J. G. Richardson (Ed.), *Handbook of theory and research for the sociology of education.* New York: Greenwood Press.

Bourdieu, P. & Passeron, J. C. (1977b). *Reproduction in education, society, and culture.* London: Sage.

Boysen, T. C. (1992). Irreconcilable differences: Effective urban schools versus restructuring. *Education and Urban Society,* 25 (1), 85-95.

Bronfenbrenner, U. (1979). *The ecology of human development: Experiments by nature and design.* Cambridge: Harvard University Press.

Cicourel, A. V. & H. Mehan. (1985). Universal development, stratifying practices and status attainment. *Research in social stratification and mobility, 4:* 3-27.

Cohen, E. (1983). Talking and working together: Status interaction and learning. In P. Peterson, L. C. Wilkinson, & E. M. Hallison (Eds.), *The social context of education.* Orlando: Academic Press.

Cole, M. & Griffin, P. (1987). *Contextual factors in education.* Madison: Wisconsin Center for Education Research.

Comer, J. P. (1980). *School power.* New York: The Free Press.

Comer, J. P. (1988). Educating poor minority children. *The Scientific American, 259* (5), 2-48.

Cookson, P. W., Jr., & Persell, C. H. (1985). *Preparing for power: America's elite boarding schools.* New York: Basic Books.

Erickson, F. & J. Schultz. (1982). *The counselor as gatekeeper.* New York: Academic Press.

Farkas, G., R. P. Grobe, R. P., Sheehan, D. & Shuan, Y. (1990). Cultural resources and school success: Gender, ethnicity, and poverty groups within an urban school district. *American Sociological Review, 55,* 127-142.

Freire, P. (1973). *Education for critical consciousness.* New York: Continuum.

Garbarino, J., Dubrow, N., Kostelny, K. & Pardo, C. (1992). *Children in danger: Coping with the consequences of community violence.* San Francisco: Jossey-Bass, Inc.

Giroux, H. A. (1983). *Theory and resistance in education: A pedagogy for the opposition.* New York: Bergin and Garvey.

Granovetter, M. S. (1982). The strength of weak ties: A network theory revisited. In P. V. Marsden & N. Lin (Eds.), *Social structure and network analysis* (pp. 105-130). Beverly Hills: Sage Publications.

Greenberg, J. B. (1989). *Funds of knowledge: Historical constitution, social distribution and transmission.* Paper presented at the annual meeting of the Society of Applied Anthropology, Santa Fe, New Mexico.

Heath, S. B. (1986). *Ways with words.* Cambridge: Cambridge University Press.

Ianni, F. A. (1989). *The search for structure: A report on American youth today.* New York: The Free Press.

Lareau, A. (1989). *Home advantage: Social class and parental intervention in elementary education.* New York: Falmer Press.

Levin, H. (1988*). Accelerated schools for at-risk students.* Stanford University: Center for Policy Research in Education

Lin, N. (1982). Social resources and instrumental action. In P. V. Marsden & N. Lin (Eds.), *Social structure and network analysis* (pp. 105-130). Beverly Hills: Sage Publications.

McDermott, R. P., Gospodinoff, K. & Aron, J. (1978). Criteria for an ethnographically adequate description of concerted activities and their contexts. *Semiotica, 24* (3/4), 245-275.

McDonough, P. M. (1994). Buying and selling higher education. *Journal of Higher Education, 65 (*4), 427-447.

McLaughlin, M. W., Irby, M. A. & Langman, J. (1994). *Urban sancturaries: Neighborhood organizations in the lives and futures of inner-city youth.* San Francisco: Jossey-Bass Publishers.

Mehan, H. (1992). Understanding inequality in schools: The contribution of interpretive studies. *Sociology of Education, 65,* (1), 1-20.

Mehan, H., Villanueva, I., Hubbard, L., Lintz, A., Okamoto, D., & Adams, J. (1995). *Constructing school success: The consequences of untracking low-achieving students.* Cambridge: Cambridge University Press.

Moll, L., Amanti, C., Neff, D., & Gonzalez, N. (1992). Funds of knowledge: Using a qualitative approach to connect homes and classrooms. *Theory Into Practice, 31* (2), 132-141.

Natriello, G., McDill, E. L., & Pallas, A. M. (1990). *Schooling disadvantaged children: Racing against catastrophe.* New York: Teachers College Press.

Nestmann, F. & Hurrelman, K. (1994). *Social networks and social support in childhood and adolescence.* New York: de Gruyter.

Ninio, A. & Bruner, J. (1978). The achievement & antecedents of labeling. *Journal of Child Language*, 5, 5-15.

Oakes, J. (1986). *Keeping track.* New Haven: Yale University Press.

Padilla, A. (1980). *Acculturation: Theory, models, and some new findings.* Colorado: Westview Press.

Pearlin, L. I. (1989). The sociological study of stress. *Journal of Health and Social Behavior, 30,* 241-256.

Sennett, R. & Cobb, J. (1972*). The hidden injuries of class.* New York: Vintage Books.

Simpson, C. H. & Rosenholtz, S. J. (1986). Classroom structure and the social construction of ability. In J. G. Richardson (Ed.), *Handbook of Theory and Research for the Sociology of Education.* New York: Greenwork Press.

Stanton-Salazar, R. D. (in press). The development of coping strategies among urban Latino youth: A focus on network orientatation and help-seeking behavior. In M. Montero-Sieburth & F. A. Villarruel (Eds.), *Latino adolescents: Building upon our diversity.* New York: Garland Press.

Stanton-Salazar, R. D. (1997). A social capital framework for understanding the socialization of racial minority children and youth. *Harvard Educational Review 67* (1): 1-40.

Stanton-Salazar, R. D. & Dornbusch, S. M. (1995). Social capital and the social reproduction of inequality: Informational networks among Mexican-origin high school students. *Sociology of education, 68* (2), 116-135.

Tharp, R. & Gallimore, R. (1988). *Rousing minds to life: Teaching, learning and schooling in social context.* Cambridge: Cambridge University Press.

Vásquez, O. A. (1992). Language as a resource: Lessons from la clase *mágica.* In B. Arias & U. Casanova (Eds.), *Bilingual education: Politics, research, and practice* (pp. 199-223) (92nd Yearbook of the National Society for the Study of Education).

Vásquez, O. A. (1994). The magic of *La Clase Mágica*: Enhancing the learning potential of bilingual children. *Australian Journal of Language and Literacy, 17,* (2), 120-128.

Vásquez, O. A., Pease-Alvarez, L., & Shannon, S. (1994). *Pushing boundaries: Language and culture in a Mexicano community.* New York: Cambridge University Press.

Vásquez, O. A.(1996). A model system of institutional linkages: Transforming the educational pipeline. In A. Hurtado, R. Figueroa, & E. E. Garcia (Eds.), *Strategic Interventions in Education: Expanding the Latina/Latino Pipeline* (pp. 137-166). The University of California Latino Eligibility Project.

Vygotsky, L. (1986). *Thought and language.* Cambridge: MIT Press.

Villanueva, I. (1990). *Cultural practices and language use: Three generations of change.* Unpublished doctoral dissertation, University of California, San Diego, La Jolla.

Werner, E. E. & Smith, R. S. (1982). *Vulnerable but invincible: A longitudinal study of resilient children and youth.* New York: McGraw-Hill.

Williams, T. & W. Kornblum. (1985). *Growing up poor.* Lexington: Lexington Books.

Willis, P. (1977*). Learning to labour: How working class kids get working class jobs.* Westmead, England: Saxon House Press.

Wood, D., Bruner, J. S. & Ross, G. (1976). The role of tutoring in problem solving. *Journal of Child Psychology and Psychiatry, 17,* 89-100.

Zweigenhaft, Richard L. & Domhoff, G. W. (1991). *Blacks in the white establishment?: A study of race and class in America.* New Haven: Yale University Press.

10. *The Persistence of African American College Students: How National Data Inform a Hopwood-Proof Retention Strategy*

Patricia Somers

INTRODUCTION

Over the past two decades, students have made important gains in educational achievement and attainment (National Center for Educational Statistics, 1999). For example, more high school students are taking core and advanced placement courses. In turn, more are attending post-secondary institutions when they graduate from high school. However, these gains reflect the average for all students, and ignore important differences by ethnicity.

There are substantial differences in the educational achievement and attainment of African American and white students. Parent's educational attainment, a key factor in positive educational outcomes rose significantly for African Americans. In 1997, 78 percent of mothers and 79 percent of fathers of 15-18 year-old African American students had at least a high school diploma, up from 36 percent and 26 percent in 1972 (National Center for Educational Statistics, 1999). These changes alone may have contributed to the increased educational attainment of African American students in the past 20 years (Jencks, Smith, Acland, Bane, Cohen, Gintis, Hines, and Michelson, 1972).

While the rates of high school completion are similar, African American students who complete high school were less likely to enroll in college and complete a baccalaureate degree than white students. While the percentage of African Americans who attend postsecondary education has risen in the past 20 years, the increase has not kept pace with enrollment patterns for white students. The college going rate for African American students rose to 79 percent of that for white students in 1997, an increase of only 10 percent since 1971 (National Center for Educational Statistics, 1999).

The college completion rates for both white and African American students has risen since 1971. However, the rate of completion is rising faster for whites than for African Americans. Because of this disparity, completion rates for African American students have remained at about one-half the rate of white students for the last 20 years (National Center for Educational Statistics 1999).

The shifting legal sands over affirmative action have focused attention on the admission of African American students to postsecondary educational institutions. While this battle rages in the courtrooms and legislatures of America, less attention has been given to the academic achievement of African American students once they have enrolled in higher education. What are the factors that influence the persistence of majority and African American students? What are the similarities and differences? How can this information be used to inform new initiatives on persistence?

This chapter describes a national study which compares the variables influencing African American and white college student persistence, provides social commentary on the differences, and evaluates retention strategies for universities based on guidelines in recent court cases.

Legal Background

What *Bakke* (1978) did in the Supreme Court for higher education admission programs--race could be a "plus" factor--*Hopwood* (1996) undid in the Fifth Circuit Court by ruling that race could not be a "plus" factor. From being merely vogue in the 60s, affirmative action programs escalated to the accepted way of doing business in educational institutions (and other arenas) in the 70s and 80s. However, in the 90s, affirmative action programs sustained a direct attack. As a result of cases like *Hopwood*, some affirmative action programs were examined, challenged, overruled, and ultimately discarded, and more legal challenges are underway.

Considering the fact that *Hopwood* was a Fifth Circuit Court ruling, not a Supreme Court decision, its influence on affirmative action programs was extensive. When the Fifth Circuit Court judges (in *Hopwood*) ruled that the University of Texas Law School could not use race as a "plus" factor in determining admission and further stated that the need for diversity and remedying past discriminations could not justify the admissions program currently in place at that institution, a cornerstone of anti-affirmative action ideology was firmly cemented into law. The impact of that ruling reached far beyond the Fifth Circuit and higher education. Likewise, *Taxman* challenged and reversed affirmation action lay-off policies in employment and *Boston Latin School* (Boston Latin, 1999) challenged and overturned affirmative action admissions programs in K-12 education.

The courts have not been the only battleground where the anti-affirmative action war has been waged. Legislators and voters have been called upon to make decisions regarding the use of affirmative actions programs. What *Hopwood* and others have accomplished in the courts, Proposition 209 has accomplished by popular initiative. As Californians voiced their desire to change the state's constitution in order to dismantle California's use of affirmative action in employment and college admissions, so possibly those citizens may have been reflecting the sentiments of an entire nation--Proposition 209 was quickly followed by Initiative 200 in the state of Washington. Only time will reveal if other states will join this movement.

The impact of *Hopwood* and its progeny on college students is enormous. Race cannot be used as a factor in admissions, financial aid, or any program. Only "benign" factors not involving ethnicity (family income, residence, etc.) can be used as criteria for programs at colleges and universities. Thus, the search for "non-discriminatory" factors that influence student persistence, but will especially benefit African American students, is crucial to the success of such programs in the post-*Hopwood* era.

Review of Literature

The research on persistence was given a big boost by the National Postsecondary Student Aid Study (NPSAS) of 1987. Prior to the development of NPSAS, much of the research had been at the institutional level or using small, select national samples. NPSAS provided an opportunity to study persistence using a large, national sample with an extensive set of economic, demographic, and college experience variables.

A series of studies using NPSAS (1987 and 1990) were done by St. John and his associates (St. John 1994; St. John and Starkey 1995a, 1995b; Hippensteel, St. John, and Starkey 1996). For instance, St. John, Paulsen, and Starkey (1996) examined the influence of finances on college choice and persistence decisions. St. John (1992) focused on persistence by traditional college students whose persistence was negatively influenced by the tuition amount. Several studies (Andrieu 1990, 1991; Andrieu and St. John 1993; St. John and Andrieu 1995) examined within-year persistence of graduate students.

Cofer, Somers, and Associates have used NPSAS:93 and NPSAS:96 in a series of persistence studies that added debtload and other variables to the St. John model. DeAngelis (1997) extended the work of Andrieu and St. John on graduate student persistence using NPSAS:93. Cofer and Somers (1997, 1998, 1999a, 1999b) first used thresholds of debt in the analysis, and found that debt had a significant and negative influence on persistence of undergraduates at public and private colleges and students at two-year colleges using NPSAS:93 and 96.

Studies of minority student persistence have used some of the same variables that were found in NPSAS studies. In a meta analysis of studies from the 1970s and early 1980s, Lenning (1982) identified six factors that influenced minority persistence: ability, background, aspirations and motivation, personality and values, institutional variables, and college experiences. Thomas (1986) found that loans had a greater negative impact on the persistence of African American students than any other group. Nora, Cabrera, Hagedorn, and Pascarella (1996) found college experiences, achievement, and environmental pull contributed most to persistence of minority students. Stith and Russell (1994) indicated that the faculty student interaction was key in African American student persistence. Porter (1989) discovered that African Americans were more likely to persist at private colleges, SES had some influence, and grants and family resources were the primary means of financing college, except for African American students, who used mostly loans. Janus (1997) identified financial aid as a major component in persistence. Blanchette (1997) found that an additional grant of $1,000 per semester would increase persistence of African Americans by 7%, but that loans would not influence persistence. She also said that income, parents' education, and test scores were all good predictors of minority student persistence.

Conceptual Framework

The framework for this study came from sociology and economics. Sociological theory (Alexander and Eckland 1980; Blau and Duncan 1967; Eckland and Alexander 1980; Parsons 1959; Thomas, Alexander, and Eckland 1979; Sewell and Shah 1967; Sewell and Hauser 1975; Trent and Medskar 1968; Wolfle 1985) suggests that background, family, academic ability, and aspiration variables should be included in any research on student attainment. From economic theory (Becker 1964; Denison 1964; McPherson 1982; Rusbult 1980; Schultz 1960) comes the notion that students invest in their education. Student aid and demand studies (Corrazzini, Dugan, and Grabowski 1963; Hoenack and Weiler 1975; Hopkins 1974; Stafford, Lindstedt, and Lynn 1984; Tannen 1978) indicate that students "purchase" more education when prices are lower and less when prices are higher. Subsidies, in the form of student financial aid, lower the net cost of attendance. The research cited in the literature review generally used models that integrated these theories, as represented by background, price, and college experience variables.

Method

The method employed for this study follows that of St. John and Associates (Andrieu 1990, 1991; Andrieu and St. John 1993; Cofer 1988; Cofer and Somers 1997, 1998, 1999a, 1999b; DeAngelis 1998; Hippensteel, St. John and Starkey 1996; St. John 1992,1994; St. John and Andrieu 1995; St. John and Starkey 1995a, 1995b; Starkey 1993).

The National Postsecondary Student Aid Study of 1996 was used for the study. All four-year undergraduate students were included in the sample. The sample was bifurcated into two cohorts: white students and African American students. No other ethnicity groups were included for this analysis. The sample size was 1,482 for African American students and 11,292 for white students.

The dependent variable was within-year progression of students from the fall 1995 to the spring semester 1996. Thirty-five independent variables within six factors were included in the analysis. The factors were background, aspiration and achievement, institutional characteristics, college experiences, current year price and subsidies, and accumulated debt load.

For a model where the outcome variable is dichotomous (such as this study), the standard regression formula (Ordinary Least Squared method) can seriously mis-estimate the dependent variable. Instead, a technique known as logistic regression (Aldrich and Nelson 1984; Cabrera 1994) was used. Since a student chooses to persist or not, the outcomes are dichotomous: either yes or no (coded as 1 or 0). The resulting graph of the relationship is not a straight line, but a curved line bounded by 0 and 1.

The beta coefficients were converted to delta-p's using a method recommended by Petersen (1984). The delta-p measured change in the dependent variable. For dichotomous variables, the delta-p provides a measure of the extent to which the outcome is likely to change if a student had the specified characteristic. For example, a delta-p of 0.050 for females was interpreted as increasing the probability of enrollment by 5.0 percentage points for this group. With continuous variables, the delta-p was interpreted as meaning that a change in a unit measure will change the probability of the outcome by a certain percentage. For example, a delta-p statistic of .0450 per $1000 of financial aid indicates that the probability of attendance or persistence increases by 4.5 percent per $1000 of financial aid awarded. The delta-p was particularly useful in financial aid policy studies because of its ease in application.

Results
While previous NPSAS studies have shown that background variables are important in student persistence, we found that this was the case for white students but not for African Americans. No background variables were significant for African American students in this study (Table 1). Younger, low income, dependent, and married white students were all more likely to persist. Male and older white students were less likely to persist.

For white students, parent's educational level (some college or above) and student aspirations for a degree were positively associated with persistence. For African American students, only the aspiration for an advanced college degree was significant and positively associated with persistence.

The college experience variables presented an interesting picture. African American students were more likely to persist if they were sophomores, juniors, or seniors, lived on campus, or attended full-time. They were less likely to persist if they had low GPAs. White students, on the other hand, were more likely to persist if they lived on campus, attended a private college, had high GPAs, or attended a doctoral institution. They were less likely to persist if they had a low GPA or took a remedial class. However, when effect size was compared, the delta Ps for African Americans were double or triple that for white students.

Table 1: Variables Affecting Persistence of African American and White College Students

Variable	African Americans		Whites	
	Coefficient	Delta P	Coefficient	Delta P
Gender	-2.2678	-0.0357	-0.1197*	-0.0121
Under 22	0.3549	0.0378	0.1125**	0.0104
Over 30	0.2641	0.0291	-0.1477**	-0.0151
High income	0.5402	0.0537	0.4585	0.0371
Low income	0.0110	0.0013	0.0095**	0.0009
Dependent	0.5009	0.0505	0.3167*	0.0271
Married	-0.2200	-0.0288	0.1339**	0.0123
Mother-Coll.	0.0557	0.0066	0.2283*	0.0202
Father-Coll.	0.0585	0.0069	0.2845*	0.0246
Aspire to B.A.	-0.1519	-0.0194	0.2035*	0.0182
Aspire adv. degree	0.8347**	0.0745	0.6479	0.0487
High test score	-0.0160	-0.0019	0.1766*	0.0159
Low test score	-0.0695	-0.0086	0.0439**	0.0042
Soph.	0.8790**	0.0772	0.6561	0.0491
Jr.	0.8557**	0.0758	0.5736	0.0443
Sr.	1.5610**	0.1077	1.1646	0.0720
Live on campus	0.5785*	0.0567	0.2465*	0.0217
Private college	0.4535	0.0466	0.1572*	0.0143
Full time student	0.9901**	0.0835	0.9864	0.0651
High GPA	0.4847	0.0492	0.1244**	0.0115
Low GPA	-0.5801*	-0.0857	-0.4029*	-0.0456
No GPA	-1.5202**	-0.2878	-1.0402	-0.1477
Remedial course	0.3877	0.0408	-0.0815**	-0.0081
Doc institution	0.1271	0.0147	0.0675**	0.0064
Work full time	-0.4214	-0.0591	-0.0843**	-0.0084
Tuition $	-0.0002**	0.0000	-0.0001	0.0000
Total grant $	0.3033**	0.0329	0.1500	0.0137
Yrs total loan $	0.1544**	0.0177	0.1398	0.0128
Work study $	0.0014	0.0002	0.5011*	0.0399
High debt	-0.5552	0.0814	-0.5195*	-0.0614
Mid debt	0.0104	0.0013	-0.3617*	-0.0403
Low debt	-0.5977*	-0.0888	-0.4374*	-0.0501

Note: $*p < .05.$ $**p < .01.$

The price and debt variables were also an interesting contrast. African American students had a small positive delta P for tuition, which meant that for every $1,000 increase in tuition they were slightly more likely to persist. As in previous studies, persistence of African Americans was positively associated with grants and work-study, although the magnitude of this effect was smaller. Further, the amount of current year loans was positively associated with persistence by African American students. A low level of accumulated debt was negatively associated with persistence, indicating loan avoidance by some African American students. White student persistence was positively associated with receiving work-study funds and negatively associated with all three levels of debt. This model predicted 87% of the persistence decisions for African American students and 88% for white students.

Discussion

The results have interesting implications. Surprisingly, none of the background variables were significant for African American students, while six of the background variables were significantly associated with persistence for white students. This is in direct contrast with many previous studies that found background variables significant for African American students. Why the change?

College experiences do make a difference in student persistence. For African American students in particular, certain college experiences encourage persistence. This suggests strategies that could be used to enhance persistence for all students while being particularly beneficial for African Americans that would likely survive legal challenges.

We were also surprised to find a positive coefficient for tuition for African American students. Is increased cost the "price of admission" to the middle class for African American students?

These findings generally indicate shifts from previous research on African American student persistence. We discuss this more in the following section, and suggest implications for practice at the end of the chapter.

Another perspective from which to analyze these results involves comparison with barriers to access. Demographic, socio-economic, and legislative trends have reduced the effects of college access barriers that have served to 'sift' students from various socioeconomic backgrounds into certain entry points into higher and postsecondary education (Carnegie Council 1980). Similarly, as this chapter has addressed, just as barriers exist for access to higher and postsecondary education, barriers also exist for persistence in higher and postsecondary education.

Two primary aspects of social stratification exert influence here; institutional stratification, and the stratification concomitant with students' social origins. First, Trow (1984) identified that a definite stratification system exists in U.S. higher education, and used Merton's (1968) concept of the 'Matthew Effect' to illustrate the effects of cumulative advantage and disadvantage for institutions of higher education. As Hearn (1980) described, "In an on-going and largely irreversible process, existing status hierarchies among institutions are reproduced and elaborated." As a result, a series of socioeconomic links begin to form a chain; the institution a student attends influences educational attainment (Wegner and Sewell 1970), and the amount of education obtained affects eventual socioeconomic attainments (Sewell 1971).

Second, in the context of the findings for African-American students that contradict some of the previous research, students' social origins are also at work here. On one hand, the educational experiences that serve as barriers to persistence for students from historically underrepresented backgrounds in higher and postsecondary education are well documented. These include Luttrell's (1989) research on working-class women in adult basic education programs, and Warren's (1995) autobiographical essay describing the college campus as a 'cultural shock,' among others.

On the other hand, a shift to an increasingly conceptual sociological approach to investigating educational outcomes supports the findings in this study. According to Astin (1993), student background variables do not exert statistically significant influence on outcomes, and this was confirmed in a recent study of satisfaction with college for first-generation college students, low-income students, and students with disabilities (Vander Putten, 1998). These contradictions in the relevant research warrant further investigation.

Despite recent legal intrusions to the contrary, diversity issues continue to be embraced on most college campuses. The strength, courage, and dreams of these new students provided the motivation for colleges and universities to view their institutional missions in a different light. Unfortunately, the gaps between black and white identified earlier in this chapter continue to widen, as do those between rich and poor. As Pogue (1990) stated:

> Our prisons and the conditions that give rise to imprisonment are doing a better job of recruiting and graduating men and women who are African American, Latino American and Native American than are most of our

institutions of higher education. For a host of well-known reasons, it is projected that by the year 2000, some 70 percent of African American males will be in prison, dead, on drugs, or alcoholics (p. 2).

As a result, it is important to recognize that the phenomenon of success in American students at all educational levels is less well understood than are the dimensions of failure. One notable example of this philosophical approach is that by the time educationally disadvantaged children matriculate into postsecondary education, they have often been long-identified as students who are at 'high-risk' for dropping out of school, i.e., failure. In reality, these students have been successful, or 'survivors' in their educational careers leading up to their entry, persistence, and graduation from postsecondary education.

Implications for Practice

African Americans at predominantly White universities do not persist as well as their counterparts attending historically black institutions. Gloria, Kurplus, Hamilton, and Wilson (1999) found that on white campuses, African American students persisted at (66.3%) of the rate for HBCUs.

This demonstrates the need for an effective and aggressive persistence program at white campuses in particular. In tailoring an effective program, a cursory review of studies implicated the key variables to be included in a sound retention program: aggressive advisement, tutorial services, faculty and peer mentors, African American role model(s), and financial aid initiatives. The goal of the retention program should be, at a minimum, to encourage and cultivate respect for authority, interest and contentment in college, degree aspiration, and positive social interactions.

Court cases like *Hopwood* and initiatives like Proposition 209 in California have gutted affirmative action programs in colleges and universities. While compensation for past discrimination in admissions is more limited now, this research indicates that once African American students are admitted, there are a number of ways in which their persistence can be improved. And, a number of these strategies are "Hopwood-proof," in that they address concerns of all students, but are likely to be much more effective for African American students. We divide these strategies into two parts: college experiences and price.

Our study found that African American students were more likely to persist if they were sophomores, juniors, or seniors, and less likely if they were first-year students. This points to the crucial nature of the first year experience and the importance of special programs that integrate students into the social and academic environment of campus. Advising and academic support programs are important in encouraging persistence. Indeed, in a previous study, we found that at-risk students were at least as likely to persist as all other students if they were appropriately placed in remedial programs (Cofer and Somers 1997).

Likewise, we found that both African American and white students were more likely to persist if they lived on campus. However, the effect size for African American students was twice that for white students. Incentives for living on campus should be made available to all students. With equal incentive for all students regardless of race and gender, special mixing of roommates could be used to optimize persistence. These incentives might include residence hall "scholarships."

Academic integration into the life on campus is likewise important to persistence. In this study, as in other studies, students with lower GPAs were less likely to persist. Methods to bring students into the academic mainstream of campus include work study positions in academic departments (a positive variable in the persistence of white, but not African American, students), academic organizations, and contact with faculty. Kobrak (1992) validated the importance of having faculty involved in the efforts to assist minority students. Stressing the need for more faculty involvement and less administrative involvement, Kobrak pointed out:

> University presidents thus have opted to channel most of their retention efforts for disadvantaged Black students through administrators housed in a branch of their institution's centralized staff, usually in units reporting directly to the president's or provost's office. These specially created offices have often attracted deeply committed individuals. Many have achieved some, but not enough, success (p. 514).

While the pairing of white students is also important to persistence, the pairing of African American students with faculty and staff mentors (minority or majority) is particularly important in building an academic community, which in turn promotes persistence. There is one note of caution in this, however. A previous study (Cofer, Somers, and Wilkinson 1997) found that scholarly productivity of African American faculty might be influenced by the additional time they spend mentoring students as compared to their white colleagues. If faculty are expected to mentor students, this commitment must be included in the peer review, promotion, and tenure evaluation.

The cost of higher education influences the persistence of African American students. In our study, full-time students were more likely to persist and students who worked more than 30 hours per week were less likely to persist. The economics of these figures is clear: with additional aid that would allow students to attend school full time, persistence would improve.

Our research also points to several price-related variables that can be integrated into a persistence program. First, tuition has a small positive effect on the persistence of African American students. This suggests that keeping tuition increases small and matching any increases with financial aid would promote the persistence of African Americans and lower income students regardless of ethnicity.

Second, African Americans and all low-income students would respond positively to institutional grants. The grants would help keep the cost of attendance affordable for all students.

Third, work-study can be used more effectively to promote student persistence. Campus employers of work-study students should be coached on how important their role is in the integration of the student into campus life. This type of aid can also encourage the persistence of African American students if campus employers understand their important role in the persistence process.

Fourth, African American students should not be "loaded up" with debt. Finding other sources of money for the financial aid package will encourage persistence of all students. Moreover, an institutional loan program, particularly one that would "forgive" part of the loan or have a reasonable income contingent repayment plan for graduates with low paying jobs would also be an effective persistence tool.

Finally, as indicated at the beginning of this chapter, it is important to continue to improve the educational achievement of the parents of African American students. As the parental educational level increases, so do the aspirations of the children. With higher aspirations, more African American students will apply to colleges.

Summary

This chapter reviewed a national study of student persistence and found that college experiences, current price, and accumulated debt all influenced the persistence of African American students. We indicated a number of ways that these data could be used to develop effective persistence programs. Moreover, since the programs would benefit white students while being very effective for retaining African American students, these persistence strategies could well withstand legal challenges.

REFERENCES

Aldrich, J. H., and F. D. Nelson. 1984. *Linear Probability, Logit and Probit Models.* Beverly Hill, CA: Sage Publications.

Alexander, K. L., and B. K. Eckland. 1975. Basic attainment processes: A replication and extension. *Sociology of Education* 48:457-95.

Andrieu, S. C. 1990. Graduate student persistence: The development of a conceptual model. Paper presented at the Mid South Educational Research Association Annual Meeting, New Orleans, Louisiana.

Andrieu, S. C. 1991. The influence of background, graduate experience, aspirations, expected earnings, and financial commitment on within-year persistence of students enrolled in graduate programs. Ph.D. diss., University of New Orleans, New Orleans, Louisiana.

Andrieu, S. C., and E. P. St. John. 1993. The influence of prices on graduate student persistence. *Research in Higher Education* 34 (4): 399-425.

Astin, A. 1993. *What matters in college? Four critical years revisited.* San Francisco: Jossey-Bass.

"Background: Boston Latin School Sued to Admit White Teenage Girls!" 1999. In Adversity.Net [database on-line], [updated 28 March 1999; cited June 9, 1999]. Available from http://www.adversity.net/c4_tbdhtml

Bakke v. Board of Regents of the University of California. 1978. 438 U.S. 265.

Becker, G. S. 1964. *Human Capital: A Theoretical and Empirical Analysis with Special Reference to Higher Education.* New York: Columbia University Press.

Blanchette, Cornelia. 1994. Higher education grants effective at increasing minorities' chances of graduating. Testimony before the Subcommittee on Education, Arts, Humanities, Committee on Labor and Human Resources, U.S. Senate. Ed370505.

Blau, P. M., and O. D. Duncan. 1967. *The American Occupational Structure.* New York: John Wiley and Sons.

Bowen, H. 1977. *Investment in learning: Individual and Social Value of American Education.* San Francisco: Jossey-Bass.

Cabrera, A. F. 1994. Logistic regression analysis in higher education: An applied perspective. *Higher Education: Handbook of Theory and Research.* Ed. J. C. Smart. New York: Agathon Press, 225-56.

Carnegie Council on Policy Studies in Higher Education. 1980. *Three thousand futures: The next twenty years for higher education.* San Francisco: Jossey-Bass.

Cofer, J. 1998. Decade of indecision: The impact of federal policy on student persistence, 1987-1996. Ed.D. diss., University of Arkansas at Little Rock, Little Rock, Arkansas.

Cofer, J., and P. Somers. 1997a. Mortgaging their future: Debtload and undergraduate persistence. Paper presented at the Association for the Study of Higher Education Annual Meeting, at Albuquerque, New Mexico.

Cofer, J. & P. Somers. 1997b. Productivity Funding and Student Enrollment. Paper presented at American Educational Research Association Conference, Memphis, Tennessee.

Cofer, J., and P. Somers. 1998. I Sold my Soul to the Company Store: How Debtload Influences Student Decisions in Public and Private Colleges. Paper presented at the American Educational Research Association Annual Meeting, San Diego, California.

Cofer, J., P. Somers, and L. Wilkinson. 1997. Faculty Productivity: An Analysis from the National Study of Postsecondary Faculty. Association for the Study of Higher Education Annual Meeting, Albuquerque, NM.

Cofer, J. & P. Somers. 1999a. Deeper in Debt: The Impact of the 1992 Reauthorization of the Higher Education Act on Within-year Persistence. Association for Institutional Research Forum, Seattle, WA.

Cofer, J. & P. Somers. 1999b. A National Study of Persistence at Two-year Colleges. American Educational Research Association Conference, Montreal, Canada.

Corrazinni, A. D., D. Dugan, and H. Grabowski. 1972. Determinants of distributional aspects of enrollment in U. S. higher education. *Journal of Higher Education* 43:39-50.

DeAngelis, S. 1997. The influence of background aspirations, financial aid and expected earnings on within-year persistence of graduate students. Ed.D. diss., University of Arkansas at Little Rock, Little Rock, Arkansas.

Denison, E. F. 1964. *Measuring the Contribution of Education, and the Residual, to Economic Growth.* Paris: Organization for Economic development and Cooperation.

Eckland, B. K., and K. L. Alexander. 1980. The National Longitudinal Study of the high school class of 1972. *Research in the Sociology of Education and Socialization* 1:189-222.

Gloria, Alberta, Sharon E. Robinson Kurplus, Kimberly D. Hamilton, and Marcia S. Willson. 1999. African American students' persistence at a predominantly white university: Influences of social support, university comfort, and self beliefs. *Journal of College Student Development* 40 (3): 257-68.

Hearn, J. (1980). Academic and nonacademic influences on the college destinations of 1980 high school graduates. *Sociology of Education* 64:158-171.

Hippensteel, D. G., E. P. St. John, and J. B. Starkey. 1996. Influence of tuition and student aid on within-year persistence by adults in 2-year colleges. *Community College Journal of Research and Practice* 20:233-42.

Hoenack, S. A., and W. C. Weiler. 1977. The demand for higher education and institutional enrollment forecasting. Unpublished paper, University of Minnesota, Minneapolis.

Hopkins, T. D. 1974. Higher education enrollment demand. *Economic Inquiry* 12:53-65.

Hopwood v Texas. 1996. 78 F.3d 932 (5th Cir.), 116 S. Ct. 2580.

Jencks, C., M. Smith, R. Acland, C. Bane, A. Cohen, C. Gintis, R, Hines, and M. Michelson. 1972. *Inequality: A reassessment of the effect of family and schooling in America.* Basic Books: New York, New York.

Luttrell, W. (1989). Working-class women's ways of knowing: Effects of gender, race, and class. *Sociology of Education* 62:33-46.

Merton, R. (1968). The Matthew effect in science: The reward and communication systems of science. *Science* 199:55-63.

McPherson, M. S. 1982. Higher education investment or expense? *Financing Higher Education: The Public Investment.* Ed. J. C. Hoy, and M. H. Bernstein. Boston: Auburn House.

National Center for Educational Statistics. 1999. *The Condition of Education: 1998.* Available online at http://www.nces.ed.gov.

Parsons, T. P. 1959. The social class as a social system. *Harvard Educational Review* 29:297-318.

Petersen, T. 1984. A comment on presenting results of logit and probit models. *American Sociological Review,* 50(1):130-31.

Porter, Oscar. 1989. The influence of institutional control on the persistence of minority students: A descriptive analysis. Paper presented at Annual Meeting of American Educational Research Association, San Francisco, California.

Rusbult, C. E. 1980. Satisfaction and commitment in friendships. Representative Research in *Social Psychology* 11:78-95.

Schultz, T. W. 1960. Capital formation by education. *Journal of Political Economy 86:571-83.*

Sewell, W. H., and R M. Hauser. 1975. Causes and consequences of higher education: Models of the status and attainment process. *Schooling and Achievement in American Society* 9-27. Ed. W. H. Sewell, R. M. Hauser, and D. L. Featherman. New York: Academic Press.

Sewell, W. H., and V. P. Shah. 1967. Socioeconomic status, intelligence, and the attainment of higher education. *Sociology of Education* 40:1-23.

St. John, E. P. 1992. The influence of prices on within-year persistence by traditional college-age students in four-year colleges. *Journal of Student Financial Aid* 22 (1):27-38

St. John, E. P. 1994. The influence of student aid on within-year persistence by traditional-age students in 4-year colleges. *Research in Higher Education* 35 (4): 455-80.

St. John, E. P., M. B. Paulsen, and J. B. Starkey. 1996. The Nexus between college choice and persistence. *Research in Higher Education* 37 (2): 175-220.

St. John, E. P., and S. C. Andrieu. 1995. The influence of price subsidies on within-year persistence by graduate students. *Higher Education* 29(2):143-68.

St. John, E. P., and J. Starkey. 1995a. The influence of prices and price subsidies on within-year persistence by students in community colleges. *Educational Evaluation and Policy Analysis* 17 (2) 149-65.

St. John, E. P., and J. Starkey. 1995b. An alternative to net price: Assessing the influence of prices and subsidies on within-year persistence. *Journal of Higher Education* 66 (2): 156-86.

Stafford, K. L., S. B. Lindstedt, and A. D. Lynn. 1984. Social and economic factors affecting participation in higher education. *Journal of Higher Education* 55:590-607.

Starkey, J. 1993. The influence of price on persistence by non-traditional-age undergraduate students. Paper presented at the American Educational Research Association Annual Meeting, Atlanta, Georgia.

Stith, Patricia and Fitz Russell. 1994. Faculty/student interaction: Impact on student retention. Paper presented at Association for Institutional Research Forum, New Orleans, Louisiana.

Tannen, M.B. 1978. The investment motive for attending college. *Industrial and Labor Relations Review* 31:489-97.

Taxman v Piscataway. 1998. 91 F.3d 1547.

Thomas, G. E., K. L. Alexander, and B. K. Eckland. 1979. Access to higher education: The importance of race, sex, social class and academic credentials. *School Review* 2:133-156.

Trent, J. W., and L. L. Medskar. 1968. *Beyond High School.* San Francisco: Jossey-Bass.

Trippi, Joseph F., and Stanley B. Baker. 1989. Student residential correlates of black students grade performance and persistence at a predominantly white university campus. *Journal of College Student Development* 30 (2):136-43.

Trow, M. (1984). The analysis of status. In B. Clark (Ed.), *Perspectives on higher education: Eight disciplinary and comparative views* (pp. 132-164). Berkeley: University of California Press.

Vander Putten, J. (1998). *Student satisfaction with college: Looking into the TRIO mirror.* Paper presented at the American Educational Research Association Annual Meeting, San Diego, CA.

Warren, G. (1995). Another day's journey: An African-American in higher education. In

In B. Dews and C. Law (Eds.) *This fine place so far from home: Voices of academics from the working class*, 106-123. Philadelphia: Temple University Press.

Wolfe, L. M. 1985. Postsecondary educational attainment among whites and blacks. *American Education Research Journal* 22:501-25.

This research was sponsored by a grant from the American Educational Research Association which receives funds for its "AERA Grants Program" from the National Science Foundation and the U.S. Department of Education's National Center for Education Statistics and the Office of Educational Research and Improvement under NSF grant #RED-9452681. Opinions reflect those of the authors and do not necessarily reflect those of the granting agency.

11. *Academic Achievement of Latino Immigrants*

Lawrence Sáez

INTRODUCTION

Why is it that Hispanics lag behind in financial achievement and educational attainment compared to other ethnic groups? According to the 1990 U.S. Census Bureau, the median family income for Hispanics in current dollars was $23,431, lower than the median family income of $35,353 for all Americans. Nearly 50 percent of Hispanics 25 years old and over had a high school degree compared to over 77 percent for non-Hispanics. Less than 10 percent of the same age group had a bachelor's degree or higher, compared to 21 percent for non-Hispanics (U.S. Department of Commerce, 1990a, 1990b, and 1990c). Some attribute the comparative lack of financial and educational success of Latinos to a variety of cultural factors. These cultural factors include hypotheses of cultural pathology as well as those known as hypothesis about "cultural discontinuity" or "cultural incompatibility." In this essay, I will argue that although cultural factors may offer a more persuasive anecdotal account for the comparative financial and educational shortcomings of Latinos, the determining factor has been the socio-economic character of Hispanic immigrants. My analysis will suggest that the variable of socio-economic status (SES) goes further than cultural explanations in explaining the differences within different Hispanic groups. Moreover, in order to promote parity in the educational attainment and financial success of Hispanics in the US, this article offers recommendations relating to immigration policy.

Cultural explanations for success and failure
Latino culture is a popular theme in the explanation for the comparative
lack of success of Hispanics in this country. In this paper, educational
attainment will be defined by increased college and high school
graduation rates. Financial success will be defined by household and
individual poverty rates. Traditionally, there have been two types of
broad cultural explanations for the comparative lack of financial
success and educational attainment of Hispanics. One of these
explanations may be termed the "cultural dysfunction" hypothesis. The
other cultural explanation for the lack of financial and educational
success of Hispanics has been termed the "cultural deprivation,"
"cultural discontinuity," or "cultural incompatibility" hypotheses.
Although the so-called cultural dysfunction and the variants of the
cultural deprivation hypotheses reached opposite conclusions regarding
the lack of educational attainment and financial success of some
ethnic/racial groups, they shared an affinity in the notion that specific
cultural traits explained differences in educational and financial
performance between groups.
     One dominant theme of cultural explanations is the so-called
"cultural dysfunction" hypothesis. Cultural dysfunction assumes that
the lack of educational and financial success of some groups is
primordial, namely that they are inherently ingrained in a specific
culture. These themes have a long tradition and are variants of
Weberian hypotheses about the superiority of the Protestant ethic.
These Weberian cultural critiques have generally emphasized some
concrete traits that have prevented Hispanic groups from achieving
success. One principal exponent of the cultural dysfunction hypothesis
is the social critic Thomas Sowell. Sowell (1975) has argued that those
cultures that embrace "such traits as work, thrift and education - more
generally achievements involving planning and working for self-denial
in the present on emphasizing the logical and mundane over the heroic"
(p. 130). Moreover, Sowell (1994) also wrote that cultures "differ in
the relative significance they attach to time, noise, safety, cleanliness,
violence, thrift, intellect, sex and art. These differences, in turn, imply
differences in goal choices, economic efficiency, and political stability"
(p. 379). Other hypotheses of cultural pathology include arguments
about a "culture of failure" that presumably exists within Hispanic (and
African American) culture.
     The other cultural explanations for the lack of financial and
educational success of Hispanics have been termed the "cultural
deprivation," "cultural discontinuity," or "cultural incompatibility"

hypotheses (Phillips, 1992; Carter and Segura, 1979).   These hypotheses assume that the lack of educational or financial success of some groups is societally constructed.   The cultural discontinuity hypothesis has its roots on sociological research that has argued that the low achievement working class children could be attributed to an absence of early environment practices and to difficult child rearing practices that resulted in linguistic deficits.   Norman Friedman (1967) and Robert Anderson (1984) have applied these sociological findings to educational research.   Friedman (1967) has suggested that this culturally based explanation assumes that minority or immigrant children suffer from identifiable cognitive or social deficits. Anderson has argued that "a person's culture is a principal determiner of what he or she can come to know." (p. 8)

Variants of the cultural discontinuity or cultural incompatibility have been narrowed to account for the lagging educational attainment of Hispanics.   This type of argument about cultural deprivation figures prominently in public policy debates against bilingual education (Ogbu, 1978; Ogbu, 1993).   Another focus of these hypotheses is that Latinos do not succeed because there are incompatibilities between Latino culture and the host culture (Suarez-Orozco, 1989; Delgado-Gaitán, 1991; Trueba, 1983; Trueba, 1988; Guerra, 1970; Valencia, 1970).   One author (Cortese, 1992) has even suggested that "the cooperative orientation of Mexican American children may not be conducive to success in school." One recent book (Sosa, 1998) that highlighted this theme argued that "culture and our beliefs...actually holds us back in this country."

Conversely, culture has been used to explain a host of external factors that presumably account for the relative failure of Latinos in the United States.   One hypothesis is that the host culture adds extra barriers to success for Latinos in the form of a variety of native racism (Muñoz, 1986).   Other research (Dunn, Griggs, and Price, 1993) has suggested that environmental stimuli (such as room temperature and time classroom interaction) affect the learning style of different ethnic groups differently.

John Ogbu (1987) has proposed another provocative variant of the cultural discontinuity hypothesis.   He has argued that minority school failure can be explained by whether or not immigrants came to the United States voluntarily or involuntarily.   Although Ogbu's cultural discontinuity hypothesis forms part of a broader hypothesis for the comparative lack of educational achievement of African Americans, it falls within a macro level cultural explanation for the comparative lack of educational achievement of other disadvantaged ethnic groups, such as Latinos.

Cultural explanations and their problems
At first glance, cultural explanations offer a persuasive account for the financial and educational success of some ethnic groups and the comparative failure of others. The unsophisticated variants of cultural explanations often become part of societal stereotypes about some ethnic/racial groups. However, even in its most benign light, academic cultural explanations for the success of some ethnic groups and the failure of others also falter under closer scrutiny. First, explanations of cultural pathology fail to explain striking differences within the Hispanic community. They also fail to explain the lack of educational attainment and financial success of Latinos compared to other similar ethnic/racial minority groups in the U.S.

One of the problems with the explanation of cultural dysfunction is that it is not a persuasive explanation for the comparative lack of financial and educational success of some Latino groups and not others. Just as there are striking differences in the educational attainment and the financial success between Latinos and other ethnic groups, there are also wide variations within the Hispanic community.

U.S. government statistics have recently tended to focus on three groups within the Hispanic community: Mexican Americans, Puerto Ricans, and Cuban Americans. Educational attainment within the Hispanic community is lowest among Dominican, Salvadoran and Mexican immigrants. On the other hand, individuals of Argentinean, Cuban and Costa Rican ancestry had the highest. For the government-selected groups, the differences in high school and college graduation rates are striking (U.S. Department of Commerce, 1998, 54). [See Table 1]

Table 1   Comparison of percentage high school and college graduation rates among selected groups (1998 estimates).

	High School	College
U.S. Average	81.7	23.6
Mexican	48.6	7.4
Puerto Rican	61.1	10.8
Cuban	65.2	19.7

Source: *U.S. Department of Commerce, Census Bureau, 1998.*

As Table 1 shows, the educational attainment among the selected Hispanic groups falls below the national average. Individuals of Mexican ancestry clearly had the lowest educational attainment in both high school and college graduation rates. In contrast, Cubans had the highest educational attainment rates.

Similarly, the financial success within the Hispanic community has been lowest among individuals of Dominican, Salvadoran and Mexican ancestry. In contrast, individuals of Argentinean, Cuban and Costa Rican ancestry had the highest. For these selected groups, the differences in individual and family poverty rates are striking (U.S. Department of Commerce, 1998).

Table 2   Comparison of individual and family poverty rates among selected groups (1998 estimates).

	Family	Individual
U.S. Average	11	13.7
Mexican	27.7	31
Puerto Rican	33.1	35.7
Cuban	12.5	17.3

Source: *U.S. Department of Commerce, Census Bureau, 1998.*

As Table 2 shows, among the selected groups, individuals of Mexican ancestry clearly had the highest level of family and individual poverty rates, whereas Cubans had the lowest. These three groups fell above the national average. It is noteworthy that although Cuban Americans had the highest educational attainment and financial success among these three government-selected Latino groups, they were not the most successful groups among all Latinos.

As argued earlier, variance among Hispanic groups cannot be explained using cultural explanations. What accounts for these differences? What seems unclear is how the purported "cultural deprivation" of Latinos of Dominican and Salvadorian ancestry could be so radically different from those of Cuban or Argentinean ancestry. Surely culture cannot properly explain the differences, otherwise disparities between Dominicans and Cubans would not occur. These types of disparities in the school performance of children with a common cultural ethnic minority background vary greatly in other cross-national studies (Swann Report, 1985; Duncan, 1987).

Wide variance in the educational attainment and financial success of Latino groups is also exhibited in other similar ethnic/racial minority ethnic groups in the US. Thus, another problem with using culture to explain the success of some Hispanic groups and the relative failure of others is that there are wide variations in success and failure within Asian ethnic groups as well. For instance, if we disaggregate the financial and educational achievements of Asian Americans, we find even more striking differences. Although in 1990 Asian families had the highest median family income, individuals of Hmong ancestry had the lowest per capita income in the country ($2,692). Moreover, over 61 percent of Hmong families lived under the poverty line (U.S. Department of Commerce, 1993a, pp. 158-159). If cultural factors account for the success of Asian immigrants in general, what accounts for Laotian, Cambodian and Hmong failure?

Paradoxically, the apparent success of Asian immigrants in general does not square well with explanations of cultural deprivation or cultural incompatibility. Using these heuristic paradigms, Asian immigrants should be far removed from success in the United States. Using the assumptions of cultural dysfunction or cultural deprivation and its variants, the cultural and linguistic barriers faced by Asians in the US would be almost insurmountable. The opposite appears to be true. For instance, in 1990 Asian families had the highest median family income ($38,450) among all ethnic groups. How then can the comparative success of Asian immigrants be explained?

Since cultural factors cannot explain their failure, an alternative hypothesis has been presented to explain Asian success using cultural factors. Some authors (Petersen, 1971; Hirschman and Wong, 1981; Chiswick, 1983; Winnick, 1990) have been very eloquent in their outline of specific common cultural traits among Asian communities relating to work ethic, thrift, and educational values. These ambiguous explanations to account for the success of Asians often fall under the rubric of "Confucian values." However, these cultural explanations for Asian success also falter because they fail to explain the wide variation in the success of some groups of Asian ancestry and not others. Are these so-called "Confucian values" less pronounced among the Hmong and more with the Vietnamese? The explanation of Confucian values also fails to explain why some Asian groups (primarily individuals of South Asian ancestry) are successful educationally and financially in the U.S. yet have not been exposed to such Confucian values.

Cultural explanations, based on hypotheses of cultural incompatibility, often purport that racism is an explanatory factor for the lack of educational attainment and financial success of minority groups in the US. An obvious problem with explanations about the incompatibility of Latino students and the host culture is that while racism may be prevalent, it is difficult to explain why racism could affect some groups more than others. Thus, if racism were a causal factor in explaining the lack of Latino educational achievement or financial success, then individuals of Costa Rican ancestry would not be treated any differently from those of Salvadorian ancestry.

Finally, the explanations based on voluntary or involuntary migration (such as John Ogbu's voluntary hypothesis) fail to provide an adequate explanation for apparently anomalous, but sizably significant ethnic populations. Ogbu's hypothesis could possibly account for the marginal differences among different immigrant groups. However, as an explanatory tool the voluntary or involuntary animus of immigrants can be difficult to pinpoint and may even lead to contradictory explanations. For instance, if we examine refugees from the immigrant population, their desire to immigrate could be explained by virtue of their willingness to immigrate to escape persecutions in a civil war as well as those who involuntarily migrate due to forces beyond their volition.

Socio-economic character of Latinos

What truly differentiates financial success and educational attainment of ethnic groups in America is not so much native racism or the various cultural hypotheses outlined here, but the socio-economic status (SES) of its immigrants. As was suggested earlier, the educational attainment is highly variable within some Latino communities. These differences in educational attainment can be directly traced to the SES of foreign-born individuals from any given country. The SES of immigrants, I believe, correlates more closely to their educational attainment in the US.

Immigration statistics show that there are wide variations in SES among Hispanic immigrants. According to the U.S. Immigration and Naturalization Service, there were 921,089 legal immigrants from Mexico, Central America and South America in fiscal year 1990 (U.S. INS, 1991, pp. 86-87). Each country differed considerably in the number of immigrants and the type of skills that a percentage of the immigrants from a given country possessed (See Table 3).

Table 3 Comparison of the professional skills of legal immigrants among selected countries of origin. (professional skills are in %'s).

Country of origin	Number of immigrants	Professional/ Technical specialties	Executive/ managerial specialties	Laborer
Mexico	679,068	0.8	1.3	24
El Salvador	80,173	1.5	1.9	22
Dominican Rep.	42,195	3.1	1.9	12
Costa Rica	2,840	3.5	1.4	12
Cuba	10,645	4.1	1.6	16
Argentina	5,437	9.1	7.8	7

Source: *U.S. I.N.S., 1991.*

As Table 3 shows, Mexico had the largest number of immigrants, while Costa Rica had the lowest (among the selected countries). What is striking was that some immigrant groups had a high percentage of immigrants with advanced professional and technical skills and a high percentage of immigrants with top level executive occupations, whereas others had a high number of immigrants with low-skilled manual labor occupations. Table 3 shows that nearly a quarter of all Mexican immigrants and over a fifth of Salvadorian immigrants had laborer occupations in 1990. In contrast, immigrants from Argentina had a noticeably high proportion of immigrants with professional and technical skills and executive occupations.

The wide variance among these selected groups also persists at other stages. For instance, the differences in the initial conditions of legal immigrants are maintained once these legal immigrants become naturalized (U.S. INS, 1991, pp. 156-157).

Table 4 Comparison of the professional skills of naturalized immigrants among selected countries of origin. (Professional skills are in %'s).

Country of origin	Number naturalized	Professional technical specialties	Executive/ managerial specialties	Laborer
Mexico	17,564	3.8	4.3	17
El Salvador	2,410	6.5	3.6	11
Dominican Rep.	5,984	4.7	3.8	12
Costa Rica	10,291	5.8	3.9	10
Cuba	589	8	4.5	9.5
Argentina	1,466	12.5	7.7	7.5

Source: *U.S. I.N.S., 1991.*

As Table 4 shows, the number of legal immigrants who decide to become naturalized U.S. citizens drops off considerably. However, among those who decide to become naturalized, the differences in the percentage of immigrants with a high and low SES were maintained. Nearly a fifth of all immigrants from Argentina who became naturalized U.S. citizens had high-skilled technical and executive occupations. In contrast, nearly a fifth of all immigrants from Mexico had low-skilled laborer occupations.

Given their initial disparities in SES among legal immigrants and naturalized citizens, it is no surprise that generations later, Mexican-Americans and Dominican-Americans lag behind other Hispanic groups in terms of financial success and educational attainment. The social characteristics of selected Hispanic groups are alarming. For instance, among foreign-born Mexican individuals (aged 25 or over) residing in the U.S., nearly a third had less than a fifth grade education (U.S. Department of Commerce, 1993b, p. 82). If the socio-economic character of Mexican, Salvadorian and Dominican immigrants was primarily composed of high school and college graduates (as opposed to semiliterate individuals with less than a sixth grade education) then they would surely duplicate the financial and educational achievements of Cubans, Costa Ricans and Argentineans.

The conclusion that the educational level of migrants affects their success in the US is supported by other studies. For instance, according to Katherine Hayes (1992), the educational background of the parents of the migrant child accounts for Latino educational underachievement. Similarly, Forsyth (1994) has shown that Central American and South American immigrants are better educated than those of Mexico. Forsyth's findings can be generalized to subgroups within each of these categories. For instance, among foreign-born Central American immigrants, eight percent of persons 18 to 24 years from Costa Rica had a completed college education, and twenty-eight percent had completed high school. Among Salvadorans aged 18 to 24 years, however, only 1.5 percent had completed a college education and less than 20 percent had completed high school (U.S. Department of Commerce, 1993b, pp. 83-87).

These differences in educational attainment were also striking within Hispanic immigrants from the Caribbean. Among foreign-born Cubans aged 18 to 24, seven percent had completed college and 28 percent had completed high school. In contrast among foreign-born Dominicans of the same age group, only 3 percent had completed college and 25 percent high school (U.S. Department of Commerce,

1993b, pp. 83-87).   Inter-regional differences were clear as well. Thirteen percent of foreign-born Argentine had completed college and 32 percent had completed high school (See Table 5).

Table 5 Educational attainment for selected foreign-born individuals. (Figures represent percentage graduation rates of selected populations, age group 18 to 24)

Country of origin	High school	College
Mexico	19	1.1
El Salvador	20	1.5
Dominican Republic	25	3
Costa Rica	28	7
Cuba	28	8
Argentina	32	13

Source: *U.S. Department of Commerce, Census Bureau, 1990b.*

As Table 5 shows, the educational attainment of these selected foreign-born individuals increased incrementally by country of origin, in both high school and college graduation rates among individuals 18 to 24. Among foreign-born individuals, Mexicans, Salvadorans and Dominicans had the lowest educational attainment in high school and college, whereas Cubans, Costa Ricans and Argentineans had the highest. These differences in the educational attainment of different Latino groups are troubling given different levels of education have been shown to affect the earnings of ethnic groups over a length of time (Ashraf, 1994; Trejo, 1997).

In addition to the wide variation in the educational level of some Latino groups, the income levels of these selected groups were also striking. Among foreign-born Cubans, 11. 5 of families and 14.9 percent of persons fell below the poverty line. These numbers were 34 of families and 30.5 percent of persons falling below the poverty line for foreign-born Dominicans, 14.5 percent of families and 16 percent for foreign-born Costa Ricans, 22 percent of families and 25 percent of foreign-born persons from El Salvador and 7 percent of families and 11 percent of Argentine persons (See Table 6).

Table 6. Poverty rates for selected foreign-born individuals. (Figures represent percentage poverty status of selected Hispanic origin groups).

Country of origin	Family	Individuals
Mexico	27.4	29.8
El Salvador	22	25
Dominican Republic	34	30.5
Costa Rica	14.5	16
Cuba	11.5	14.9
Argentina	7	11

Source: *U.S. Department of Commerce, Census Bureau, 1993b.*

Table 6 shows the poverty rate for selected groups of foreign-born individuals. Dominicans and Salvadorans had the highest family and individual poverty rates whereas Cubans and Argentineans had the lowest.

The aforementioned statistical figures for foreign-born individuals are conclusive. The patterns of variance among legal immigrants were duplicated for naturalized citizens. The educational attainment and financial success indicators used here also showed that the pattern of variance among foreign-born Latino individuals was salient.

Discussion and policy implications
The findings obtained from this paper support the premise that socioeconomic status (SES) is the principal factor to explain Latino financial success and educational attainment. In contrast to the cultural explanations considered in this analysis, SES has been found to be an important predictor of the financial success and the educational attainment of Latinos.

These conclusions have been generalized in the literature about minority educational attainment. In a through review of the literature on social disadvantage and educational attainment, Mortimore and Blackstone (1982) confidently concluded that the "persistence of a negative relationship between local disadvantage and educational attainment has been well documented in the research literature." Similar findings regarding social background as a major explanatory factor in underachievement of other ethnic groups had been tentatively established in other research efforts on other ethnic groups and cross-national comparisons with the children of immigrants (Karraker, 1992; Razack, 1995; CERI, 1987).

This study focused on the factors that accounted for the disparities in the financial success and educational attainment of the Latino populations. As shown here, these disparities emanate from striking differences in the educational and professional attainment of legal immigrants. This study goes further to propose specific policy recommendations to alleviate these disparities in the future.

Proponents of cultural explanations have offered some proposals that assume cultural assumptions. One popular policy recommendation is to create a classroom environment that will accommodate the cultural differences of immigrants and facilitate their transition into American society. For instance, Martha Montero-Sieburth (1996) has argued that teachers and educators "will need to recognize that Latino students are distinct from other students, that the traditional methods of teaching and managing may not be relevant today and that understanding Latinos in their own right requires accepting their cultural and linguistic backgrounds as a starting point of dialogue" (p. 84).

Other policy recommendations that account for culturally based remedies can appear startling. For instance, one set of cultural-matching teaching strategy proposals (Castañeda, 1974, pp. 35-36) urged teachers to highlight cultural differences by preparing and eating Mexican food in the classroom. This set of proposals also urged teachers to show sensitivity to appropriate gender roles by respecting "boy's attempts to be 'manly' when they show bravery" and "girls' attempts at self-adornment." Other pedagogical proposals have been rooted in cultural differences to learning. For instance, Delgado-Gaitán and Trueba (1985) have suggested that "copying was found to be an effort on the part of the Mexican children to collectivize their learning experience." Thus they concluded that "teachers need to re-examine the peer interaction structures in the classroom that encourage copying, evaluate the type of curriculum assigned, and assess the students' native cultural preferences, language...and their potential for higher language and cognitive development through peer exchange of ideas" (Delgado-Gaitán and Trueba, 1985, p. 74).

If culture cannot explain the differences in income and educational attainment among Hispanics, then the effectiveness of culturally based remedies should be suspect *a priori*. A case in point maybe the continuing debate about the effectiveness of bilingual education. Some culturally based proposals (Lucas, Henze, and Donato, 1990) include endorsement of English as a Second Language (ESL) programs or more direct stages via Transitional Bilingual Education (TBE) programs and structured immersion. However, the literature on the effectiveness of bilingual education as a remedy are mixed. The studies that advertise the success of a given bilingual education program seldom examine SES as an explanatory factor. The most comprehensive surveys to evaluate the effectiveness of bilingual education programs find that either most of the studies are methodologically flawed and/or fail to control for socioeconomic status (Lam, 1992; Willig, 1985; Baker and Kanter, 1983; Burt, 1978; Zappert and Cruz, 1977). In those studies in which SES was examined as a contributing factor in the success of bilingual education, there was a strong positive relationship between the success of a given bilingual education program and the high level of SES of its participants (López, 1998; López and Mora, 1998).

The political reaction to bilingual education in the policy arena has been increasingly antagonistic.   Although Latino children accounted for over eighty percent of the students eligible for bilingual education in California, the benefits of bilingual education were not immediately apparent to first generation Latino immigrants. Moreover, as a system of integrating immigrants, bilingual education was soundly rebuffed by California voters with the passage of Proposition 227. During California's 1998 referendum on the elimination of bilingual education programs, over thirty percent of Hispanics voted in favor of the proposal. A full year after the passage of the measure, only ten percent of parents had applied for a waiver of Proposition 227 timelines for their children. In addition, some first generation Latino parents in New York had filed lawsuits to have their children released from bilingual education classes.

Opponents of bilingual education also offer culturally based remedies, typically favoring English-only immersion programs for new immigrants.   Unfortunately, advocacy of English-only immersion programs had not received the evaluative scrutiny of bilingual education programs. Therefore, it was uncertain whether English-only immersion programs worked any better than bilingual education programs.

Given that the SES of foreign-born individuals are a crucial differentiator in the success of Latinos, then it is maybe best to consider another possibility, namely to target the source of Latino underachievement in the United States by changing immigration laws. In his controversial book, *Friends or Strangers*, George Borjas (1990) pointed to some of the wage differential problems among Latino immigrant groups. He tentatively endorsed the enactment of a point system (modeled after Canadian and Australian immigration laws) in the awarding of visas. However, he wavered in his support for this policy and failed to provide a specific set of policy proposals that would act as "skills filter" to attract Latino immigrants with a higher level of SES.

The proposed changes to immigration law are aimed at selecting immigrants with a higher SES. These recommendations assume that cultural differences do not account for differences in educational and financial outcomes of Latinos. Current immigration laws favor immigrants who have family ties with individuals already here rather than professional skills. This trend is changing and some incremental steps are already being taken in this direction. For instance, the 1990 Immigration Reform and Control Act (IRCA) gradually shifted the selection of legal immigrants away from family relationship in favor of skilled workers. However, these changes did not go far enough. The 1990 IRCA rearranged the categories and number of family-based and employment-based visas. Over 50 percent of visas for legal immigrants were allocated under one of the four categories of the family preference system. These categories included: family preference category for sons and daughters of US citizens; spouses and unmarried children of legal permanent residents category; married sons and daughters of US citizens; and a category for brothers and sisters of US citizens.

Similarly, the 1990 IRCA rearranged the number and category content of employment-based visas. Currently about 140,000 immigrants per year receive an employment-based visa. Employment-based visas are divided into five preferences. However, most of the visa quotas for employment-based immigrants are allocated for immigrants with extraordinary abilities and professional skills.

Despite the modest changes made by the 1990 IRCA, the bulk of visas granted to numerically limited legal immigrants are far superior for family preference immigrants than for any other category. A few countries constitute the majority of family-based visas (China, Mexico, and the Philippines). The majority of family-based visas are granted to immigrants with low socio-economic status. One of the consequences of the family preference system in U.S. immigration law is that the Latino population in the United States has been replenished with an influx of low-skilled immigrants from Mexico who have benefited under the family-based preference system.

Perhaps new legislative initiatives can be proposed to encourage skilled immigrants from Latin American countries. My proposal is to further reduce or even eliminate one of the preferences for the spouses and children of unmarried children of legal permanent residents, which is similar to proposals that either reduce or eliminate one of the preferences for the brothers and sisters of US citizens. Another proposal is to eliminate the number of unused visas from one family or employment based category for use by another preference tier.

Under the current system, over 50,000 visas are granted under the diversity immigrant category. This unorthodox immigration quota (distributed by an annual lottery) is reserved for immigrants from countries that traditionally have a low number of family-based immigrants. One proposal would be to increase the number of skilled immigrants from Mexico, Central and Latin America (or other geographic areas) through a lottery system modeled after the diversity immigrant category. Alternatively, the diversity immigrant category could be adjusted to demand more rigorous educational and work experience requirements.

At first glance, my proposals may appear to be overly restrictive and punitive. The intent of these proposals is not to punish or reduce the number of immigrants from Mexico, Central America, and Latin America. Instead, the intent of these proposals is to improve the quality of legal immigrants by selecting individuals from a higher socio-economic background. These proposals are pragmatic and can easily be implemented in Congress. There is a manifest need for skilled workers, primarily in the information technology field. In 1988, the Congress approved compromise legislation providing for a three-year increase in the number of visas available for non-immigrants with specialty occupations (H-1B visas). This proposal would provide a more optimal solution to the SES gap among Latino immigrants as well as to the demand for highly skilled technical workers. Moreover, other labor market demands could be met through these targeted immigration proposals in other fields where there are temporary labor shortages (for instance, teachers).

Admittedly, these proposals would not single-handedly reverse the underclass status of many Latinos already living in the United States. The aim of these proposals is not to control the effects but to serve as a remedy for Latino underachievement in educational attainment and financial success. In this paper I have linked Latino success in the United States with the SES of Latino immigrants. In the long run, the proposed incremental changes in immigration laws to favor skilled workers from Central and Latin America would most optimally prompt immigrants with high SES to reside in the United States.

Conclusion

The evidence is clear on the relationship between the socio-economic character of immigrants and their eventual financial achievement and education attainment in the US. Other alternative explanations, either regarding identity problems, societal prejudice, or inherent cultural factors do not provide a complete picture for the disparity between Hispanics and other ethnic groups. Financial success and educational attainment seems to be compatible with all kinds of values and cultures. Clearly, further research should continue to explore the differences within various branches of the Latino communities. However, cultural explanations for the lack of financial success or educational attainment of any Latino group must not overlook the significance of SES and initial conditions of legal immigrants. In an era of renewed nativist efforts, calls for more measured immigration changes are certain to be unpopular. However, more dramatic steps need to be taken to prevent Hispanics from becoming a permanent underclass.

REFERENCES

Anderson, R. 1984. "Some Reflections on the Acquisition of Knowledge." *Educational Researcher*, 13 (9): 5-10.

Ariselle, J. and Laura Ferreiro. 1998. "Is Bilingual Education Losing Support in the Hispanic Community?" *CQ Researcher*, 8 (35) (September 18): 225.

Ashraf, J. 1994. "Differences in Returns to Education - An Analysis by Race." *American Journal of Economics and Sociology*, 53 (3): 281-290.

Baker, K. and Adriana de Kanter. 1983. "Federal Policy and the Effectiveness of Bilingual Education." in Keith Baker and Adriana de Kanter (eds.), *Bilingual Education: A Reappraisal of Federal Policy*. Lexington, Massachusetts: D.C. Heath.

Borjas, G. 1990. *Friends or Strangers: The Impact of Immigrants in the U.S. Economy*. New York: Basic Books.

Boxell, B. 1998. "Proposition 227: Popularity Extends Past Racial Lines." *Los Angeles Times*, May 29: A3.

Carter, T. and Roberto Segura. 1979. *Mexican Americans in School: A Decade of Change*. New York: College Entrance Examination Board.

Castañeda, A. 1974. "The Educational Needs of Mexican Americans." in Alfredo Castañeda, Richard James, and Webster Robbins, *The Educational Needs of Minority Groups*. Lincoln, Nebraska: Professional Educators Publications.

Centre for Educational Research and Innovation (CERI). 1987. *Immigrant's Children at School*. Paris: OECD.

Chiswick, B. 1983. "An Analysis of the Earnings and Employment of Asian American Men." *Journal of Labor Economics*, 1 (2): 197-214.

Cortese, A. 1992. "Academic Achievement in Mexican Americans: Sociolegal and Cultural Factors." *Latino Studies Journal*, 3 (1): 31-47.

Delgado-Gaitán, C. and Henry Trueba. 1985. "Ethnographic Study of Participant Structures in Task Completion: Reinterpretation in 'Handicaps' in Mexican Children." *Learning Disabilities Quarterly*, 8 (1): 67-75.

-----. 1991. *Crossing Cultural Borders*. London: The Falmer Press.

Dulay, H. and Marina Burt. 1978. *Why Bilingual Education? A Summary of Research Findings*. San Francisco, California: Bloomsbury West.

Duncan, C. 1987. "Understanding Multicultural/Anti-Racist Education for Practice." in T.S. Chivers, *Race and Culture in Education*. Berkshire, England: NFER-Nelson.

Dunn, R., Shirley Griggs, and Gary Price. 1993. "Learning Styles of Mexican-American and Anglo-American Elementary School Students." *Journal of Multicultural Counseling and Development*, 21 (4): 237-247.

Forsyth, A. 1989. "Immigration and Economic Assimilation." in Paul Ong (ed.), *The Widening Divide: Income Inequality and Poverty in Los Angeles*. Los Angeles, California: The Research Group on the Los Angeles Economy.

Friedman, N. 1967. "Cultural Deprivation: A Commentary in the Sociology of Knowledge." *Journal of Educational Thought*, 1 (2): 89-99.

Grossman, H. 1984. *Educating Hispanic Students*. Springfield, Illinois: Charles Thomas Publishers.

Guerra, M. 1970. "Why Juanito Doesn't Read." in Henry Johnson and William Hernandez, eds. *Educating the Mexican American*. Valley Forge: Judson Press.

Hayes, K. 1992. "Attitudes Toward Education - Voluntary and Involuntary Immigrants from the Same Families." *Anthropology and Education Quarterly*, 23 (3): 250-267.

Helweg, A. and Usah Helweg. 1990. *An Immigrant Success Story - East Indian in America*. Philadelphia: University of Pennsylvania Press.

Hirschman, C. and Morrison Wong. 1981. "Trends in Socio-Economic Achievement Among Immigrants and Native-born Asian Americans." *The Sociological Quarterly*, 22 (4): 495-513.

Hutchenson, R. 1998. "Immigrant Parents Lead Efforts to End Bilingual Education." *Knight-Ridder, Washington Bureau*, May 31.

Karraker, M. 1992. "Socioeconomic or Race Differences: Explaining Black and White Adolescent Females' Plan for Education." *Urban Education*, 27 (1): 41-58.

Lam, T. 1992. "Review of Practices and Problems in the Evaluation of Bilingual Education." *Review of Educational Research*, 62 (2): 181-203.

López, M. 1998. "Does Bilingual Education Affect Educational Attainment and Labor Market Outcomes?" *Unpublished manuscript*.

----- and Marie Mora. 1998. "Bilingual Education and Labor Market Earnings Among Hispanics. Evidence Using High School and Beyond." Paper presented at the Association for Public Policy Analysis and Management, 19th Annual Research Conference.

Lucas, T., Rosemary Henze, and Ruben Donato. 1990. "Promoting the Success of Language-Minority Students: An Exploration of 6 High Schools." *Harvard Educational Review*, 60 (3): 315-340.

Montero-Sieburth, M. 1996. "Teachers', Administrators' and Staff's Implicit Thinking About 'At-Risk' Urban High School Latino Students." in Francisco Rios, ed. *Teacher Thinking in Cultural Contexts*. Albany, New York: State University of New York Press.

Mortimore, J. and Tessa Blackstone. 1982. *Disadvantage and Education*. London: Heinemann Educational Books.

Muñoz, D.G. 1986. "Identifying Areas of Stress for Chicano Undergraduates." in Manuel Olivas, (ed.), *Latino College Students*. New York: Teachers College Press.

Ogbu, J. 1978. *Minority Education and Caste*. New York: Academic Press.

-----. 1987. "Variability in Minority School Performance: A Problem in Search of An Explanation." *Anthropology and Education Quarterly*, 18 (4): 312-334.

-----. 1993. "Differences in Cultural Frame of Reference." *International Journal of Behavioral Development*, 16 (3):483-506.

Petersen, W. 1971. *Japanese Americans: Oppression and Success*. New York: Random House.

Phillips, S. 1992. "Participant Structures and Communicative Competence: Warm Springs Children in Community and Classroom." in Dell Hymes, Cortney Cazden, and Vera John (eds.), *Functions of Language in the Classroom*. New York: Teachers College.

Razack, S. 1995. "The Perils of Talking About Culture: Scholarly Research on South and East Asian Students." *Race, Gender, and Class*, 2 (3): 67-82.

Sosa, L. 1998. *The Americano Dream*. New York: Dutton Press.

Sowell, T. 1975. *Race and Economics*. New York: David McKay.

-----. 1994. *History and Cultures*. New York: Basic Books.

"Spanish Speakers Fight to Overturn Bilingual Education." *MacLean's*, 111 (22), June 1, 1998: 34.

Suarez-Orozco, M. 1989. *Central American Refugees in U.S. High Schools*. Palo Alto, California: Stanford University Press.

Swann Report. Great Britain. Department of Education and Science. 1985. *Committee of Enquiry in the Education of Children from Ethnic Minority Groups. Education for All, CMND 9453*. London: HMSO.

Trejo, S. 1997. "Why Do Mexican Americans Earn Low Wages?" *Journal of Political Economy*, 15 (6): 1235-1268.

Trueba, H. 1983. "Adjustment Problems of Mexican American Children: An Anthropological Study." *Learning Disabilities Quarterly*, 6 (4): 395-415.

-----. 1988. "Culturally-Based Explanations of Minority Students' Academic Achievement." *Anthropology and Education Quarterly*, 19 (3): 270-287.

U.S. Department of Commerce, Bureau of the Census. 1990a. *Current Population Reports*. Washington, D.C.: U.S. Government Printing Office.

-----. 1990b. *U.S. Census of Population, U.S. Summary*. Washington, D.C.: U.S. Government Printing Office.

-----. 1990c. *Current Population Survey (CPS)*. Washington, D.C.: U.S. Government Printing Office.

-----. 1993a. *Asians and Pacific Islanders in the United States*. Washington, D.C.: U.S. Government Printing Office.

-----. 1993b. *Persons of Hispanic Origin in the United States*. Washington, D.C.: U.S. Government Printing Office.

-----. 1998. *Statistical Abstract of the United States*. Washington, D.C.: U.S. Government Printing Office.

U.S. Immigration and Naturalization Service. 1991. *Statistical Yearbook of the Immigration and Naturalization Service, 1990.* Washington, D.C.: U.S. Government Printing Office.

Valencia, R., ed. 1991. *Chicano School Failure and Success.* London: The Falmer Press.

Willig, A. 1985. "A Meta-Analysis of Selected Studies on the Effectiveness of Bilingual Education." *Review of Educational Research,* 55 (3): 269-317.

Winnick, L. 1990. "America's Model Minority." *Commentary,* 90 (2): 22-29.

Zappert, L. and Roberto Cruz. 1977. *Bilingual Education: An Appraisal of Empirical Research.* Berkeley, California: Berkeley Unified School District.

12. *Nurturing the Mind to Improve Learning: Teacher Caring and Student Engagement*

Karen Osterman and Stephanie Freese

Introduction

Student disengagement is a pervasive and serious problem with important implications for student learning (Steinberg, 1996). Affecting all ability levels, disengagement has significant implications for all students, but particularly for those who are least likely to succeed in public schools.

Engagement is a multidimensional variable including behaviors, emotions, and psychological orientation (Connell & Wellborn, 1991; Newmann, 1992). Students who are engaged are interested in learning, enjoy challenges and persist in completion of tasks. They are psychologically involved with and committed to the learning process. The disengaged student, in contrast, is emotionally distant from his or her education. In some cases, disengagement is not apparent: students can complete assignments and achieve good grades while remaining completely detached from their work. In other cases, disengagement is evident in behavioral problems, either withdrawal or aggression.

The costs of disengagement are multiple. Based on a national survey of over 1,300 high school students, a Public Agenda report concluded that "most view their high school careers as an exercise in the art of 'getting by" (Johnson & Farkas, 1997, p. 11). According to Roth & Damico, (1994), even kids who 'go through the motions,' attending class, doing homework, behaving well and passing tests describe school as 'boring' and demonstrate little pride or commitment to their work. They "come to school, occupy a seat and make few waves until they accumulate enough credits to graduate" (p. 9).

For these students, their level of disengagement affects the quality of their learning. For others, the cost of disengagement is much higher. Using student interviews and observations, Altenbaugh, Engel, and Martin (1995) and Wehlage, Rutter, Smith, Lesko, and Fernandez (1989), found that disengagement was an important factor in students' decisions to drop out of school. The central finding was that dropouts felt alienated and estranged from their schools, teachers and peers, as well as from their homes, neighborhood, and society in general. They perceived schools as uncaring environments and experienced no sense of school membership. The decision to drop out, according to Leithwood & Aitken (1995) was simply the "final step in a long process of gradual disengagement and reduced participation" in school life (p. 56).

On the positive side, engagement was linked to academic success. Studies in elementary and secondary schools consistently show that engagement has strong relational and predictive links with standards measures of academic performance as well as with lower frequency of school deviance and higher educational aspirations (Connell, Halpern-Felsher, Clifford, Crichlow, & Usinger 1995; Connell & Wellborn 1991; Newmann, Wehlage, & Lamborn,1992; Wentzel, 1998).

Factors that influence the level of student engagement
A growing body of research links student engagement to the quality of students' relationships with teachers. Specifically, when students feel that teachers care for them as individuals and as students, they are more likely to be engaged in the learning process. When students perceive that teachers care, they themselves are more likely to care about learning and more likely to succeed.

The rationale for this is grounded in motivational theory. Engagement is an indicator of motivation, and recent research has begun to see motivation as a social phenomenon (Wigfield, Eccles, & Rodriguez, 1998). This social cognitive perspective on human motivation shifts away from a focus on characteristics of the individual as determinants of motivation, to a focus on individuals in their context and the way that the particular context impacts on perceptions and behavior. Basically, this line of thinking argues that individuals have needs that must be met in the social context.

According to some motivational researchers, there are three basic psychological needs that are essential to human growth and development: the needs for competence, autonomy, and relatedness (Connell & Wellborn, 1991; Deci and colleagues, 1991; Ryan, 1995). The need for competence is the need to experience oneself as capable of achieving certain outcomes. The need for autonomy refers to an individual's ability to exercise choice and control in one's environment, and the need to feel securely connected with others in the environment and to experience oneself as worthy of love and respect. Even if one is not aware of needing these experiences, the satisfaction of these needs affects psychological development and the overall experience of well-being and health (Ryan, 1995).

There is extensive empirical research that establishes a strong and direct link between students' psychological experience and student engagement (Connell et al.,1995; Connell & Wellborn, 1991; deCharms, 1976; Ryan, 1995; Ryan & Powelson, 1991). If these psychological needs for competence, autonomy, and relatedness are met, students will be more motivated and more engaged. Conversely, if individual student needs are not met on an ongoing and continuous basis, the predictable outcome is diminished motivation, impaired development, alienation or disengagement, and poor performance (Deci et al., 1991).

The need for relatedness or belongingness is essential and also more neglected, particularly in the impersonal environment of secondary schools. The experience of belongingness is associated with important psychological processes and behavioral differences (Osterman, 1998). Children who experience a sense of belongingness have a stronger supply of inner resources. They perceive themselves to be more competent and autonomous. They have a stronger sense of identity but are also willing to conform to and adopt established norms and values. These inner resources in turn predict engagement and performance.

Those students who experience a sense of relatedness behave differently. They have more positive attitudes toward school, classwork, teachers, and their peers. They are not only more apt to like school, but they are also more engaged. They participate more in school activities and they invest more of themselves in the learning process. They have a stronger sense of their own social competence and they are more likely to interact with peers and adults in prosocial ways.

Feelings of rejection/alienation are the flip side of the relatedness coin. Findings regarding the effects of non-acceptance and specifically rejection are consistent and clear. Rejection or the sense of exclusion or estrangement from the school community is predictably associated with behavioral problems in the classroom (either aggression or withdrawal), lower interest in school, lower achievement, and dropout.

As indicated, the experience of support or belongingness is related to multiple outcomes. Among these different outcomes, however, the research is strongest regarding the relationship between the experience of relatedness and student engagement. Regardless of academic level or demographic differences, students who experience a sense of relatedness are more engaged in the learning process. Conversely, those who do not feel cared for are more likely to be disengaged. This finding is highlighted in the research on student dropout.

A study by Wehlage & Rutter (1986), analyzing data from the High School and Beyond study for the sophomore 1980 cohort, found that teacher interest in students was one of the key factors associated with student alienation and rejection of school. Ochoa (1994) surveyed and interviewed high school students in San Diego to elicit their perceptions on dropout prevention. Here, students focused on the need for teachers to "show a more caring attitude (yet demand and push their students to achieve) but in a manner that allows students to feel secure and seek their help" (p. 51). Using observations and interviews, Miller, Leinhart, & Zigmond (1988) documented the experiences of six students: three learning disabled and three non-learning disabled students. Teacher involvement with and responsiveness to the students in the study helped keep the students engaged.

All of this research highlights the critical role of teacher support. While peer and family support had an important influence on student perceptions and behavior, teacher support had the most direct impact on student engagement. How kids feel about school and their coursework was in large measure determined by the quality of the relationship they had with their teachers in specific classes.

Connell & Wellborn (1991) collected data from students, parents, and teachers from grades 3-6 in a rural/suburban community, grades 4-6 in a working class, suburban school district, and grades 7-10 in a predominantly minority urban setting. The samples included 245, 542, and 700 students, respectively. The study found that emotional security (relatedness) with parents, teachers, and classmates was significantly associated with teacher ratings of engagement. While positive relationships with each group were important, a sense of emotional security with teachers had the strongest correlation with engagement. The study also considered the relative impact of adult educators, family, and peers and demonstrated that the support relationship with adults in school had a greater effect on students' psychological state than support from home or peers.

Three other studies utilizing Connell & Wellborn's conceptualization of engagement found equally strong relationships between different sources of support and student engagement. Freese (1999) surveyed 338 juniors and seniors from two middle-income suburban high schools to assess the strength of the relationship between teacher caring and student engagement in academic classes. Her findings showed that teacher caring accounting for 47% of the variance in student engagement. Interestingly, and consistent with previous research (Siskin & Little, 1995), she also found that perceptions of teacher caring and student engagement varied significantly by academic department with the most positive responses regarding English classes and the least positive about science classes.

Ryan, Stiller, and Lynch (1994) found strong positive relationships between the way that students represented their relationships with teachers, parents, and peers and measures of academic motivation, including engagement, and self-esteem. The strongest correlation in the study were between felt security with teachers and engagement ($r=.43$, $p<.001$) as measured by self-report on a 16 item engagement scale and between utilization of teachers to deal with school problems and positive coping ($r=.40$, $p<.001$). In other words, students who felt more security with teachers were also more engaged and students who viewed teachers as sources of support were more willing to rely on teachers for support and demonstrated stronger coping behaviors. Conversely, those students who were "unlikely to turn to others for help showed poorer school adaptation and motivation and lower self-esteem and identity integration" (p. 243). The researchers also addressed another continuing question: Are students who are more secure at home likely to be those who are more secure at school? The data, they reported, show that "teacher representations adds variance to outcome predictions even after controlling for parent's inputs" (p. 244).

Wentzel (1998) assessed the ways in which parent, teacher, and peer support are related to academic performance and to various measures of adolescent motivation including psychological distress, interest in school, academic and social goal orientations, and interest in class. With a sample of 167 sixth grade students from a 6-8 middle school in a suburban, middle class and predominantly white community, she found that while family support contributed to variance in school interest, perceived teacher support made the strongest contribution. Teacher support was also the only source of support contributing significantly to student interest or engagement in class. As indicated elsewhere, teacher support was an independent and positive predictor of interest in class, interest in school, and social responsibility or willingness to comply with school norms.

Another study sheds light on the pathways between student engagement, students' experience of relatedness, and risk behavior (Connell et al., 1995). Theoretically, the researchers proposed that perceptions of support and involvement from significant others shaped students' beliefs about themselves in school. These self-perceptions affected behavior and specifically engagement. Engagement contributes directly to performance and adjustment and the individual's experience of support, "as significant others react to the individual's behavior in the setting"(p. 44). Analyses of longitudinal data gathered from 443 urban African American adolescents from grades 7-9 through grades 10-12 revealed that students who avoided risk behaviors in junior high school (attendance, suspensions, grades, test scores, grade retention) and were more engaged were more likely to remain in high school three years later. As predicted, engaged students reported more positive perceptions of competence, autonomy, and relatedness in the school setting than did students who were less engaged. Path analysis showed that the experience of support significantly predicted students' level of school engagement; this, in turn, predicted lower levels of risk behavior.

Adult support is important. Using path analysis, Connell and colleagues demonstrated that adult support in school affects students' sense of competency, autonomy, and relatedness and that these effects were "over and above the effects of the adult support students receive at home" (Connell et al., 1995). Higher levels of support from teachers contributed to higher levels of perceived competence, autonomous self-regulation, and feelings of greater emotional security with adults and peers at school. The development of these psychological processes was linked to higher levels of engagement.

Quite simply, while family support is very important, the support that students received from teachers had a stronger and more direct influence on student engagement. Students who experienced teacher support in schools were more likely to be engaged in the learning process, to have more favorable attitudes toward school, and far less likely to engage in behaviors that would jeopardize their academic success.

These findings were significant for two reasons. Schools and the public often attribute disengagement and poor performance to factors intrinsic to the child, the home environment, and the peer culture. This research certainly challenges that perspective showing that the school directly contributes to engagement over and above the contribution of family and peers and that parents, teachers, and peers affect student behavior in very discreet ways. The link between relatedness and engagement is also particularly significant because of the predictive links between engagement and performance.

Caring in the School and Classroom

The literature on caring helps us to understand how teachers convey a sense of support. Conceptually, caring has many definitions. From an organizational perspective, caring involves the "ways in which individuals and institutions protect young people and invest in their ongoing development" (Chaskin & Rauner, 1995, p. 668). Noddings, well known for her emphasis on caring in schools, describes it as "apprehending the other's reality" or an "attitude that warms and comforts the cared-for" (1984, p. 19). Hult (1979), focusing specifically on the school and classroom, described three dimensions of the teachers' role associated with caring: recognizing the student as unique individual; as a member of the human race; and as a role occupant. Regardless of the approach, the implication was that teachers acted so that student's experience a sense of support, a sense that they were cared for.

Teacher caring has been demonstrated in the simple civilities of daily life. In the research of Sizer (1984), Altenbaugh et al., (1995), and Noblit, Rogers & McCadden (1995), we find relatively consistent descriptions of caring teachers: They are "out to help you," "they "want you to learn," they "sit down with you and work personally with you," and "they talk to you." As Altenbaugh et al. (1995) explained "One doesn't have to be a psychologist to fill this role - just a common sense person with antenna out to capture the 'unsaid' in students' lives" (p. 164).

Bosworth (1995) interviewed more than 100 students and observed 300 middle school students in order to explore the indicators of caring in young adolescents. She described the ways in which students construct teachers' caring behavior as well as the ways teachers can demonstrate caring. In her study, helping emerged as the most common theme when students discussed their conception of caring. "To help" is synonymous with "to care" for 30% of these middle school studnents.

Wentzel (1997) asked 375 eighth grade students from a suburban middle school to identify three things teachers do to show that they care about you. According to these students, teachers show they care when they: make class interesting; communicate openly both listening and talking; treat students honestly and fairly; and keep promises. Also important behaviors include recognizing students' individuality, expressing interest in personal as well as academic areas of their lives, and paying close attention to their work, providing support and feedback. This last point is particularly important. Caring should not be confused with leniency, niceness, or being perpetually agreeable. Both Gilligan (1982) and Noddings (1984) rejected a sentimental or self-sacrificing notion of care, encouraging care-givers instead to act in the best interests of their students. Having rigorous expectations for students was quite compatible with the concept of caring, and as reports from students indicated, teachers who were strict and demanding were often perceived as caring because, through their actions, enabled students to succeed. They recognized students' academic and personal needs and worked to address them.

The study by Freese (1999), described above, provides additional insight. Analysis of survey responses identified two positive factors: showing consideration or understanding of the student; and knowing the whole student. According to these high school students, caring teachers showed consideration and understanding and had a relationship that extended beyond the boundaries of the classroom. The heaviest weightings showed that students most strongly associated teacher caring with three teacher behaviors: having patience when they made mistakes; encouraging them to do their best; and being polite. Students clearly wanted teachers to understand them, encourage them, and show respect. Students expected their teachers to make human connections with them and to treat them fairly, with dignity and courtesy. They also looked to their teachers to give them individual help when needed. It was evident that students wanted their teachers to know them as individuals who had lives outside of school and not just as recipients of academic information. Teacher behaviors negatively correlated with student perceptions of caring dealt primarily with understanding and expectations, rather than understanding the pressures they faced either not making expectations clear or having expectations that were impossible to meet.

Despite their relatively simple expectations regarding the quality of their relationships with adults in schools, students did not experience schools --whether elementary or secondary--as caring institutions. While the research on students' experience of support or acceptance in classrooms and schools was not extensive, existing research showed that some students were more likely to feel a sense of support than do others. Boys, for example, were less likely to experience a sense of belongingness in school than did girls (Wentzel & Caldwell, 1997; Goodenow, 1993, a,b). Students from low-income schools also tended to experience their schools as less caring than do students from higher income schools. In two studies of high schools, students in low income urban schools reported lower sense of belonging than did students from affluent suburban districts (Goodenow & Grady, 1993, Goodenow, 1993a). Even at the elementary level, a study of 12 elementary schools in six districts found that "about 25% of the upper-grade students reported they experienced their school as an uncaring place" and that "schools with high percentages of poor children are significantly less likely to be described as caring places than those serving mostly middle-class students" (Watson, Battistich, & Solomon, 1997, pp. 573,574).

While students in schools serving low-income communities were less likely to experience schools as supportive, there was also evidence to show that this need for support was even greater and had a more positive impact in those schools than in more affluent schools. Examining students' sense of community, defined as supportiveness and the ability to exercise influence in the classroom or school (Battistich, Solomon, Kim, Watson, & Schaps, 1995) also found a negative relationship between poverty and students' sense of community. While the sense of community was consistently associated with a wide range of positive motivational and behavioral outcomes, they found that the relationship was strongest in high poverty schools.

Within classrooms, students also experienced different levels of support. While a substantial body of research has established that students receive differential treatment from teachers on the basis of characteristics such as race or culture, gender, class, ability, and appearance, research also suggests that teacher perceptions of student ability, engagement, and academic performance influence their relationships with students.

At the high school level, students interviewed by Altenbaugh et al. (1995) reported teacher favoritism. The favorites, one explained, were "the kids that were real smart in class. The other ones, they just ignored altogether." Those teachers who had favorites would show it in different ways but "They were always nicer to those students and always mean to the others... If a kid missed a day of notes, he would give it to him and help him out, but he wouldn't the other students" (p. 87).

Elliott & Voss (1974), Schwartz (1981), Oakes (1985), and Gamoran and Berends (1987) all found differential treatment among lower tracked students. Elliott & Voss (1974) described an alienating tracking system for troublemakers and failures. Schwartz (1981) observed teachers distancing themselves from low-ranked pupils and, by examining end of the year elementary student reports, found an increasing polarization between low and high track students with teacher comments about low-track students being exceedingly brief and negative. Interestingly many of the negative comments - disruptive, nonconformist, withdrawn, daydreamers, non-participants - are indicators of disengagement. Oakes (1985) found differences between tracks in perceptions and incidence of teacher punitiveness and the level of teacher concern. While none of the groups of students described their teachers as very punitive or unsupportive, students in low tracks felt that teachers were more likely to use hurtful behavior, making fun of some students, hurting their feelings, or getting mad when they ask a question.   High track classes consistently saw their teachers as more concerned about them and less punitive.   Observers found more incidences of positive behaviors such as the use of humor, positive touching, or expressions of enthusiasm in high track classes while there were more negative behaviors--making demeaning or angry remarks, negative touching, and negative expressions--in low track classes.

Gamoran and Berends (1987), in their review of the research on tracking, found that teachers were more positive towards high track than low track students and that prosocial behavior of high track students seemed to have more influence on teacher perceptions than actual achievement. The Connell et al. study (1995) found that while engagement predicted academic performance, it was student engagement that directly influenced the level of perceived support from adults. Students receive support "depending on their level of engagement, with more engaged students receiving more support" (p.58).

The findings here are paradoxical.   While the level of student engagement was influenced by the quality of the relationship between students, teachers tended to distance themselves from students who were disengaged with the ironic result that those students with the greatest need for support were least likely to get it.   This is indeed a vicious cycle with serious implications for students.

Implications and Recommendations
The research findings have serious implications for policy and practice. Disengagement affects children regardless of age, race, or ethnicity, becoming more apparent at middle and high school level.   Because of its association with academic success and dropout, it is most problematic for children at risk.

Educational theory has consistently emphasized the significant role that feelings play in the learning process.   Recent research affirms this belief establishing a strong relationship between student perceptions of teaching caring and support and their level of engagement.   Student engagement, too, is an important and direct predictor of school commitment and success. Nonetheless, this research stands in stark contrast to the reality of school for many students.

While students may experience the lack of support at any level, the problem is particularly serious in secondary schools. As children move from elementary through high school, motivation declines progressively with the greatest declines occurring as children enter the middle school (Anderman & Maehr, 1994).   Students' attitudes toward school worsen, they become less interested in specific subjects, and their perception of their ability and their expectations for success decrease. While some attribute these changes to adolescence, Anderman & Maehr and others argue that these changes can be directly related to changes in characteristics of the school, including the impersonal quality of teacher-student relationships. While needs for a sense of belongingness are perhaps greatest during adolescence, opportunities to develop meaningful relationships within the school community diminish at the secondary level.

There are many factors that influence the quality of relationships between teachers and students and prevent the development of a strong sense of community. At the classroom level, research establishes that teachers at the secondary level perceive their primary role as information providers and do not feel responsible for adolescents' social or emotional needs (Frymier & Gansneder, 1989). This emphasis on academics, however, is consistent with the predominant goals and values of schools and society. "Society in general and parents as a group" said John Goodlad (1984), "assume that the primary function of schools□is to teach academics" (p.61). If anything, this singular focus has only intensified in the last 15 years, and teachers' concern with academic accomplishment is a predictable reflection of societal values.

This emphasis on academics is also reflected in the culture of schools and in organizational policies and practices. According to Maehr & Midgeley (1996), schools place undue emphasis on ability, establishing norms of competition and individualism. Schools and teachers want children to succeed; implicitly and explicitly, they reward and recognize those who do. Unfortunately, those who do not demonstrate above average ability receive, a message that their efforts, and they themselves, are of less value. While paying lip service to more humanistic goals in this competitive academic environment, schools as educational institutions pay scant attention to the emotional needs of students, individually or collectively (Anderman & Maehr, 1994; Goodlad, 1984; Hargreaves, Earl, & Ryan, 1996; Maehr & Midgley, 1996; Noddings, 1992).

Many organizational practices associated with secondary schools were designed to maximize academic accomplishment of students. Unfortunately, some of these same practices contributed to the depersonalization of the learning process. Some critics, for example, have highlighted the negative impact of school size, traditional scheduling practices, and ability grouping. While these features were originally intended to address academic goals, they also fragmented students' experience, fostered divisiveness and competition, and reduced opportunities for sustained and personal interaction between teachers and peers.

With respect to tracking or ability grouping, Oakes (1985) has described tracking as a "legitimation of inequality" (p. 137), a practice that, as Schwartz (1981) illustrated, directly affects the nature and quality of peer relationships. Departmentalization, almost a universal given in secondary schools, is another organizational pattern that is associated with academic rigor and depersonalization (Hargreaves, & Macmillan, 1995). Siskin and Little (1995) reported that subject matter specialization forms a "locus of professional values and commitments" (p. 174), highlighting the conflict that existed between "subject-centered" and "student-centered" teachers. With some exceptions, math and foreign language emerged as the most linear and sequential (subject-centered), while English was typically viewed as more open and flexible (student-centered). Freese's study (1999) similarly found that there were significant differences in students' perceptions of teacher caring by department level with students reporting English and social studies teachers as most caring, with foreign language and math teachers perceived as least caring.

Despite departmental differences, however, patterns of instruction at the secondary level were highly consistent and allowed few opportunities for dialogue between teacher and students, whether of an academic or personal nature. Goodlad (1984) and Anderman & Maehr (1994) reported that there was little, if any time, devoted to discussion within classes. Gamoran & Nystrand's (1992) study of discourse in 54 high school classes found that the group discussion incorporating student contributions averaged 15 seconds per 50-minute period. Thirty-three classes had no discussion time at all; only four had more than a minute. These patterns were unaffected by class size; when classes were smaller, students spent more time in individual seatwork. Opportunities for personal dialogue between teachers and students were even more restricted, given the unrelenting demands of tight schedules and pressures to equate teaching with the transmittal of information.

As research shows, there is a direct and significant relationship between teaching caring, student engagement, and student learning. The recommendations growing out of this line of research were both simple and complex. If students are to succeed, schools must address the emotional needs of students and recognize that the ability to convey a sense of caring to students is an essential aspect of teaching. Given the predominant value system in society and the deeply engrained structures and practices at the secondary level, this is no small challenge. Nonetheless, there are steps that can be taken.

At the school level, it is important for schools to recognize the importance of personalization and to develop a culture that supports positive interaction between teachers and students and among all members of the school community. The importance of caring must be articulated clearly and forcefully in mission statements, modeled by school leaders, and included as an integral aspect of personnel policies and practices. It must be clear that schools exist to serve students. The importance of adult support should be reflected in job descriptions, selection criteria, supervisory standards, and staff development initiatives, not only for teachers but also for the entire staff, from lunch aides to maintenance workers. Within the school, it should be clear that the guidance is a responsibility that crosses role divisions; and hopefully, there will be opportunities for personnel --teachers, counselors, social workers, psychologists--to share information about students' needs and performance. In addition, the school should support activities that facilitate interaction between students and adults, both in and out of the classroom.

It is important also that the relationship between psychological needs and behavior is recognized and incorporated into academic and disciplinary policies. There should be an understanding that behavioral or attitudinal problems might well be an indicator of students' growing need for support. Accordingly, there should be an effort to increase personal as well as academic support when students experience difficulty in their work or when their behavior jeopardizes their chances for success.

Schools can also consider ways to modify learning arrangements to support and encourage supportive teacher and student interaction. Organizational options intended to increase students' sense of community include smaller schools, "houses" departmental teaming, block scheduling, inter-age grouping, and looping (maintaining intact classes over several grade levels). All of these changes would extend the time that students remained with the same peers and teachers. Theoretically, these structural changes would increase interaction and give students and teachers the opportunity to develop a more personal sense of understanding; but, if they are to have a positive impact, reorganization must be accompanied by changes in the nature of instruction.

At the classroom level, it is important to examine assumptions about teaching and learning in the context of theory and research. Caring is not inconsistent with high academic standards and accomplishment; in fact, caring is essential to the learning process. From educational psychology or learning theory, we know that caring, support, and personalization play an important role in motivation and learning. Dewey (1958) and Vygotsky (1981, cited in Wertsch, 1985) have emphasized the importance of social interaction in the learning process. Constructivism also tells us that the learning process must build on prior experiences and knowledge. For this to take place, learning situations must provide opportunities for students to articulate and represent their knowledge. This enables teachers to assess student learning, better enabling them to identify student needs and tailor instruction appropriately. Dialogue supports the learning process on an academic level; it also enables teachers and students to develop a deeper understanding of one another. Battistich, Watson, Solomon, Schaps, & Solomon (1991) maintain that having the opportunity to express personal opinions in a safe and respectful environment gives children the opportunity to discover that others care. Through such experiences, they develop feelings of trust, mutual respect, and solidarity. Gamoran & Nystrand (1992) similarly affirm that "regardless of the activity in which students participate, discourse is a critical indicator of the extent to which school offers membership" (p. 40). Activities that support peer interaction within the classroom and school also facilitates the development of more positive relationships between teachers and students. Students who experience acceptance within the school community are more likely to be committed to school and engaged in learning. They are also more likely to accept and conform to school regulations and interact in more positive ways with teachers and peers (Osterman, 1998).

To establish and maintain dialogue and to enhance learning, it is necessary to share and build on personal experience. To convey a sense of caring through dialogue depends on cultural sensitivity. Eaker-Rich & Van Galen (1996) point out that teachers must avoid manifesting care in culturally bound ways that serve to reinforce class, race, and gender roles and limit, rather than support, students' personal and academic growth. Without a deep understanding of and appreciation for cultural differences, teachers and other adults might either misread student behaviors in a way that affects their relationship or they might utilize strategies that may not be perceived as caring. "To be effective at caring in settings of diversity," the authors maintain, "we must move from a 'caring about', which connotes a generalizability and an objectification of the one receiving care, to a practice of 'caring for', which implies a recognition and rationality with the one receiving care" (Eaker-Rich & Van Galen, 1996, p. 233).

Autonomy support within the classroom is another strategy that supports student learning and facilitates positive relationships between teachers and students. Critiques of secondary education often focus on the contrast between adolescents' growing needs for autonomy and actual decreases in opportunities for student autonomy within the classroom (Anderman & Maehr, 1994 ; Goodlad, 1984; Hargreaves et al., 1996). As in the case with teacher support, research also shows that the level of autonomy support from teachers has an important positive affect on students' motivation and behavior (deCharms, 1976; Deci et al. (1991). When students experience autonomy, they are more likely to develop stronger self-concepts, assume greater responsibility for their own learning, and also experience the teacher as more supportive. Involving children in decision-making and problem solving conveys a sense of respect that is so essential to the concept of caring and helps to establish warm and supportive personal relations (Battistich et al., 1991).

Changes outside of the school environment can also support a renewed emphasis on humanistic aspects of schooling. Teacher preparation programs must highlight the emotional component of teaching and help pre-service teachers to develop the skills of observation and communication so that they will be sensitive and responsive to the emotional needs of their charges. Policy makers, too, must reexamine goals and assess policies in light of what we know about the important role that emotional needs play in the learning process.

All students can learn and more will learn if we as educators are able to provide a supportive caring environment that will nurture hearts as well as minds.

REFERENCES

Altenbaugh, R. J., Engel, D. E., & Martin, D. T. (1995). *Caring for kids: A critical study of urban school leavers.* Bristol, PA: The Falmer Press.

Anderman, E. M., & Maehr, M. L. (1994). Motivation and schooling in the middle grades. *Review of Educational Research, 64*(2), 287-309.

Battistich, V., Solomon, D., Kim, D., Watson, M., & Schaps, E. (1995). Schools as communities, poverty levels of student populations, and students' attitudes, motives, and performance: A multilevel analysis. *American Educational Research Journal, 32*(3), 627-658.

Battistich, V., Watson, M., Solomon, D., Schaps, E., & Solomon, J. (1991). The child development project: A comprehensive program for the development of prosocial character. In W. M. Kurtines & J. L. Gewirtz (Eds.), *Handbook of moral behavior and development: Application* (Vol. 3, pp. 1-34). Hillsdale, NJ: Lawrence Erlbaum Assoc.

Bosworth, K. (1995). Caring for others and being cared for: Students talk caring in school. *Phi Delta Kappan, 76*(9), 686-693.

Chaskin, R. J., & Rauner, D. M. (1995). Toward a field of caring: An epilogue. *Phi Delta Kappan, 76*(9), 718-719.

Connell, J. P., Halpern-Felsher, B. L., Clifford, E., Crichlow, W., & Usinger, P. (1995). Hanging in there: Behavioral, psychological, and contextual factors affecting whether African American adolescents stay in high school. *Journal of adolescent research, 10*(1), 41-63.

Connell, J. P., & Wellborn, J. G. (1991). Competence, autonomy, and relatedness: A motivational analysis of self-system processes. In M. R. Gunnar & L. A. Sroufe (Eds.), *Self Processes and development* (Vol. 23,). Hillsdale, N.J.: Lawrence Erlbaum Assoc.

deCharms, R. (1976). *Enhancing motivation: Change in the classroom*. New York: Irvington.

Deci, E. L., Vallerand, R. J., Pelletier, L. G., & Ryan, R. M. (1991). Motivation and education: The self-determination perspective. *Educational Psychologist, 26*(3 & 4), 325-346.

Dewey, J. (1958). *Experience and education*. New York: The Macmillan Co.

Eaker-Rich, D., & Van Galen, J. (Eds.). (1996). *Caring in an unjust world: Negotiating borders and barriers in schools*. Albany: State University of New York Press.

Elliott, D. S., & Voss, H. L. (1974). *Delinquency and dropout*. Lexington, MA: Lexington Books.

Freese, S. (1999). *Is teacher caring related to student engagement in high schools?* Unpublished Doctoral Dissertation, Hofstra University, Hempstead, NY.

Frymier, J., & Gansneder, B. (1989). The Phi Delta Kappa study of students at risk. *Phi Delta Kappan, 71*(2), 142-146.

Gamoran, A., & Berends, M. (1987). The effects of stratification in secondary schools: Synthesis of survey and ethnigraphic research. *Review of Educational Research, 57*(4), 415-435.

Gamoran, A., & Nystrand, M. (1992). Taking students seriously. In F. M. Newmann (Ed.), *Student engagement and achievement in American secondary schools* (pp. 40-61). New York: Teachers College Press.

Gilligan, C. (1982). *In a different voice: Psychological theory and women's development*. Cambridge, MA.: Harvard University Press.

Goodenow, C. (1993a). Classroom belonging among early adolescent students: Relationships to motivation and achievement. *Journal of Early Adolescence, 13*(1), 21-43.

Goodenow, C. (1993b). The psychological sense of school membership among adolescents: Scale development and educational correlates. *Psychology in the Schools, 30*(January), 79-90.

Goodenow, C., & Grady, K. E. (1993). The relationship of school belonging and friends' values to academic motivation among urban adolescent students. *Journal of Experimental Education, 62*(1), 60-71.

Goodlad, J. I. (1984). *A place called school.* New York: McGraw-Hill.

Hargreaves, A., Earl, L., & Ryan, J. (1996). *Schooling for change: Reinventing education for early adolescents.* Bristol, PA: Falmer Press, Taylor & Francis, Inc.

Hargreaves, A., & Macmillan, R. (1995). The balkanization of secondary school teaching. In L. S. Siskin & J. W. Little (Eds.), *The subjects in question: Departmental organization and the high school* (pp. 141-171). New York: Teachers College Press.

Hult, R. E., Jr. (1979). On pedagogical caring. *Educational Theory, 29*, 237-244.

Johnson, J., Farkas, S., & with Bers, A. (1997). *Getting by: What American teenagers really think about their schools* . New York: Public Agenda.

Leithwood, K., & Aitken, R. (1995). *Making schools smarter.* Thousand Oaks, CA: Corwin Press, Inc.

Maehr, M. L., & Midgley, C. (1996). *Transforming school cultures.* Boulder, CO: Westview Press.

Miller, S. E., Leinhardt, G., & Zigmond, N. (1988). Influencing engagement through accomodation: An ethnographic study of at-risk students. *American Educational Research Journal, 25*, 465-487.

Newmann, F. M. (Ed.). (1992). *Student engagement and achievement in American secondary schools.* New York: Teachers College Press.

Newmann, F. M., Wehlage, G. G., & Lamborn, S. D. (1992). The significance and sources of student engagement. In F. M. Newmann (Ed.), *Student engagement and achievement in American secondary schools* . New York: Teachers College Press.

Noblit, G. W. (1993). Power and caring. *American Educational Research Journal, 30*(1), 23-38.

Noblit, G. W., Rogers, D. L., & McCadden, B. M. (1995). In the meantime: The possibilties of caring. *Phi Delta Kappan, 76*(9), 680-685.

Noddings, N. (1984). *Caring: A feminine approach to ethics and moral education*. Berkeley, CA: University of California Press.

Noddings, N. (1992). *The challenge to care in schools: An alternative approach to education*. New York: Teachers College Press.

Oakes, J. (1985). *Keeping track*. New Haven: Yale University Press.

Ochoa, A. M. (1994). *Evaluation of student perceptions on dropout prevention: San Diego High School student survey* . San Diego.

Osterman, K. (1998). *Student community within the school context: A research synthesis.* Paper presented at the Annual Meeting of the American Educational Research Association, San Diego, CA.

Roth, J., & Damico, S. B. (1994). *Broadening the concept of engagement: Inclusion of perspectives on adolescence.* Paper presented at the Annual Meeting of the American Educational Research Association, New Orleans, LA.

Ryan, R. M. (1995). Psychological needs and the facilitation of integrative processes. *Journal of Personality, 63*(3), 397-427.

Ryan, R. M., & Powelson, C. L. (1991). Autonomy and relatedness as fundamental to motivation and education. *Journal of Experimental Education, 60*(1), 49-66.

Ryan, R. M., Stiller, J. D., & Lynch, J. H. (1994). Representations of relationships to teachers, parents, and friends as predictors of academic motivation and self-esteem. *Journal of early adolescence, 14*(2), 226-249.

Schwartz, F. (1981). Supporting or subverting learning: Peer group patterns in four tracked schools. *Anthropology & Education Quarterly, XII*(2), 99-121.

Siskin, L. S., & Little, J. W. (Eds.). (1995). *The subjects in question: Departmental organization and the high school*. New York: Teachers College Press.

Sizer, T. R. (1984). *Horace's compromise: The dilemma of the American high school*. Boston, MA: Houghton Mifflin.

Steinberg, L. (1996). *Beyond the classroom*. New York: Simon & Schuster.

Watson, M., Battistich, V., & Solomon, D. (1997). Enhancing students' social and ethnical development in school: An intervention program and its effects. *International Journal of Educational Research, 27,* 571-586.

Wehlage, G., & Rutter, R. (1986). Dropping out: How much do schools contribute to the problem? *Teachers College Record, 87*(3), 374-92.

Wehlage, G. G., Rutter, R. A., Smith, G. A., Lesko, N., & Fernandez, R. R. (1989). *Reducing the risk: Schools as communities of support.* Philadelphia: The Falmer Press, Taylor & Francis Inc.

Wentzel, K. R. (1997). Student motivation in middle school: The role of perceived pedagogical caring. *Journal of Educational Psychology, 89*(3), 411-419.

Wentzel, K. R. (1998). Social relationships and motivation in middle school: The role of parents, teachers, and peers. *Journal of Educational Psychology, 90*(2), 202-209.

Wentzel, K. R., & Caldwell, K. (1997). Friendships, peer acceptance, and group membership: Relations to academic achievement in middle school. *Child Development, 68*(6), 1198-1209.

Wertsch, J.V. (1985). *Vygotsky and the social formation of mind.* Cambridge, MA: Harvard University Press.

Wigfield, A., Eccles, J. S., & Rodriguez, D. (1998). The development of children's motivation in school contexts. In P. D. Pearson & A. Iran-Nejad (Eds.), *Review of Research in Education* (Vol. 23). Washington,D.C.: American Educational Research Association.

13. *Predictors of Academic Achievement Among African American Adolescents*

Teresa A. Fisher

The academic achievement of African American students is a national concern for educators and researchers. To explain differences in achievement scores of African American and White students, the dominant research strategy has been to conduct large cross-racial studies. Some of the findings in comparative analysis reveal that Black students have lower standardized achievement test scores than any other racial or ethnic group (Osterlind, 1997; Smith, 1995), and a higher percentage of students performing in the low achievement groups in both math and reading (U.S. Department of Education, 1998). Additionally, an analysis of the 25 largest school districts in the U.S. indicate that in most gifted programs, Black students are drastically under-represented (Ford, 1995), while over-represented in special education programs (Patton, 1998; Russo and Talbert-Johnson, 1997).

Based on this research, the low academic performance of Black adolescents in comparison to whites have been attributed to such factors as need-achievement (McCleland, 1985; Smith, 1983) aspirations (Cosby, 1971; Eckstromm et al, 1986) locus of control (Stipek, 1993) and general self-concept (Osborne, 1995; Shokraii, 1996).

Interventions based on this research would assume that promoting the attitudes and beliefs of high achieving Whites result in high achievement in Black children as well. However, the findings from cross-racial studies have contributed little to the understanding of academic achievement behavior of Black adolescents. They have typically involved representative samples, which has meant the comparison of Blacks from low socioeconomic households and poor neighborhoods with the majority population. This analysis has produced a bleak and one-sided view of the academic motivation of Black adolescents, therefore having results confounded by race and socioeconomic status. When representative samples of Black youth are utilized, it is assumed that Black students are a homogenous group, all having the same predictors for academic success.

Most importantly, these studies do not account for racial differences in factors leading to achievement and school success. This strategy assumes that whatever factors predict achievement in Whites will also predict achievement for African Americans. They ignore the fact that racial ethnic groups are frequently treated very differently within the same academic structure (Taylor, 1994). Comparative studies are designed with the belief that students from majority and minority populations share the same historical and political context for achievement. Typically, the socio-political circumstances can present different achievement barriers for White and African American students. The attitude and beliefs required to successfully negotiate educational contexts may be very different for high achieving Blacks and high achieving Whites. In order to understand the predictors of academic success for various racial/ethnic groups, it may be more appropriate to examine groups individually. This would avoid converging the social factors that differentially impact achievement behavior.

Comparative studies have been focused on explaining why Black adolescents perform so poorly in school. More research is needed which examines factors that contribute to the academic success of Black students. Although as a whole, Black students tend to perform lower on academic achievement measures than the majority population, they have nevertheless made significant educational progress over the past decade. There have been gains among Black youth in reading, math, and science performance.

The percent of elementary and secondary students performing at the highest proficiency levels steadily increased across the three academic areas (U.S. Department of Education, 1998). Additionally, when education ambition is used as a measure of achievement, Black students reported higher educational aspirations than white students (Boykin, 1983; Cosby, 1971; Smith, 1983). In spite of this educational progress, very little research has been done to determine causes for improvement or describe the factors that distinguish low from high achieving Black students.

This study was designed to obtain a more comprehensive picture of the academic predictors of Black adolescents by studying school achievement within a diverse Black student population. The purpose of the research was to identify factors that would help explain differences between high and low achieving Black adolescents. As compared to cross-racial studies, intra-race studies provide a more precise picture of academic predictors, because educational barriers due to race are held constant. When studies focus on a population with a common socio-political, historical, and cultural background, it provides an opportunity to better understand how specific racial groups learn to negotiate academic situations (Ogbu 1992).

In this study there was a particular focus on factors that can be affected by educational interventions. Based on a review of recent research, four constructs were identified which show promise of differentiating Black adolescents who do well academically from those who do not. The constructs included were self-concept of academic ability, perceptions of opportunity for success in school, perceptions of future opportunity structure and social support from significant others. Following is a review of research supporting the potential of these factors to predict academic achievement behavior in African American adolescents.

SELF-CONCEPT OF ACADEMIC ABILITY

The present study refers to self-concept of academic ability as the development of one's self-evaluation of his/her academic potential (Brookover, LeRue, Hanachek, Thomas, & Erickson, 1965). In recent years, academic self-concept has been strongly validated as a separate entity of the overall general or global self-concept (Byrne, 1984; Fleming & Courtney, 1984; Marsh, Barnes & Hocevar 1985; Marsh & Shavelson, 1985; Shavelson & Marsh, 1986). This finding has provided the opportunity for researchers to observe relationships specifically for academic self-concept, one of which has been academic achievement. Numerous studies have shown that academic achievement has a much higher correlation with academic self-concept than with the general construct of self-concept (Byrne, 1984; Hansford & Hattie, 1982; Marsh, 1987). In addition, the research indicates that the earlier individuals establish a positive self-evaluation of their academic ability, the more likely a long history of successful achievement related events will be maintained (Hansford & Hattie, 1982; Byrne & Shavelson, 1986.)

A limited number of studies have looked at the relationship of self-concept of academic ability and academic achievement among African American adolescents. One of the forerunners was Epps (1969), who investigated personality variables among 2,538 Black adolescents from inner-city high schools. In this particular study, self-concept of ability had the strongest relationship to student grades. These results have been supported on a smaller scale by Kleinfeld (1972) and Jordon (1981). They found that Black high school students' self-evaluation of their academic potential had a major influence on the amount of effort they exerted toward achieving in school. Presently, evidence indicates that academic self concept may be an important predictor of Black adolescent achievement.

PERCEPTIONS OF OPPORTUNITY FOR SUCCESS IN SCHOOL

In school settings, students not only have to believe that they have the requisite abilities, but also need to perceive that they have the opportunity to succeed in their present academic environment. In order for students to perceive that their ability and efforts will lead to success, they must have an overall feeling of comfort and a supportive atmosphere for achievement. This construct encompasses the student's belief that they can achieve their academic goals by being treated fairly, feeling comfortable enough to show their competence, and receiving recognition for accomplishments.

These psychological and academic support factors are components of school climate that have a major impact on student achievement (Maehr & Braskamp, 1986; Maehr & Fyans, 1989). Studies have shown that when students perceive their academic goals can be achieved in their present school setting, they put forth greater effort toward achieving, than students who do not perceive the school environment was conducive for their goals (Ames & Archer, 1988; Edwards, 1976; Lee, 1984; Mackler, 1970; Waxman & Huang, 1995).

Research indicates that school climate may have differential effects on the academic achievement of ethnic groups (Maehr & Fyans, 1989). Literature reviews by Clark (1983), and Hale (1982) have revealed that feeling comfortable and being recognized for their efforts, is more central to achievement for successful Black students than successful non-minority students. A closer look at this construct could reveal useful knowledge about the academic behavior of African American adolescents.

PERCEPTION OF FUTURE OPPORTUNITY STRUCTURE

African American youth often perceive the future opportunity structure as more limiting than majority group members. For Blacks, access to high status occupations has often been denied due to the vocational barriers induced by prejudice. Black students are aware that they are likely to have a smaller salary than whites for the same work and education level and twice as likely to be unemployed (Ogbu, 1986). The impact of this perception on academic achievement has only recently received attention. A few studies have suggested that Black children are aware of these barriers early in life and subsequently adopt the belief that successful school achievement may not lead to one's desired career (Boykin, 1983; Clark, 1983; Jackson, 1981; Ogbu, 1974; Gottfredson, 1981). These student beliefs can be established as they interact with significant adults in their life. Children who observe adults that are distressed by a lack of equitable wages or adequate promotions, find it difficult to be positive toward school and do not put forth the effort to earn good grades. Whereas, adults who feel that their occupational success corresponds with their level of education, typically have children who display successful academic behavior (Mickelson, 1990.)

It is likely that the belief that one's achievement efforts may not be effective in obtaining future success probably contributes significantly to the low level of scholastic performance of some of our Black youth. The perception of future opportunities appears to be a viable component in the development of academic achievement motivation among Black youth.

SOCIAL SUPPORT FROM SIGNIFICANT OTHERS

A positive relationship with a significant other has been found to be a crucial factor in the achievement behavior of Black adolescents (Cramer et al., 1966; DeStefano, 1986; DeSantis, 1990;Hare, 1979; Scanzoni, 1977). Individual effort are not always sufficient to overcome the obstacles to academic success. The majority of this research has examined the impact parents, teachers, and peers can have on the academic achievement behavior of Black youth. All three support groups have demonstrated a positive influence on school performance when their academic expectations of students were high.

Evidence reveals that when parents and teachers overtly express their support for minority students' goals and accomplishments, the students do better academically than those without such support. The encouragement has typically been in the form of parent-school contact, reinforcing student input regarding their future plans, and verbally indicating their belief in student success. In addition, common educational plans among significant peers have been found to have a large impact on minority student achievement. The following is an overview of research on the centrality of social support to the academic performance of African American adolescents.

Parental support has been cited as one of the most important components for academic success among Black adolescents (Clark, 1984; Comer, 1988; Gill, 1996; Mannan, 1992; Shanahan & Walberg, 1985;

Tucker et al., 1996). Students whose parents support their educational goals, have high expectations and provide verbal reinforcement have higher levels of academic performance than students without this encouragement.

A study by Scanzoni (1977) revealed that one of the most significant variables distinguishing high achievers from low achievers was the amount of interaction their parents had with their children's schools. A high percentage of parent contact with the schools (i.e., school visits) appeared to serve as an incentive for students to take their classes more seriously. In addition, the parents' increased contact with the teachers reinforced the student's belief that the parents were genuinely concerned with their academic plans. These findings were supported in a national study by Shanahan and Walberg (1985).

The notion that parents display preferential treatment according to the sex of their child is controversial. There is evidence that Black females out perform their male counterparts in school due to the higher levels of encouragement they receive from their parents (Epstein,1973; Gruin & Gaylord, 1976). Others have suggested that African American parents practice sex role stereotyping similar to the majority culture (Astin, 1975; Patterson & Sells, 1973), and thus restrict the achievement behavior of Black females and reinforce their tendency to aspire to, traditional feminine occupations. Finally, other observations of African American families have revealed that children are socialized with the view that the sexes are equal (Carter & Picou, 1975; Hale, 1982).

The evidence is not yet conclusive regarding the theory that Black females are socialized within their families to have higher achievement goals than Black males. Considering the strong influence that parents can have on academic behavior, there is a need to further investigate social support factors within the African American family that contribute to gender differences in achievement.

Teacher expectations have played a major role in the academic behavior of students. Researchers have documented that teachers' inferences about their students' present and future academic behavior affect student performance (Brophy, 1983; Rosenthal, 1985; Scott-Jones & Clark, 1986). Most of the studies that included this factor have involved an investigation similar to the "Pygmalian in the classroom" experiment conducted by Rosenthal and Jacobson (1968). In their experiments, the manipulations of teachers' expectations had a tremendous impact on students' academic development.

Significant differences in teacher behavior according to the race of the student have also been observed. Rubovits & Maehr (1971) revealed that when compared to white students, teachers gave less overall attention to

African American students, encouraged them less frequently to talk about their ideas, ignored a large percentage of their comments and questions, gave them less praise, and criticized them more. Other researchers have indicated that teachers who show little support and have low expectations of Black students' abilities tend to nurture student failure by reinforcing prejudicial beliefs and attitudes regarding their academic capabilities and their race. The evidence indicates that teachers are in a unique position to have an impact on the low school performance of Black adolescents, by maintaining high expectations and reinforcing student achievement efforts.

Significant peer relationships have been found to be very important in African American student achievement (DeStefano, 1986; Houser & Garvey, 1983; O'Brien, 1990; Wilks, 1986). In the National Study by Cramer, Bowerman, and Campbell (1986), high school students listed their peers as the third most influential persons (after parents and teachers) who have an impact on their educational goals. A student is most likely to have high educational expectations if their friends are also academically oriented, and interested in pursuing higher education. Overall, the study indicated that there is a very strong tendency for peers to establish similar educational goals.

The aspiration and educational plans of peers can have a powerful influence on a student's academic achievement. This has been partly attributed to the peer culture phenomena (Lee, 1984). A peer group can help establish the individual's goals, implant values, and shape his/her attitude toward self. To remain in a peer group, a student will have to conform to the behavior that is expected of all members. For example, if students have to maintain high aspirations and good grades to be accepted into a peer group, they will adapt to the behavior necessary to obtain this goal. The need for recognition, respect, encouragement, and acceptance by others implies that peers are in a unique position of influencing values and behaviors for one another.

In general, relationships with significant others have been found to be relevant for achievement in African American students. More research is needed among African Americans from various socioeconomic backgrounds to provide a detailed picture of Black students' relationships with their significant others and the effects of these experiences on individual differences in achievement.

In summary, the present investigation empirically examined the strength of the constructs for predicting academic achievement (cumulative GPA) among Black adolescents. Variables are identified that were expected to help distinguish Black students who are academically successful from

those who are unsuccessful. The following hypotheses guided this study:
1. Students from upper-class homes will have a higher GPA than students from lower-class homes.
2. Students with positive academic self-concepts will have a higher GPA than students with negative academic self-concepts.
3. Students who have positive perceptions about their opportunity to succeed in their academic setting will have a higher GPA than students with negative perceptions.
4. Students who believe that their future opportunities for success are excellent will have a higher GPA than students who believe their future success is limited.
5. Students who have positive perceptions of educational support from their parents, teachers and peers will have a higher GPA than students with negative perceptions of educational support.

METHOD
Participants
Data came from 368 Black adolescents attending three urban high schools located in the Midwest. The high schools were predominantly Black (2% non-minority). The sample consisted of 194 sophomores (189 females, 105 males); and 174 juniors (52 females, 122 males), and all students were between 15-17 years of age and participated in a college preparatory program. An analysis of the 1990 census tract data by population characteristics revealed that the three schools had comparable census data. The areas in which the students live were compared according to average occupation level, family income, and percentage of population below the poverty level.

Variables and their measurement
The questionnaire consisted of demographic information as well as the four scales that assessed the independent variables of interest. Each measure except the Self-Concept of Ability Scale, used a four-point likert-type rating scale (from strongly agree to strongly disagree). The Self-Concept of Ability measure, used a five-point likert scale that varied responses according to the nature of the question. Most of the questions included response selections of among the best to among the poorest. Following are the descriptions of the individual measures.
    Academic: Self concept. (SELF) The Self-Concept of Ability Scale developed by Brookover et al. (1965) was used in the present study

to assess self-evaluations of academic ability. This scale measures how students feel about school in general as well as how they view their academic skills in relation to those of their peers (e.g. How do you rate yourself in school ability compared with your close friends?). The internal consistency reliability for this instrument is .85 in this study.

Perception of opportunity to succeed in school. Students' perceptions of their opportunities for success in their school environment was assessed by eight questions from an adapted version of the Inventory of Personal Investment (Braskamp & Maehr, 1983). The purpose of the original scale was to assess whether or not employees perceived that they had the opportunity to obtain what they expected to in their work environment. The adapted questions used in the present study, measured students' perceptions of their opportunity to succeed in a school environment. For example, "When I work hard, my teachers notice." For this study, the Perceived Opportunity for Success in School Scale had an internal consistency reliability of .65.

Perception of opportunity structure. Student perceptions of future opportunities were measured by a shortened version of the 14-item Awareness of Limited Access to Opportunity Scale (Landis, Dinitz, & Reckless, 1963). The scale was developed to measure one's perceived barriers regarding future opportunities in the areas of education, career, power, influence wealth and neighborhood. (e.g., Doing well in school will help me earn a good income). The correlation between the short version of this scale and the longer version is .89. For this study, the Awareness of Limited Access to Opportunity Scale had an internal consistency reliability of .65.

Perceived support form parents, teachers and peers. The parent, teacher and peer support items were adopted from Farmer's Career Motivation and Achievement Planning Questionnaire (C-MAP; Farmer et al., 1981). All three scales have parallel items which reflect the students' perception of significant other support for their academic efforts (e.g., My parents, teachers, friends-encourage me to do my best in school). In this study, the parent, teacher and peer support scales had internal consistency reliability coefficients of .55, .71 and .83 respectively.

Socioeconomic status (SES). Students were asked to respond to five socioeconomic indicators that were incorporated in the questionnaire: mother's occupation and educational level, father's occupation and education level, and annual family income. The parents' occupations that were reported were scored using Duncan's Socioeconomic Index (SEI) (Hauser & Featherman, 1977: Stevens & Cho, 1985). The index described socioeconomic distances between occupations. Duncan scores were derived from a combination of average education and salary level for each occupation.

Academic achievement. The cumulative grade point averages (GPA) were used to assess student's academic achievement behavior.

PROCEDURE
The variables were assessed through a 10-page questionnaire and interview procedure. Four English teachers from each school (2 sophomore and 2 junior classes) were briefed regarding the classroom administration of the questionnaire. Students completed the questionnaire in approximately 30 minutes. Ten students were randomly selected from each school to be interviewed individually. The purpose was to provide anecdotal information from students that would help explain differences between Black students who were academically successful in school and those who were not.

RESULTS
The data analysis was conducted in two major phases. Analysis of variance was utilized to examine mean differences in academic achievement for gender and socioeconomic groups. SAS's general, linear model (GLM) was implemented to counteract the effect of unequal numbers of observations for the different levels of variables.

The second process involved multiple regression analysis to establish which independent variable made the most contribution to the variance in academic achievement. In addition, of particular interest was identifying the combination of variables that formed the best prediction for the student's grade point average. The student's GPA was regressed on academic self-concept, perception of opportunity to succeed in school, perception of opportunity structure, and measures of significant other support (parents, teachers, peers).

Descriptive Analysis
Initial analysis consisted of the mean levels and correlations for the independent variables. Table I specifies the means, standard deviations, as well as the minimum and maximum values. A low score for all measures except SES and GPA, indicates a positive perception by the student.

Table 1: Means and Standard Deviations for Variables in the Study

Variable	N	Mean	SD	Actual Values		Potential Values	
				Min	Max	Min	Max
Grade Point Average (GPA)	315	2.50	.79	.10	4.00	0	4.00
Perceived Parent Support	367	1.69	.32	1.00	2.64	1.0	4.00
Perceived Teacher Support	367	1.70	.44	1.00	3.25	1.0	4.00
Peer Perceived Support	368	1.80	.49	1.00	3.67	1.0	4.00
SES (Standard Scores)	225	.00	.71	1.38	1.97	0	2.35
Opportunity For Academic Success in School	367	1.9	.4	1.00	3.25	1.0	4.00
Awareness of Limited Opportunity	368	1.73	.42	1.00	3.38	1.0	4.00
Academic Self-Concept	364	2.09	.58	1.00	4.56	1.0	5.00

Correlations

The correlational analysis in Table 2 supported the hypotheses that students with positive perceptions of academic self-concept and opportunity for success in school would have higher GPA's than students with negative perceptions on these variables. The academic self-concept scale had the highest inter-variable correlation with GPA ($r = -.69$, $p < .001$). When inter-variable correlations were examined separately by sex, the scale remained the highest correlation with GPA (males, $r = -.72$, $p < .001$; females, $r = -.60$, $p < .001$). Since low scores on the scale indicated a positive academic self-concept, the results demonstrated the higher the student's academic self-concept, the higher the GPA.

There was a significant negative correlation between GPA and the opportunity scale (GPA, $r = -.22$, $p < .001$). Students who believed they had opportunity for success in their academic environment (indicated by a low score on the scale) had a tendency to have high GPA's.

The hypothesis that students who scored low on the Awareness of Limited Access to Opportunity Scale (Limit) would have a higher GPA than students who score high was not supported by the correlation data. The inter-variable correlation of GPA and limit was very low and insignificant (GPA, $r = .02$). The variables that had significantly high correlations with the Limit Scale were the teacher ($r = .37$, $p < .001$), parent ($r = .27$, $p < .001$), and peer ($r = .25$, $p < .001$) support scales. Students who perceived their significant others as giving them very little academic support had a tendency to believe they had limited access to future opportunities.

The prediction that students who had positive perceptions of parent, teacher and peer academic support would have higher GPA's than students with negative perceptions was not confirmed. All of the correlations between the significant other support scales and academic achievement were low and insignificant while relationships among the three scales were strong.

Analysis of Variance
Surprising results were obtained when analysis of variance procedures were conducted for SES and GPA. The hypothesis that students from high socioeconomic backgrounds would have higher GPA than students from low SES backgrounds, was not supported. Table 3 indicates that the students' socioeconomic status has a significant ($p < .05$) effect on their grade point average. There was a significant negative correlation between GPA and SES ($r = -.17$, $p < .05$). Students from low-income families had higher GPA than students from upper-class homes. More elaboration on this unusual finding can be found in the discussion section.

Table 2: Zero-order Intercorrelations of the Variables

Zero-order Intercorrelations of the Variables

	GPA	Parent Support	Teacher Support	Peer Support	Opport	Limit	SES	SELF
GPA								
Parent Support	.05							
Teacher Support	.05	.39***						
Peer Support	-.03	.30***	.37***					
Opport	-.22***	.26***	.45***	.32***				
Limit	.02	.27***	.37***	.25***	.15**			
SES	-.17*	-.03	.13	-.05	-.04	.01		
SELF	-.69***	.15**	.22***	.06	.15*	.17**	-.01	

* = P .05
** = P .01
*** = P .001

NOTE: Low scores on all measures except GPA and SES indicate students are positive on this construct.

The results of the ANOVA did support the hypothesis that females would have significantly higher grade point averages than males (see Table 3). The mean GPA for male students is 2.14, as compared to 2.51 for females.

Table 3: Analysis of Variance of GPA by Socioeconomic Status and Sex

Analysis of Variance of GPA by Socioeconomic Status and Sex

Sources	df	SS	F
SES	2	3.96	3.34* (L)
within SES Groups	198	117.46	
SEX	1	9.76	16.61*** (F)
within SEX Groups	313	184.03	

NOTE: (L) = Students with low SES are higher.
(F) = Females have higher GPA.
* = P<.05
*** = P<.001

<u>Multiple Regression</u>
Table 4 presents the results of the multiple regression analysis for the full model of predictor variables. Academic Self-Concept emerges as the most powerful predictor of academic achievement. The second most important predictor is the academic support students' perceive from their parents. This finding supports the research highlighting the significant role parents play in the development of academic achievement.

Table 4: Coefficients of the Full Regression Model of Academic Achievement

Coefficients of the Full Regression Model of Academic Achievement

Independent Variables	<u>Coefficients</u>
Self	-.99***
Limit	.21*
Opport	.04
Teach	.09
Parents	.28**
Peers	.06

$R^2 = .52$

Standard error = .55

N = 310

* = $p<.05$
** = $p<.01$
*** = $p<.001$

To examine the unique contribution of the individual's personal (self, opportunity, limit) and social support (parents, teachers, peers) variables on academic achievement, separate regression analyses was conducted. First, academic achievement was regressed on the social support variables. These factors' contribution to the total variance was not significant, $(R^2=.009$, p< .38). Next, academic achievement was regressed on the three personal factors. This regression equation was significant $(R^2= .505$, p<.001). Academic Self-Concept was the significant predictor (B=.99, p < .001). Although the opportunity scale (Perception of Opportunity for Success in School) did not contribute significantly to the overall equation, it was a significant contributor when used solely as a predictor for academic achievement $(B=-.44, p, .0001)$, accounting for .047% of the variance. It appears that the correlation between self, opportunity, and limit undermined the individual contribution of opportunity (See Table 2). The dominant predictor, self, accounted for almost all of variance when used as a single predictor for academic achievement $(R= .47, p< .0001)$. Further exploration with the personal variables, using ANOVA procedures, revealed that students who are high on all three personal variables (self, opportunity, limit) had significantly higher GPA's than students who were low on all three or who were high on just one or two of the variables.

DISCUSSION
The preceding section presented some expected as well as unanticipated findings. The results will be interpreted with the help of the interviews in order to paint an anecdotal picture of the concerns and issues that arose in this study.

One of the most interesting findings in this study was that students with low SES had significantly higher GPAs than students from high SES backgrounds. In addition, the correlation between SES and GPA was lower than expected (.r = -.17, p< .05). There are several plausible explanations for this low but significant correlation, including the fact that all students participated in a college preparatory curriculum. An advanced curriculum can motivate and challenge students to do their best in school. It also serves to bring high and low SES groups closer together in regards to their academic foundation.

Given that all students experienced similar academic curricula, it is speculative why students classified as being from high and middle income families did not achieve up to their expected norm, thereby bringing down the mean GPA for their economic group. Research which supports these results indicate that African American parents with high and middle income levels often have a difficult time transmitting academic motivation to their offspring (Hale, 1982). Most discussions around this issue have centered around the fact that students do not always receive adequate models for goal setting and problem solving.

An additional reason accounting for a higher mean GPA than expected for low SES students may have been that low SES families have a very strong belief that academic success as a means to social and economic mobility (Edwards, 1970; Scanzoni, 1977). The low SES students in this study may have been working very hard academically to prepare for a future that would be better than their present low economic environment.

It is also feasible to believe that these results are a reflection of the national trend observed for African Americans (Farley, 1984). A national study conducted by Farley revealed that the academic achievement gap between Blacks at the top and the bottom of the income distribution was getting smaller. In other words, Black students at both ends of the income range have similar academic gains. This indicated that the socioeconomic status may not have been as large a factor as it used to be in describing the academic achievement behavior of low income and high income African Americans.

The significant gender differences in achievement that were found and supported by the interview data suggests that these differences can be partly attributed to the consequences of sex-role socialization in African American families. The interview data reveals that Black parents reinforce behaviors in females that are compatible with academic achievement, whereas males are reinforced for portraying macho images. For instance, it was believed that parents gave more attention to their daughters' college and career plans than they did to the future plans of their sons'.

The male interviewees indicated that they felt as though their parents did not push them to work hard academically. Several of the male students described their parents as having a laissez-faire attitude toward their performance in school. In addition, the male students believed they were expected to engage in activities that made them appear tough. They were reinforced by parents and peers to participate in sports and other masculine extracurricular activities. Males in this study also received strong support from their peers for "acting cool." This meant they had to condemn education and disapprove of the status quo in the school system. The pressure to "act cool" and maintain a tough image may have prevented males in this study from joining academic enrichment programs or seeking help for their course work when needed, thereby contributing to their low academic performance.

These findings support research which suggests Black students are differentially treated by sex, in their school setting as well as in the home (Irvine, 1991: McAdoo & McAdoo, 1985). Females overwhelmingly reported more than males that teachers were a major source of academic encouragement and motivation. The interviews revealed the two major stereotypes that teachers often had about Black males were that they were disruptive and not interested in learning (Brophy & Good, 1974; Hale, 1982). The following was a quote from one of the interviewees (it sums up the sentiment of several male students). The quote clearly reveals how this stereotype held by some teachers, can be perceived by students and subsequently effect their learning process:

> "Teachers believe that Black males want to come to the classroom to disrupt and not to learn. Some teachers act like we want to hurt them physically. Students can perceive this uneasiness from teachers—it makes students uneasy as well. When this happens, my mind starts wandering, and it becomes very difficult to concentrate, and stay interested in the lesson."

Teachers with whom this investigator had spoken, insisted that Black boys appeared rebellious while Black girls tended to be compliant. It is quite possible that teachers believe there is a bigger misfit between Black boys and school than Black girls and school. The current study demonstrates that academic self-concept had the highest inter-variable correlation with GPA as well as accounting for the most variance. These results are supportive of past research that show self-concept of academic ability correlating significantly with achievement behavior among African American students in grade school, high school (Epps, 1969), and college (Gurin & Epps, 1975). All of the studies reveal a positive correlation between academic self-concept and numerous measures of academic behavior (i.e., GPA, standardized tests, educational aspiration/expectations). The present study adds to this existing research by showing the value of academic self-concept for distinguishing high and low achieving African American adolescents.

The females in this study had higher mean academic self-concept scores than males. This may be due to their positive perceived support from significant others. It is believed that one of the major methods students use to form their academic self-concept is by internalizing the perceived evaluations of significant others (Brookover et al., 1965; Klienfeld, 1972). In this study it was speculated that females had higher self-assessments of their academic ability because the academic evaluations they perceive from their parents, teachers, and peers were higher than those perceived by the Black males in the study.

An additional explanation for females having higher mean academic self-concept scores than males can be attributed to their higher academic performance. As African American females compare their academic performance to their male counterpart, they form a positive self-evaluation of their academic ability (Hare, 1979). Research evidence indicates that once the self-evaluation is complete, Black females can maintain this high academic evaluation, even when they do not have the highest GPA among an ethnically diverse group of students (Hare, 1987; Rosenberg & Simmons, 1971).

One of the least explored constructs, perception of opportunity for success in school, demonstrated its viability for predicting academic achievement among African American adolescents. These findings support existing literature that observed student success based on their perception of psychological and social factors in their academic setting (Cramer et al., 1986; Lee, 1984; Waxman & Huang, 1996). Students who were academically successful (i.e. GPA and standardized test scores), had positive relationships with teachers, received encouragement from their teachers, and believed that their academic goals could be obtained in their present school setting.

The Perceived Opportunity for Success in School Scale had the largest correlation with the Teacher Support Scale ($r = .45$, $p<.001$). This is logical since teachers are the primary source from which students base their perceptions about the school environment. Teachers who demonstrated academic and personal interest in students and had high educational expectations of them, had more students in their classes with positive school experiences than teachers who did not recognize students for their effort and accomplishments (Cramer et al., 1986; Ogbu, 1986; Mackler, 1970). The students perceptions of their opportunity for academic success identified in this study, can be categorized as mutual respect, supportive atmosphere for displaying competence and recognition for accomplishments and effort. These appear to be crucial components for academic achievement among African American adolescents, and should be useful in further research exploring school culture.

The prediction that students who do not perceive they have limited opportunities in the future will have a higher GPA than students who believe that they have limitations, was not confirmed by the data. In other words, the Awareness of Limited Access to Opportunity Scale (Limit) did not distinguish between students who were high achievers and low achievers. The correlation between the Limit Scale and GPA was very low and insignificant. These results do not support other research findings which state that Blacks who are aware of limitations have lower achievement behavior than students who do not perceive future limitations (Cramer, et al., 1986; DeStafano, 1986; Jackson, 1981; Scanzoni, 1985). This investigator attributes the results in this study to the students using their immediate environment as a frame of reference. Black students who attend predominantly Black schools tend to be somewhat naive regarding possible future limitations they can have as a result of their race and institutional racism (Feagin & Feagin, 1978; Jones, 1979). All the students came from environments in which they are exposed to successful African American adults (i.e. prominent politicians, public servants, educators and athletes). The Black professionals that they saw may have had a tendency to create the perception that African Americans were not limited in their social and professional arenas.

Additional explanations for the insignificant relationship between the Limit Scale and GPA may be attributed to the lack of sensitivity of the scale or the fact that the measure was too narrowly defined for the population.

The strong relationship that was predicted for academic achievement and academic support by significant others, was not realized in this study. While the intercorrelations between the two types of variables, social support and GPA, were low and insignificant, the Parent Support Scale appeared to make a contribution to academic achievement in the full regression model. This result was not sustained when exploring the regression equation for the social support variables only. It is possible that the significant other scales encouraged socially acceptable responses that may have caused students to answer in a similar manner. Such an occurrence would restrict the range of scale scores and make it very difficult for the scales to distinguish high GPA students from those with a low GPA.

Although the instruments did not reflect a significant relationship, the interview results indicate the importance of social support for academic achievement among African American adolescents. Students were asked two major questions regarding this issue. The first one was, "What has helped you do your best in school?" Academic encouragement from one or both parents was stated as the most crucial factor. Teacher support was the second influential factor that contributed to their academic motivation. The second question, "What has prevented you from doing your best in school?", revealed a similar order of significance. Students who perceive a lack of academic support from significant others had less desire to achieve in school than students with such support. Lack of parental support was listed as the most damaging with teachers and peers running a close second and third.

IMPLICATIONS FOR PRACTICE

This study clearly identifies educational and social factors that make a difference between Black adolescents who succeed in school and those who do not. Two educational domains suggested for implementation of these factors are the school and the home.

The major predictor of academic achievement was the student's academic self-concept. In order for this knowledge to have an impact on student performance, it would be important to work with teacher education/staff-development programs. Teachers need to be encouraged to help students develop positive self-evaluations of their academic potential. This would involve teachers giving students constructive feedback continuously, and helping them realize that their efforts are the key to present and future achievement. These results also suggest that schools develop interventions to help minority youngsters see themselves as good students, instead of the typical interventions that focus on self-esteem in general.

An additional educational modification that can be adopted from this study is the importance of increasing a student's perception of the opportunity to succeed in their current academic setting. This would require intense work with teachers on helping to enhance the overall learning climate in the classroom. Teachers would have to feel comfortable with their role in working with all students including those from diverse backgrounds. As the interview data indicated, students can perceive if teachers are uncomfortable, which will cause many students not to take the academic setting serious enough to do their best. The perception of a comfortable academic climate will enable students to feel free enough to try behaviors that demonstrate their various levels of academic competence. In order to perpetuate this behavior among all students, teachers need to not only feel comfortable in the classroom, but learn to treat students fairly, be conscious of the student's perception of their learning environment and provide recognition for all student effort. Hence, encouraging students to put forth consistent effort, regardless of the outcome is vital.

As mentioned earlier, the second educational domain that can have a major impact on academic achievement is the home life of African American adolescents. This study indicated that parents could provide a sound base that can contribute significantly to the academic performance of their children. One of the key ingredients for this sound foundation is for parents to treat their sons and daughters equally. Encouraging their boys as well as girls to set high academic goals. In addition, parents need to serve as positive role models for their sons and daughters.

FUTURE RESEARCH

The goal of the present research was to look at individual perceptions and social support factors as predictors for African American adolescent achievement. As indicated, two of the three constructs (academic self-concept and perception of opportunity for success) and one of the social support variables (parents) show promise of distinguishing African American students who succeed academically from those who do not. While one's perception of future opportunities and the teacher and peer support variables did not result in significant predictors, they should be reexamined by researchers using measures that do not encourage socially acceptable responses. The interviews and data from other studies indicate that these variables may be key components in understanding school performance differences among African American adolescents (Mickelson, 1990).

Future directions should include the relationship between measures of racial identity attitudes and academic achievement among African American adolescents. Within group differences in racial identity attitudes of Black high school students may be related to the various ways that they perform in school (McCurtis & Thomas, 1997). It has also been shown that the African American's level of identity (i.e, immersion) can be a fundamental component of providing the most effective intervention strategies and services. Additionally, the issue of color may be more salient for African Americans than any other minority group, and white youth are less likely to experience the chronic stress and problems associated with racial identity (Ford, Harris, Webb & Jones, 1994).

Furthermore, future research should continue to explore the model of academic achievement that this study suggests. Students can perform successfully in an environment in which positive self-evaluations of academic potential are developed and reinforced by a comfortable academic climate and home life that is supportive of academic pursuits.

REFERENCES

Ames C. & Archer, J. (1988). Achievement goals in the classroom: students' learning strategies and motivation processes. *Journal of Educational Psychology* 80, 260-267.

Astin, A.W. (1975). *Preventing students from dropping out._*San Francisco, CA: Jossey-Bass

Boykin,W.(1983).Academic performance of Afro-American children. In J. Spence (Ed), *Achievement and achievement motives*. San Francisco: W. H. Freeman & Co.

Braskam, L. & Maehr. M.(1983).*Inventory of personal investment.* (Instrument developed at University of Illinois, Urbana, Illinois).

Brookover, W. B., LeRue, J.M., Hanachek, D. E., Thomas, S., & Erickson, E. (1965). *Self-concept of ability and school achievement, II* (U.S.O.E. Cooperative Research Rpt, Project o 1636). East Lansing: Michigan State University.

Brophy, , J.E. (1983). Research on the self-fulfilling prophecy and teacher expectations. *Journal of Educational Psychology* 75, 631-661.

Brophy, J., & Good, T. (1974). *Teacher-student relationships: Causes and consequences.* New York: Holt, Rinehart and Winston, Inc.

Byrne, B. M. (1984) The general/academic self-concept nomological networks. A review of construct validation research. *Review of Educational Research*, 54, 427-456.

Byrne, B.M. & Shavelson, R.J. (1986) On the structure of adolescent Self-concept. *Journal of Educational Psychology*, 78, 474-481.

Carter, T. , & Picou, J. (1975) Status attainment theory and Black male youth. In J. Picou & R. Campbell (Eds.), *Career behavior of special groups, research and practice.* Columbus, OH: Charles E. Merrill.

Clark, R. (1984). *Family life and school achievement: why poor Black children succeed and fail.* Chicago: The University of Chicago Press.

Comer, J.P. (1988). Educating poor minority children. *Scientific American*, 259, 42-48.

Cosby, A. (1971). Black-White differences in aspirations among deep South high school students. *Journal of Negro Education.* 40, 17-21.

Cramer, R., Bowerman, C., & Campbell, R. (1986). *Social factors in educational achievement and aspirations among Negro adolescents* (Vols. I and II). (Cooperative Research Project No. 1168) Washington, DC: Office of Education, U.S..

DeSantis, J.P. (1990). Black adolescents' concerns that they are academically able. *Merrill Palmer Quarterly.* 36 (20), 287-99.

Dye, J.S. (1989). Parental involvement in curriculum matters. *Educational Research, 31,* (1), 20-35.

DeStefano, L. (1986). *Factors associated with academic success or future in academically able minority high school students.* Unpublished doctoral dissertation, University of Pittsburgh, PA.

Ekstrom, R.E., Goertz, M. E., Pollack J.M., & Rock, D.A. (1986). Who drops out of school and why: Findings from a national study. *Teachers College Record*, 87, 356-373.

Edwards, H. (1970). *Black students.* New York: The Free Press.

Edwards, 0. (1976). Components of academic success: A profile of achieving Black adolescents. *Journal of Negro Education,* 45, 408-422

Epps, E. G. (1969). Correlates of academic achievement among Northern and Southern urban Negro students. *Journal of Social Issues,* 25, 55-70.

Epstein, F. (1973). Position effects of the multiple negative: Explaining the success of the Black professional women. *American Journal of Sociology,* 78, 912-935.

Farley, R. (1984). *Blacks and whites narrowing the gap?* Cambridge, MA: Harvard University Press.

Farmer, H., Keane, J., Rooney, G., Vispoel, W., Harmen, L., Lerner,B., Linn, R., & Maehr, M. (1981). *Career motivation and achievement planning (C-MAP).* (Instrument can be obtained from Helen S. Farmer, University of Illinois, Urbana, Illinois)

Feagin, J. , & Feagin, C. (1978). *Discrimination American style: Institutional racism and sexism.* Englewood Cliffs, NJ: Prentice-Hall.

Fleming, S.S. & Courney, B.E. (1984). The dimensionality of self-esteem. Hierarchal facet model for revised measurement scales. *Journal of Personality and Social Psychology* 46, 404-421

Ford, D.Y., Harris, J., Webb, K.S., & Jones, D.L. (1994). Rejection or confirmation of racial identity: a dilemma for high achieving Blacks? *The Journal of Educational Thought,* 28, (1), 7-33.

Ford, D. (1995). Desegregating gifted education: a need unmet. The *Journal of Negro Education,* 64, 52-62.

Gill, S. & Reynolds, A.J. (1996). *Role of parent expectations in the school success of at-risk children.* (ERIC Document Reproduction No. ED 401 019).

Gottfredson, L.S. (1981). Circumscription and compromise: A developmental theory of occupational aspirations. *Journal of Counseling Psychology,* 28, 545-579.

Gurin, P., & Epps, E. (1975). *Black consciousness, identity and achievement.* New York, NY: J. Wiley and Sons.

Gurin, P. , & Gaylord, C. (1976). Educational and occupational goals of men and women at Black colleges. *Monthly Labor Review,* 99, 10-16.

Hale, J. (1982). *Black children, their roots, culture and learning styles.* Provo, UT: Brigham Young University.

Hansford, B.C. & Hattie, J.A. (1982) The relationship between self and achievement/ performance measure. *Review of Educational Research.* 52, 123-142.

Hare, B. (1979). *Black girls: A comparative analysis of self perception and achievement by race, sex, and socioeconomic background.* Unpublished monograph. Center for Social organization of Schools (Report No. 271), Johns Hopkins, University, Baltimore, MD.

Hare, B. (1987). Structural inequality and the endangered status of Black youth. *Journal of Negro Education*, 56 (l): 100-110.

Hauser, R., & Featherman, D. (1977). *The process of stratification.* New York: Academic Press.

Houser, B.B. & Garvey, C. (1983). The impact of family, peers and educational personnel upon career decision-making. *Journal of Vocational Behavior*, 23, 35-44.

Irvine, J.J. (1991). *Black students and school failure.* New York: Praeger.

Jackson, L. (1981). *The effect of desegregation and achievement motivation on academic achievement levels of Black high school students.* Dissertation Abstracts International, 42, (6-B), 2600.

Jones, J. (1979). Conceptual and strategic issues in' the relationship of Black psychology to American social science. In W. Boykin (Ed.), *Research directions of Black psychologists.* New York: Russell Sage Foundation.

Jordon, T. (1981). Self-concepts, motivation and academic achievement of Black adolescents. *Journal of Educational Psycholoqv*, 73, 509-517.

Kleinfeld, J. (1972). The relative importance of teachers and parents in the formation of Negro and white students' academic self-concept. *Journal of Educational Research*, 65(5), 211-212.

Landis, J. R., Dinitz, S., and Reckless, W. (1963). Implementing two theories of delinquency: Value orientation and awareness of limited opportunity. *Sociology and Social Research*, 47: 408-416.

Lee, Courtland, C. (1984). An investigation of psychosocial variables related to academic success for rural Black adolescents. *Journal of Negro Education*, 53(4): 424-434.

Mackler, B. (1970). Blacks who are academically successful. *Urban Education*, 5: 210-237.

Maehr & Braskamp. (1986). *The Motivation Factor: A Theory of Personal Investment.* Lexington, MA: D.C Heath

Maehr, M. and Fyans, L. (1989). *"School Culture", Student Ethnicity and Motivation.* Paper presented at the annual meeting of the Association For Educational Research.

Mannan, G. & Blackwell, J. (1992). Parent involvement: barriers and opportunities. *Urban Review*, 24, 219-226.

Marsh, H. W. (1987). The big fish-little-pond effect on academic self-concept. *Journal of Educational Psychology.* 79, 3, 280-295.

Marsh, H. W., Barnes, J., & Hocevar, D. (1985) Self-other agreement on multidimensional self-concept ratings: Factor analysis and multitrait-multimethod analysis. *Journal of Personality and Social Psychology*, 49, 1360-1377.

Marsh, H.W., and Shavelson, R.J. (1985). Self-Concept: Its multifaceted, hierarchal structure. *Educational Psychologist*, 20, 107-125.

McAdoo, H., & McAdoo, J. (Eds.). (1985). *Black children: Social educational and parental environments.* San Francisco: Sage Publications.

McClelland, D. (1985). *Human Motivation.* Glenview, ILL: Scott, Foresman and Company.

McCurtis-Witherspoon, Karen & Thomas, Anita, J. (1997). Racial identity attitudes, school achievement, and academic self-efficacy among African American high school students. *Journal of Black Psychology*, 23, 7-33.

Mickelson, R.A., (1990). The attitude-achievement paradox among Black adolescents. *Sociology of Education*, 63, 44-61.

National Center for Educational Statistics, (1988). *High school and beyond: National longitudinal study of high school;* Washington, D.C.; U.S. Department of Education.

O'Brien, B.R. (1990). *The use of family members and peers as social resources during adolescence.* (ERIC Document Reproduction No. ED 327 297).

Ogbu, J. (1974). *The next generation: An ethnography of education in an urban neighborhood.* New York, NY: Academic Press.

Ogbu, J. (1986). The consequences of the American caste system. In U. Neisser (Ed.), *The school achievement of minority children: New perspectives*, 19-50.

Ogbu, J.U. (1992). Understanding cultural diversity and learning. *Educational Research*, 21: 5-14.

Osborne, J. (1995). Academics, self-esteem and race: A look at the underlying assumptions of the misidentification hypothesis. *Personality and Social Psychology Bulletin*, 2(5), 449-455.

Osterlind, S.J. (1997). *A national review of scholastic achievement in general education courses.* ASHE-ERIC Higher Education Reports, 25 (8), 1-94.

Patterson, M. , & Sells, L. (1973) . Women dropouts from higher education. In A.S. Ross & A. Calderwood (Eds.), *Academic women on the move*, (173-185). New York: Russell Sage

Patton, J.M. (1998). The disproportionate representation of African Americans in special education: looking behind the curtain for understanding and solutions. *The Journal of Special Education*, 32, 25-31.

Rosenberg, M., & Simmons, R. (1971). Black and white self-esteem: The urban school child. *American Sociological Review*, 38, 553-568.

Rosenthal, R., & Jacobson, L. (1968). *Pygmalian in the classroom: Teacher expectations and pupil's intellectual performance*. New York: Holts, Rinehart, and Winston.

Rubovits, P. , & Maehr, M. (1971) . Pygmalion analyzed: Toward an explanation of the Rosenthal-Jacobson findings. *Journal of Personality and Social Psychology*, 19, 197-203.

Russo, C. & Talbert-Johnson, Carolyn (1997). The overrepresentation of African American children in special education: resegregation of educational planning? *Education and Urban Society*, 29, 136-148.

Scanzoni, J. (1977). *The Black family in modern society: Patterns of stability and security*. Chicago: University of Chicago Press.

Scott-Jones, D., & Clark, M. (1986). The school experiences of Black girls. *Phi Delta Kappan*, 67, 520-526.

Shanahan, T., & Walberg, H. (1985). Productive influences on high school student achievement. *Journal of Educational Research*, 78, (6), 357-363.

Shavelson, R.J., & Marsh, H.W. (1986) On the Structure of Self Concept. In R. Schwarzer (ed.), *Anxiety and Cognitions*. Hillside, NJ. Erlbaum Associates.

Shokraii, N. H. (1996). *The self-esteem fraud: Why feel good education does not lead to academic success*? (ERIC Document Reproductions Service No. ED 402 105).

Smith, T.M. (1995). The educational progress of Black students. Findings from *The condition of education, 1994*. (ERIC Document Reproduction No. ED 385 619).

Smith, E. (1983). Issues in racial minorities' career behavior. In W. Walsh and S. Osipow (Eds.), *Handbook of vocational Psychology*, (Vol. 1) Hillsdale, NJ: Lawrence Erlbaum Associates.

Stevens, G., & Cho, D. (1985). A revised socioeconomic index of occupational status. *Occupational Status Index*, 364-395.

Stipek, D.J. (1993). *Motivation To Learn* (2nd ed.). Boston: Allyn and Bacon.

Taylor, R. (1994). Risk and resilience: Contextual influences on the development of African American adolescents. In M. Wang, & e. Gordon (Eds.), *Educational resilience in inner-city America*. (pp.119-130). Hillsdale, NJ: Lawrence Erlbaum Associates.

Tucker, C.M., Harris, Y.R, Brady, B.A., & Herman, K.C. (1996). The association of selected parent behaviors with the academic achievement of African American children and European children. *Child Study Journal*, 26(4), 253-276.

U.S. Department of Education: (1998). National Center for Education Statistics, *The Condition of Education*. Washington DC., U.S. Government Printing Office.

Waxman, H.C., & Huang, S. Y. (1996). Motivation and learning environment differences in inner-city middle school students. *Journal of Educational Research*, 90 (2): 93-102.

Wilks, J. (1986). The relative importance of parents and friends in adolescent decision-making. *Journal of Youth and Adolescence*, 15: 323-334.

ACKNOWLEDGEMENT
The support of the teachers, administrators and students of the schools who participated in the study is gratefully acknowledged. I want to thank my colleagues from the University of Illinois, Urbana-Champaign, Lenore Harmon, Mildred B. Griggs and William Trent for their suggestions and assistance. I am especially appreciative of my research assistants at Arizona State University Marla Bennett and Laura Huser and to the administrative support staff, Sheila Saunders and Emily Traiforos.

Correspondence concerning this paper should be addressed to Teresa A.Fisher, Assistant Professor, Arizona State University, Psychology in Education, P. O. Box 870611, Tempe, AZ., 85287-0611 or phone (480) 940-8038. E-mail address: T.A.Fisher@asu.edu.

14. *Black Students' Academic Performance and Preparation for Higher Education*

Ramona S. Thomas

For a variety of reasons, ranging from recent challenges to affirmative action and admissions policies to issues of educational stratification and inequity, the academic preparedness of high school graduates for higher education, particularly those from historically underrepresented groups (e.g., Black, Latino, and low-income students) continues to receive national attention. The concern is that many high school graduates from these groups are academically limited and do not possess the knowledge and skills needed for higher education (College Entrance Examination Board [College Board] 1983). Despite decades of educational goals, policies, and reform, as well as gains in the achievement and attainment levels of Black students, questions about their academic performance persist.

Driven by the need to investigate and document the role of schools in students' college-going behavior, this chapter examines whether Black students who plan to pursue higher education receive the academic preparation necessary to be admitted into and succeed in a four-year college. The purpose of this study is to: (1) describe and highlight the academic preparation and performance of Black high school students, and (2) examine Black students' college enrollment and the significance of their academic preparation (and achievement) in their enrollment. I focus on Black students because academic achievement and preparation issues for these youth remain the most pressing. They tend to be significantly under-represented among high school graduates who are academically well prepared for college (Miller 1995). In addition to raising important questions, I hope to stimulate discussion about Black students' academic experiences in an effort to bring about change that will ultimately enhance their experiences and improve their performance and college participation.

Related Research
This section provides a brief review of the literature on students' academic preparation and achievement in high school. This includes research on high school programs or tracking and how it influences student outcomes; the importance of students' academic preparation (e.g., curriculum, course taking, and opportunity to learn) and achievement in high school; and the influence of academic preparation and achievement factors on students' college enrollment.

The framework for this chapter comes from a model of student college choice, which emphasizes how the process of college choice occurs and how it varies for different groups (Hossler & Gallagher 1987). Student college choice is an ongoing, longitudinal process that begins at an early age, for most students, and results in a student's decision to attend an institution of higher education. Combined models of student college choice emphasize social and economic factors that affect a student's college choice process and typically have three stages (Hossler, Braxton & Coopersmith 1989). The first, "predisposition," is a developmental phase in which students decide whether they want to continue their education past high school. During the second stage, "search," students explore potential college options and acquire and examine college information. During the last stage, "choice," students formulate an application and decide which institution they will attend, or given their alternatives, whether they will attend college at all (Hossler et al. 1989; Hossler & Gallagher 1987; Paulsen 1990).

This chapter raises questions that are central to both the predisposition and choice stages. This study examines the academic preparation and performance of Black students who expect to pursue higher education; that is, those who have decided to continue their education beyond high school. Students' predisposition toward higher education has been found to relate to their academic preparation and performance in high school (Hossler et al. 1989). However, another important part of this study focuses on the choice stage, particularly whether and to what extent Black high school graduates attend college right after high school, especially four-year institutions of higher education. Using student college choice as a framework for this study provides more flexibility because it helps account for a *process*, for which many factors are significant. More importantly, the model acknowledges that the college choice process varies for different groups of students.

Not surprisingly, academic achievement continues to be one of the more common predictors in the empirical attempts to explain the lower college participation rates of Black high school graduates. Research indicates that academic achievement has a strong, positive, and consistent relationship to the probability of attending college (Kane & Spizman 1994; Manski & Wise 1983; Stage & Rushin 1993). Moreover, students' grades and their performance on standardized tests have been identified as significant predictors of their college attendance after high school (Ganderton & Santos 1995; Stage & Rushin 1993).

However, almost all measures of academic outcomes, such as standardized test scores, high school graduation, and participation in college preparatory classes, continue to be strongly correlated with ethnic background and social class (Wilson & Corcoran 1988). On standardized tests, such as the National Assessment of Educational Progress (NAEP) and the Scholastic Assessment Test (SAT) [formerly the Scholastic Aptitude Test], Blacks have historically been overrepresented among low-achievers and underrepresented among high-achieving students. Note, however, that the SAT was not initially designed as an indicator of achievement, but to help predict how well students would perform in college (National Center for Education Statistics [NCES] 1998b). What is important is that differences among racial groups develop relatively early in students' school careers (Miller 1995).

The literature indicates that students' high school program is another important predictor of students' college enrollment, particularly because it serves as an indicator of their academic preparedness for higher education. However, the process of tracking, which divides students by assigning them to a program and provides them with a different series of courses according to their track placement (O'Neil 1992; Oakes 1985, 1986a), contributes to differences in their preparation. Some schools rely on indicators of achievement such as grades, standardized test scores, or previous track placement, while others use more subjective measures such as teacher evaluations or student choice (Hallinan 1994). Research evidence reveals clear disparities in students' program assignments; Black students are often underrepresented in college preparatory programs and overrepresented in low-ability programs, while the reverse is true for White students (England et al. 1988; Oakes 1985, 1995; Oakes & Guiton 1995).

Furthermore, students' expectations about college may not be reflected in the curriculum or courses they are assigned to in high school. This becomes a major obstacle in that many students who aspire to attend college do not participate in academic programs; instead, they take classes that do not provide the kinds of challenges needed to prepare them for higher education (Lewis 1994). The high proportion of White and affluent students in college preparatory curricula or courses provides them with access to certain educational futures (i.e., college or university participation) and the overrepresentation of Black and Latino students in nonacademic programs and courses denies them, by exclusion, an opportunity to receive educationally and socially important knowledge (Hallinan 1994; Oakes 1985).

In a review of research on opportunity to learn and a study of assessment programs in 142 public school districts, Stevens and Grymes (1993) found that student differences in academic achievement are not being related to an analysis of opportunity to learn. Moreover, most school districts lag behind in analyzing information on opportunity to learn. Little is known whether there is much concern about addressing opportunity to learn for quality education purposes in general and for equity purposes for poor and minority students in particular (Steven & Grymes 1993). They concluded that investigating students' opportunity to learn would be a viable way to determine whether equity exists for all students in our public schools. We need to know more about what happens in schools and classrooms that causes some students to perform well academically and others not (Steven & Grymes 1993).

To address concerns about low academic performance and low-quality education, in 1983, the National Commission on Excellence in Education recommended that all high school students complete a "New Basics" curriculum. This is essentially a core curriculum that consists of four years of English; three years each of social studies, science, and math; and half a year of computer science. The Commission also recommended that students bound for college follow the New Basics curriculum, but along with two years of a foreign language. Since then variations of the recommended curricula have emerged, which typically omit the foreign language requirement, the computer science requirement, the third year of science and math, or some combination of the above.

Recent research in this area has focused greater attention on the curriculum and courses students take in high school. For example, one study found that high school curriculum reflected 41 percent of the academic resources (a composite measure of content and performance) students bring to higher education (Adelman 1999). (Test scores reflected 30 percent and class rank/grade point average 24 percent.) More importantly, the influence of a high quality curriculum on completing a college degree was more positively pronounced for Black (and Latino) students than any other indicator of academic content and performance. This influence was also much greater for Black and Latino students than for White students (Adelman 1999). In general, data show that all students are following a more rigorous curriculum and taking more academic courses that they were 10 years ago (NCES 1998a). Moreover, while the percentage of Black high school graduates who have taken four years of English and three years each of social studies, science, and math, they are less likely to meet these requirements than Whites and Asians (NCES 1998a; NCES 1998b). In addition, these data show that high school students who take more rigorous course loads have higher achievement than those taking a less rigorous curriculum (NCES 1998a).

While this brief review of related research is by no means an exhaustive one, it provides a framework for the primary questions that emerged about Black students' academic experiences in high school and their subsequent college enrollment. First, what is students' academic preparation like in high school? That is, what courses do students need to graduate, what courses are available in their school, and how many courses do they complete in the major subject areas (English, math, science, and social studies)? Moreover, how do students perform in high school? Second, what are the characteristics of the students who attend college right after high school and what factors, particularly those relating to their preparation and achievement in high school, are important in their college enrollment? While all students experience high school differently; that is, no two students will have the same experiences, the expectation is that there are clear distinctions in the academic preparation of students for higher education.

Methods
Data Source and Measures

Data from the National Education Longitudinal Study of 1988-1994 (NELS) were used to examine the two major research questions. NELS is a nationally representative longitudinal study of high school students that was designed to investigate students' educational development at different grade levels, and the familial, social and institutional factors that may affect their development. This data set was used because it is one of the more recent national longitudinal studies and it contains extensive information about students' educational aspirations, experiences in school, and postsecondary activities. In addition, the design and implementation of NELS permit results that can be generalized to Black high school graduates across the country. The 1988 base-year survey of NELS employed a two-stage, stratified probability design, resulting in a nationally representative sample of over 25,000 eighth-grade students from 815 public and 237 private schools. Data were also collected directly from the students' parents, teachers, school principals, and transcripts. Follow-up surveys were conducted at two-year intervals to provide additional data on participants during tenth and twelfth grade, and two years after high school. For more information on the design and implementation of NELS, please see Haggerty and colleagues (1996) or Ingels and colleagues (1994).

The data fall primarily into in six categories of variables: (1) student demographic and background characteristics including race, gender, socioeconomic status (SES), and parent education; (2) students' educational expectations, that is, how far they expected to go in school; (3) students' academic performance before high school, as measured by their grades and test scores; (4) students' academic preparation for higher education, including graduation requirements, course offerings, and the curriculum and courses completed; (5) students' academic performance while in high school, based on standardized test scores and grades; and (6) students' college enrollment in the fall right after high school. Please see the Appendix for details about the construction of the variables used and discussed in this chapter.

Sample

As NELS contains extensive information on a variety of different student groups, the sample selected for this study was restricted to participants who, before attending high school, indicated that they planned to pursue some form of higher education; attended public high school; attended the same high school in tenth and twelfth grade; did not drop out of high school; and participated in the first four waves of NELS. These selection criteria served several purposes. First, they focused primarily on youth who were presumably college bound or at the very least expressed a desire to attend college. Second, they eliminated issues involving students who may have changed high schools or who dropped out of school. This is particularly important, as dropouts are likely to be different from those who graduate, regardless of whether they continue their education beyond high school. In addition, American Indian students were omitted from this study, which resulted in a sample of 7,133 students: 740 Blacks (10%), 638 Asian/Pacific Islanders (9%), 861 Latinos (12%), and 4,894 Whites (69%).

Data Analysis

Given the multiple categories of variables and the longitudinal design of this study, the analytical tasks were to describe Black students' preparation for higher education, their achievement, and their college enrollment. Racial comparisons are provided primarily because in spite of the ideological efforts to overlook race in public education, it is often through race (and social class) that we detect clear discrepancies and inequities in education.

To describe students' academic preparation and performance in high school, many cross tabulation procedures were performed using SPSS, which resulted in two-way and multi-way tables with measures of association between variables. (The Pearson chi-square test (χ^2) was often used to test the association between variables.) Examples of some of the associations tested include the relationship between race and academic performance. In addition, analysis of variance (ANOVA), which tests the null hypothesis that several group means are equal in the population, was used to identify significant differences in student achievement and courses taken by race, for example.

To understand the role of students' academic preparation and performance in their college enrollment decisions, logistic regression was used to analyze the influence of students' background, prior performance, and other factors on their college enrollment. Logistic regression analysis estimates the coefficients of independent variables in a probabilistic model that best predict the outcome of a dichotomous dependent variable. It is similar to linear regression but requires fewer assumptions in that violations of assumptions of normality and equality of variances of the independent variables still provide a robust analysis. Logistic regression coefficients can be used to estimate odds ratios for each of the independent variables in the model. The regression models used indicator-variable coding, which recodes variables and creates a comparison (or reference) group for each categorical variable, so that the coefficients for the new variables denote the effect of each category compared to the referent group.

All statistical analyses in this chapter were weighted by a longitudinal panel weight designed specifically for NELS participants. "F3PNWT" was used because it applies to students who completed questionnaires in the first four waves. More importantly, use of this weight allows projections to the population of eighth graders in spring 1988 who were seniors in 1992. This panel weight was readjusted to equate the weighted sample size with the unweighted sample size (also known as a relative weight), so that the results for the representative sample are the same as in the population. As the weighted sample is designed to be representative of the population, it contained more Black and White students and fewer Asians and Latinos than the unweighted sample.

Results

Before discussing the findings, it seems befitting to provide some background information on the students under investigation. There were twice as many students from affluent backgrounds in this sample than poor students. By race, however, Black and Latino students were more than twice as likely to be poor than their Asian and White peers. This was true of parent education as well. Black and Latino students were more likely, than Whites and Asians, to have parents with only a high school education (or less). They were also less likely to have parents with a college or graduate degree than Whites and Asians.

There were noticeable differences in students' academic performance before they attended high school (i.e., in eighth grade). For example, Asian students were more likely to be in the high ability group for English, followed by Black, White, and Latino students. For math, Black and Latino students were less likely to be in the high ability group and more likely to be in the middle (or low) ability group than Whites and Asians. However, the percentage of students who were not grouped by ability at all was about 20% of all students for English and roughly 12% for math.

In addition, for both grades and test scores, Black students were more likely to be in the lowest quartile (and even the two middle quartiles), and less likely to be in the highest quartile compared to students from other races. ANOVA procedures with tests for multiple comparisons verified that the differences in the students' grades were statistically significant ($F = 51.9$, $df = 3$, $p < .001$). While Asian students had the highest grades, on average, Black students' grades were significantly lower than those in other racial groups. Similar findings held true for the students' standardized test scores in eighth grade; there were significant differences between the racial groups ($F = 284.0$, $df = 3$, $p < .001$), with Black students performing below students from other racial groups.

With this background information about students' academic performance while still in middle school, I became curious about their program placement once enrolled in high school. Students' self reports of their program during the sophomore year were used, which helped reduce the problem of whether senior-year reports, which were also available in NELS, were a response to achievement rather than a cause (Gamoran 1992). The primary focus here was to see whether students' high school programs reflected their college expectations.

Overall, 43% of the students were assigned to an academic (college preparatory) program in high school, while 40% and 7% were placed in general and vocational programs, respectively. (Five percent were in other programs and 5% did not know their high school program.) Consistent with the literature on tracking, there was a significant relationship between students' race and their high school program ($\chi^2 = 232.3$, $df = 12$, $p < .001$). Black and Latino students were less likely to be placed in academic programs in high school (38% and 32%, respectively) than Asians and Whites (48% and 44%, respectively). However, the opposite was true for students' placement in vocational programs; Black students were assigned to vocational programs at higher rates (14%) than Latino, Asian, and White students (9%, 8%, and 6%, respectively). Interestingly, 12% of the Black students who expected to graduate from college were assigned to vocational programs. Moreover, Black students who planned to earn a graduate degree were less likely to be assigned to an academic program (48%) than White and Asian students with similar expectations (60% and 57%, respectively).

Students' Academic Preparation and Performance in High School

With a clearer understanding of students' background, their academic performance before high school and their high school program assignments, it seemed important to know more about students' academic experiences while in high school. For example, what courses did students need to graduate and what courses were available in their schools? Administrators' reports of their high schools' graduation requirements were cross tabulated with students' racial background, which revealed some interesting relationships between race and the number of years required in each subject area. For example, in English, Black and Latino students were more likely than Asian and White students to attend high schools that required four years of English (Table 1). Similar results were found in math; Black and Latino students were more likely than Asian and White students to be enrolled in high schools that required three or more years of math to graduate (Table 1). In science and history, the results were more varied. However, Black students were more likely than other students to attend high schools that required only one year or less of history and other social studies (not shown in Table 1).

Given the difference in graduation requirements, one could reasonably expect further differences in course offerings at the students' schools and, perhaps more importantly, in the number of courses students ultimately take in these subject areas. To get a sense of what courses were available to students in their respective high schools and whether specific course offerings seemed to differ by race, administrators' reports of the school's regular course offerings in science and math were cross-tabulated with students' race. In science, the courses included general science, first- and second-year biology, chemistry, and physics, while the math courses included general math (grades 9 and 10-12), first- and second-year algebra, geometry, trigonometry, senior math (both with and without some calculus), calculus, and advanced placement (AP) calculus. The findings reveal that Black students were consistently less likely to have access to most of the science courses listed above than the overall sample and White students in particular (Table 1). (Note that only affirmative responses to the variables (i.e., yes, applies, met criteria, etc.) and only significant associations are displayed in Table 1.) The same was true in math (Table 1), but the differences in access were larger at the more advanced levels (i.e., senior math and AP calculus).

The small percentage of students who actually had access to AP calculus, along with the differences in course offerings by race, led to an interest in the number of advanced placement and other kinds of courses students had access to. One unexpected finding was that White students attended high schools that offered fewer advanced placement courses, on average, than Asian, Latino, and Black students, respectively ($F = 22.7$, df = 3, $p < .001$). Not surprising was that Black, and particularly Latino, students attended high schools with greater proportions of students receiving remedial reading and math courses, compared to White and Asian students. The results were significant for both reading ($F = 218.7$, df = 3, $p < .001$) and math ($F = 246.3$, df = 3, $p < .001$). Moreover, while nearly 15% of the students in this study had taken at least one remedial reading or math course in high school, Black students were more likely to have been enrolled in a remedial course (Table 1).

Table 1. Students' Academic Preparation for Higher Education
by Race

	All Students (%)	Black (%)	Asian (%)	Latino (%)	White (%)
Graduation Requirements					
English (4 years)	88.6	97.1	87.2	94.2	87.0
Math ($\geq$ 3 years)	43.7	54.9	39.5	58.5	43.7
Science ($\geq$ 3 years)	23.1	24.7	21.1	20.2	23.3
History ($\geq$ 3 years)	39.2	33.8	37.9	43.2	39.7
Course Offerings					
Science					
General (grade 9)	48.5	42.3	38.4	37.0	50.7
Biology (2nd year)	49.7	40.5	41.8	42.9	52.0
Chemistry (1st year)	94.5	93.4	92.7	91.6	95.0
Chemistry (2nd year)	33.9	28.9	20.9	28.4	35.7
Physics (1st year)	91.6	89.6	93.6	89.3	92.0
Math					
General (grade 9)	79.7	74.8	73.2	78.3	80.6
Algebra (1st year)	97.8	97.4	97.2	95.5	98.0
Geometry	96.9	96.2	96.8	94.7	97.2
Trigonometry	82.2	78.3	86.3	79.2	82.8
Senior (no calculus)	53.4	43.6	47.6	44.9	55.8
Senior (some calculus)	52.1	45.5	49.8	49.7	53.3
AP Calculus	9.5	6.2	8.8	10.1	10.0
Remedial (Ever Been in)					
English	14.5	17.6	12.0	14.9	14.1
Math	16.3	20.2	13.0	18.7	15.6
New Basics Curriculum					
4E+3SS+2S+2M	69.1	67.6	74.6	65.5	69.5
4E+3SS+3S+3M	47.5	42.0	56.6	36.5	49.1

Note: Percentages are provided to indicate the distribution of the affirmative responses (i.e., yes, applies, met criteria) for the variables listed by students' race. For New Basics Curriculum, E = English, SS = social studies, S = science, and M = math.

The average number of units students completed in high school in the major subject areas also varied by race. A unit refers to the Carnegie unit, which is a standard measure that denotes one credit for the completion of a one-year course (NCES 1998). Black students took fewer years of English (4.0) than Whites (4.1) and although the difference appears quite small, it was statistically significant (F = 3.6, df = 3, p < .05). Asian students completed more years of math (3.6) than White students (3.3) and Black and Latino students (3.1 for both). On average, Black students took fewer units of math than students in other racial groups; these differences were statistically significant when compared to Whites and Asians (F = 20.4, df = 3, p < .001). The findings were similar for science (F = 56.9, df = 3, p < .001). Again, Asian students completed more years of science (3.5) than White, Black, and Latino students (3.1, 2.8, and 2.7, respectively). As in math, the difference in the number of years of science completed by Black students was statistically significant when compared to Asians and Whites, but not Latino students. In social studies, the results follow a similar pattern (F = 12.0, df = 3, p < .001): Asian students completed the most years (3.5), on average, followed by Whites, Blacks, and Latinos (3.5, 3.4, and 3.3, respectively). Although Latino students took fewer years of social studies than Asians, Whites, and Blacks, there were no other statistically significant differences in the average number of years of social studies taken among Asian, White, and Black students.

Given the differences in graduation requirements, course offerings, and average number of years taken in English, math, science, and social studies by race, it was important to determine whether students completed a curriculum that would, theoretically, prepare them for higher education. Two variations of the New Basics curriculum prescribed curriculum were analyzed. The first variation included four years of English, three years of social studies, and two years each of science and math. The second was the same, except for an additional year each of science and math. Overall, 69% of all high school graduates in this study met the threshold for the first New Basics curriculum (with the two years of math and science), but the percentage of students meeting these criteria differed by race (Table 1). Asian graduates were more likely to complete this curriculum (75%), followed by White, Black, and Latino students (70%, 68%, and 66%, respectively). When the prescribed curriculum contained the additional year of math and science, far fewer students met the threshold (48% overall). Moreover, there were clear racial differences in who actually met these criteria (Table 1).

Thus far, this section has focused on students' preparation for higher education, but what about their academic performance or achievement during high school? How well did students perform in the courses they took and on standardized tests while in high school? Were there any differences by race or high school program? The results of several ANOVA revealed that the racial differences in students' academic achievement did not change over time. Asian students, as a group, continued to outperform students from other racial backgrounds on standardized test scores (55.8), followed by Whites (54.3), Latinos (49.3), and Blacks (46.2), who continued to score the lowest of the four racial groups. The differences in mean test scores were statistically significant (F = 209.8, df = 3, p < .001), except between Asians and Whites. The results were identical for students' average grades in English, math, science, and social studies. In every subject, Asian students' grades were higher, on average, than students from other racial backgrounds and Black students' grades were the lowest. The differences in students' grades among the racial groups were statistically significant for all four subjects (F = 127.8, df = 3, p < .001 for English; F = 111.2, df = 3, p < .001 for math; F = 101.1, df = 3, p < .001 for science; and F = 122.3, df = 3, p < .001 for social studies). This indicates that Asian students' grades, on average, were significantly higher than Whites, whose grades were significantly higher than Latinos, whose grades were significantly higher than Blacks.

Similar findings emerged when the comparison was not race, but high school program. On average, students in academic programs had higher standardized test scores (56.5) than students in general (52.0) and vocational programs (45.7). These differences were statistically significant (F = 248.1, df = 4, p < .001). The results were the same when students' average grades in English, math, science, and social studies were analyzed by high school program. In every subject, students in academic programs had higher grades, on average, than students in general and vocational programs. The differences in average grades among the different programs were statistically significant for all four subjects (F = 141.7, df = 4, p < .001 for English; F = 100, df = 3, p < .001 for math; F = 116.4, df = 3, p < .001 for science; and F = 192.3, df = 3, p < .001 for social studies). Therefore, students in college prep programs had significantly higher grades than students in general programs, who had significantly higher grades than those in vocational programs.

High School Graduates' College Enrollment
Before examining the college enrollment of the graduates in this study, it seemed important to examine whether and how students' expectations to pursue higher education changed over time. While students were initially selected, in part, because of their educational expectations, the goal was to examine whether these expectations changed since eighth grade and if so, how they changed. One could reasonably expect students to change their college plans for a variety of reasons. For example, they may have clearer career or occupational goals or more information about higher education. Some students, after facing numerous challenges in high school, may decide that college is not what they want to do right after high school or there may be financial reasons why students would postpone going to college. Nevertheless, comparing students' educational expectations in eighth grade and twelfth grade shed light on changes in students' educational expectations since middle school.

Not surprisingly, there was a strong association between students' educational expectations in eighth and twelfth grade. Although many students had the same or higher educational expectations in twelfth grade as they had in eighth grade, others had lower expectations. Overall, 27% of students who said that they would attend college in eighth grade still expected to do so as seniors, but 29% of them expected to graduate from college and 14% expected to earn a graduate degree. Among those who expected to finish four years of college when they were in eighth grade, 44% had the same plans in twelfth grade, while 31% expected to earn a graduate degree. Interestingly, 13% of these students expected to attend less than four years of college.

Among those expecting to earn a graduate degree in eighth grade, 57% still planned to do so as high school seniors, while 30% expected to finish four years of college. For each racial group, there were also significant relationships between their educational expectations in eighth grade and twelfth grade, which was not surprising. Among Black students who planned to graduate from college (while in the eighth grade), 38% still planned to finish college as seniors and 36% reported plans to earn a graduate degree. However, 17% of the Black students reported as seniors, that they would pursue less than four years of college or go to trade school. Among Asian students who planned to finish four years of college in eighth grade, 35% planned to do so as seniors, while 46% expected to earn a graduate degree. Note, however, that 12% of the Asian students, as seniors, planned to attend college for less than four years. Among Latino students who expected to finish college in eighth grade, 36% reported expectations to do so as seniors.

Thirty percent of these students expected to earn a graduate degree, while 25% planned to attend less than four years of college or go to trade school. Among White students who planned to finish college in eighth grade, 46% still expected to do so as seniors, 30% expected to earn a graduate degree, and 19% planned to go to college or trade school.

Overall, 70% of the high school graduates in this study made an immediate transition to some form of higher education. Nearly half (46%) attended a four-year college or university, 19% attended a two-year school, and 5% enrolled in a trade school. Thirty percent did not enroll in college at all. Students' educational expectations in twelfth grade were quite foretelling of their subsequent enrollment. For example, over half of the students who expected to graduate from college and over two-thirds of those who expected to earn a graduate degree enrolled in a four-year college or university (Table 2). Note that 20% of the students who were unsure of how far they would go were also enrolled in four-year institutions. Conversely, nearly 90% of the students who expected to go no further than high school were not enrolled in college. This was also true of 72% of the students who expected to attend less than four years of college or trade school (Table 2).

There were several significant associations between students' college enrollment and their background characteristics. For example, by race, Asian and White graduates were more likely to enroll in four-year colleges and universities than Blacks and Latinos (Table 2). Moreover, nearly 40% of Black and Latino graduates did not attend college right after high school compared to 22% of Asian and 28% of White graduates. Note that Black graduates attended community colleges at lower rates than students from other racial backgrounds. There were larger differences in college enrollment by SES; students from affluent backgrounds were much more likely to attend a four-year college or university (Table 2). Not surprisingly, the reverse was true of low-SES students; half of them did not attend college right after high school. Similarly, students with college-educated parents were much more likely to attend a four-year institution than graduates whose parents only went as far as high school or some college. Potential first-generation college students were more likely not to enroll in college at all (Table 2).

Table 2. College Enrollment Status in October 1992 by Selected Student Background Characteristics and Academic Performance

	Four-Year Inst. (%)	Two-Year Inst. (%)	Trade School (%)	Not Enrolled (%)
College Expectations				
Don't Know	19.9	20.2	6.2	53.8
High School (or less)	2.8	5.0	2.8	89.5
Some College	3.7	13.0	11.2	72.1
Finish College	51.6	20.9	4.4	23.1
Graduate Degree	68.5	14.6	3.5	13.4
Background Characteristics				
Race/Ethnicity				
Black	39.2	15.9	5.9	38.9
Asian	52.3	19.7	5.7	22.2
Latino	30.7	20.5	7.1	41.7
White	48.6	18.9	4.9	27.6
Gender				
Male	43.7	18.3	4.7	33.3
Female	48.3	19.1	5.8	26.8
SES				
Low	25.0	17.6	6.8	50.6
Middle	40.0	21.1	5.4	33.4
High	65.9	15.6	4.2	14.3
Parent Education [‡]				
High School (or less)	28.5	19.4	5.2	46.9
Some College	39.6	21.6	6.2	32.6
College Graduate	60.8	15.8	4.2	19.2
Graduate Degree	73.6	13.8	4.3	8.3
High School Preparation				
Program				
General	39.8	19.5	5.6	35.2
Vocational	21.9	22.3	8.6	47.2
College Preparatory	60.2	17.6	4.0	18.2
New Basics Curriculum				
4E+3SS+2S+2M	51.8	19.2	4.7	24.2
4E+3SS+3S+3M	64.1	16.5	4.0	15.3
Test Scores				
Lowest Quartile	15.4	22.8	6.6	55.2
Two Middle Quartiles	38.6	22.9	5.6	32.9
Highest Quartile	73.1	11.7	2.8	12.4

Note: Row percentages are displayed to indicate the distribution of college enrollment for each of the attributes listed. Therefore, row percentages sum to 100%. For College Expectations and Parent Education variables, "Some College" also includes trade school. For New Basics Curriculum, E = English, SS = social studies, S = science, and M = math.

[‡] A fifth category ("don't know") is excluded from these results due to the small number of cases in this category (.5%).

Significant relationships emerged between students' academic preparation in high school and their college enrollment. The results for high school program support the literature on tracking in that students in college preparatory programs were more likely to attend a four-year college or university than their peers in vocational and general programs (Table 2). At least twice as many students placed in vocational or general high school programs did not go on to college right after high school compared to those in academic programs. Graduates who took three years of math and science, as part of the recommended New Basics curriculum were more likely to enroll in a four-year college or university after high school (Table 2). There was also a significant relationship between students' performance on standardized tests and their college participation. Over 70% of the students in the highest test quartile attended a four-year institution compared to 39% of students in the two middle quartiles, and 15% in the lowest quartile (Table 2).

A similar analysis was performed for Black students to identify the characteristics of those who made an immediate transition to higher education. The findings revealed that Black high school graduates who enrolled in a four-year college or university right after high school were more likely to be female, come from upper-middle class backgrounds, have parents with some college education, have been in a college prep program in high school, fall in the third quartile on standardized tests, and have had educational expectations of earning a graduate degree as high school seniors. Black graduates who attended community colleges or other two-year schools after high school differed from their peers who attended four-year institutions. While they too were more likely to be female and have parents with some college education, these graduates were more likely to come from low-income backgrounds, have been placed in an academic or general program, and fall in the lowest or second lowest test quartile. As high school seniors, one-third expected to finish college, while 46% expected to earn a graduate degree. Black high school graduates who did not enroll in an institution of higher education at all were similar to their peers who attended two-year colleges. However, over half were male. They were more likely to come from low-income backgrounds and about equally likely to have parents with some college or only a high school education. These graduates were also more likely to have been in a general high school program and to fall in the lowest test quartile. However, as high school seniors, 29% expected to finish college and 24% expected to earn a graduate degree.

These analyses are informative because they confirm that certain measures of students' academic preparation and performance relate to their transition to higher education, such as their high school program, the curriculum they completed, and their scores on standardized tests. Nevertheless, these analyses tell us little about the strength of these relationships or about the relative importance of these measures in students' college enrollment. Logistic regression analysis helped identify what factors were significant in graduates' college enrollment right after high school. The models regressed students' college enrollment on six blocks of variables (background, prior performance, high school program, academic preparation, educational expectations, and academic performance in high school). The first set of analyses focused on students' enrollment, while the second focused on whether students attended a four-year or two-year institution. One set of regression analyses was performed for all students and a second set was analyzed for Black students separately.

The estimated coefficients of the variables in the final regression models predicting students' college participation revealed that, overall, students' academic preparation and performance in high school were more important in predicting what type of institution students attended rather than whether or not they simply enrolled in college (Table 3). SES and gender were the only two significant variables in the model predicting college enrollment for all students. The results indicate that the odds of enrolling in college after high school were significantly reduced by factors ranging from .34 to .63 for students who were not from affluent backgrounds (Table 3). In addition, being male reduced the odds of going to college by a factor of .15.

Several additional factors were important in predicting whether graduates attended a four-year college or university. For example, race emerged as a significant variable. Somewhat surprisingly, the odds of attending a four-year institution were increased by a factor of 2.4 for Black students, when compared to Whites. The effects of SES were similar to those found for college enrollment; that is, coming from the lowest two SES quartiles significantly reduced the odds of attending a four-year institution when compared to graduates from the highest quartile. Certain academic preparation variables and educational expectations also emerged as significant predictors of the level of higher education graduates pursued. The number of science units taken and the type of New Basics curriculum completed, particularly the one with three years of math and science, significantly increased the odds

Table 3. Summary of Estimated Parameters in Logistic Regression Analysis on College Enrollment

	All Students		Black Students	
	College Enrollment (N = 5,306)	4-Year Inst. (N = 3,777)	Coll. Enrollment (N = 516)	4-Year Inst. (N = 308)
	β	β	β	β
Background Characteristics				
Race (White)				
Asian	-.01	-.37	—	—
Latino	.07	.04	—	—
Black	-.02	.88***	—	—
Gender (Female)	-.16*	.10	-.18	.35
SES (Highest Quartile)				
Lowest Quartile	-1.00***	-.45**	-.89*	-.34
2nd Quartile	-.73***	-.63***	-.41	-.37
3rd Quartile	-.42***	-.20	-.16	-.04*
Prior Performance (in 8th grade)				
Grades	-.07	.25**	-.27	.63
Test Scores	.02	.02	.05	.05
Academic Preparation				
High School Program	-.18	-.05	-.23	-.41
English Units	-.03	.06	.20	-.01
Math Units	.38	.14*	.40**	-.17
Science Units	.16	.39***	.02	.26
Social Studies Units	-.04	.06	.01	-.30
NB: 4E+3SS+2S+2M	-.14	-.19	-.32	-.49
NB: 4E+3SS+3S+3M	.08	.38**	-.08	.10
Educational Exp. (≥ 4 years)				
High School (or less)	-1.48	-.98***	-1.29**	-.47
Some College	.83	-1.61***	-.86**	-1.32**
High School Performance				
Test Scores	-.01	.03**	-.02	-.05
Grades				
English	-.17	-.10**	-.02	-.07
Math	.06	-.04	.01	-.14
Science	-.04	-.01	.02	.07
Social Studies	-.13	-.02	-.21**	-.11

Note: Cases with missing data were excluded from these analyses. The category in parentheses is the referent group for that variable. Asterisks denote the significance levels for the Wald statistic, which tests that the coefficient β is 0 (* $p < .05$, ** $p < .01$, and *** $p < .001$). NB = New Basics Curriculum, where E = English, SS = social studies, S = science, and M = math. For the Educational Expectations variable, "Some College" also includes trade school. Negative coefficients for the grades variables should be interpreted cautiously; they were coded such that a lower numerical value represented a higher grade. Therefore, when significant, there exists a positive relationship between grades and college enrollment.

of attending a four-year college or university by factors of .47 and .46, respectively (Table 3). In addition, students' educational expectations as high school seniors were predictive of their enrollment in a four-year institution; the odds were significantly reduced by factors of .62 and .80 for students who expected to go no further than high school or some college, respectively. Lastly, students' performance in high school helped predict whether graduates would enroll in a four-year college or university. Increases in test scores and English grades were both associated with increased odds of attending a four-year college or university. (Note that prior grades were also associated with increased odds of going to a four-year institution.)

Interestingly, the results differed when the same regression analyses were performed for Black students only. It is clear that fewer factors were significant in predicting Black students' college enrollment, including academic preparation and performance predictors. For example, increases in the number of years of math taken increased the odds that Black students would attend college after high school. The odds of college enrollment were reduced for Black students with lower educational expectations, compared to those who expected to finish at least four years of college. Increases in Black students' grades in social studies were also associated with increased odds of enrolling in college right after high school. In attempting to predict whether Black students would attend a four-year college or university, only two variables were remotely significant: SES and college plans and the direction of their effects are similar to those in the other models.

Conclusions and Discussion
One purpose of this chapter was to describe and highlight Black students' academic preparation and performance in high school. The findings revealed that Black students were more likely than their Asian and White peers to be assigned to a program in high school that did not reflect their educational expectations. They were more likely to be placed in general and vocational programs and less likely to be assigned to an academic program. Black students were also less likely to attend high schools with specific science and math classes that would have made them more competitive for college and university admission (e.g., physics, trigonometry, and AP calculus). Instead, they were more likely to attend schools with higher proportions of students in remedial classes. Ironically, Black students appeared to be held to greater graduation requirements in English and math than other students, but, on average, they completed the lowest number of years in these and

other subjects. They were also less likely to meet the New Basics curriculum specified by the Commission. Their performance in high school showed similar results. On average, Black students tended to score lower than other racial groups on standardized tests and had lower grades in the four major subjects than students from other racial/ethnic backgrounds.

A second purpose of this study was to examine Black students' college enrollment and the significance of their academic preparation and achievement in their college participation. The findings revealed that about 55 percent of the Black students in this study enrolled in a four-year or two-year institution of higher education right after high school. (Another six percent enrolled in a trade school.) However, they were less likely to enroll in a college or university than other students, Asians and Whites in particular. Black graduates who attended four-year institutions right after high school were more likely to be female, come from upper-middle class backgrounds, have parents with some college education, be in an academic program in high school, and fall in the third quartile on standardized tests. Those who attended two-year schools were different from their counterparts who enrolled in four-year colleges in that they were more likely to be low-income, score in the lowest test quartile, and be in an academic or general high school program. Interestingly, none of these factors was significant, except perhaps for SES, in predicting whether Black high school graduates actually enrolled in college or the level of higher education they initially attended. More importantly, the academic preparation and performance were generally weak or insignificant predictors of Black high school graduates' immediate transition to higher education.

One implication of this study for high school students, especially Black students interested in continuing their education beyond high school, is that academic preparation and performance at the secondary level is not uniform. While it is not surprising that disparities exist between different racial/ethnic groups, this should not imply that this is true at *every* public high school in the country. Nevertheless, this study raises important questions about the nature and extent of such disparities in students' academic experiences across and within public high schools, particularly as they relate to tracking, graduation requirements, and course offerings in schools. They also give rise to issues of students' access to guidance counseling and to information about their secondary education and higher education in general. Moreover, there are questions about the students' roles in their own secondary and higher education. These include the practicality of students' educational expectations, versus their aspirations or desires; their motivation to do well in school; and specific actions they take to secure their college enrollment (e.g., courses, college admissions tests, and applications to specific institutions).

The results of this study raise questions for practitioners, primarily teachers, guidance counselors, and school administrators who are often held partly responsible for students' secondary education. The first focuses on the quality of the curriculum and courses offered in public high schools, which seem to need constant revisiting. For example, the analyses conducted here indicate that many students are not meeting the New Basics curriculum recommended by the Commission. The findings also raise questions about what kinds of courses qualify toward graduation and more importantly, whether students are even meeting the graduation requirements specified by their respective high schools. These issues may be especially relevant for schools and districts enrolling high concentrations of minority and economically disadvantaged students. Other issues emanating from the results of this study extend beyond program assignments and course offerings to those that also affect students' academic preparation and achievement. This includes classroom practices, school personnel interactions with and expectations of students, and student access to and the quality of academic and college advising. Overall, this study points to the need for some kind of immediate intervention, as the pervasive and continuing relationship between achievement and attainment and ethnic and social background continues and remains an important problem in American education (Wilson & Corcoran 1988).

Lastly, this study has generated additional questions for future research on Black high school students' transition to higher education. First, does the insignificance of academic preparation and achievement variables in Black students' college enrollment mean that other factors are more important on their college participation? *How* does the college choice process work for different groups of students and for Black students in particular? Moreover, what role do students' families play, besides that of SES and parent education? What about the role of student motivation, the effort students invest in education, and the influence of their families, peers, and teachers? These questions suggest a need to investigate academic preparation and achievement, particularly as they relate to student college choice, through other methods of research. For example, although secondary analyses of large data sets like NELS are helpful, they sometimes lack depth. Future longitudinal investigations should also include qualitative methodologies that enable students to explain, first hand, how they experience high school academically and what factors are important in their college-going decisions.

While there are many unknown factors that bear upon college enrollments, we must admit that educational attainment does not occur in a social vacuum. Education is a social institution that reflects patterns of race relations throughout American society. It mirrors conditions that prevail in other components of the social system (Blackwell 1990). Many policy analysts think raising minority achievement in high school is the only way to raise college enrollment. However, experience suggests that raising Black students' test scores is not enough (Carnoy 1994). When addressing the academic preparation of high school students for college, we should realize that in many school systems, school boards, administrators, and teachers have a hierarchy of concerns. Unfortunately, the academic preparation of high school students for postsecondary education often has the lowest priority (Lewis 1994). Improving the overall preparation (not only test scores) of students for college is still necessary to fulfill the national promise of equal access to higher education and to improve the quality of high school (College Board 1983). Consequently, there needs to be a clear climate of commitment to improving students' educational opportunities at the secondary level (Carnoy 1994), as inadequate preparation deprives these students a fair chance to take advantage of higher education (College Board 1983).

References

Adelman, C. 1999. *"Answers in the tool box: Academic intensity, attendance patterns, and bachelor's degree attainment."* Washington: U.S. Department of Education, Office of Educational Research and Improvement.

Blackwell, J. E. 1990. "Blacks and Hispanics in the educational pipeline." In *U.S. race relations in the 1980s and 1990s: Challenges and alternatives,* edited by G. E. Thomas. New York: Hemisphere.

Carnoy, M. 1994. Why aren't more Black Americans going to college? *Journal of Blacks in Higher Education* 6:66-69.

College Entrance Examination Board. 1983. *Academic preparation for college: What students need to know and be able to do.* New York: College Entrance Examination Board, Office of Academic Affairs.

Commission on Pre-college Guidance and Counseling. 1986. *Keeping the options open: An overview. Interim report of the commission on precollege guidance and counseling.* New York: College Entrance Examination Board.

England, R. E., K. J. Meier, and L. R. Fraga. 1988. Barriers to equal opportunity: Educational practices and minority students. *Urban Affairs Quarterly* 23:635-46.

Gamoran, A. 1992. The variable effects of high school tracking. *American Sociological Review* 57:812-28.

Ganderton, P. T., and R. Santos. 1995. Hispanic college attendance and completion: Evidence from the high school and beyond surveys. *Economics of Education Review* 14:35-46.

Haggerty, C., B. Dugoni, L. Reed, A. Cederland, and J. Taylor. 1996. *NELS:1988-1994: Methodology report.* Washington: National Center for Education Statistics.

Hallinan, M. T. 1994. School differences in tracking effects on achievement. *Social Forces* 72:799-820.

Hossler, D., J. Braxton, and G. Coopersmith. 1989. Understanding student college choice. In *Higher education: Handbook of theory and research,* edited by John C. Smart, Vol. V, 231-88. New York: Agathon Press.

Hossler, D., and K. S. Gallagher. 1987. Studying student college choice: A three-phase model and the implications for policymakers. *College and University* 62:207-21.

Ingels, S. J., K. L. Dowd, J. D. Baldridge, J. L. Stipe, V. H. Bartot, and M. R. Frankel. 1994. *NELS:88 second follow-up: Student component data file user's manual.* Washington: National Center for Education Statistics.

Kane, J., and L. M. Spizman. 1994. Race, financial aid and college attendance: Parents and geography matter. *American Journal of Economics and Sociology* 53:85-97.

Lewis, R. A., Jr. 1994. Public relations and politics in the public schools: Barriers to academic preparation for college. *The Journal of American History* 81:1088-92.

Manski, C. F., and D. A. Wise. 1983. *College choice in America.* Cambridge: Harvard University Press.

Miller, L. S. 1995. *An American imperative: Accelerating minority educational advancement.* New Haven: Yale University Press.

National Center for Education Statistics. 1998a. *The condition of education 1998.* Washington: U.S. Department of Education, Office of Educational Research and Improvement, National Center for Education Statistics.

National Center for Education Statistics. 1998b. *Digest of education statistics, 1998.* Washington: U.S. Department of Education, Office of Educational Research and Improvement, National Center for Education Statistics.

National Center for Education Statistics. 1999. *The condition of education 1999.* Washington: U.S. Department of Education, Office of Educational Research and Improvement, National Center for Education Statistics.

O'Neil, J. 1992. On tracking and individual difference: A conversation with Jeannie Oakes. *Educational Leadership* 50: 18-21.

Oakes, J. 1985. *Keeping track: How schools structure inequality.* New Haven: Yale University Press.

Oakes, J. 1986a. Keeping track, part 1: The policy and practice of curriculum inequality. *Phi Delta Kappan* 68:12-17.

Oakes, J. 1995. Two cities' tracking and within-school segregation. *Teachers College Record* 96:681-90.

Oakes, J., and G. Guiton. 1995. Matchmaking: The dynamics of high school tracking decisions. *American Educational Research Journal* 32:3-33.

Paulsen, M. B. 1990. *College choice: Understanding student enrollment behavior.* ASHE-ERIC Higher Education Report No. 6. Washington: The George Washington University, School of Education and Human Development.

Stage, F. K., and P. W. Rushin. 1993. A combined model of student predisposition to college and persistence in college. *Journal of College Student Development* 34:276-82.

Stevens, F. I., and J. Grymes. 1993. *Opportunity to learn: Issues of equity for poor and minority students.* Washington: U.S. Department of Education, Office of Educational Research and Improvement, National Center for Education Statistics.

Weinstein, R. S. 1996. High standards in a tracked system of schooling: For which students and with what educational supports? *Educational Researcher* 25(8):16-19.

Wilson, B. L., and T. B. Corcoran. 1988. *Successful secondary schools: Visions of excellence in American public education.* London: Falmer Press.

Appendix – Variable Definition and Construction
Demographic and Background

Race is categorical and comes from the RACE variable. The four values for this variable were Asian/Pacific Islander, Latino, Black, and White.

Gender is dichotomous and comes from the SEX variable. The values were male and female.

Socioeconomic status (SES) measures students' socioeconomic status and comes from the BYSESQ variable. In NELS, SES was constructed into one composite scale (BYSES) based on father's and mother's education level, father's and mother's occupation, and family income (questions on the base-year parent questionnaire). Composite SES scores were then recoded and grouped into SES quartiles in the data file (1 is the lowest and 4 is the highest) based on the weighted marginal distribution of responding parents, which resulted in the BYSESQ variable.

Parent education is a composite variable that comes from the BYPARED variable and measures the level of education attained by the student's parents (using parent data from the base-year questionnaire). The original values were recoded to include the following: (1) do not know; (2) high school or less (including an equivalency degree and those who did not finish high school), (3) some college (including the completion of an associate or trade school degree), (4) college graduate, and (5) graduate degree (master's degree, Ph.D., M.D., or other).

College Expectations/Plans
Students' Expectation/College Plans variables capture students' reports of their educational expectations in eighth and twelfth grade based on a similar item on the base-year and second follow-up student questionnaires (items BYPSEPLN and F2S43, respectively). These items asked students, "as things stand now, how far in school do you think you will get?" The item on the base-year survey (BYPSEPLN) was one of several criteria used to select participants (those who reported "will attend college," "will graduate from college," or "will attend a higher level of school after graduating from college" were included). Students' responses for F2S43 were recoded to include the following values: (1) high school or less, (2) trade school, (3) some college (less than four years, including two-year degrees), (4) graduate from college (baccalaureate degree), and (5) graduate degree (master's or higher).

Prior Performance/Achievement

Grades (8th grade) consist of two measures of students' grades, while in eighth grade. The first comes from BYGRADS, which is an average of students' self-reports for grades in English, mathematics, science, and social studies. Students' responses were converted to a five point scale (mostly As = 4, Bs = 3, Cs = 2, Ds = 1, mostly below D = .5) and the mean of all nonmissing values of the four items equally weighted was compute. The values are continuous and were rounded to one decimal place. The second measure comes from BYGRADSQ, which is the quartile distribution of BYGRADS. It was constructed by recoding BYGRADS into quartiles (1 is the lowest and 4 is the highest) based on the weighted marginal distribution of students.

Test Scores (8th grade) include two measures of students' performance on the standardized tests in reading and math administered through NELS. Students completed a series of curriculum-driven cognitive tests in reading, mathematics, science, and social studies, intended to measure achievement at their grade level when surveyed and their cognitive growth between eighth and twelfth grades. Measures come from the BY2XCOMP and BY2XQURT variables (from the base-year survey). BY2XCOMP contains a composite (reading and math) score; the values for this variable are continuous (30.71 is the lowest score and 75.81 is the highest score possible). BY2XQURT is the quartile distribution of BY2XCOMP (1 is lowest and 4 is the highest quartile).

Ability Groups in the major subjects (English, math, science, and social studies) capture whether students were assigned to an ability group and if so, what group. Measures for students' ability groups in math, science, English, and social studies come from the items BYS60A, BYS60B, BYS60C, and BYS60D, respectively. These were based on students' self reports on the base-year questionnaire in 1988, which asked, "sometimes students are put in different groups, so that they are with other students of similar ability... What ability group are you in for the following classes: mathematics, science, English, and social studies?" The values for these variables are (1) high, (2) middle, (3) low, (4) are not grouped, and (5) do not know.

Academic Preparation

High School Program identifies the program a student was assigned to in high school (track placement). It comes from the F1HSPROG, which indicates the high school program a student was assigned to. The source was an item on the student questionnaire during the first follow-up survey in 1990. The original values were recoded to include the following: (1) do not know, (2) other, (3) vocational, (4) general, and (5) academic/college preparatory.

Ability Grouping variables in the major subjects (English, math, science, and social studies) measure whether a student's high school assigned students to classes based on ability or achievement. Measures come from the variables F1C61A, F1C61B, F1C61C, and F1C61D. The source was an item on the school administrator survey in 1990, which asked, "does your school use homogeneous grouping (according to ability or achievement) for placement of tenth-grade students in the following classes: English, mathematics, social studies, and science?" The values for these items were "yes," "no," and "does not apply."

Graduation Requirements variables capture how many years of English, math, science, and social studies students needed to complete high school. Measures come from variables F1C70A, F1C70B, F1C70C, F1C70D, and F1C70E. These were based on an item on the school administrator survey in 1990, which asked "how much coursework is required in each of the following subjects to meet high school graduation requirements: English, mathematics, science, history, and other social studies?" Original values were recoded to the following: (1) course is not offered, (2) none, (3) one year or less, (4) two years, (5) three years, and (6) four years.

Course Offerings variables identify whether specific courses in science and math were available (offered) at the students' high school. The measures come from several items on the school administrator survey in 1990, which asked administrators to identify whether the specific courses were offered in their schools. These included: F1C75D2 (general science grade 9), F1C75F2 (biology 1st-year), F1C75G2 (biology 2nd year), F1C75H2 (chemistry 1st-year), F1C75I2 (chemistry 2nd- year), F1C75J2 (physics 1st-year), F1C75K2 (physics 2nd-year), F1C75R2 (general math grade 9), F1C75S2 (general math grade 10-12), F1C75X2 (algebra 1st-year), F1C75Y2 (algebra 2nd-year), F1C75Z2 (geometry), F1C75AA2 (trigonometry), F1C75CC2 (senior math no calculus), F1C75DD2 (senior math some calculus) F1C75EE2 (calculus), and F1C75FF2 (advanced placement calculus). The values for these items were "applies" and "does not apply."

Number of AP Courses Offered measures how many advanced placement courses were offered at a student's school. It comes from the variable F1C76, which was based on an item on the school administrator survey in 1990 that asked, "including mathematics, science, English, history and other subjects areas, what is the total number of Advanced Placement courses offered at your school?" The values for this variable are continuous.

Percent of Students in Remedial Courses variables measure the percentage of a student's peers who receive remedial courses in reading in math at his/her school. The source is variables F2C25B and F2C25C on the second follow-up survey of high school administrators in 1992. These measures were part of a series that asked administrators, "what percentage of the total student body in your school receives the following special services... remedial reading and remedial math?" The values for these two variables are continuous.

Course Units variables in the major subjects measure the Carnegie units completed by students. The measures come from variables F2RHEN_C, F2RHMA_C, F2RHSC_C, and F2HSO_C, which indicate the total number of Carnegie unites in English, math, science, and social studies, respectively. The source of these items is the transcript survey conducted as part of the second follow-up survey in 1992. The values for these four variables are continuous.

Curriculum Completed variables indicate whether students completed a variation of the curriculum recommended by the National Commission on Excellence in Education. The source for these variables are F2RNWB4A (4 years of English, 3 years of social studies, and 2 years each of science and math) and F2RNWB5A (4 years of English and 3 years each of social studies, science, and math). These come from the transcript survey (part of the second follow-up survey in 1992). The values for these two variables are "failed threshold" and "met threshold."

Academic Performance

Test Scores (12th grade) resemble those discussed above for eighth graders, except they measure students' performance in twelfth grade during the second follow-up survey in 1992. There were six forms of the cognitive test battery, each containing a different combination of reading and math difficulty levels. Respondents' scores on the base-year and first follow-up reading and math cognitive tests determined their test battery for the second follow-up. This customized the difficulty of the reading and mathematics tests to the senior's ability and, given limitations in testing time, provided a more accurate measurement than a single-level test design. The measures come from F22XCOMP (a continuous variable where 27.86 is the lowest score and 71.04 is the highest score available) and F22XQURT (the quartile distribution of F22XCOMP).

Grades measure students' average grades in the major subjects. They come from variables F2RHENG2, F2RHMAG2, F2RHSCG2, and F2HSOG2, which provide a student's average grade in English, math, science, and social studies, respectively. The source of these items is the transcript survey (part of the second follow-up survey in 1992). For each subject, the composite is an average where '01.00' represents the highest grade (comparable to 'A+') and '12.01-13.00' represents the lowest grade (comparable to 'F'). Values for these four variables are continuous.

College Participation

College Enrollment is a dichotomous variable that measures high school graduates' immediate transition to higher education; that is, whether they enrolled in an institution of higher education during the fall following graduation (October 1992). It was constructed from the variable ENRL1092, which gives a student's enrollment status as of October 1992 (part of the third follow-up survey of students). (This variable was one in a series of month-by-month enrollment status variables from June 1992 through August 1994). Enrollment status is defined here as a concatenation of the full/part-time status with the type of institution attended. The original values were recoded to correspond to two levels of enrollment status: yes or no.

College Type is a categorical variable that identifies the type of institution attended right after high school. It was constructed from the same variable as college enrollment (ENRL1092), but the original values were recoded into the following categories: (1) four-year college or university, (2) two-year school, (3) trade school, and (4) not enrolled.

Note: The opinions expressed in this chapter are solely those of the author and not the Spencer Foundation.

III.

Improving Learning in Postsecondary Education

15. *Creative Pedagogy to Enhance the Academic Achievement of Minority Students in Math*

Angela H. Brown

Much has been written about the stereotypes, myths, and facts surrounding race, gender, and mathematics and the decision not to pursue careers in mathematics as a result of those issues. Failure of minorities to catch up with the dominant groups in the area of mathematics achievement in spite of those stereotypes, myths, and facts has been thoroughly documented (Becker 1995; Brown 1997; Carl 1995; Etzkowitz et. al. 1994; Mallory 1997; Secada 1995). Stanic and Hart (1997), in their discussion of attitudes, persistence, and mathematics achievement, came to the conclusion that minorities' attitudes and behaviors needed to be studied over time to provide more insight into academic achievement and attrition in mathematics. One way to empirically follow-up on this recommendation for longitudinal research was to study minorities that had made a career of teaching mathematics. Specifically, it would be instructive to understand the stories of African American women who rose from their marginal status in mathematics classrooms to be successful in the area of mathematics. Surely, those persons who were able to teach mathematics at the post-secondary level constituted persons who were successful in mathematics. African American women post-secondary mathematics teachers represent a group whose experiences have not been well documented in the literature. This chapter, drawing upon the classroom experiences of seven African American women post-secondary mathematics teachers, sought to provide insights into the academic attrition and achievement of minority students in mathematics. This will be accomplished by examining the stories of those who successfully negotiated the maze of stereotypes, myths, and facts surrounding race, gender and mathematics in mathematics classrooms.

Methodology
The theoretical perspective that guided the analysis was Black feminism (Collins 1991). Black feminist thought authenticates the independent specialized knowledge that can be produced by African American women and invites them to respect their own subjective knowledge base (Collins 1991). This perspective placed importance on engaging in "theoretical interpretations of Black women's reality by those who live it" (Collins 1991, 22). Collins went on to propose that historical and material conditions have informed the unique perspectives of African American women and that the everyday lives of African American women were shaped by a connection between consciousness and experience.

     Although the purposeful sample consisted of seven African American women from four southeastern states who taught mathematics at either a technical school or a community college, they were not a homogeneous group. Each participant brought distinct flavors to the table, including a wide range of educational backgrounds, skin color, marital status, family background, and job experiences. Women ranged in age from thirty to forty-five, and their teaching experiences ranged from five to twenty years. Past teaching experiences came from many types of institutions, including junior high schools, high schools, vocational schools, technical schools, community colleges, four-year colleges and universities. Additionally, they came from a wide range of educational backgrounds. For instance, one attended schools in the North and had only worked with educational institutions that were predominantly White, while others worked primarily for predominantly Black institutions. They had attended small community colleges, predominantly White research universities, historically Black colleges and universities, and religiously affiliated institutions that were either integrated or

Creative Pedagogy to Enhance the Academic   367
Achievement of Minority Students in Mathematics:
Lessons from African American Mathematics Teachers

segregated. Some had all of their educational experiences in the same city or in the same state while others' experiences were across several states. These distinct factors help to show the power of the common themes that emerged in their stories.

A qualitative methodology was chosen for the study because the author had an interest in studying the process undertaken by these African American women mathematics teachers (Bogdan and Biklen 1992) and the ways that these women post-secondary mathematics teachers made sense out of their professional lives (Bogdan and Biklen 1992). Merriam (1988) states that a qualitative methodology is merited if one wants to know how certain things happen, how people interpret their experiences, or how people structure their social worlds. Therefore, a qualitative methodology was chosen because of the need to provide the most thorough understanding of the African American women mathematics teachers' experiences by speaking directly with them about the details of their work. Additionally, it was realized that observations are an important vehicle with which to gather a more accurate picture of the experiences of African American women post-secondary mathematics teachers. A qualitative design that included interviews and classroom observations of African American women post-secondary mathematics teachers provided various alternatives for understanding their experiences. Consequently, because the goal was to understand the process of human behavior and to experience a particular phenomenon, the concreteness of observations helped to explore more deeply the human condition (Bogdan and Biklen 1992).

Accordingly, a qualitative design was used to investigate what themes emerged about academic achievement and attrition in the stories of African American women who taught mathematics on the post-secondary level. The constant comparative technique used in this paper was qualitative research that constantly compared against other data to see generative tentative themes. Those themes were then compared to each other and other instances to see if the themes were consistent across the sample and within the data set. This method is ongoing and interactive throughout the research process, while the researcher searches for patterns in order to understand the participants and the phenomena being studied. According to Merriam (1998), the constant comparative method is one in which continuous comparison of interview transcripts and observation data are compared from each teacher in the sample and, through those comparisons, themes are constructed and analyzed. The constant comparative technique's goal is to compare information from the data collection in order to see patterns and regularities.

Using a constant comparative technique (Bogdan and Biklen 1992), those in the sample were interviewed and observed. The specific design involved an initial interview of two to four hours. The initial semi-structured interview focused on the teachers' prior history as mathematics students, previous experiences in teaching mathematics, and descriptions of issues and beliefs in their teaching practices. This was followed by an observation of each woman teaching. During the observations, detailed field notes (Bogdan and Biklen 1992) were taken of classroom interactions. A second interview, usually about one-hour long, asked the teacher to provide explanations for teaching practices.

The use of multiple data collection strategies such as interviews and classroom observations allowed for examination of the data from different viewpoints, to construct a better understanding of and insight into the complexity of the phenomena being studied (Coffey and Atkinson 1996). In this study, the combination of observations and interviews provided two lenses for viewing the phenomena being studied. Observations provided a check on what was reported in interviews. Interviews, on the other hand, permitted the observer to go beyond external behavior to explore the internal states of people who have been observed (Patton 1990). Hence, interviews with African American women post-secondary mathematics teachers, as well as observations of their teaching, provided a more accurate description of their experiences because the validity of the data was enhanced by using multiple data collection methods (Glesne and Peshkin 1992).

The data analysis used the constant comparative method (Bogdan and Biklen 1992) to identify themes that addressed academic attrition and achievement. The data used for the analysis included two interviews and detailed field notes from the classroom observations. The themes that emerged were used both to describe and analyze the data. Merriam (1998) proposed that the themes that emanate should have the following properties. The purpose of the research should be reflected. All of the relevant data, according to Merriman, should be placed in the themes that were generated. The theme should be named to capture the meaning of the data that is represented. Also, the

Creative Pedagogy to Enhance the Academic   369
Achievement of Minority Students in Mathematics:
Lessons from African American Mathematics Teachers

themes of data should make sense together. My data analysis reflected these guidelines. Additionally, the rule of thumb advocated by Merriam which states that "the set of themes should seem plausible given the data from which they emerge, causing independent investigators to agree that the categories make sense in light of the data" (185) was followed.

Validity in qualitative research is based on how closely a researcher's statement corresponds to the participants' own interpretation or construction of their realities. In qualitative research, researchers do not set out to prove or disprove hypotheses; instead they focus on inductive analysis whereby the data provides an unearthing of understanding and relationships.

Triangulation and listing my own biases were strategies I employed to ensure internal validity. Prior to entering the field the expectations, assumptions, and preconceived notions relating to the study were listed. The listing was revisited often during the process of data collection and data analysis. Additionally, the participants were presented a copy of the findings and asked for their reactions. Since validity is concerned with the degree to which the interpretations of the data made sense, this process was a necessity. No negative reactions were given for these findings, nor did any participant question any of the emergent themes. Hence, the findings were consistent with the participants' interpretations and the research was valid.

Reliability is the degree of consistency in the process of the study across researcher and methods. It should be noted the purpose of qualitative research is not to produce research that can be generalized to other situations, but to explain the phenomena being studied by those who are encompassed by the phenomenon. Nevertheless, the details of the research have been kept so that others could follow the procedures and processes undertaken to collect this research. This audit trail increases the chances that this study could be replicated. Also, a semi-structured interview was used and according to Silverman (1993), this method provides more reliability than an unstructured interview. Reliability in this study was confirmed by those who had looked at the findings and agreed that the results made sense and were consistent with the data collected.

Findings

These African American women post-secondary mathematics teachers reflected upon and drew from their own experiences in the classroom as learners to inform their teaching practices and strategies. As these women spoke of what they did in their mathematics classrooms, they referred to the practices of their own teachers and their experiences as learners. It became apparent that these African American women mathematics teachers exhibited an experiential mode of teaching based on the ways that their teachers had taught them and interacted with them. For instance, Georgia professed, "I teach the way I learn best... the way the teachers in which I learned the most taught." Similarly, Norris said:

> What I generally do is I see myself as the type of teacher I wish I had. The teachers that I copy are the ones I had a lot of respect for.......I pick up what made them stand out to me...... I want to be that way so I can have a positive effect on my students.

Some of their former mathematics teachers recognized their abilities or gave them opportunities to determine their aptitude. Other former mathematics teachers laid the burden of their own prejudice, racism, and sexism on them. If these African American women post-secondary mathematics teachers perceived a strategy or behavior exhibited by a former teacher as effective in reaching them, then they modeled that strategy or behavior. However, if a former teacher displayed a teaching practice that was inhibitive to their learning, then these African American women mathematics teachers modified it to produce a teaching strategy that would aid students in accessibility to certain information during their educational journey.

The factors that affected these African American women as learners in mathematics classrooms caused them to adopt teaching strategies that they believed would enhance students' academic achievement in mathematics. First, these African American women post-secondary mathematics teachers believed that the teacher had to have the right attitude about teaching and learning. Second, the mathematics had to be made accessible to their students. And finally, those same teachers believed that their students needed to be emotionally empowered.

Creative Pedagogy to Enhance the Academic   371
Achievement of Minority Students in Mathematics:
Lessons from African American Mathematics Teachers

Form the right attitude for fostering mathematics achievement
As learners of mathematics, these African American women believed that they were marginalized because of their race and gender. One of the obstacles they had to overcome in order to achieve success in mathematics were the attitude of some teachers who felt that these African American females were not among the elite students who should be privileged in the mathematics classroom. That marginalization had prevailed upon them as mathematics teachers to seek equity in the classroom and to teach students in the way that they wished they had been taught. Therefore, they believed that it was their job as mathematics teachers to reach all of their students, even those whom others might have consider to be on the margin of mathematical privilege and perceived ability because of their minority status.

Reba expressed her teaching philosophy this way, "I feel that all students can learn, given the opportunity and I'm here to give them the opportunity." In Reba's narrative she spoke of teachers who she felt did not give her the opportunity she needed to learn mathematics. For instance, Reba told of a high school mathematics teacher who showed little patience, often leaving his students to review material on their own. This and other instances recounted in her narrative, made it apparent that Reba would see the effective teacher as one who gave all students opportunities for learning.

Annie articulated her teaching philosophy this way, "A teacher's main objective should be to motivate, stimulate, and activate." Annie's philosophy was a result of her wanting more from her teachers and not getting it. Annie attributed this lack of interest and engagement on her teachers' part to her minority status. According to Annie, [mathematics] teachers have to expect their students to perform. Then teachers must instill in their students a desire to perform. Ultimately, Annie felt a teacher should motivate students to perform at higher levels.

Georgia's classroom marginalization was two-fold. She felt that she was discriminated against in the mathematics classroom both because she was a woman and because she was confident in her mathematics ability. As a result of her marginalization and struggles, Georgia believed that everybody could learn, and she recognized that the degree and style of their students' learning could be different from hers. Therefore, she expressed her teaching philosophy this way, "It is my job to give them the time, patience, environment, teaching, and attitude for them to learn."

Norris' teaching philosophy has two parts, one relative to the student and the other relative to her. Both the teacher and the student had to engage in the process for students to be successful. Norris said, "I go into the classroom and give students the opportunity to work hard..... They work hard, and I'm there to help them be successful." Norris' teaching philosophy is not surprising considering the many tales she recounted from her days as a student in mathematics. For instance, Norris told of a White male algebra teacher who refused to give her the extra attention that she needed when she did not quickly understand algebra:

> If I would have just been given the time or given a little extra push, I would not have made a C in the course.... I wasn't comfortable with a C. I felt I could have done better if given the opportunity.... But I didn't get that from him.

It is evident that Norris' teaching philosophy of valuing all students regardless of perceived ability flows from her experiences as a student of mathematics.

Similarly, Angela spoke at length of the negative experiences she had in her graduate and undergraduate mathematics classrooms at a predominantly White research university. She remembered being made to feel dumb and being an outsider in the classroom. Angela felt that she had a marginalized status as a student in her college mathematics classrooms. She says:

> So my whole mathematics career her at the university was so hard, it made me doubt what I knew that I could do..... I would cry so much.... It was so disheartening..... And when I tried to see some of my White mathematics teachers, it was like I was taking up their time and they really weren't that helpful and they weren't that nice when I was with them.

From these experiences, Angela developed a teaching philosophy in which all learners are invited to partake in mathematics in sundry ways regardless of their positionality.

Consequently, the attitudes upheld by these African American women resulted from the combined effects of each teacher's vast range of experiences as a mathematics student. Overall, these African American women educators had a philosophy comprised of reaching

Creative Pedagogy to Enhance the Academic   373
Achievement of Minority Students in Mathematics:
Lessons from African American Mathematics Teachers

those who were marginalized, bringing them to the center alongside those who were already privileged in the mathematics classroom. All these African American women post-secondary mathematics teachers felt that they as mathematics teachers were the instruments to bridge students to mathematics learning. Each of their philosophies involved motivating students. But most importantly, all of their philosophies were aimed at preventing marginalization and bringing everyone to the center of the environment.

Looking at the stories and themes that emerged from the experiences of these African American women who have been successful at mathematics, one should take away several lessons relating to mathematics achievement. First, the teacher holds a critical role in helping minorities achieve in the mathematics classroom. Second, a teacher's attitude toward the students in her or his classroom can affect a student's achievement in mathematics. Third, teachers need to examine carefully their beliefs and actions to be sure they are not marginalizing minority students, but encouraging achievement in the mathematics classroom by: 1) disregarding stereotypical beliefs about minorities' potential mathematics achievement; 2) setting high standards for all students; 3) providing opportunities for minorities and others to succeed in the mathematics classroom; and 4) inviting students to be a productive part of the mathematics classroom.

Developing a climate for fostering mathematics achievement
The climate in which the learning process took place was seen by these African American women post-secondary mathematics teachers as another factor affecting students' mathematics achievement. From their experiences as students in the mathematics classroom, all of these mathematics teachers had strong beliefs about the type of climate needed to foster mathematics achievement. For instance, Annie exclaimed, "I try to put as much energy and pizzazz in my class to make it come alive.... Most importantly what I want is for my students to be comfortable." Similarly, Addie declared, "students should be in a supportive environment and that's why I try to affirm them." Likewise, Ethel professed, "I want my students to be in an environment that is non-threatening." Reba remarked, "I want my

students to be engaged in the classroom dynamics."   Georgia proclaimed, "students should feel supported in the classroom."

Additionally, in discussing her views on classroom climate, Norris stated:

> I don't think it's so important that your students like you as a person, but I think it helps. So I take kind of an extra effort for the students to like me..... My personality, because when students are comfortable with you and your personality, they're comfortable in your classroom and are more successful.

On a similar note, Addie recalled one of her former mathematics teachers and how frightening and threatening he was. She remembered how this person adversely influenced her achievement in the classroom, and so she sought to be just the opposite. As a result of that classroom experience, Addie tried to foster a spirit of acceptance and approachability in her classroom. "I'm just trying to think of ways to make them relax but still be able to learn.... Relax them [learners] and you keep them [learners]" was Addie's formula. She also reflected on how her former professors, based on their own race, had expectations that were non affirming. For example, Addie said, "It was like I had to work twice as hard just because I was Black.... I mean, it's almost like a whirlwind.... You're fighting the White instructors and you have to prove yourself to the Black ones." Addie promoted the idea that her students could be themselves in the classroom without her having any prejudices.

Angela, who remembered her own sense of marginalization in the mathematics classroom and being made to feel dumb, worked diligently to affirm her students and make math accessible to them. It was noted that, in the observation of Angela's mathematics classroom, when students answered problems incorrectly, she did not tell them they were wrong but worked through the problems step by step and emphatically stated which parts might have been confusing. Similarly, if a student gave an incorrect response in her class, Addie asked him or her to think about the answer and then proceeded to help him or her recall previous mathematical knowledge that would aid in finding a more appropriate response. She would then give the student another problem to work through so that she or he could respond with a right answer. This method was also seen in the observation of Reba's classroom. When Norris' students answered wrong she tried to lead them down the path to a more appropriate reply. She would then

Creative Pedagogy to Enhance the Academic   375
Achievement of Minority Students in Mathematics:
Lessons from African American Mathematics Teachers

model a similar problem or concept to drive home what was wrong with the incorrect response. When Georgia's students answered incorrectly she would say, "Wait a minute" and review the rules. This led the student in question to give a more suitable answer. Georgia would then give him or her another question so that the student could gain confidence in his or her ability to articulate a correct solution.

In their attempt to create a climate conducive to mathematics achievement, these African American women post-secondary mathematics teachers were all of the opinion that students should be encouraged to ask questions freely and to seek their teachers as needed. Ethel recounted an episode from her graduate school days. She remembered how painful it was to be in a learning environment where she could not ask questions. Therefore, Ethel wished to promote an atmosphere in which students were not afraid to ask her questions. Angela, remembering how her own college mathematics teachers silenced her, listened attentively to all students and would stop in the middle of whatever she was discussing to attend to even the smallest questions and in some instances the repetitive or challenging questions. In Reba's observations, students would interrupt and ask questions frequently without hesitation. In Addie's class, students would ask questions and Addie would first acknowledge and affirm them for asking the question before she answered it. Norris explained that "I encourage students to stop me, not at the middle of my words but at the end of the statement, to dialogue with me about conceptual and skill questions."

A community spirit of learning was one component of the classroom climate that these African American women mathematics teachers felt helped to foster mathematics achievement. It was evident in the classroom observations of Norris, Angela, and Addie that they liked to promote a community spirit of learning. Students could be seen working problems together in class or discussing the homework assignments in groups. Norris said she didn't formally tell the students that they had to work together, but she acknowledged the fact when she saw it happening and told the students that she liked it. Similarly, Reba tried to foster a community spirit of learning and she stated that she liked to have a comfortable classroom "I have to become comfortable with the class," Reba stated, "and over a period of time we had a lot of fun in there and the best classes are the ones where the students become comfortable with each other." Evidence of this was seen in observing her class during the review of homework. Her students would bounce ideas off each other and exchange notebooks to look at their neighbors' problems and offer possible suggestions as to what was wrong with the problem. Reba, in her classroom discussions, often questioned her students. Georgia, Angela and Addie also spoke of teaching in classrooms where psychological safety was important.

Moreover, all of these African American women mathematics teachers loved to teach classes where the students engaged in interaction with them on many levels. In one college mathematics classroom, Georgia was expected to sit quietly in some classes and soak up the mathematics like a sponge. Georgia hated that method and preferred a more interactive manner and as such, she now uses an interactive mode of teaching. In observing her classes it was obvious that this classroom engagement of students in interactive lessons helped facilitate the learning of the difficult concepts she was teaching that week.

Similarly, Addie's stories showed many experiences where she felt that the lack of interaction in the classroom between herself and the teacher, inhibited her mathematics achievement. Therefore, Addie sought to know her students and to allow them to know her as they engaged in learning. For instance, an observation of Addie's mathematics class revealed many things. Addie was very cordial and non threatening in her manner, with her students, and extremely caring and enthusiastic about their correct responses and effort. She called on all the students in her class and rarely stayed at the front of the room; instead she strolled about the classroom visiting every student's desk. Addie dialogued with each student as she or he went to and from the board. When students were explaining their board work she would even sit with the other students. Her responses to students' answers were very affirming with words like "good, excellent, and great job" used repeatedly throughout the lesson. The students seemed to reciprocate Addie's affectionate behavior.

Annie talked about her lack of motivation in the classroom and how her teachers were boring and she was pretty much a loner in the classroom. These experiences prompted Annie to try to stimulate her students tremendously. Throughout her narrative she spoke often of how she needed to make lessons entertaining. During the observation, the researcher noted her teaching practice of making

Creative Pedagogy to Enhance the Academic   377
Achievement of Minority Students in Mathematics:
Lessons from African American Mathematics Teachers

mathematics entertaining. For Annie, the most important feature of climate setting was to make sure her students had fun in her classes, because she felt if they were motivated and stimulated they would learn more.

These mathematics teachers felt that humor played a positive role in creating a classroom climate that fostered mathematics achievement. Six of the African American women post-secondary mathematics teachers utilized humor in their classrooms as a way of making students feel comfortable and as a means to make transitions from awkward moments. Annie was the only one who used humor differently in that she used it to help a student realize the error of her or his ways when she or he did something incorrect in the classroom. She additionally used humor to point out common student errors or the causes of errors.

Norris said "humor is a way to get students to connect with you and this gives you the opportunity to teach them something." Later in her narrative she remarked:

> A lot of times I make jokes and allow them [her students]
> to make a joke every now and then. This contributes to a
> kind of easy atmosphere and they kind of take to your
> personality that aids in the learning process.

Also, when teaching difficult concepts or ones students found troubling, Angela used humor to lighten the mood. Moreover, Angela felt that humor was the best way to get learners not to give up or feel defeated when covering complex concepts.

Looking at the stories and themes that emerged from the experiences of these African American women who have been successful at mathematics, we should take away several lessons relating to mathematics achievement. The teacher has an awesome responsibility in creating a climate that enables minorities to achieve in the mathematics classroom. The classroom climate is a crucial element that affects minorities' achievement in mathematics. According to these African American women post-secondary mathematics teachers, there were eight classroom climate components necessary to aid in the achievement of minority students: 1) Teachers themselves had to actively create the climate; 2) The climate need to facilitate open dialogue between the student and the teacher; 3) The climate should facilitate open dialogue and spirit of cooperation among students; 4) Students need to be actively engaged in the classroom; 5) Teachers need to affirm students in the classroom even when students were incorrect in their responses, because students needed to feel supported; 6) Teachers need to help students feel comfortable in the classroom; and 7) Teachers need to promote a community spirit of learning.

Meeting students' affective needs to enhance achievement potential
These African American women mathematics teachers found that in order to foster mathematics achievement, they needed to empower their students not only intellectually but also emotionally.   They believed a teacher must empower students with the mental attitude and confidence about learning.   Because each of these women felt they were most successful when teachers not only encouraged them but prepared them for future challenges, they in turn tried to empower their students. These African American women mathematics teachers also had teachers whom they felt were obstacles to their success in the classroom, as well as in further endeavors, and because of those negative influences they tried hard to inspire students to learn.

These African American women mathematics teachers wanted students to know they can learn. Moreover, these teachers wanted their students to be stimulated to seek learning for a lifetime in addition to seeing the value of what they were learning through the course content. These teachers also realized that their learners were human and as such, did not exist in a vacuum and in numerous instances, had many dilemmas to juggle in their educational tenure. These African American women worked on educating the whole student and not just teaching mathematics. Often these mathematics teachers spoke of being a teacher versus being a mathematics teacher. For instance, Georgia remarked, "I do much more than teach mathematics... I am not just a mathematics teacher.... I am a teacher."   Consequently, these African American teachers not only taught mathematics but supported their students' emotional well-being.

Moreover, these African American women mathematics teachers spoke of counseling their learners, getting learners to value themselves, building self-esteem among their learners, and developing their students' ability to learn mathematics. Ethel said, "I do a lot of counseling... Students come in every day and tell me what's going on in their lives and what can I do to make it better." Georgia remarked,

Creative Pedagogy to Enhance the Academic   379
Achievement of Minority Students in Mathematics:
Lessons from African American Mathematics Teachers

"I try to make you [the students in her classes] feel good about yourself." Sometimes to accomplish this Georgia must nudge students to come to her office so they can get to know each other. She professed, "you are a different person in my office, one on one... we can cut to the chase and get down to your needs."

Addie explained, "I want them to feel good about themselves... Because once they feel good about themselves, they can get to the point that they can learn." Addie used many positive adjectives to reinforce students' efforts in her class. When a young African American male came up with a different way to do a problem than the way she had taught, she embraced his creative way and used it several times before the end of the lesson. Furthermore, in reviewing a previously learned concept, Addie engaged her students in helpful test taking tips. Also, several students had been absent in Addie's class because of illness. She wanted to catch them up on the missed lessons while assessing the level of learning acquired by those students who had been present. Addie had those students explain the missed concepts during the lesson.

Georgia felt she could have been more successful as a student of mathematics if some of her mathematics teachers had been caring. As a result of this, she tried to present herself as a caring teacher and made sure she was presenting the new material and not just expecting students to learn it on their own. Also, Georgia talked about several teachers in her narrative and made her experiential base of teaching known. When discussing her experiences with several teachers, the word "nurture" emerged throughout her story. These teachers, some Black and some White, helped Georgia to build her self esteem and hunger for learning. As she spoke of her own teaching practices, "nurture" was the word she repeatedly used. Georgia felt her teaching practices should set students on fire for learning and should help build their self-concept.

Reba considered it her duty to assist her students in setting and reaching professional goals. Annie spoke of many instances that involved counseling her learners. For example, one student was diagnosed with a particular illness that necessitated a change of lifestyle, so the two of them dialogued on the topic. Norris summarized some of the feelings that her students expressed on evaluations, "You're someone they go to for help."

These African American women were not only teaching the principles of mathematics, but they were also teaching their learners about how to become proficient learners. They taught their students the discipline necessary for becoming adept beyond the classroom for a lifetime of learning. For example, Annie emphasized organization and logical reasoning, Norris and Georgia emphasized hard work and setting goals, whereas Angela emphasized making connections. Similarly, Norris helped her students learn how to read mathematics books. She felt that if students were able to read mathematics books, then they would seek the help they needed in any mathematics book.

Norris also maintained that "if a student enters college and they test into basic math, you have to give them special attention to meet their special needs." Addie, Angela, and Georgia expressed similar sentiments in their stories. Addie remarked, "It could be the difference between the student staying in the program or giving up." She explained that sometimes when students get into basic mathematics course at the post-secondary level, that they experience a sense of "I cannot make it." She felt that it was up to her to see that they did make it and that their attitudes reflected this new source of empowerment. Angela discussed the sense of power she got when she taught developmental mathematics because she was the one who could help turn around learners who had previously been unsuccessful in mathematics.

Along the same lines, Norris fondly remembered one of her mathematics teachers. She spoke of a White male college mathematics teacher who had made a big difference in her mathematics achievement. Not only was he very attentive to her in class, but he encouraged her to take more challenging courses. In thinking about her teaching practices, Norris wanted to make a difference in her students' lives by inspiring them to greater achievement. She felt that she had to deal with the students' emotional needs as well as their need for skill and concept development.

Looking at the stories and themes that emerged from the experiences of these African American women who have been successful at mathematics, three major lessons became paramount: 1)Teaching is more than the transmission of facts and concepts; it also involves nurturing and empowering; 2) Teachers need to attend to the affective needs of their students in order to maximize their students'

Creative Pedagogy to Enhance the Academic   381
Achievement of Minority Students in Mathematics:
Lessons from African American Mathematics Teachers

academic achievement; and 3) Teachers need to be attentive, accessible, and affirming.

Making Mathematics Accessible
These African American women felt that their achievement in the mathematics classroom was enhanced when teachers made the mathematics accessible to them, and their achievement was inhibited when it was not. Therefore, one of the foci of their teaching practices that became apparent in the interviews and observations was their perceived responsibility to make mathematics accessible to all learners.

One strategy of these African American women mathematics teachers' mission to make mathematics accessible was flexibility. Each teacher felt that flexibility was necessary to reach divergent ranges of student needs and abilities. Each teacher recognized that each student had something to bring to the learning environment and made room for differences among their student populations. These teachers typically deviated from the traditional male norm of the teacher as the omniscient center of knowledge and the learner in a passive role.

Flexibility could also be witnessed in the following remarks by Reba, "I listen to them... Sometimes they will tell me I didn't understand the way you did a certain problem... I'll show them two ways of doing it." Annie related it this way, "I just come alive... I like thinking of ways to explain things so that even the slowest person will understand." Annie further highlighted her flexibility when she remarked, "What I attempt to do is that I take the math, and I almost have to translate to them in a funny kind of way of English because math is in itself another type of language." In the observation of Annie's class when students did not respond to her prompts, Annie rephrased them and asked questions in terms of something she knew they knew. Angela confirmed that when she felt that one group or one person might be monopolizing the class, she switched gears and went to a different method that would allow less vocal people to be affirmed.

All of these mathematics teachers went beyond the textbook in order to help their learners. This was not surprising considering past experiences as learners who were marginalized in the classroom. This marginalization occurred not only through the actions of the teachers but also through the classroom materials. So in order to empower their own students and make the mathematics accessible, they saw the need to incorporate personal experiences into the lessons as a way of making learning purposeful and rewarding. None of these African American women mathematics educators promoted simple rote memorization, drill, and practice. They found it necessary to supplement the prescribed textbooks with problem sets, review sheets, student experiences, and their own experiences.

In making mathematics accessible, these African American women post-secondary mathematics teachers used various modes of assessment in the learning process. They talked of reading the looks on students' faces and responding with appropriate questions, comments, and dialogues. For instance, Annie remarked, "If I noticed that you have a question, you better ask because if I notice that you look puzzled I'm going to ask you a question.... So you better be asking me a question." Addie, Norris, Georgia, and Angela also noted how they would change their verbal cues or lesson plans based on the student's facial expressions and spend more time on a topic. Georgia said, "Some students are not vocal and they will never raise their hands and ask a questions because they are scared. But they often send other signals to let you know they are perplexed." Norris rendered similar comments, "I have some students who don't talk much and so use their facial expressions to help guide me through discerning their stupefaction or understanding concepts and algorithms." These adult educators used homework in sundry ways as a means of determining students' abilities, problems, concerns, weaknesses, and confusions.

In each of the narratives and classroom observations, it was obvious that these African American women teachers felt that modeling behaviors, good and bad, was key to making mathematics accessible. Ethel stated, "I go through lots of examples until I see that the majority of them are following me." Annie explained that "I tell them, well I'm going to explain all levels of problems to get them to appreciate the fact that if you know the rules, you can play the game because the rules are going to work in any level, on any kind of problem." An observation of Annie's class revealed her modeling good visual pictures to go along with the algorithmic processes. Norris modeled how to get a better understanding of mathematics. She taught her students how to read the book, listen in lecture, and work hard. Norris believed it was important to go through the formal

Creative Pedagogy to Enhance the Academic   383
Achievement of Minority Students in Mathematics:
Lessons from African American Mathematics Teachers

language the book used to discuss properties and rules and then paraphrase in real words or language that was familiar to her students. For Norris, modeling played a big part in teaching word problems. She took her students through train of thought patterns about the set up of equations to answer word problems. Norris explained,

> So I go through one at a time of the different types of word problems… I write down the strategies for each different type of problem… I tell them exactly what generally is given in those types of problems… And I instruct them to write complete sentences stating their variables and their conclusions… I write on the board the format I want them to use.

These African American women mathematics teachers not only modeled behaviors that were appropriate for mathematics, but ones which were appropriate for lifelong learning across varying situations. Modeling was evident in Angela's practice. Her first evidence of modeling was expressed in her initial handouts to her learners. In these handouts she modeled a good method of note taking, as well as successful ways to study mathematics. Annie declared, "You have to be organized or you will not survive in math, nor in life being unorganized, being lazy." In keeping with this belief, Annie modeled modes of organization. She actively engaged students in outlining the mathematical concepts on the board and structured them in such a way as to facilitate efficient learning. According to Annie, "mathematics has to be written down as your mind functions…. you envision it systematically, it's going to go into your head systematically." Modeling was seen as an opportunity for these teachers to share their enthusiasm for mathematics, and for learning in general with their students and hopefully to spark in the learners that same enthusiasm for the subject matter.

These mathematics teachers made learning mathematics accessible by focusing on the learner through interactive lessons that emphasized input and feedback from the students. Student ownership of the learning process was integral in their way of promoting positive learning experiences. Each of these teachers started her classes by allowing students to discuss the homework. Hence, emphasis was immediately placed on students' needs. Norris explained, "When you come into my classroom at the beginning, you will hear students saying they have questions about the homework or tests." Accordingly, she addressed their concerns first thing. Annie began her classes by asking students to put up the numbers of the problems that they felt she needed to discuss. The students who put up the problem numbers on the board then engaged in a dialogue with Annie about the problems in question. In the midst of this dialogue, other students chimed in when they felt they could be of assistance or needed more clarification of the problem in question. Annie also asked her students to explain a homework problem she just discussed so that she could further engage the students in understanding the assignment.

In Angela's classroom, she allowed students to help fellow students with homework problems. Then she followed up with more problems in an effort to ascertain understanding. Since Addie had small classes, she had a standing rule that each student must go to the board everyday, and in her bigger classes each student must go at least once a week. Also, she had her students put all the homework problems on the board. Addie allowed students to volunteer for the problems they would like to put on the board and then assigned any remaining problems to students who had not volunteered to go to the board. She then had the students check each other's board work and explain a problem that they did not put on the board. Addie said this not only aided in getting the students involved but also helped them to learn to spot mistakes and to become comfortable dialoguing about the math. In Reba's narrative she noted that sometimes in the homework stage, she may patiently work the same problem several times until she is quite sure the student really understands the problem.

An additional way that all of these mathematics teachers made their lessons learner-focused was by allowing students to ask questions at any point during the lesson. All of these women noted that they often read the faces of their students and used student reactions to draw the students in or to ask the students specific questions. Norris, Angela, Addie, Reba, and Ethel liked to have students give choral and individual responses to prompts in their lectures. The observer noted that Angela listened to all of her students, even those who were not as fast or as vocal as others. Angela acknowledged each and every student's presence in the classroom. Georgia's classroom observation yielded similar behaviors by the teacher. There were several students in class who were quick to volunteer to answer questions and who readily asked questions of the content that Georgia was teaching. However, some students were

Creative Pedagogy to Enhance the Academic   385
Achievement of Minority Students in Mathematics:
Lessons from African American Mathematics Teachers

silent, and Georgia purposefully tried to bring them into the class discussion by calling on them and asking their opinions on the answers of their classmates. One White female student who normally was very active in the lessons was silent for a long portion of the class and Georgia solicited questions from her because she knew that in her case silence meant confusion. Norris, remembering her own sense of being left out in classes, listened and acknowledged all of her students in whatever way they wished to contribute. Some of her students mumbled the answer or nodded their heads and some even wrote the answers on their papers and asked Norris to check it. No matter what form of participation her students took, Norris was quick to acknowledge their answers even if they weren't vocal. Annie did not like to do this in her lecture, but she does like to follow this notion of prompting students for responses during her summation and her introduction to the lesson. Addie, Norris, and Angela liked to have their students work problems at their seats while they walked about the room assisting in and/or questioning their learners' progress.

Furthermore, neither Norris, Addie, nor Angela liked to remain in the front of the room. During the bulk of their lessons, you would probably find them out among their students discussing concepts and promoting a discussion of the topics in question. Ethel and Annie periodically walked out among their students during their lessons, but neither of them circulated throughout the entire room like Addie, Norris, and Angela. Annie stated that she liked to circulate among her learners, but this was not evident in the observation. Annie maintained that her lack of circulation among her students for the entire classroom had to do with the arrangement of the room. Reba was eight months pregnant at the time of her interviews and stated that her condition contributed to her lack of circulation. She, however, recalled that prior to the pregnancy she was more likely to go out and about her learners in the midst of the lesson. The observer noted that Georgia never walked out among her students, not even in the mathematics computer lab; her students always came to her desk.

Looking at the stories and themes that emerged from the experiences of these African American women, several lessons relating to mathematics achievement emerged: 1) Teachers must actively seek to make mathematics accessible to their students; 2) There are many ways to make mathematics accessible; 3) The classroom should be student centered; 4) Teachers need to be flexible; 5) Teachers need to go beyond the textbook and utilize multiple resources; 6) Teachers need to use many modes of assessment; 7)Teachers need to model behaviors for their students; and 8) Students need to be invited to participate in lessons and to ask questions.

Concluding thoughts

According to Willis (1995), "certain groups within the community are privileged by the way mathematics currently is constituted and few people give up privilege easily" (p. 72). Examining the stories of these African American women post-secondary mathematics teachers, we see that because of their minority status they had not been privileged in the mathematics classroom as learners. However, they sought to change this norm in their own mathematics classrooms. One strategy that teachers embraced was that of examining their own practices to see if they were perpetuating the so-called myth of the mathematical elite or to see if they were providing environments that facilitated achievement for all. Teachers need to follow the examples of these African American women who have been marginalized in the classroom. These women now seek to transcend the myths of minorities being a part of the mathematically non elite by knowing that it is our job as teachers to promote equity in the classroom and to give all students, regardless of their majority or minority status, the opportunity and help to learn mathematics.

Despite the fact that many persons have discussed the need for equity in the mathematics classroom (Atwater, Radzik-Marsh, and Strutchens 1994; Bailey 1995; Treagust, Duit, and Fraser 1996; Willis 1995), there is still a tradition among teachers to adhere to a long-standing male model of teaching mathematics that puts the teacher as the center of the classroom and the learners as incidental sponges of knowledge (Becker 1995; Etzkowitz, Kemelgor, Neuschatz, and Uzzi 1994). Many educators advocate that mathematics needs to be accessible not to just a select few but for all learners, and as teachers need to search for ways to accomplish this (Bailey 1995; Secada 1995). These African American women teachers had teaching practices that were accessible and empowering, and that deviated from the traditional methods of teaching mathematics. Reflecting on their own experiences as learners, they did not adhere to the male model of teaching mathematics, but instead used a more student-centered approach (Becker 1995). This emphasis on students and their

Creative Pedagogy to Enhance the Academic 387
Achievement of Minority Students in Mathematics:
Lessons from African American Mathematics Teachers

experiences concured with Cuevas' position that "educational opportunity must accompany the need for equitable access to the content and experiences the students will have in the mathematics classroom" (1995, p. 65). Also, this emphasis on students' experiences served as an avenue for empowering those students in the mathematics classroom who were often not privileged by the present norm of teaching mathematics. This supports the viewpoints of Atwater, Radzik-Marsh, and Strutchens (1994).

Most importantly this study highlights the important roles that teachers hold in fostering academic achievement. Cummins (1989) proposed:

> Minority students are disempowered educationally in very much the same way that their communities are disempowered by interactions with societal institutions. The converse of this is that minority students will succeed educationally to the extent that the patterns of interactions in school reverse those that prevail in the society at large. In short, minority students are "empowered" or "disabled" as a direct result of their interactions with educators in schools (p. 58).

The findings of this study supported Cummins' claims. Along the same lines, Mallory (1997) argued that the classroom culture of mathematics affected how African American students viewed themselves in the mathematics classroom, which ultimately affected their academic achievement. The findings of this study also supported Mallory's position. However, the actions of the women in this study illustrated that it was possible for the teachers to create a mathematics classroom culture that fostered academic achievement. These African American women mathematics teachers, because they were marginalization as students of mathematics, were committed to eliminating psychological barriers to the study of mathematics and so they subscribed to practices that were built on students' experiences and that included developing a climate conducive to learning.

Finally, all of the strategies depicted within this chapter are not mathematics specific but can be applied to any content area. Accordingly, simply because these women were mathematics teachers and drew from their experiences as mathematics students, should not prohibit these strategies from being used to foster academic achievement in other subject areas.   For instance, one strategy illustrated in this chapter was that teachers have to actively create the classroom climate and the climate should be one that facilitates open dialogue between the student and the teacher.   Just like these mathematics teachers, a science teacher could utilize this strategy of creating a classroom climate of open communication to reach the students in his or her class. Therefore, as one of the African American woman mathematics teachers from this study, I challenge educators to embrace the lessons gleaned from the experiences of the post-secondary mathematics teachers presented in this chapter.

REFERENCES

Atwater, M. M., Radzik-Marsh, K., and Strutchens, M. (Eds.). 1994. *Multicultural education: Inclusion of all.* Athens, Georgia: The University of Georgia.

Bailey, P. 1995.   Opportunities within the new mathematics curriculum. *Multicultural teaching to combat racism in school and community,* 13 (3): 3-6.

Becker, J. R. 1995. Women's ways of knowing in mathematics. In *Equity in mathematics education: Influences of feminism and culture* edited by P. Rogers and G. Kaiser, p. 163-174. Washington, D.C.: The Falmer Press.

Bogdan, R. and Biklen, S. 1982. *Qualitative research for education: An introduction to theory and methods.* Boston: Allyn and Bacon.

Brown, A. H. 1997. *Making the invisible visible by challenging the myth of the universal teacher: African American women post-secondary mathematics teachers.*   (Doctoral dissertation, University of Georgia, 1997). *Dissertation Abstracts International, 58-06A,* 2023.

Carl, I. M. (Ed.). 1995. *Prospects for school mathematics.* Reston Virginia: The National Council of Teachers of Mathematics, Inc.

Coffey, A. and Atkinson, P. 1996. *Making sense of qualitative data: Complementary research strategies.*   Newbury Park, CA: SAGE Publications.

Collins, P. H.   1991.   *Black feminist thought: Knowledge, consciousness, and the politics of empowerment.* New York: Routledge.

Creative Pedagogy to Enhance the Academic   389
Achievement of Minority Students in Mathematics:
Lessons from African American Mathematics Teachers

Cuevas, G. J. 1995. Empowering all students to learn mathematics. In *Prospects for school mathematics* edited by I. M. Carl, pp. 62-77. Reston Virginia: The National Council of Teachers of Mathematics, Inc.

Cummins, J. 1989. *Empowering minority students.* Sacramento, CA: California Association for Bilingual Education.

Etzkowitz, H., Kemelgor, C., Neuschatz, M., and Uzzi, B. 1994. Barriers to women's participation in academic science and engineering. In *Who will do science?: Educating the next generation* edited by W. Pearson, Jr. and A. Fechter, p. 43-67. Baltimore: The Johns Hopkins University Press.

Glesne, C. and Peshkin, A. 1992. *Becoming qualitative researchers: An introduction.* White Plains, New York: Longman.

Mallory, C. E. 1997. Including African American students in the mathematics community. In *Multicultural and gender equity in the mathematics classroom: The gift of diversity,* edited by J. Trentacosta, and M. J. Kenney, p. 23-33. Reston, VA: National Council of Teachers of Mathematics.

Merriam, S. B. 1998. *Qualitative research and case study applications in education.* San Francisco: Jossey-Bass Publishers.

Merriam, S. B. 1988. *Case study research in education.* San Francisco: Jossey-Bass Publishers.

Patton, M. 1990. *Qualitative evaluation and research methods.* Newberry Park, CA: SAGE Publications.

Secada, W. G. 1995. Social and critical dimensions for equity in mathematics education. In *New directions for equity in mathematics education,* edited by W. G. Secada, E. Fennema, and L. B. Adajian, p. 146-164. New York: Cambridge University Press.

Silverman, D. 1993. *Interpreting qualitative data: Methods for analyzing talk, text, and interaction.* Thousand Oaks, CA: SAGE Publications.

Stanic, G. M. A. and Hart, L. E. 1995. Attitudes, persistence, and mathematics achievement: Qualifying race and sex differences. In *New directions for equity in mathematics education* edited by W. G. Secada, E. Fennema, and L. B. Adajian, p. 258-278. New York: Cambridge University Press.

Treagist, D. F., Duit, R., and Fraser, B. J. (Eds.). 1996. *Improving teaching and learning in science and mathematics.* New York: Teachers College Press.

Willis, S. 1995. Mathematics: From constructing privilege to deconstructing myths. In *Gender informs curriculum: From enrichment to transformation* edited by J. Gaskell and J. Willinsky, p. 262-284. New York: Teachers College Press.

16. *Minority Student Persistence: A Model for Colleges and Universities*

Watson Scott Swail and Dennis Holmes

INTRODUCTION

Goal Five of the Goals 2000: Educate America Act[1] states that "the number of United States undergraduate and graduate students, especially women and minorities, who complete degrees in mathematics, science, and engineering will increase significantly."[2] However, it is increasingly clear that Goal Five will not be attained by the year 2000, and without significant intervention into the development of minority scientists, engineers, mathematicians, and technologists, it is unlikely that it will be achieved at all.

Although the number of African American, Hispanic, and American Indian students entering and earning degrees from America's colleges and universities has steadily increased over the past decade, these populations continue to be underrepresented at all levels of higher education.[3] And the under-representation is most severe among bachelor's degree recipients than among undergraduate enrollments. Data from the National Center for Education Statistics show that 45 percent of African American and Hispanic students graduate within five years of matriculation to a four-year institution, compared to 57 percent of white students.[4] Moreover, over the past two decades the number of non-Asian minority students receiving bachelor's degrees in the sciences has stagnated.[5]

Even though large investments have been made by government and private sectors to reduce these gaps over the past 30 years, and although access and persistence rates have increased for all groups, the gaps nonetheless remain stubbornly wide. If the massive federal programs since the mid-60s have done little to reduce—let alone eliminate—the access and persistence gaps between minority and white students, part of the answer must ultimately lie at the doorstep of the institution.

Much of the research over the past quarter century examining student retention issues has focused on isolating the role of specific variables, such as counseling, instruction, campus culture, and student behavior. Other research has explored the effects of particular programs or interventions on curbing the attrition of students from undergraduate degree programs. Although research has led to the development of retention programs at institutions across the country, these interventions have generally operated in isolation from other programs and activities on campus. Little effort has been placed on developing a comprehensive campus-wide student retention program. A campus-wide approach to student retention that coordinates the specific and unique elements of a college is required to best address the particular needs of minority students.

This paper will present a research-based model that focuses on the persistence of minority students in science, engineering, and mathematics programs. The model provides practical considerations for the adoption of policies at the institutional level to help increase the persistence of students in those fields. In addition, we will conclude with a discussion of the model in terms of institutional and public policy.

BACKGROUND
What is now known as the "pipeline issue" has become the focus of considerable attention in the past decade. The pipeline refers to the pool of persons who are eligible to enter a particular field or occupation. Mathematically speaking, the pipeline acts like a vortex, in which the entrance to the pipeline encompasses a large majority of the population during their youth. As time goes on, however, various factors, including socio-economics, motivation, and aptitude, pull

people out of a particular pipeline, effectively reducing the flow of persons toward the intended field or occupation.

In terms of science, engineering, and mathematics, the pipeline of minorities is considerably smaller than that for white males by the time of high school graduation. The reduction of the SEM pipeline is affected by a number of factors, and the scientific/mathematical talent pool, as Berryman[6] refers to it, diminishes at successive points before, during, and after secondary school.

An abundance of research has shown that minority children and females are negatively influenced by the sciences early in life through societal stereotypes.[7] These researchers and others contend that a lifetime of social growth represents the act of conditioning one's expectations and place within society. As Clewell et al.[8] state, the interest of minorities and females in the sciences is essentially squelched by the time they reach the seventh grade. By high school, many minority students generally feel unsupported, unprepared, or simply unmotivated to take SEM courses required for admission to a four-year institution. For students managing to complete the appropriate course work, other factors, including poor teaching, inadequate laboratory facilities, and lack of real-world application, make the transition to higher education most difficult.[9]

Despite the doubling of minority students entering college since 1976,[10] problems associated with high attrition rates continue to plague the SEM pipeline. Although we have identified the significant attrition problems facing minority students in U.S. colleges and universities, the issue of student retention plagues all student groups, regardless of race. Thus, the identification of retention variables, development of intervention programs, and the creation of institutional policy to reduce student attrition, are important areas of study for all colleges and universities.

Over the past twenty-five years, the issue of student retention in higher education has received much attention in the educational policy arena, mostly due to the realization that the rate of student departure from higher education is disturbingly high.[11] Benchmark studies by Tinto,[12] Astin,[13] Pantages and Creedon,[14] Cope and Hannah,[15] Beal and Noel,[16] and others are largely responsible for the elevation of minority-student retention on the college agenda.

During this period, considerable discussion centered around the identification of retention factors for minority students in U.S. colleges and universities. Studies conducted by Astin,[17] Blackwell,[18] Whimbey, Carmichael, Jones, Hunter, and Vincent,[19] and Fullilove and Treisman[20] resulted in the proposal of theories regarding minority retention in higher education. Research has also shown that factors affecting minority students vary from those of white students, and has concentrated on such issues as minority achievement and retention on predominantly white campuses,[21] achievement and retention on minority campuses,[22] and issues emphasizing the retention of SEM students, both on minority and predominantly-white campuses [23]

To date, research regarding student retention has focused in three areas. The first regards the size and breadth of the retention problem. While literally hundreds of studies have been conducted on retention, the most robust data come from the National Center for Education Statistics longitudinal studies, in particular, National Longitudinal Studies (NELS72), High School & Beyond (HSB82), and National Educational Longitudinal Study (NELS88). Although gaps in access and completion have declined in the past few decades, minority students are still less likely to attend postsecondary education, attend four-year schools, and even less likely to persist to degree.[24] Participation rates have increased for minority students in science, mathematics, and engineering fields, but they are still underrepresented compared to their percentage of the U.S. population.[25] Research suggests that for non-Asian minorities, choice of a science, mathematics, or engineering major is significantly influenced by such barriers as inadequate financial support, poor academic preparation in high school, and lack of science and engineering discipline-specific learning opportunities.[26]

The second focus of retention research during this period has been on the determination of factors and variables correlated with retention in higher education. Lenning,[27] in his synthesis of the studies of Cope and Hannah,[28] Lenning, Beal, and Sauer,[29] Pantages and Creedon,[30] and Ramist,[31] developed six categories of student retention, which include student academic ability, demographics, aspirations and motivations, personality and values, institutional variables, and student/institution interaction. Factors identified through the literature include the causal effects of campus climate,[32] socio-economic backgrounds,[33] and the presence of role models and mentorships[34] on minority student retention.

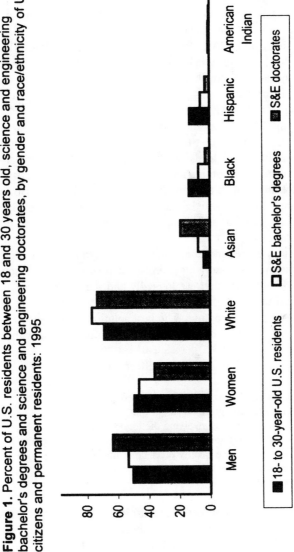

Figure 1. Percent of U.S. residents between 18 and 30 years old, science and engineering bachelor's degrees and science and engineering doctorates, by gender and race/ethnicity of U.S. citizens and permanent residents: 1995

SOURCE: National Science Foundation (1999). "Despite Increases, Women and Minorities Still Underrepresented in Undergraduate and Graduate S&E Education." *Data Brief.* Arlington, VA: National Science Foundation.

The third focus of the research has been on the development of retention models and programs. Since the introduction of pioneering retention models by Tinto,[35] Bean,[36] and Noel,[37] numerous retention programs have been developed and implemented in colleges and universities across the United States. Exemplary student retention programs include the Delaware State College Project Freshman Attrition Reduction (FAR) Program,[38] the University of California at Berkeley Mathematics Workshop Program,[39] and the Baylor College of Medicine Science Enrichment Program.[40] Retention programs, in general, incorporate such strategies as tutoring, mentoring, counseling, and skill development.

Most of the programs reviewed in the literature, such as those cited above, operate at the departmental level (e.g., Chemistry, Physics, English) and focus on the freshman student population. In addition, retention programs are most often independent of each other and are not linked with other retention efforts on campus. However, it is important to acknowledge that an extensive body of literature suggests that campus-wide retention efforts are the most effective retention strategies.[41]

First, a retention effort should be viewed as a kind of gigantic, campus-wide problem-solving exercise. It then naturally follows that there are certain steps that are logically and inevitably taken. Second, the essential task is to find a way to mobilize the collective wisdom that already exists on campus. The best solutions to the problems on a campus—and solutions do exist—for the most part reside with its own people.

Smith, Lippitt, and Sprandel concur:

> In our experience over the past few years, we have now come to recognize clearly that retention cannot be improved without involving the total campus system. This means involving everyone in a planned change effort that will improve the quality of campus life by drawing upon our institutional ability to function as a strong community.[42]

Pascarella suggests that institutions need to "organize salient constituencies"[43] on campus to orchestrate reform that evokes a positive change in student persistence. Institutions must not only develop the capacity to assess their current status, but also develop specific strategies to institutionalize the retention program. Although studies by Noel et al.[44] and Smith, Lippitt, and Sprandel[45] have discussed how institutional change can support student retention, there has been very little focus upon program institutionalization and sustainability.

METHOD OF INQUIRY

The research model presented in this paper was developed in two stages. The first stage included an extensive review of pertinent literature. An important outcome of this process was the development of a series of research-based institutional practices that had been shown to effectively increase minority student persistence. These were placed into five categories: student services, academic services, curriculum and instruction, recruitment and admissions, and financial aid.

The second stage involved the formation of a national panel of experts and scholars in the area of minority student persistence. Based on nominations from established scholars and practitioners, 16 experts—including vice presidents of educational foundations, senior scholars at national associations, and nationally-recognized researchers and professors—were selected to participate. Participating in a two-stage Delphi technique, the panel responded to the five-category framework introduced above.

The first Delphi round formed the foundation of the study by allowing panelists to comment on the five-category framework. Panelists were asked to rate individual objectives of the framework on a four-point Lickert-type scale and add comments regarding each objective. After the responses were analyzed, a second round was conducted and focused on ranking and clarifying the objectives within the framework.

Panelists were asked to comment and modify the framework based on their specific expertise and experience. The result of this two-stage Delphi inquiry is a research-based model that outlines a series of practices likely to reduce student attrition in the science, engineering, and mathematics fields.

THE RESEARCH-BASED MODEL

Studies and issues regarding minority student persistence are not new, and many of the practices identified and outlined in the research-based model have been presented before by other researchers. Three main differences in this model from previous efforts include: the focus on science, engineering, and mathematics; the broad scope of coverage across a variety of campus issues; and the specific recommendations for institutional practice. The model provides administrators and practitioners with a menu of activities, policies, and practices to consider during the planning and implementation of a comprehensive campus-based retention program.

The retention framework is classified into five components based upon an extensive review of current literature. Four of the five components, **financial aid, recruitment and admissions, academic services**, and **student services**, are generally major offices in most four-year institutions. The fifth component, **curriculum and instruction**, are receiving more attention and consideration at colleges, and was added to this study because of the direct impact it has on student retention.

The framework components are further broken down into categories based on areas of specialization, and subsequently into specific objectives.

It is important that practitioners understand the relationship between framework components. Most notably would be the ability of campus offices to work together toward common goals and focus on student needs.[46] From an organizational perspective, it is difficult to imagine how any of the components could work effectively without linkages to other areas. For instance, financial aid offices often work closely with recruitment and admissions offices, while academic services must work in tandem with curriculum and instruction. The framework attempts to develop additional linkages, such as those between student services and academic services, where the notion of Tinto's theory of academic and social integration[47] is most relevant. The linkage of recruitment practices with pre-college academic support programs is a good example of how a campus-wide support network can help students persist toward graduation. Thus, interrelation of the five components within the framework should be a major consideration for practitioners and developers.

As viewed in Figure 2, the research-based model is supported by a student-monitoring system. The system, identified from literature and panel discussion as an important benchmark, is a resource that supports the linkage of campus components or services. Such a system, when developed to capture data that reflects the true nature of student and faculty life, provides institutions with a snapshot of student

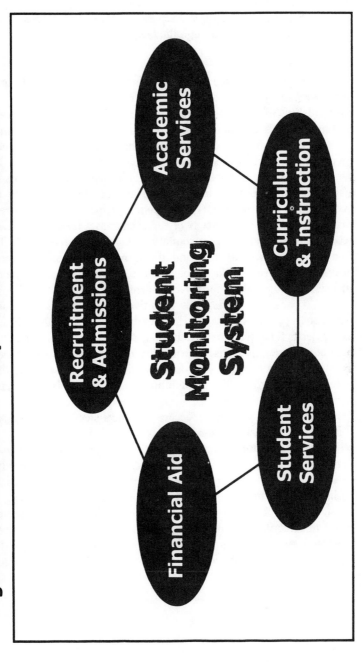

Figure 2. Institutional Components for Student Persistence

experience in terms of academic and social development.[48] It is with this knowledge that campus offices and personnel can generate more appropriate methods of supporting student needs.

Presented below is a discussion of the main issues of each component as generated through the Delphi process.

Component One: Financial Aid

Four categories were used to describe financial aid. The use of grants and scholarships, student loans, financial counseling, and assistantships/work study programs were all identified in the literature and supported by the panel to be important factors in student retention.

Although research has shown that grants are a much better predictor of student persistence compared to loans,[49] the finite limitations on grant/scholarship availability suggest that loans and work-study options must remain open avenues for students to gain access into the nation's post-secondary institutions. Princeton, Stanford, and a host of other Ivy League campuses have made news in recent years by making large commitments to need-based aid.[50] Other campuses, however, do not find themselves in the same financial position as the Ivies, and therefore must develop alternative ways to increase institutional aid for needy students.

Loans, although not positively correlated to student persistence (especially for African Americans),[51] are often the only available options for many students. Thus, it is important that institutions carefully devise an equitable and supportive loan operation for students and families. The delivery of accurate and easy-to-follow information regarding loan availability and regulations is an important factor for families.

A major barrier to access and persistence is the lack of information for parents and students regarding grants, loans, and scholarship opportunities. Colleges must be proactive in advising families of the price[52] of college, selection criteria, and availability of financial aid opportunities. The application process must also be designed such that it does not deter families from applying for financial aid.[53] Recent studies by the U.S. Department of Education[54] found that families from all sectors of society, including all income brackets and racial groups, had trouble completing the Free Application for Student Aid (FAFSA) form. While families, colleges, and even the Congress have long called for simplification of the student aid system, very little progress has been made in this area.

One other area for consideration is the availability of emergency loans for students who occasionally require additional financial support mid-way through a semester due to unanticipated costs associated with books, health care, and travel. The availability of quick turnaround funds for students can help students focus on their studies and persist through the semester.

Assistantships and work-studies are an important part of a student's college education, especially for science majors. Astin[55] found that work-study programs could increase student persistence by 15 percent. These opportunities provide students with money, experience in the field, and perhaps most important, networking capabilities for future employment and research possibilities. However, recent research by NCES[56] supports Astin's finding that there is a threshold where the amount of work per week distracts students from their studies and lowers the chances of student persistence.[57]

Financial counseling is the foundation for each of the three areas previously discussed. Counseling allows campuses to reach out to families and students and offer a variety of avenues to finance college attendance. College financing is arguably one of the most important and costly endeavors a family may make. Financial aid staff must be cognizant of the burden these decisions place on families, and support them during the decision-making process.

Major Objectives for Financial Aid

1) *Information dissemination.* In order to make informed decisions, appropriate information must get to students and families regarding student financial aid. The use of new technologies to deliver this information, such as computer networks and computer-interactive systems can help families plan for college and learn more about the college environment and requirements. Institutions must devise efficient and coherent communication paths to interested families in a method that is both informative and supportive. Yet access to these new technologies, especially computers and the Internet, is heavily influenced by family income. Thus, traditional information or access to computer-aided information must be made available.

2) *Increase availability of need-based aid.* Colleges should attempt to revise current lending practices to increase availability of grants,

scholarships, work-studies, and loans to needy families. Although a national trend is afoot to increase merit-based aid on campus, colleges should consider the impact of those decisions and maximize aid to needy students. The revision of current national financial aid policies, although out of the realm of an individual college's control, should continue to be a crucial focus area for national collegiate associations.

3) *Consideration of front-loading aid packages.* Some research has shown that front-loading student aid packages (i.e., coordinating financial disbursement so that students receive more money during the freshman year with diminished amounts in subsequent years) results in a more efficient use of loan money.[58] Additionally, it broadens the capacity of the program to include a greater number of persons that may receive loan opportunities. However, the panel responses regarding front-loading practices were predominantly negative.

Component Two: Recruitment and Admissions

The three categories under the classification of recruitment and admissions include student identification, admissions, and orientation.

Tinto[59] and other researchers[60] discuss the importance of matching student goals and expectations to a college's mission. The role of the recruitment and admissions offices must be clarified to: (a) first identify students whose career and educational goals are closely matched to the institutional mission; and (b) admit only those students to the college. The objectives within the recruitment and admission component reflect this current view held by practitioners and researchers.

Focus areas under this category include the recruitment of students who have been involved in pre-college preparatory programs; promotional visits to local-area secondary schools; the development of outreach programs within the target area of the institution; and the utilization and promotion of alumni clubs to recruit students.

Although traditional admissions practice incorporates the evaluation of students to see if they meet the institutional "fit," colleges should, in turn, accept the reciprocal responsibility of ensuring that the institution fits the student. Colleges should utilize a number of assessment/evaluation practices in the admissions office to determine the extent of student-institution congruence. Although SATs and other norm-referenced tests are widely used for gatekeeping by the majority of four-year colleges, they are by no means the only measures of student ability or aptitude. Even the College Board

Figure 3. Financial Aid Component

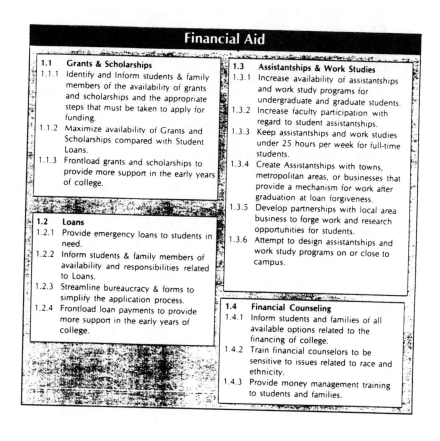

Financial Aid

1.1   Grants & Scholarships
1.1.1 Identify and Inform students & family members of the availability of grants and scholarships and the appropriate steps that must be taken to apply for funding.
1.1.2 Maximize availability of Grants and Scholarships compared with Student Loans.
1.1.3 Frontload grants and scholarships to provide more support in the early years of college.

1.2   Loans
1.2.1 Provide emergency loans to students in need.
1.2.2 Inform students & family members of availability and responsibilities related to Loans.
1.2.3 Streamline bureaucracy & forms to simplify the application process.
1.2.4 Frontload loan payments to provide more support in the early years of college.

1.3   Assistantships & Work Studies
1.3.1 Increase availability of assistantships and work study programs for undergraduate and graduate students.
1.3.2 Increase faculty participation with regard to student assistantships.
1.3.3 Keep assistantships and work studies under 25 hours per week for full-time students.
1.3.4 Create Assistantships with towns, metropolitan areas, or businesses that provide a mechanism for work after graduation at loan forgiveness.
1.3.5 Develop partnerships with local area business to forge work and research opportunities for students.
1.3.6 Attempt to design assistantships and work study programs on or close to campus.

1.4   Financial Counseling
1.4.1 Inform students and families of all available options related to the financing of college.
1.4.2 Train financial counselors to be sensitive to issues related to race and ethnicity.
1.4.3 Provide money management training to students and families.

strongly advises that the SAT should only be used in conjunction with other measures, such as GPA, class rank, and other non-cognitive measures, such as essays and interviews.[61]

Finally, campus orientation component of this area is an important part of student integration on campus, both socially and academically. Orientations should look beyond the student and offer opportunities to families and significant others, as the college experience is truly an experience for the entire family and not just the person in attendance. The Lubin House experience at Syracuse University[62] remains an exemplary model of satellite orientation practice and should be studied carefully by prospective colleges. Additionally, on-site orientations and extensive communications with families should become standard practice of any college.

Major Objectives of Recruitment and Admissions

1) *Pre-College Programs.* To ensure the efficiency of campus offices related to student recruitment, coordinators should capitalize on student data and involvement in pre-college programs offered by the institution. Students in these programs generally have already shown college aspiration, academic potential, and have been oriented to the college. Therefore, pre-college programs offer institutions an opportunity to recruit and assess student ability based upon previous contact with students and schools.

2) *Alternative Assessment Methods.* Colleges should revise current selection criteria to include a variety of assessment techniques,

Figure 4. Recruitment & Admissions Component

Recruitment & Admissions

2.1 Student Identification

2.1.1 Work with pre-college programs to identify potential recruits.

2.1.2 Monitor the participation of students enrolled in pre-college programs.

2.1.3 Attempt to match student academic and career goals with the institutional mission of the campus.

2.1.4 Use work study and teacher prep students to make visitations to middle and high schools to recruit students, and inform students about the need for study skills, good academic preparation, and advantage of taking AP courses.

2.1.5 Develop and focus outreach programs on the prime-targeted population of the university.

2.1.6 Further coordinate recruitment with the Alumni association to identify future students.

2.2 Admissions

2.2.1 Incorporate portfolios, interviews, and other non-cognitive assessments.

2.2.2 Balance the weight of SAT, ACT, and other tests in selection process.

2.3 Orientation

2.3.1 Provide opportunities for pre-college students to live on campus.

2.3.2 Provide early orientation activities for families.

2.3.3 Involve all campus departments in the orientation process.

2.3.4 Provide satellite orientations for non-local students.

2.3.5 Ensure personal communications with students and families via phone and visitations.

2.3.6 Create freshman orientations that are required and for credit.

including portfolios, interviews, and perhaps other non-traditional methods of pre-testing. While some panelists cited literature suggesting that SATs were culturally biased and problematic for non-white students,[63] most empirical research finds the SAT as the best available predictor of student success, especially in SEM and medical education.[64]

3) *School Visitations.* The use of work study students, graduate assistants, and other student personnel to make visits to local high schools (especially alma maters) in the capacity of recruiter is a cost-effective way of reaching out to the community. This practice is appealing because of the close connection between college students and high school students as opposed to trying to bridge the gap via recruitment personnel. These interactions also help generate a peer relationship between the college and high school that may be an important part of a student's decision to attend college or a particular campus.

4) *On-Campus Living Orientation.* Providing high school students enrolled in pre-college programs with on-campus experiences, especially living opportunities, was strongly supported by the panel as a method of recruitment and orientation. This practice has practical application for both students and colleges, first by giving students opportunities to test the college environment and become more familiar and comfortable with the college, and second, to allow colleges a much better chance of recruiting students who have had extended visits to the campus.

5) *Freshman Orientations Course Credit.* The panel suggested that freshman orientations should be given course credit in order to justify its importance to students in relation to their academic pursuits. Some universities have designed three-credit hour programs for first semester students, while others have designed one-credit hour orientation opportunities. Although the establishment of mandatory orientations without credit is a standard practice on many campuses, students often resent this use of their time. This is particularly true when orientations are poorly planned and offer students little in terms of increased knowledge regarding university services and regulations.

Component Three: Academic Services

The academic services component is the most diversified and expansive component explored within the framework. The focus of academic services in terms of student retention and persistence is on providing supplementary support to students in addition to classroom/lecture practice. This component is divided into six categories, including: academic advising, supplementary instruction, tutoring/mentoring activities, research opportunities, pre-college programming, and bridging programs.

Academic advising is important to the direction that students will follow during their college experience. Forrest[65] and Beal[66] are among those researchers who suggest that academic advising is an important part of an effective student retention program. To be effective, it is important that students receive guidance that reflects their needs while also incorporating the knowledge of campus programming and bureaucratic practices. Prospective advisors need to be trained accordingly to handle a variety of issues during advising sessions.

Beal[67] also noted the importance in using faculty as student advisers. This has many potential benefits, including role modeling and mentoring in addition to the academic guidance that may be offered. However, as one panel member of this study noted, there is a major difference between formal advisements that are scheduled and informal advisements or conversations that take place in hallways and classes. Both practices are important and should be supported by institutions and offices to ensure that students receive adequate academic advising and support during their college careers.

Supplementary instruction programs are becoming more prominent in colleges and universities. More colleges are developing alternative learning activities beyond that of regular classes to aid student learning. The Supplementary Instruction (SI) program developed by Deanna Martin at the University of Missouri-Kansas City is perhaps the most widespread program in use. However, in addition to providing remedial activities and supplementary support, departments must also continue to develop better strategies that increase knowledge acquisition and improve the learning process for all students.

Tutoring and mentoring practices form another support network for students. Colleges must make tutoring support available and affordable to students with such need. Faculty members should also make themselves available for academic assistance. Again, this "out-of-classroom" contact between students and faculty members has been substantiated by many researchers as an important factor in student persistence,[68] and has ramifications on the student's personal, social, and intellectual development.[69]

Students in science, engineering, and mathematics programs also benefit greatly from research opportunities. The link between classroom theory and real-world practice has positive implications upon a student's retention of knowledge while also making him or her more marketable after graduation. The development of local business partnerships and encouragement of on-campus research can create excellent opportunities for students.

Pre-college programs have long been an effective educational practice by post-secondary institutions. The MESA (Mathematics, Engineering, and Science Achievement) and MSEN (Mathematics and Science Education Network) programs are examples of how pre-college programs can help build the science pipeline by motivating students toward those areas. The newly created federal GEARUP (Gaining Early Awareness and Readiness for Undergraduate Programs) initiative has heightened the awareness and interest among colleges regarding pre-college programs. Colleges can benefit greatly from the establishment of these programs and the ensuing partnerships with K-12 schools and community organizations.

Bridging programs are an off-shoot of the pre-college program, but are more specific in nature. Colleges can utilize a student's senior year or summer before matriculation to help develop the learner's knowledge and ability to meet freshman program requirements. Study skills, time management, and course-related study are popular content strategies.

Major Objectives for Academic Services

1) *Academic Advising.* Colleges should implement a regular and standard practice of academic advising for students required by each office. The panel noted that student attitude is an important issue related to persistence, and that a pro-active system would require scheduled meetings to catch problems before they occur.

2) *Diversity in Instruction.* Supplementary instruction programs should utilize a combination of successful instructional techniques that support learning preferences of the entire student audience. The panel supported related literature suggesting that a diverse assortment of teaching methods were more effective in reaching students whose learning preferences are even more diverse.[70]

Figure 5. Academic Services Component

Academic Services

3.1 Academic Advising
3.1.1 Provide academic advising and counseling for students on regular basis.
3.1.2 Provide appropriate training in academic advising for faculty.
3.1.3 Use faculty for the academic advising students when possible.
3.1.4 Keep log of student/faculty-staff interactions in a computerized monitoring system.

3.2 Supplementary Instruction
3.2.1 Encourage the use of peer study groups to foster learning and incorporate more labs with classwork.
3.2.2 Incorporate a variety of instructional methods to support student learning.
3.2.3 Utilize peers as instructional personnel for supplementary instruction when possible to assist students.
3.2.4 Offer supplementary courses that focus on academic support skills (e.g., study skills, note taking, listening, writing, reading, time management) and academic content (e.g., biology, calculus, etc.).
3.2.5 Monitor all supplementary instruction activities by students and log into the computerized database.

3.4 Research Opportunities
3.4.1 Support faculty to work with students on research projects.
3.4.2 Integrate regular research activities into curricula.
3.4.3 Develop industry partners for research opportunities.
3.4.4 Encourage business and industry to participate on campus through in-class demonstrations and experiments.

3.5 Pre-College Programs
3.5.1 Develop pre-college programs at the elementary and secondary education levels.
3.5.2 Monitor student progress in pre-college programs.
3.5.3 Offer pre-college programs on and off-campus.

3.6 Bridging Programs
3.6.1 Provide on-campus residency for students during bridging programs.
3.6.2 Provide summer academic and social support for admitted students before the commencement of the freshman year.
3.6.3 Monitor all student progress in bridging programs.

3.3 Tutoring/Mentoring
3.3.1 Provide regularly scheduled and easy access tutoring for students with regard to course work.
3.3.2 Use Research Assistants (RA), Teaching Assistants (TA), and exemplary undergraduates as tutors.
3.3.3 Encourage faculty to support the academic needs of students outside of class time.
3.3.4 Encourage peer tutoring and group studying within class population.
3.3.5 Create reward structure for faculty involvement as mentors.
3.3.6 Identify and encourage the identification and use of minority students, faculty, and staff as mentors for students.

3) *Bridging Programs.* Colleges should focus on developing academic bridge programs between senior year in high school and the freshman year in college. On-campus intervention programs afford students a number of potential benefits, including the opportunity to (a) become acclimated to the campus, (b) work through some of the freshman problems before the fall semester begins, (c) receive academic support in areas of weakness, and (d) become accustomed to the pace associated with academic learning at the college level.

4) *Pre-College Programs.* To help develop the pipeline of students interested in attending college, institutions should place considerable resources into the development of pre-college programs. These programs, provided at levels as early as elementary school, help motivate students and get them thinking about the possibility of college. Clewell, Anderson, and Thorpe,[71] in their study of barriers to women and minorities in science, state that the middle school years are particularly decisive points in a adolescent's life regarding whether they follow through with science or disregard it as a field of study. Colleges and universities can help expose students to the excitement of science while also exposing them to college life. As one panel member stated, "You can not start too soon."

5) *Encourage Informal Faculty-Student Contact.* Colleges should try and promote informal contact between faculty members and students to build trust, support, and motivation during the college experience. Out-of-class contact with a student can create a bond and a sense of self-worth that can positively effect a student's locus of control and impact future decisions regarding college. Extra assistance on projects, informal discussions regarding academic subjects, and special social gatherings can encourage this type of interaction.

Component Four: Curriculum and Instruction

The continued development of curricula and pedagogical practice is perhaps the most important and fundamental need that colleges must address in terms of student retention. The need to revise current practices, especially in gatekeeper courses, stems from what Tobias acknowledges as the practice of designing courses that are "unapologetically competitive, selective and intimidating, [and] designed to winnow out all but the 'top tier' "[72] To combat some of these issues, the curriculum and instruction component has been divided into four categories: curriculum review and revision, instruction strategies, assessment strategies, and faculty development and resources.

Of primary importance to academic offices should be the continuous process of curriculum review and revision. This process should, in fact, become a mainstream part of curriculum development. Especially in terms of science, engineering, and mathematics, academic content must reflect the current dynamics of industry practice to be worthwhile and effective. Therefore, to prepare students for employment within SEM fields in the near future, it follows that SEM curricula must not only relate to current industry trends and practices, but also to anticipated practices and procedures (e.g., cutting edge technology/research). colleges should attempt to gain access to new equipment and provide instruction that utilizes state-of-the-art instructional technologies to ensure that materials are presented in a fashion that is commensurate with student learning preferences. The communication age has radically altered traditional learning and teaching styles, especially for students currently in elementary and secondary classrooms. Computers are second nature to new students matriculating to college or attending pre-college programs. Within a few years, virtual reality, a technology embodied as the ultimate in applied scientific and medical training, will also be second nature to undergraduates. Thus, colleges must allocate resources to the development of new teaching strategies that incorporate the latest in educational and industrial technology. Without these considerations, students may find that their knowledge is antiquated with the needs of society upon their graduation, when they should be on the cutting edge.

With the revision of curricular and instructional approaches also comes the need for a revision of assessment practices on campus. If new curricular practices are focusing on a higher level of knowledge and understanding on the part of the learner, assessment practices must be able to assess this higher learning. Thus, traditional methods of student evaluation are not appropriate to meet the needs of emerging teaching practice. The incorporation of instruments which: a) measure student comprehension rather than memorization; and b) use of a variety of assessment methods, including short answer, essay questions, and observation, may offer a more accurate picture of student development and comprehension.

The instructional capacity of faculty to deliver materials in an exciting, interesting, and motivating manner is also essential to the quality of education delivered by an institution. The use of diverse strategies by teaching faculty should be representative of institutional practice. Research has shown that student progress benefits from the use of smaller classes and group practice. The hands-on and group collaborative approach made popular by the Emerging Scholars Program at Berkeley[73] has shown that students, with specific reference to African Americans, are more inclined to produce academically at higher levels than students not involved in these programs. In effect, instructors must begin to employ practices more popularly related to K-12 education in order to reach students effectively.

Finally, if the three previous areas are to become standard practice, faculty must receive appropriate training and support. Faculty development activities, with specific focus on teaching and assessment strategies, must become a basic foundation for instructional practice at colleges. Additionally, faculty should be rewarded and given opportunities to develop new techniques that may benefit other educators.

Major Objectives for Curriculum and Instruction

1) *Instructional Practices.* Colleges should attempt to utilize various methods of delivering content to students, focusing on comprehension rather than rote memorization. The use of hands-on, exploratory, and peer learning groups are a few methods of motivating students to learn. An important comment from the panel suggested that a good balance between several methods is the optimum in style, allowing students to learn through a variety of ways rather than traditional rote memorization.

2) *Curricula Review.* Colleges should develop an integrated process of curriculum review to ensure that all curriculum pieces are up-to-date and relevant to the society's needs. At many universities, individual faculty members are left in isolation to decide what to include in a course syllabus, leaving much to be desired in terms of "quality control." This is a greater issue considering that most faculty have little or no background in learning theory or educational practice. Therefore, a systemic and cyclical review process that allows for faculty to review all curricula on a rotating basis would help control the content delivered in classes. Additionally, it also serves to keep curricula current.

3) *Professional Development.* Colleges need to provide extensive and ongoing professional development to faculty and staff to incorporate new teaching strategies and assessment techniques. With regard to the

Figure 6. Curriculum & Instruction Component

Curriculum & Instruction

4.1 Curriculum Review & Revision

4.1.1 Develop an ongoing review process of curricula utilizing faculty input and outside consultation.

4.1.2 Design curricula with interdisciplinary and real-world emphasis to stimulate interest and deeper understanding on behalf of the students.

4.1.3 Design curricula with knowledge of computer-aided instructional techniques and other technological innovations for instruction.

4.2 Instructional Strategies

4.2.1 Incorporate interactive, relevant, hands-on, exploratory instructional practices, utilizing individual and small/large group strategies to maximize learning and motivate students.

4.2.2 Provide homework, out-of-class assignments, and in-class assignments for students.

4.2.3 Utilize educational technologies to complement instruction.

4.3 Assessment Strategies

4.3.1 Develop assessment instruments that require students to utilize higher order thinking skills.

4.3.2 Conduct extensive student testing and assessment on a regular basis to monitor student progress.

4.3.3 Utilize a variety of assessment techniques to encourage a diverse assessment strategy that allows for differences in student preferences. (e.g., paper-pencil, observation, homework, lab work, portfolio development, etc.).

4.3.4 Develop computer monitoring capability for instant trend analysis for student growth and development in terms of student assessment.

4.4 Faculty Development/Resources

4.4.1 Provide appropriate instructional training for teaching faculty.

4.4.2 Develop an appropriate faculty reward system.

4.4.3 Develop a center for teaching excellence to support teacher development.

4.4.4 Make available and identify grant opportunities for classroom research.

discussion of curriculum revision and assessment, faculty cannot be expected to teach specific, if not more standard, courses without opportunities to share and learn from others with different experience. The panel was extremely supportive of the substantial literature regarding professional development, and one panelist in particular suggested that the absence of professional development activities would restrict any new initiatives from taking hold. If colleges and universities are serious about teaching as a focus of their mission, then it is incumbent upon them to provide support for their instructional staff.

4) *Faculty-Reward Structure.* The development of a faculty reward structure as a specific objective was an addition to the framework by the panel. Throughout the study, panelists discussed the importance of building in rewards for faculty to motivate them to change. Apart from the development of a cohesive policy statement regarding reward structures, the administration must actively participate in revision of the institutional mission, and ultimately the reward structure, to generate long-term support from the staff. Faculty and staff need to see that their efforts are rewarded and taken seriously by administration.

5) *Assessment Techniques.* Campuses should design and implement new assessment techniques which are multi-faceted and regard the integrity of human learning and understanding. Teaching and learning practices that require students to evaluate, synthesize, analyze, and create, also require new methods of assessing student progress.[74] Although the literature suggests that these practices are important, the panel questioned the capability and the readiness of the faculty to become this deeply involved. As one panelist asked, how is a college that has not taken teaching seriously going to take to higher level assessment practices? With this in mind, it is evident that colleges currently struggling with similar issues must work to develop a foundation upon which further reform can take place. The faculty must be swayed to the new ways, and this requires support in terms of training, leadership, rewards, and the freedom to make mistakes.

Component Five: Student Services

As Tinto[75] and others have suggested, the "social integration" of students with the institution is an important factor in their ability to persist. The role of the student services office has evolved to deal with many of the issues facing students on campus. The atmosphere and climate of a university, reflected by how the institution treats and supports students and by the positive nature of peer relations on campus, is important to the self-esteem and confidence a student generates about him or herself. Neisler[76] concluded that personal, emotional, and family problems, in addition to feelings of isolation and adjustment to college life, are strong barriers to retention for African American students. Therefore, the campus must focus on developing an atmosphere that is supportive, safe, and pluralistic. The outcomes of this study found that campus climate, accessibility to campus, campus housing, and career and personal counseling are areas that should be considered in terms of their effect on student retention.

Campus climate is not some intangible, abstract concept that 'just happens.' More accurately stated, campus climate is the development of the beliefs and practices of the administration, faculty, staff, and students belonging to that institution. Therefore, it can be created, and to some degree, controlled. To develop a positive campus climate supportive of learning and human development, campuses should promote diversity on campus and extol the virtues of shared culture.[77] This practice allows colleges and universities to better reflect the changes in society and promote pluralism. Ensuring safety for students and providing social opportunities for students to forge new friendships and build trust with their fellow classmates are examples. The existence of student groups and organizations can also support a positive climate by integrating students into the campus environment.

Accessibility to campus is also an important concept for institutions to consider. Administrators must consider the use of flexible scheduling practices to allow students with different schedules to be able to enroll in classes required for graduation. The use of weekends and evenings are alternative methods for class scheduling, and offering classes in subsequent semesters rather than flip-flopping semesters can make the path to graduation much more palatable to students. An additional consideration is the linkage of public transportation systems to campus. Students who have difficult times accessing the campus are less likely to persist. However, the utilization of distance learning technologies may also help alleviate these problems.

On-campus housing is an important element directly related to student persistence due to the integration of the student to the campus.[78] However, colleges must ensure that housing is accessible and affordable for the student population, and offer choices in terms of type of housing. Additionally, campuses should also consider the changing demographics of college students. Native Americans, for example, are well known for the advanced age of their college students (unofficial reports of 28-years of age). This trend in advancing age of the student population suggests that institutions must start thinking in terms of average student age on campus and add housing for spouses and children of students.

Finally, counseling services are also related to student retention. Studies of the effects of counseling and at-risk students,[79] African Americans,[80] and first-generation students[81] confirm that counseling services are important components of student retention programs. Colleges need to deal with the added stress and burden that today's students bring with them to campus. Counseling services should provide support for students in terms of social needs and career counseling. In providing these services, colleges must make the services accessible to the student population and provide alternative methods of counseling to suit particular needs of the population.

Major Objectives for Student Services

1) *Diversity and Multiculturalism.* Colleges can build a pluralistic environment by promoting diversity and multiculturalism through special programming and activities. Studies by Astin[82] and Justiz[83] found that campuses embracing diversity and multiculturalism attracted student populations that were very positive, capable of change, and were academically skilled. Although the panel was extremely supportive of this objective, they were also cautious, noting that the experience must be real and not just exist by name. As one panelist stated, "almost all campuses say they do the above," but few act upon such need.

2) *Flexible Scheduling.* Allowing the scheduling of classes in a variety of timeslots allows a broader constituency of students to attend classes. Many universities have fixed schedules that allow for little flexibility in course selection, mostly because of budget reasons. However, there are instances when this occurs due to the inflexibility of faculty to try different schedules. Adding Saturday courses, or moving courses around the schedule, may allow students to enroll in more of the classes they need during a semester rather than wait for a rotation where they have no conflict.

Figure 7. Student Services Component

Student Services

5.1 Campus Climate

5.1.1 Provide and support a pluralistic environment for students by promoting diversity and multiculturalism through special programs, activities, and curricula.

5.1.2 Provide a safe campus environment for all students, faculty, staff, and visitors.

5.1.3 Provide non-classroom opportunities for faculty-student interaction.

5.1.4 Provide social opportunities for students through entertainment, sports, extracurricular activities, special events, and academic-related social events.

5.1.5 Support the organization of student clubs, associations, and fraternal organizations on campus.

5.2 Accessibility/Transportation

5.2.1 Offer classes in a variety of timeslots to permit flexible scheduling by students.

5.2.2 Ensure transportation link with local area metro system for increased access to campus.

5.2.3 Offer classes on weekends and special Friday-Saturday combinations.

5.2.4 Offer classes in concurrent semesters to allow for student flexibility in scheduling.

5.2.5 Utilize distance learning technologies to allow for a broader audience and support those students who cannot attend on -campus classes.

5.3 Housing

5.3.1 Ensure affordable housing and meal plans.

5.3.2 Encourage on-campus housing for students.

5.3.3 Provide an appropriate number of housing slots to meet the needs of the student body.

5.3.4 Develop housing patterns that may incorporate choice of major or other demographic issues.

5.4 Counseling

5.4.1 Provide psychological and social counseling to students to support added stresses in society.

5.4.2 Provide career counseling to ensure that students, in accordance with academic advising, are following the proper path to reach their goal.

5.4.3 Provide counseling services that are cognizant of the cultural and racial issues facing students.

5.4.4 Develop and disseminate appropriate publications, brochures, and mailings that inform students of issues and programs.

5.4.5 Offer a variety of counseling opportunities and techniques, including individual, group, computer, video counseling sessions.

3) *Career Counseling.* Colleges must ensure that students are sent on an academic track that will direct them toward their career destination. Occasionally, students are advised to take certain courses that in reality are poor choices and may extend their attendance. Career and academic counselors need to be well-versed in the requirements, schedules, and policies regarding graduation as well as a keen knowledge of what business and industry are looking for. This can only be done through an expansive knowledge of the student by qualified counselors.

4) *Faculty-Student Interaction.* Informal contact between faculty members and students are part of a rich atmosphere of sharing and caring at college campuses. Students feel much more relaxed and cared for when faculty are committed to their success. The sister version of this objective was presented under the academic services component. As stated previously, the social integration of students is paramount to student persistence, enjoyment, and achievement in college. The willingness and acceptance of staff to "rub shoulders" with students beyond the confines of the classroom can have long-lasting effects.

5) *Room and Board.* Affordability and comfortability are important considerations for students in terms of housing and meals. Campuses should look at numerous plans that allow students to choose the type of housing which best meets their financial ability and living requirements. This impacts mature students with families, economically disadvantaged students, and those students living far from home.

POLICY IMPLICATIONS AND RECOMMENDATIONS

The framework offers institutions a set of options to consider during program development. We close this paper with perspectives on the following selected policy issues.

Institutional Leadership. Ultimate success of a campus-wide retention effort will depend on a number of leadership issues. First, retention programs must have unequivocal support from the Office of the President or Provost, involve the entire campus in shaping program operations, and keep ideology focused on the student. Increasing student-retention rates is a complex issue requiring the involvement of the entire campus. Although departments and offices may conduct their own programs, it is not until the entire campus directs a unified effort at reducing attrition that large-scale changes can be seen. The development of a **Cross-University Retention Task Force** sends both a message of urgency as well as a sign of support from the administration. This task force can help plan across the departmental silos inherent in most university systems.

Funding Priorities. No large-scale program is free or cheap. If increased student persistence is the end goal, appropriate funding must be made available in the general budget. Once departments and offices start arguing over where funding should be pulled from, the program is likely doomed. Funding sends an important leadership message to all faculty, and helps crystallize campus priorities.

Faculty Reward Systems. If faculty members are to turn more of their attention to student needs and teaching as a whole, the institution must incorporate these actions into the tenure structure. Current reward systems at most institutions are structured in a way that deter faculty members from focusing on teaching. Tenure and promotion decisions are, by and large, based on a history of research and scholarship, which includes a candidate's record of academic publishing and success in obtaining sponsored-research funds. Although teaching is often considered in such decisions, it lacks the clout of tangible evidence provided by publication and research. It isn't that instructional staff aren't interested in helping students achieve and persist, but the pressure to produce in other non-academic areas restricts involvement.

Student-Teacher Interaction. Faculty support isn't just a tenure issue. Instructional faculty require time to develop the student-teacher interactions that can make a difference. Most faculty believe they are overburdened with advisees, faculty and dissertation committees, and other bureaucratic affairs. To make real differences in these interactions, such burdens must be reduced.

Flexible Planning. Student retention programs must be designed to match the characteristics and conditions at each campus. Programs that work well on one campus do not necessarily work well on another campus. The students, faculty, and institutional mission bring different aspects to the campus that makes it unique and special, and these characteristics must be considered in the planning cycle.

Institutional Research. Feedback is perhaps the most important aspect of program development, implementation, and sustainability. The campus institutional research (IR) office is potentially the greatest resource for campus leadership and faculty. With appropriate fiscal and material support, IR offices can provide responsive feedback regarding the impact of major initiatives or programs down to the student level. Empirical information should be the foundation of any retention effort, and careful planning must be taken to ensure that appropriate indicators are selected and high-quality data collected. Additionally, systems must be put in place to ensure that this information is disseminated on a systematic basis to inform key stakeholders about progress toward goals.

Academic Preparation and Admissions. Recent affirmative action litigation is forcing campuses to rethink their admissions practices. One brief year after Proposition 209, California institutions are showing dramatic decreases in the admission rates of Black and Latino students. One answer to this problem for colleges is to further encourage and develop the academic preparation of minority students. The divisions between PreK-12 and postsecondary education are becoming more blurred all the time. College and universities are coming to the understanding that they need to play a stronger role during the pre-college years. Short of radical educational reform, institutions interested in admitting students of greater academic capacity must wade into the pool themselves. Pre-college outreach programs have enjoyed great success in increasing the academic ability and motivation of young students at the elementary-, middle-, and high-school levels.

College Affordability. How much college costs is a major factor in whether students go to college, as well as where they go. Over the past two decades, most four-year colleges have had to increase tuition and fee charges to remain viable. Simultaneously, institutions have also increased institutional aid packages in an attempt to keep college affordable for low-income students. However, high-tuition, high-aid policy makes it difficult for colleges to remain affordable for the most needy students. That said, college has become much less affordable for students since 1980. Tuition and Fees at four-year public and private institutions has risen about 90 percent after adjusting for inflation, student aid has increased around 40 percent and median family income[84] has only increased 9 percent.[85] Thus, for many low-income students, many of whom are non-Asian minorities, there is somewhat of an affordability crisis with regard to postsecondary education. Colleges and state systems must continue to remove cost as a major disincentive for needy students.

Technology. Recent development of web-based technologies has begun to impact how colleges and universities can deliver instruction, and how students and professors may communicate. The birth of the virtual university and proliferation of distance education courseware is forcing institutions to rethink how they do business. But the ability to benefit from technology is a product of technological access. While technology has the potential to remove barriers of time and distance, it simultaneously may widen gaps in access between low- and high-income students--between the technological have and have-nots. Technology is clearly a double-edge sword. It is difficult to image the collegiate experience without computer assistance in this day and age. However, colleges and universities must take special care to ensure that students from all backgrounds enjoy access and comfortability with technology.

REFERENCES

Association of American Medical Colleges. 1992. "Project 3000 by 2000." *Technical Assistance Manual: Guidelines for Action.* Washington, DC: AAMC.

American Association of State Colleges and Universities. 1994. *AASCU/Sallie Mae National Retention Project: 1993 Survey Results.* Washington, D.C.: AASCU.

Astin, A. W. 1975. *Preventing Students from Dropping Out.* San Francisco, CA: Jossey-Bass Inc.

___. 1977. *Four Critical Years.* San Francisco, CA: Jossey-Bass, Inc.

___. 1982. "Minorities in American Higher Education." *Recent Trends, Current Prospects, and Recommendations.* San Francisco, CA: Jossey-Bass Inc.

___. March/April 1993. "Diversity and Mulitculturalism on the Campus: How are Students Affected?" *Change.* San Francisco, CA: Jossey-Bass Inc.

Bagayoko, Diola, and Ella Kelley. Fall 1994. "The Dynamics of Student Retention: A Review and a Prescription." *Education, 115* (1).

Beal, Philip E., and Lee Noel. 1980. *What Works in Student Retention.* American College Testing Program.

Bean, J.P. 1982. "Student Attrition, Intentions, and Confidence." *Research in Higher Education, 17,* pp. 291-320.

Berryman, Sue E. November 1983. *"Who Will Do Science?"* Minority and Female Attainment of Science and Mathematics Degrees: Trends and Causes. Paper presented for the Rockefeller Foundation.

Bird, Tom. 1990. "The School Teacher's Portfolio: An Essay on Possibilities." *The New Handbook of Teacher Evaluation.* Newbury Park, CA: Sage Publications, pp. 241-256.

Blackwell, James E. 1992. "Suggested Research on the Future of Minorities in Graduate Education." *Minorities in Graduate Education: Pipeline, Policy and Practice.* Princeton, NJ: Educational Testing Service, pp. 122-129.

Burrell, Leon F., and Toni B. Trombley. 1983. "Academic Advising with Minority Students on Predominantly White Campuses." *Journal of College Student Personnel, 24,* pp. 121-126.

Carmichael, J. W., Jr. and John P. Sevenair. 1991. "Preparing Minorities for Science Careers." *Issues in Science and Technology, 7*(3), pp. 55-60.

Chickering, A.W. 1974. *Commuting Versus Resident Students: Overcoming the Educational Inequities of Living Off Campus.* San Francisco, CA: Jossey-Bass, Inc.

Clewell, Beatriz Chu, Bernie T. Anderson, and Margaret E. Thorpe. 1992. *Breaking the Barriers.* San Francisco, CA: Jossey-Bass Inc.

Clewell, B., and M. Ficklen. 1986. *Improving Minority Retention in Higher Education: A Search for Effective Institutional Practices.* Princeton, NJ: Educational Testing Service.

College Board, The. 1998. *Trends in Student Aid 1998.* New York, NY: The College Entrance Examination Board.

Collison, M. 6 July 1988. "Complex Application Form Discourages Many Students From Applying for Federal Financial Aid." *Chronicle of Higher Education,* A19, A30.

Cope, R., and W. Hannah. 1975. *Revolving College Doors: The Causes and Consequences of Dropping Out, Stopping Out, and Transferring.* New York, NY: Wiley.

Cross, Patricia H., and Helen S. Astin. 1981. "Factors Affecting Black students' Persistence in College. In Thomas " *Black Students in Higher Education.* Westport, Connecticut: Greenwood Press.

Culotta, Elizabeth. 13 November 1992. "Minorities in Science, The Pipeline Problem. Black Colleges Cultivate Scientists." *Science*, pp. 1216-1218.

Dreisbach, Melanie et al. 1982. "Testwiseness as a Factor in Readiness Test Performance of Young Mexican-American Children." *Journal of Educational Psychology*, 74(2), pp. 224-229.

Elam, Julia C., ed. 1989. *Blacks in Higher Education: Overcoming the Odds*. Lanham, MD: University Press of America.

Forrest, A. 1982. *Increasing Student Competence and Persistence: The Best Case for General Education*. Iowa City, IA: American College Testing Program National Center for Advancement of Educational Practices.

Fennema, E., and J. Sherman. February 1976. *Sex-Related Differences in Mathematics Learning: Myths, Realities, and Related Factors*. Paper presented at the annual meeting of the American Association for the Advancement of Science, Boston.

Fullilove, Robert E., and Philip U. Treisman. 1990. "Mathematics Achievement Among African American Undergraduates at the University of California, Berkeley: An Evaluation of the Mathematics Workshop Program." *Journal of Negro Education*, 59(3), pp. 463-478.

Gates, Rebecca T. 1989. "Project Far: A Blueprint for College Student Retention." *Recruitment and Retention of Black Students in Higher Education*. National Association for Equal Opportunity in Higher Education, Research Institute.

General Accounting Office. March 1995. *Restructuring Student Aid Could Reduce Low-Income Student Dropout Rate*. Report to Congressional Requesters. GAO/HEHS-95-48.

Gibbs, J.T. 1975. "Use of Mental Health Services by Black Students at a Predominantly White University: A Three Year Study." *American Journal of Ortho Psychiatry, 45*, pp. 430-445.

Goals 2000: Educate America Act. Public Law 103-227, 103rd Congress 1994.

Griffen, Oris T. 1992. "The Impacts of Academic and Social Integration for Black Students in Higher Education." *Strategies for Retaining Minority Students in Higher Education*. Springfield, IL: Charles C. Thomas, Publishers, pp. 25-44.

Hyman, A.K. 1988. "Group Work as a Teaching Strategy in Black Student Retention in Higher Education." *Black Student Retention in Higher Education*. Springfield, IL: Charles C. Thomas, pp. 71-82.

Justiz, Manuel. 1994. Demographic Trends and the Challenges to American Higher Education. *Minorities in Higher Education*. Phoenix, AZ: Oryx Press and ACE, pp. 1-21.

Kalechstein, Pearl et al. 1981. "The Effects of Instruction on Test-Taking Skills in Second Grade Children." *Measurement and Evaluation in Guidance*, 13(4), 198-201.

Landis, Raymond B. 1985. *Handbook on Improving the Retention and Graduation of Minorities in Engineering*. New York, NY: The National Action Council for Minorities in Engineering.

Lang, Marvel. 1986. "Black Student Retention at Black Colleges and Universities: Problems, Issues and Alternatives". *Western Journal of Black Studies, 10*(2).

____ and C. Ford, eds. 1988. *Black Student Retention in Higher Education*. Springfield, IL: Charles C. Thomas, Publishers

Lenning, Oscar T. 1982. "Variable-Selection and Measurement Concerns." *Studying Student Attrition*. San Francisco, CA: Jossey-Bass Inc.

____, Philip E. Beal, and Ken Sauer. 1980. *Retention and Attrition: Evidence for Action and Research*. Boulder, CO: National Center for Higher Education Management Systems.

Loo, C. M. and G. Rolison. 1986. "Alienation of Ethnic Minority Students at a Predominately White University." *Journal of Higher Education, 57*(1), 58-77.

Malcom, Shirley. 1988. "Brilliant Women for Science, Mathematics and Engineering: Getting More Than We Deserved?" *Developing Talent in Mathematics, Science and Technology: A Conference on Academic Talent*. ERIC Document Reproduction Service No. ED 307 775. Durham, North Carolina: 28-30 March 1988.

Matyas, M. L., and J.B. Kahle. 1986. "Equitable Pre-college Science and Mathematics Education: A Discrepancy Model." *The Workshop on Underrepresentation and Career Differentials of Women in Science and Engineering*, Washington, D.C., October 1986.

National Center for Education Statistics. 1998. *The Digest of Education Statistics.* Washington, DC: U.S. Department of Education.

National Science Board. 1998. *Science &Engineering Indicators – 1998.* Arlington, VA: National Science Foundation, 1998 NSB 98-1.

National Science Foundation. 1988. *Women and Minorities in Science and Engineering.* Washington, DC: National Science Foundation.

National Science Foundation. 1994. *Science and Engineering Degrees by Race/Ethnicity of Recipients: 1977-1991.* Washington, DC: National Science Foundation. NSF Publication 94-306.

National Science Foundation. 1999. "Despite Increases, Women and Minorities Still Underrepresented in Undergraduate and Graduate S&E Education." *Data Brief.* Arlington, VA: National Science Foundation.

Neisler, O.J. 1992. "Access and Retention Strategies in Higher Education: An Introductory Overview." *Strategies for Retaining Minority Students in Higher Education.* Springfield, IL: Charles Thomas, Publisher, pp. 3-21.

Nettles, M., L. W. Perna, and K. Edelin Freeman. 1999. *Two-Decades of Progress: African Americans Moving Forward in Higher Education.* Fairfax, VA: Frederick D. Patterson Research Institute.

Noel, Lee. 1978. "Reducing the Dropout Rate." *New Directions for Student Services,* Number 3. San Francisco, CA: Jossey-Bass, Inc.

___, Randi S. Levitz, and Diana Saluri. 1985. *Increasing Student Retention.* San Francisco, CA: Jossey-Bass Inc.

Padron, Eduardo J. Winter 1992. "The Challenge of First-Generation College Students: A Miami-Dade Perspective." *New Directions for Community Colleges,* (80), pp. 71-80.

Pantages, Timothy J., and Carol F. Creedon. Winter 1978. "Studies of College Attrition: 1950-1975." *Review of Educational Research,* pp. 48-101.

Pascarella, Ernest T. 1984. "Reassessing the Effects of Living On-Campus Versus Commuting to College: A Causal Modeling Approach." *The Review of Higher Education,* 7(3), pp. 247-260.

____.1986. "A Program for Research and Policy Development on Student Persistence at the Institutional Level". *Journal of College Student Personnel*, 27(2), pp. 100-107.

Pinkston-McKee. 1990. *Student Support Services Program*. ERIC Document Reproduction Service No. ED 321 645.

Quality Education for Minorities. (QEM). 1990. *Education that Works: An Action Plan for the Education of Minorities*. Cambridge, MA: Massachusetts Institute of Technology.

Ramist, L. 1981. "College Student Attrition and Retention." *College Board Report no. 81-1*. New York, NY: College Board. Eric Document Reproduction Service No. ED 200 170.

Richardson, Richard C., Jr., and Elizabeth F. Skinner. Winter 1992. "Helping First-Generation Minority Students Achieve Degrees." *New Directions for Community Colleges*, 20(4) 29-41.

Rodriguez, Esther M., and Michael T. Nettles. 1993. "Achieving the National Education Goals: The Status of Minorities in Today's Global Economy." *A Policy Report of the State Higher Education Executive Officers*. ERIC Document Reproduction Services No. ED 360 443.

Ryan, Joseph M. and Terese M. Kuhs. Spring 1993. "Assessment of Preservice Teachers and the Use of Portfolios." *Theory Into Practice*, 32(2) 75-81.

Sedlacek, W., and D. Prieto. 1990. "Predicting Minority Students Success in Medical School." *Academic Medicine*, 65(3), pp. 161-166.

Seymour, E., and N. M. Hewitt. 1997. *Talk about leaving: Why undergraduates leave the sciences*. Boulder, CO: Westview Press.

Silverman, Suzanne, and Alice M. Pritchard. 1993. *Building Their Future: Girls in Technology Education in Connecticut*. ERIC Document Reproduction Service No. ED 362 650.

Smith, L., R. Lippitt, and D. Sprandel. 1985. "Building Support for a Campuswide Retention Program." *Increasing Student Retention*. San Francisco, CA: Jossey-Bass, Inc., pp. 366-382.

Steinmiller, R., and G. Steinmiller. 1991. *Retention of At-Risk Students in Higher Education*. ERIC Document Reproduction Services No. ED342527

Suen, K. Hoi. 1983. "Alienation and Attrition of Black College Students on a Predominantly White Campus." *Journal of College Student Personnel*, 24, pp. 117-121.

Thomas, Gail E. 1986. *The Access and Success of Blacks and Latinos in U.S. Graduate and Professional Education.* A Working Paper prepared for the National Research Council.

Tinto, Vincent. 1975. "Dropout from Higher Education: A Theoretical Synthesis of Recent Research.*" Review of Educational Research*, 45, pp. 89-125.

___.1993. *Leaving College.* Chicago, IL: Chicago University Press.

Tobias, S. 1990. *They're Not Dumb, They're Different.* Tucson, AZ: Research Corporation.

Trippi, J., and H. E. Cheatham. 1989. "Effects of Special Counseling Programs for Black Freshmen on a Predominantly White Campus." *Journal of College Student Development.* 30, pp. 144-151.

Ugbah, Steven, and Shirely Ann Williams. 1989. "The Mentor-Protégé Relationship: Its Impact on Blacks in Predominantly White Institutions." *Blacks in Higher Education: Overcoming the Odds.* Lanham, MD: The University Press of America, pp. 29-42.

U.S. Student Association. 1992. *Student Retention Study.* Washington, DC: USA.

U.S. Department of Education. 1998b. Comments from Assistant Secretary of Education David Longanecker regarding quality control checks conducted by the Office of Postsecondary Education. Monthly meeting of the Higher Education Associations, Washington, DC.

Whimbey, Arthur, and J. W. Carmichael Jr., Lester WI Jones, Jacqueline T. Hunter, Harold A. Vincent. October 1980. "Teaching Critical Reading and Analytical Reasoning in Project SOAR." *Journal of Reading*, pp. 6-9.

FOOTNOTES
[1]Ibid
[2]Ibid.

[3]M. L. Nettles, W. Perna, and K. Edelin Freeman, 1999, *Two-Decades of Progress: African Americans Moving Forward in Higher Education* (Fairfax, VA: Frederick D. Patterson Research Institute)

[4] Ibid.

[5] National Science Board, 1998, *Science &Engineering Indicators – 1998* (Arlington, VA: National Science Foundation) 1998 NSB 98-1.

[6]Sue E. Berryman, November 1983, "Who Will Do Science?" *Minority and Female Attainment of Science and Mathematics Degrees: Trends and Causes,* Paper presented for the Rockefeller Foundation.

[7]Ibid; Beatriz Chu Clewell, Bernie T. Anderson, and Margaret E. Thorpe, 1992, *Breaking the Barriers* (San Francisco, CA: Jossey-Bass Inc.); E. Fennema, and J. Sherman, February 1976, *Sex-Related Differences in Mathematics Learning: Myths, Realities, and Related Factors.* Paper presented at the annual meeting of the American Association for the Advancement of Science, Boston; Shirley Malcom, 1988, "Brilliant Women for Science, Mathematics and Engineering: Getting More Than We Deserved?" *Developing Talent in Mathematics, Science and Technology: A Conference on Academic Talent.* (ERIC Document Reproduction Service No. ED 307 775. Durham, North Carolina: 28-30 March 1988); M.L. Matyas, and J.B. Kahle, 1986, "Equitable Pre-college Science and Mathematics Education: A Discrepancy Model," *The Workshop on Underrepresentation and Career Differentials of Women in Science and Engineering,* Washington, D.C., October 1986; National Science Foundation, 1988, *Women and Minorities in Science and Engineering* (Washington, DC: National Science Foundation); Suzanne Silverman, and Alice M. Pritchard, 1993, *Building Their Future: Girls in Technology Education in Connecticut* (ERIC Document Reproduction Service No. ED 362 650)

[8]Clewell et al, 1992.

[9]Association of American Medical Colleges, 1992, "Project 3000 by 2000," *Technical Assistance Manual: Guidelines for Action.* (Washington, DC: AAMC); J. W. Carmichael Jr. and John P. Sevenair, 1991, "Preparing Minorities for Science Careers," *Issues in Science and Technology,* 7(3), pp. 55-60.; Robert E. Fullilove, and Philip U. Treisman, 1990, "Mathematics Achievement Among African American Undergraduates at the University of California, Berkeley: An Evaluation of the Mathematics Workshop Program." *Journal of Negro Education,* 59(3), pp. 463-478.

[10]National Center for Education Statistics, 1998, *The Digest of Education Statistics* (Washington, DC: U.S. Department of Education)

[11]A.W. Astin, 1982, *Minorities in American Higher Education. Recent Trends, Current Prospects, and Recommendations.* San Francisco, CA:

Jossey-Bass Inc; Vincent Tinto, 1975, "Dropout from Higher Education: A Theoretical Synthesis of Recent Research," *Review of Educational Research*, 45, pp. 89-125

[12]Tinto, 1975

[13]Astin, 1982.

[14]Timothy J. Pantages, and Carol F. Creedon, Winter 1978, "Studies of College Attrition: 1950-1975," *Review of Educational Research*, pp. 48-101.

[15]R. Cope, and W. Hannah, 1975, *Revolving College Doors: The Causes and Consequences of Dropping Out, Stopping Out, and Transferring* (New York, NY: Wiley)

[16]Philip E. Beal, and Lee Noel, 1980, *What Works in Student Retention*. American College Testing Program.

[17]Astin, 1982.

[18]James E. Blackwell, 1992, "Suggested Research on the Future of Minorities in Graduate Education," *Minorities in Graduate Education: Pipeline, Policy and Practice*, Princeton, NJ: Educational Testing Service, pp. 122-129.

[19]Arthur Whimbey, and J. W. Carmichael Jr., Lester WI Jones, Jacqueline T. Hunter, Harold A. Vincent, October 1980, "Teaching Critical Reading and Analytical Reasoning in Project SOAR," *Journal of Reading*, pp. 6-9.

[20]Fullilove and Treisman, 1990.

[21]Leon F. Burrell, and Toni B. Trombley, 1983, "Academic Advising with Minority Students on Predominantly White Campuses." *Journal of College Student Personnel*, 24, pp. 121-126.; J. T. Gibbs, 1975, Use of Mental Health Services by Black Students at a Predominantly White University: A Three Year Study. *American Journal of Ortho Psychiatry*, 45, pp. 430-445; C.M. Loo, and G. Rolison. 1986. "Alienation of Ethnic Minority Students at a Predominately White University." *Journal of Higher Education*, 57(1), 58-77; K. Hoi Suen, 1983, "Alienation and Attrition of Black College Students on a Predominantly White Campus," *Journal of College Student Personnel*, 24, pp. 117-121.

[22]M. Lang, and C. Ford, eds. 1988, *Black Student Retention in Higher Education* (Springfield, IL: Charles C. Thomas); Rebecca T. Gates, 1989, "Project Far: A Blueprint for College Student Retention," *Recruitment and Retention of Black Students in Higher Education* (National Association for Equal Opportunity in Higher Education, Research Institute)

[23]Diola Bagayoko, and Ella Kelley, Fall 1994, "The Dynamics of Student Retention: A Review and a Prescription," *Education, 115* (1); Car-

michael and Sevenair, 1991; Elizabeth Culotta, 13 November 1992, "Minorities in Science, The Pipeline Problem. Black Colleges Cultivate Scientists," *Science*, pp. 1216-1218.

[24]National Center for Education Statistics, 1998.

[25]National Science Foundation, 1999, "Despite Increases, Women and Minorities Still Underrepresented in Undergraduate and Graduate S&E Education," *Data Brief* (Arlington, VA: National Science Foundation) Figure 1

[26]Clewell et al., 1992; E. Seymour, and N. M. Hewitt, 1997, *Talk about leaving: Why undergraduates leave the sciences* (Boulder, CO: Westview Press)

[27]Oscar T. Lenning, 1982, "Variable-Selection and Measurement Concerns," *Studying Student Attrition* (San Francisco, CA: Jossey-Bass Inc.)

[28]Cope and Hannah, 1975.

[29]Oscar T. Lenning, Philip E. Beal, and Ken Sauer, 1980, *Retention and Attrition: Evidence for Action and Research* (Boulder, CO: National Center for Higher Education Management Systems)

[30]Pantages and Creedon, 1978.

[31]L. Ramist,1981, *College Student Attrition and Retention*, College Board Report no. 81-1. New York, NY: College Board. (Eric Document Reproduction Service No. ED 200 170)

[32]Loo and Rolison, 1986; Suen, 1983.

[33]Quality Education for Minorities, (QEM), 1990. *Education that Works: An Action Plan for the Education of Minorities* (Cambridge, MA: Massachusetts Institute of Technology)

[34]Steven Ugbah, and Shirely Ann Williams, 1989, "The Mentor-Protégé Relationship: Its Impact on Blacks in Predominantly White Institutions," *Blacks in Higher Education: Overcoming the Odds*, (Lanham, MD: The University Press of America), pp. 29-42.; Pinkston-McKee, 1990, *Student Support Services Program*, (ERIC Document Reproduction Service No. ED 321 645)

[35]Tinto, 1975.

[36]J.P. Bean, 1982, "Student Attrition, Intentions, and Confidence," *Research in Higher Education*, 17, pp. 291-320.

[37]Lee Noel, 1978, "Reducing the Dropout Rate," *New Directions for Student Services*, Number 3 (San Francisco, CA: Jossey-Bass, Inc.)

[38]Gates, 1989.

[39]Fullilove and Treisman, 1990.

[40]Pinkston-McKee, 1990.

[41]Ernest T. Pascarella, 1984, "Reassessing the Effects of Living On-Campus Versus Commuting to College: A Causal Modeling Ap-

proach," *The Review of Higher Education,* 7(3), pp. 247-260; Lee Noel, Randi S. Levitz, and Diana Saluri, 1985, *Increasing Student Retention,* (San Francisco, CA: Jossey-Bass Inc.)

[42]L. Smith, Lippitt, R., and D. Sprandel, 1985, "Building Support for a Campuswide Retention Program," *Increasing Student Retention* (San Francisco, CA: Jossey-Bass, Inc.), pp. 369

[43]Ernest T. Pascarella, 1986, "A Program for Research and Policy Development on Student Persistence at the Institutional Level,". *Journal of College Student Personnel,* 27(2), P. 101

[44]Noel et al., 1985.

[45]Smith et al., 1985.

[46]Noel et al., 1985; Smith et al., 1985.

[47]Tinto, 1975.

[48]Vincent Tinto, 1993, *Leaving College* (Chicago, IL: Chicago University Press)

[49] Astin, 1982; General Accounting Office, March 1995, *Restructuring Student Aid Could Reduce Low-Income Student Dropout Rate,* Report to Congressional Requesters. GAO/HEHS-95-48.

[50] In early 1998, Princeton University made public that it would spend an additional $6 million a year providing aid to low-income students. Within a month, both Yale and Stanford followed suit with similar promises. Although most financial aid experts applauded the news, the underlining comment from the majority was that these institutions "could afford it."

[51] Gail Thomas' research in 1986 found that loans had greater negative impacts on African Americans than other student groups.

[52] Much of the discussion of the "cost" of college has been confusing to those within higher education, let alone parents and students. To this end, and in accordance to the recent report from the National College Cost Commission (1998), I refer to the amount that students/parents pay as "price" and "cost" to refer to the cost associated with supplying education.

[53] Astin, 1982; M. Collison, 6 July 1988, "Complex Application Form Discourages Many Students From Applying for Federal Financial Aid," *Chronicle of Higher Education,* A19, A30.

[54]U.S. Department of Education, 1998b, Comments from Assistant Secretary of Education David Longanecker regarding quality control checks conducted by the Office of Postsecondary Education. Monthly meeting of the Higher Education Associations, Washington, DC.

[55] A. W. Astin, 1975, *Preventing Students from Dropping Out* (San Francisco, CA: Jossey-Bass Inc.)

[56] NCES, 1998.

[57] Both Astin's and NCES' research found that students who worked about 15 hours generally persisted higher than other students. Those who worked more tended to have higher rates of departure.

[58] GAO, 1985.

[59] Tinto, 1993.

[60] Astin, 1975; Cope and Hannah, 1975.

[61] The College Board, in its annual *College-Bound Seniors* Press Release each September (the release of SAT and AP data), prominently makes note of the limitations of standardized test scores and the dangers of using them without other indicators. Further information on this issues may be found from www.collegeboard.org.

[62] Elam, Julia C., ed. 1989, *Blacks in Higher Education: Overcoming the Odds*, (Lanham, MD: University Press of America)

[63] Pearl Kalechstein, 1981, "The Effects of Instruction on Test-Taking Skills in Second Grade Children," *Measurement and Evaluation in Guidance*, 13(4), 198-201; Melanie Dreisbach, 1982. "Testwiseness as a Factor in Readiness Test Performance of Young Mexican-American Children." *Journal of Educational Psychology*, 74(2), pp. 224-229.

[64] [64] W. Sedlacek, and D. Prieto, 1990, "Predicting Minority Students Success in Medical School," *Academic Medicine*, 65(3), pp. 161-166.

[65] A. Forrest, 1982. *Increasing Student Competence and Persistence: The Best Case for General Education*, Iowa City, IA: American College Testing Program National Center for Advancement of Educational Practices.

[66] Beal (1978)

[67] Beal (1978)

[68] Ugbah and Williams, 1989; Oris T. Griffen, 1992, "The Impacts of Academic and Social Integration for Black Students in Higher Education," *Strategies for Retaining Minority Students in Higher Education*. Springfield (IL: Charles C. Thomas), pp. 25-44.; Astin, 1982

[69] Griffen, 1992.

[70] Whimbey et al., 1977; A. K. Hyman, 1988, "Group Work as a Teaching Strategy in Black Student Retention in Higher Education," *Black Student Retention in Higher Education* (Springfield, IL: Charles C. Thomas),pp. 71-82.

[71] Clewell et al., 1992.

[72] S. Tobias, 1990, *They're Not Dumb, They're Different*, Tucson, AZ: Research Corporation. (p. 9).

[73]Fullilove and Treisman, 1990.

[74]Joseph M. Ryan, and Terese M. Kuhs, Spring 1993, "Assessment of Preservice Teachers and the Use of Portfolios," *Theory Into Practice*, 32(2) 75-81; Tom Bird, 1990, "The School Teacher's Portfolio: An Essay on Possibilities," *The New Handbook of Teacher Evaluation* (Newbury Park, CA: Sage Publications), pp. 241-256.

[75]Tinto, 1993.

[76]O.J. Neisler, 1992, "Access and Retention Strategies in Higher Education: An Introductory Overview," *Strategies for Retaining Minority Students in Higher Education* (Springfield, IL: Charles Thomas), pp. 3-21.

[77] Manuel Justiz, 1994, "Demographic Trends and the Challenges to American Higher Education" *Minorities in Higher Education* (Phoenix, AZ: Oryx Press and ACE), pp. 1-21.

[78] Pascarella, 1984; A. W. Chickering, 1974, *Commuting Versus Resident Students: Overcoming the Educational Inequities of Living Off Campus* (San Francisco, CA: Jossey-Bass, Inc.); A.w. Astin, 1977, *Four Critical Years* (San Francisco, CA: Jossey-Bass, Inc.); Pantages and Creedon, 1978.

[79] R. Steinmiller, and G. Steinmiller, 1991, *Retention of At-Risk Students in Higher Education*, ERIC Document Reproduction Services No. ED342527.

[80]J. Trippi, J., and H. E. Cheatham, 1989, "Effects of Special Counseling Programs for Black Freshmen on a Predominantly White Campus," *Journal of College Student Development.* 30, pp. 144-151.

[81]Richard C. Richardson, Jr., and Elizabeth F. Skinner, Winter 1992, "Helping First-Generation Minority Students Achieve Degrees," *New Directions for Community Colleges*, 20(4) 29-41; Eduardo J. Padron, Winter 1992, "The Challenge of First-Generation College Students: A Miami-Dade Perspective," *New Directions for Community Colleges*, (80), pp. 71-80; Justiz, 1994.

[82] Alexander W. Astin, March/April 1993, "Diversity and Mulitculturalism on the Campus: How are Students Affected?" *Change* (San Francisco, CA: Jossey-Bass Inc.)

[83] Justiz, 1994.

[84] For families with parents aged 45-54 years old (the approximate age of families with college-aged dependents).

[85] The College Board, 1998, *Trends in Student Aid 1998* (New York, NY: The College Entrance Examination Board).

17. *Feasible Learning Opportunities for Urban Latino Students in Community College*

Philip Rodriguez, Lacreta Scott, and William Maxwell

When we first began to talk with Latino students from an English writing course, we wanted to learn what the students saw as helping them successfully complete the course. Later as we reflected on our interviews, we found that the students identified many strategies that are readily available to most of us that teach minority students, even when resources are modest. New resources are needed to make many kinds of important improvements. Yet, when a teacher or administrator first wants to expand minority opportunities, their resources may be limited. These strategies can enable any teacher to do something important in improving learning opportunities for students of color.

The strategies identified by the students were inclusion and validation, multicultural assignments, personalized feedback, collaborative learning and peer groups. Before reporting these students' views, we will review the barriers faced by Latino students, the theoretical literature concerning possible solutions, and the interview and questionnaire methods by which we conducted this study.

BARRIERS FOR LATINOS

Latino students face formidable difficulties in entering and completing programs of higher education in the United States. Latino American students have been less likely to attend four-year colleges than African

Americans, Asian Americans or White Americans.   If they gained access to a college, it was more likely to be a community college for Latino students than for these other three ethnic groups.   Those Latinos who attended community colleges were less likely to gain an Associate of Arts degree or transfer to a baccalaureate institution, as compared to Asian or White Americans (Carter and Wilson, 1997; Gandara forthcoming; Nora, 1993; Mow and Nettles, 1990).

THEORETICAL BACKGROUND
Researchers have recommended several teaching strategies for minority students. However, we believe that leading theories on college students can be applied only partially to minority students in community colleges.   Rather than testing hypotheses, we used these theories to suggest what strategies we should explore for Latino students. Some of the ideas found in these theories could be seen in the interviews as applicable; others simply did not fit students who were commuters living with their families, holding down jobs, and managing their lives on limited incomes.   The inapplicable ideas were often based on research in traditional residential four-year colleges and primarily on prosperous white majority students.

Social integration. For example, research on four-year college students has produced two hypotheses concerning the impact of integration on academic success. Close peer relations have been shown to promote the learning process, status attainment, and persistence at these campuses.   The extent of student involvement with faculty has also been a powerful influence on learning and graduation rates (Astin, 1993; Cabrera, Nora, & Casteneda, 1993; Dougherty, 1994; Kuh, Schuh, Whitt, and Associates, 1991; Mayo et. al. 1995; Nora, 1993; Pascarella and Terenzini, 1991; Stage, 1989; Tinto, 1975, 1993; Tinto and Russo, 1994).

When the two hypotheses of peer and student-faculty integration were tested in previous research in community colleges, conflicting findings were obtained. Peer integration was correlated with retention or other academic and social achievements in about half of the studies. Negative correlations, or an absence of correlation, were found in the remaining studies. Though research on student-faculty relations in community colleges has been sparse, it has also been inconclusive (Bers and Smith, 1991; Friedlander and MacDougal, 1992; Halpin, 1990; Kraemer, 1997; Moss and Young, 1995; Nora, 1987, 1993; Nora, Attinasi , and Matonak, 1990; Pascarella, 1980; Pascarella, Smart, and Ethington, 1986; Voorhees, 1987).

Learning networks among students in classrooms is a theme that parallels the peer integration hypothesis and has been proposed by several perspectives. Collaborative learning theory recommends classroom group activity be initiated to benefit both learning and retention. Several types of learning community methods, such as coordinated studies and supplemental instruction, use classroom networks as a strategy to provide feedback and social support to students. The latter approaches when fully implemented may require substantial new social or financial resources, beyond the boundaries we have set for this report. Classroom network methods in themselves, however, are very feasible and require only moderate investments of planning (Gabelnick, MacGregor, Matthews, and Leigh-Smith, 1990; Levin and Levin, 1991; Tinto, 1975, 1993; Tinto and Russo, 1994).

Validation of minority students as capable learners and members of campus social networks is a conception of college support that was developed by Rendon (1994) in her research on Latino students in community colleges. In contrast to integration theories that focus on the student's ability to join campus social circles, validation involves the interventions used by the college to reach and include minority students. Employing themes from integration theories concerning involvement with peers and faculty, the central elements in this perspective are the strategies by which the college positively affirms the intellectual and social capabilities of minority students. Validating communities can be created in courses by introducing curricula that address each of the cultural backgrounds of the members of the course, personalizing and maintaining positive classroom atmospheres, and providing one-on-one feedback to the students.

When this study was designed, the authors looked for the strategies implied by these foregoing perspectives of integration, learning networks, and validation.

THE INTERVIEWS, QUESTIONNAIRE, AND SAMPLE
The study was focused on Latino students who completed the developmental course in English writing at a large and ethnically diverse community college in a middle class suburb of Los Angeles. Each of the authors was employed at this college. Minority students together comprised a majority of the campus population. The student population was classified as approximately 43% Latino American, 26% White American, 16% Asian American, 7% Filipino American, and 7% African American.

While we certainly had preconceptions, preferences for the writing program, and incorporated ideas from the theories reviewed above, attempts were made to design the study so that one could learn from the students also about elements that had not been anticipated. An interview guide was developed with 12 open-ended questions concerning the students' purposes for taking the course, their views on important course elements, and the usefulness of these course features (See Appendix).   In addition, we prepared a closed category questionnaire with 39 items concerning the cultural and educational backgrounds of their parents, and their social relations with students and with faculty. This instrument drew items from those suggested by Mow and Nettles (1990) for research on minority students, and also from the integration measures developed for research on four-year colleges by Pascarella and Terenzini (1980). We pilot tested the instrument with several students, and revised the questions for clarity.

Our population of students consisted of those students with a Spanish surname who had enrolled in any of the sections of this course during the two previous semesters. Through the assistance of the campus computer center, we were able to identify Latino students who had completed or not competed the course. The number of students enrolling each semester was so large (usually more than 500 students per semester) that we decided to limit our study to students receiving financial aid who had taken the course with a full-time instructor within the previous two semesters, and who were still enrolled in other courses in the college at the time of our interviews. Our subsequent difficulties in finding enough students willing to be interviewed necessitated the inclusion of some students that were not receiving financial aid.

The interviews were conducted on campus the first two of the authors. The study was initiated with support from the California Community College Chancellor's Office. The staff of the Extended Opportunity Program/Services (EOP/S) office telephoned and corresponded with students to make hour-long appointments for the interviews during daytime hours at the authors' campus offices. A modest financial aid stipend of ten dollars was offered to each student completing the appointment. Interviews were successfully completed with 41 of the students who agreed to meet with the faculty interviewers. These usually lasted about 45 minutes, ranging from about 20 to 90 minutes, and were taped with the students' permission. After the interviews were completed, the students were requested to fill out the closed category questionnaire which required about 10 minutes or less to complete.

THE WRITING COURSE AND THE STUDENTS

The Course. The developmental English writing course, attended by the students in our study, was a crucial point of entry for many into the college curriculum. Latino students in their first semester of study in the college, after taking basic skills assessment tests, were often counseled to register for this course. Successful mastery of English writing skills and completion of the course opened for the students a path into regular college courses and subsequent required writing projects.

A few years earlier, a few colleagues in the English department began to share their concerns and strategies for assisting minority students. Eventually, regular discussions emerged in the department as several faculty attempted to develop their teaching for the ethnic diversity in their classrooms. The process of reform was aided by several seminars on teaching diverse populations and other faculty development opportunities that were taken by some of the faculty.

Though no uniform pattern of reform developed across the many sections of the developmental English writing course, various teachers adopted strategies such as collaborative learning, culturally diverse readings, personalized feedback, and writing assignments that addressed topics of cultural diversity. A central thread in these reforms was the teacher's attempt to recognize the personal interests and ethnic culture of each student.

Two of the authors of this study had taught in this writing course. There they had attempted to address the needs of their Latino and other minority students in the course. Despite changes and improvements made by several teachers in various sections of the course, only a little more than about 60% of the Latino students were successfully completing the course with a grade of C or better.

The Students. One of the most surprising outcomes of this study was the difficulty in bringing the students and researchers together for an interview outside the classroom, particularly among those who had not completed the writing course. Initially, we envisioned the study as exploring the perceptions of both students who had successfully passed the course and those who had not completed it. We found that it was very difficult to meet with many of the students, whether or not they had previously completed the course. Almost all of the students who had not completed the course declined our invitation to meet for an interview. Of the students who did agree to an appointment, many did not keep them. During one period of the interviewing, of the 20 students scheduled for interviews (including some that had completed the writing course and some who had not), only 4 students appeared for their appointments. For students who could not be initially reached by telephone, letters and postcards were sent and telephone calls were made in the evenings and on the weekends. We were attempting to include in our sample only students who were still continuing to attend classes at the campus one or more semesters after their enrollment in the writing course. In an attempt to interview those who had not completed the course, near the end of our period of interviewing, one of the authors went a few times to classrooms of courses the students were currently attending. Even this method for inviting the students to a later interview, proved unsuccessful. Of the 41 students who did meet with us for an interview, all had completed the course. Thus our findings in this study concern the teaching strategies that these relatively successful students saw as beneficial.

Among those who did not complete the course, though a few had agreed to an appointment for an interview, none of these students actually participated. The families of the students in our sample had in very recent generations participated in the stream of Latino immigration into Southern California. Almost all of the fathers and most of the mothers had immigrated to the United States. About a third of the students themselves had been born in another country. Three quarters of the students spoke Spanish as their native language.

The students wanted English writing and conversational skills so that they could learn and work effectively in their other courses. Some explained that they didn't know how to write a regular paper for a college course until studying in this course. One student felt he would have had to drop his current Political Science introductory course if he had not earlier learned how to prepare a term paper in this writing course.

Motivation. Students who completed this course were ambitious. A strong flavor of upward social mobility laced the comments of the students. They wanted a good education in general social skills, including communication in English, and they certainly desired training for secure, rewarding and interesting jobs. We did talk to one or two students who had completed the course mainly due to parental pressure, and there were probably other students with little interest in the benefits of the course among those we called but who simply declined to keep their appointments. The students who met with us saw their college education as a route to a better job than their parents. For three-fourths of our sample, their generation was the first in their family to attend college (about a fourth of the fathers had enrolled in at least some college courses but few had graduated). About 40% of the fathers and 30% of the mothers had not completed primary schooling. Ambition and motivation were themes that were mentioned in several of the interviews. Even though over half of the interviewees held a job (of these, the majority worked at their job 10-30 hours per week), some students blamed themselves for not working enough in the course and earning high enough grades.

FEASIBLE TEACHING STRATEGIES

Inclusion. In our interviews with the students, we heard many of the teachers described as warm and supportive. Many teachers welcomed these students into the class and called them by name. The students felt that they belonged to the class group. The following quotations from students emphasized how important it was for them that the teacher enabled them to become part of the class:

> When I first got there, I really felt like an outsider, but the teacher really made an effort to make you feel like part of the class. She called me by name. I liked that a lot.

> At first I felt like an outsider but later I felt more comfortable and got more into the class. I was also called by my name....that made it important to me.

> The teacher was very supportive. She was great. She did call me by name.

> The teacher....made it a point to call us by our name.

> I felt very much part of the class. She always made sure everyone felt as part of the class. Just like a big family. She made an effort to know your feelings. She would call us by name.

Several feasible strategies for any teacher were suggested by the students; their names, positive welcoming initiatives, familiarity with their individual attitudes, and involving them in the classroom life. These students were warmly received and recognized as individuals, their own identity was acknowledged, and their distinctive attitudes were given some place in the classroom. As individuals, they were also included into the classroom group through the teacher's references to them during the discussion, and through questions and encouragement from the teacher to share their perspectives with the class.

Multicultural readings and tasks. Teachers can validate or neglect, the cultural identity and status of their students through the readings and activities they assign in the classroom.   Community college teachers have considerable freedom to select the readings and topics pursued by their students. Instructors at this college varied in their assigned material from various cultures, yet in many of the sections of this writing class there was emphasis on Latino literature. In most of the classrooms, there was a relatively strong multicultural orientation manifested in the selection of reading assignments.   The majority of our sample of students who had completed the course reported that sizeable portions of the readings were drawn from each of the African American, Latino American, and non-Hispanic white cultures of the society (few of the readings were from Asian American or Native American traditions). When asked in the interviews if they "felt their culture was given enough attention in the assignments, readings, and discussions, " their responses were generally positive:

> Yes, definitely.

> Somewhat.

> Yes, the teacher gave us assignments such as writing about our culture, and other students had to review them and we would discuss them. But no reading about our culture.

> Yes, she had discussions. We had to write an essay about us. She never concentrated on one race. She moved from one to another, that's what I liked.

> Yes, we had to write an essay about bilingual education. No readings though.

> Yes, she [had us] read many different authors, it was a diversity [sic].

> Yes, we had a book that we had to read and it was Latino.

> Yes, we touched the Latino perspective.

> Yes, we had readings about a boy that was born here but of Hispanic origin.

About a quarter of the students reported that none, or very few of the readings and classroom topics concerned Latino culture. Compared to the students who expressed pleasure over studying their traditions and experiencing dignity accorded to their culture within the classroom, these students seemed to accept neglect of their group as part of the daily business of higher education. The feelings suggested indifference and determination, rather than disappointment. They had persevered in the course because they wanted the skills involved, and because the course was necessary for them to move forward in their schooling.

> Not really, the readings were diversified.

> No Latino writers, mainly African American or white.

> Culture-wise, not really. We read about African Americans but not about Mexicans.

> Not really. Mostly reading about white people.

> No. Even though we didn't read anything specific about my culture, we did read about African Americans.

> No, and I didn't feel left out, because English is English.

> I didn't really think about it as a culture class. It was just a class, classes don't have to be divided. It's an English class. We did view a movie and it had to do with discrimination, and we had to write about it.

The foregoing comments were made by the students that persisted in the course. The silent voices here were those who did not complete the course and did not participate in the interviews. Classroom respect and recognition for Latino culture alone, probably would not have been sufficient to guarantee success for those who left the courses. Because so much was missing in the instruction provided by one of the teachers, it was difficult to sort out the damage caused by this teacher's disrespect, yet the importance of cultural validation can be readily seen in the words of one of his students:

> I thought I was passing class although I'm not that good in English. I thought I was passing class since the teacher never told us anything. We never got our grades or papers

back.... Out of my five essays, only one was corrected...I felt uncomfortable with the instructor. He used to make jokes about others. I didn't like comments like "You are here because you are not good writers," or, "because your second language is English." One time he said that his son was a sixth-grader and that he wrote better than anyone in the class. That's good, but his son is not bilingual. His second language is not English... I did learn, but he started with a large class and at the second section of the class one-half had dropped. He was absent a lot... No Latino writers [were assigned].

None of the students who left the course before completing it appeared for an interview. This person was the only student who had failed the course who was willing to be interviewed.

Incorporating minority symbols required a subtle approach by the faculty. None of the students suggested anything that could be taken as grounds for converting a class in English composition skills into a course whose primary ends would be to celebrate their ancestral traditions. These purposeful students wanted to improve their writing skills in what, for them, was not their first language, and they wanted to use this course to advance their college and vocational careers. One Latina who was having difficulty keeping up with the course assignments complained that too much reading had been required on the history of the Spaniards. She had entered the course because she wanted to improve her grammatical skills in writing, and though she enjoyed one of the texts with Hispanic writings from many societies, she objected to all the work required to plow through a lengthy volume of history. The dignity and pleasure experienced in studying their own culture's texts was apparent in the remarks of many of these students, yet it was clear that their primary satisfactions had been improving their English writing skills.

Assignments and feedback. Both teachers and students were negotiating across cultural differences. Even in the few cases where teacher and student were both Latinos, there were great differences between them with regard to cultural perspectives and experience with the literature and writing styles of the dominant cultures being presented in the classroom. It is evident from the students' comments that bridges were laid across these cultural gaps when the teachers provided full explanations for assignments and main ideas, lot of examples, and classroom questions and discussion. The sense of inclusion in these classrooms was strengthened, not hampered, by high expectations and challenging writing assignments for which the students received feedback from the teacher and student peers. Writing essays and receiving feedback from teachers and classmates was highly applauded.

Collaborative learning. Peer feedback was also an important element of these classrooms. The students' feelings of belonging to the classroom community were enmeshed within the collaborative small group learning activities pursued in these courses. Students tried out ideas in these groups and received suggestions and feedback on their various writing projects. The frequency of these small group sessions varied, from a few times a semester to almost weekly, depending on the teacher and on the sequence of the semester. Only a few students found fault with parts of this social activity, and most considered these groups very valuable. Friendships emerged for some of the students within these groups.

> We had group discussions. Other people would give their comments about our writing that helped. We got into these groups once or twice a week.

> The group projects helped me out as well because we could give each other advice. It felt better having a peer. Someone else telling you what you did wrong. Everyone gave their ideas. The teacher would ask if we had questions or ideas to share. It also taught us that what might be a problem for you in a particular area might not be a problem for another student, and that's how you can complement each other. We would meet two or three times a month...about every other week.

> Made a lot of friends because it was a daily thing to get into small groups. We know each other by name. The only negative thing about the group was that some students are lazy. These students just let the rest of the group do everything, but it comes back to haunt them when the teacher will ask for details or summary of how the story went, plus your personal opinion. It was not the same group all the time...we switched.

> It was helpful to have groups....it was useful to meet more people. It helped to talk to other students, and hear what they felt or thought about the work....they gave me another perspective.

> The only thing I didn't like about the groups is that we would end up arguing sometimes. I was fresh out of high school and thought I was always right....I never took into consideration other opinions....I learned that everyone has different opinions and you have to accept them.

Meeting with other students within classrooms was the most important form of initial contact they had with other students on the campus.   In Table 1 the responses of the interviewees to our questionnaire indicated they found other students to be friendly, yet interacted with other students in few activities other than to studying together. Most students responded that they felt it was not difficult to meet and make friends with other students. In contrast with this ease of informal contact, very few of the students reported frequent involvement in formal extra-curricular activities such as club and student government meetings, campus art, drama or music activities.

Classroom relations with peers offered a special opportunity for teachers to involve minority students with their peers in relationships that would support their academic goals.

Some students formed study groups that they organized to meet with other students outside of class.   This extremely valuable strategy was available to almost all teachers, with only a small investment of time and encouragement to the students.   These informal groups gave students special opportunities for the social integration that had been found to be so helpful to minority students where other forms of inclusion were lacking.   In response to our interview question "Did you meet outside this class with other students from the class to study for the course?," some students responded:

> Yes, we had study groups going...we would meet at the library.   We would meet once a week after class.   The group was initiated by an older lady....I guess she was a returning student. Definitely wiser. She really got us going. She needed help getting creative ideas and we helped her.

> Yes, met with students to study in the library in the main tables. We made arrangements in advance...probably three times. We talked about essays....we set up the meetings.

> Yes, probably every two to three times of the month [sic]. We would go to the library or under the trees. In the library general section, or outside of the library.

Table 1: Peer Relations and Student-Faculty Contact

	High 1				Low 5
			Peer Relations		
It has been difficult for me to meet and make friends with other students.[a]	37%	27	29	7	-
How often have you participated in some art, drama, or music activity on campus...?	2%	2	-	10	85
How often have you attended a meeting of a club, organization or student government group...?	10%	5	5	63	17
How often have you sat around in the student center talking with other students...?	10%	10	15	24	42
How often have you studied with other students...?	12%	17	24	15	32
			Student-Faculty Contact		
It is easy to develop close relationships with faculty members on this campus.	20%	17	27	29	7
There is a lot of contact between professors and students outside the classroom.	2%	24	32	34	7
Have you socialized informally With a family member.	-	2	2	20	76
How often have you discussed career plans and ambitions with a faculty member?	2%	7	7	29	54
How often have you discussed personal problems and concerns with a faculty member?	-	-	7	32	61
Most faculty members here are sensitive to the interests, needs, and aspirations of students.	15%	42	37	5	2
At least one faculty member here has had a strong impact on my intellectual development.	34%	24	32	5	5
I am satisfied with the student-faculty relations.	10%	49	29	7	5

Total $N = 41$.   Due to rounding, some totals are equal to 99%, rather than 100%.

> Yes, we met in the library before the final. We went to like an indoor patio type...inside the library area....there was a large table that seated 10. The teacher recommended it but we set it up. We got together probably three times for our three tests.

> Yes, we would meet at school in the open area...mainly on Saturdays.

> Yes, like once or twice. We would call each other. We would meet here at school.

Many students initiated these study groups on their own. Only a few of the teachers provided the explicit guidance within the classroom that led the students to establish such groups. Yet this option was powerful, and was readily available to teachers.

Contacts with faculty. Most of the students were content regarding their contact with the faculty. They felt it was not difficult to have a relationship with the teachers. In Table 1, the questionnaire responses indicated that over half of the students were satisfied with student-faculty relations, and few disagreed with this statement of satisfaction. Over half of the students saw the faculty as sensitive to the students, and a similar proportion of the students reported that at least one teacher had had a major impact on their intellectual development. Surprisingly, when compared with the actual rate of relations, a full third of the students agreed that it was easy to develop close relationships with faculty on campus, and a quarter of the students even agreed that there is a lot of contact between professors and students outside the classroom. When we asked the students in our interviews if they ever met the teacher outside of class to discuss their work, they replied:

> Yes, twice...But she always encouraged us to see her. One of those meetings was mandatory.

> Never met out of class. Never wrote or called either.

> Yes, I missed one day. So, I met with him...

> I did not....no contact at all out of class with teacher.

> No, I did call her a few times through the class. She was easy to reach, plus she would call back right away.

> Yes, during conference time. For some assignments we had to meet with him and discuss the project.

> Yes, like 6 times. The teacher made an effort to meet with
> the students at least once a week [in class], to work on
> papers.

Experienced teachers of commuting students will not be surprised to
learn that there was little contact with the faculty outside the classroom.
Responses in Table 1 concerning actual contact with faculty indicated
that career and personal problem discussions and informal socializing
were infrequent. Despite the high levels of satisfaction with student-
faculty relations expressed by almost all of the students, over a third of
the students disagreed with the statement that there was a lot of contact.

From these observations, we proposed a hypothesis that there
were relatively unspoken cultural norms held by both students and
teachers that teachers' office hours were available but little used. Few
believe that they have the need or time for such contact outside of class.
The teachers were nominally available; they had regular and posted
office hours, and students reported that the teachers announced their
availability for office visits. Thus, we found in our conversations with
students that in-class contact was mentioned several times when we
specifically asked about out-of-class meetings with teachers. For
example, in response to our query about meeting outside class, one
student replied, "Yes, once in class." Another said, "Yes, twice in the
semester. Once in her office, and once in class." In the latter case, the
class period had ended and the student was departing from routine one
time in the semester by staying to talk further with the instructor. For
those rare moments during the semester when a student might elect to
engage the teacher outside class time, several students indicated that
their main mode of contact was meeting the instructor for a few
minutes before either had left the classroom.

For those teachers who want to individually contact minority
students, they may find that regularly ending class a bit early and
dedicating a brief period for student contact after the end of class will
be an effective way to initiate closer relations with the students.
Another strategy may be to require office meetings with students as an
important feature of a course. It may or may not be possible to increase
the frequency of office visits or other contacts with students outside
class. In any event, the classroom and required course activities were
currently the center for student-faculty relations.

The dominant themes for student meetings with teachers
concerned problems rather than possibilities. Students contacted
teachers about remedial efforts or the clarification of expectations for

assignments and for final grades. One student explained, "Yes, towards the end of the year, I wanted to see how I was doing." The students did not report going to talk to their teachers about ideas or ventures that excited them, or of things about which they were curious (other than their course marks). In Table 1 it can be seen that students rarely discussed future career issues or personal problems with the faculty. When we asked students in our interviews about meeting with the teacher, the following were typical of their responses:

> Well, he just said anytime you need help you can come to my office.

> Yes, toward the end of the year, wanted to see how I was doing.

> Yes, I met when I needed help with a paper. I felt very comfortable with her.

> Yes, several times I go over assignments, to make sure I was understanding.

Strong praise for teachers was voiced by most of the students in our interviews. (We found important dissatisfactions and grievances with a couple of students). Students were engaged individually by the teachers and given feedback on their work. Some students wished they had been challenged by more assignments, yet most felt their instructors had required sufficient work and activity.

In sum, we found much satisfaction and praise for what usually appeared to be warm, supportive teacher-student relations within the classrooms for many of the students who completed the course. By contrast, the amount of contact outside the classroom seemed limited, and we are not at all sure of the experience of those who did not complete the course.

The students who remained to complete the course felt they had made important progress in their writing skills. They regarded their writing as now closer to college standards. Some commented on improvements in English conversation as well. In addition to a sense of an increasing general mastery, some students cited improvements in various specific skills such as grammar, punctuation, vocabulary, starting an essay, time management, and formats for college and other writing.

Improvements desired. Even for the students who completed the course, many felt that they had faced difficulties. However, for most of the students who would or could come to talk with us, the difficulties mentioned were rarely the factors that are often cited as limiting performance in community colleges, such as jobs, family demands, and commuting. Instead, some of our sample of students referred to their own motivation, boredom, disinterest in the reading assignments, or "party minded" young friends. We wondered if these students were blaming themselves too much, and if responsibilities were fairly apportioned.

When we asked students what they advised changing or keeping in the course, their answers depended in part on what they had received. Some wanted more reading based on Mexican or other Latino cultural interests, or more feedback from instructors, while some wanted more training in grammar. There was general interest in keeping several of the teaching strategies described above, including the small student group activities, writing assignments, interesting readings, and the engaging teaching which had included and validated them as capable learners.

CONCLUSIONS

Students viewed as important for their success the connections that developed with their teachers and with other students. Broadly speaking, this finding bears out prevailing ideas about the importance of social and academic involvement. On closer examination of the data, it can be seen that at this community college, there was little of the formal extra-curricular peer and student-faculty activity that is traditionally attributed to four-year colleges. Nor was there substantial contact with the faculty outside the classroom. The social relations revealed by the students appeared less like those of four-year college theories and more like the images from perspectives on learning communities and on validation of minority students as suggested by Rendon.

The classrooms were the main points of contact with the college community for these minority students. In the English writing classes, the students felt that they were welcomed. Those who remained in the course felt they were known and valued. They considered themselves to be important members of the classroom. In the classroom peer groups and from many of the teachers, they received genuine personalized feedback. Students were satisfied with their contacts with and access to the faculty, primarily around the classroom. There they received support that they felt was helpful. Also, it appears that some of the faculty had done an excellent job weaving literature into their teaching curriculum that affirmed the cultural diversity of the students.

Though the motives and talents of students were of great importance, we have looked here instead at the direction and support that teachers can give to minority students. The importance of the teaching for the student was expressed by one Latina, when we asked her why she had completed the English writing course: "I had a good teacher that helped me stay in class."

One of the most stunning puzzles in our findings over which we can speculate, but which must be examined in further research, concerns the difficulties of student-faculty contact for those students who did not complete the course. We do not know if many of the students had troubling experiences in the writing course that they decided to leave before completing it. We did observe considerable evidence, even for those students who successfully completed the course, of the very low rates of student visits to faculty offices and of other contacts with faculty outside the classroom. Two of the authors who were members of the English faculty and who conducted the interviews for this study, found that despite all of the efforts these students declined out-of-class contact with us about their previous writing course experiences. This was the case even though these students were currently attending other courses in subsequent semesters. We were not able to construct from the things we observed, an explanation as to why these students had left the writing course, and why they would not later come to talk about their experiences.

REFERENCES

Astin, A. W. 1993. *What matters in college? Four critical years revisited.* San Francisco: Jossey-Bass.

Bers, T. H. and K. E. Smith. 1991. Persistence of community college students: The influence of student intent and academic and social integration. *Research in Higher Education* 32 (5): 539-556.

Cabrera, A. F., A. Nora, and M. B. Castaneda. 1993. College persistence: Structural equations modeling test of an integrated model of student retention. *Journal of Higher Education,* 64 (2): 123-139.

Carter, D., and R. Wilson. 1997. *Minorities in Higher Education, 15th Annual Status Report.* Washington, D.C.: American Council on Education.

Dougherty, K. J. 1994. *The contradictory college.* Albany, NY: State University of New York Press.

Friedlander, J., and P. Macdougall. 1992. Achieving student success through student involvement. *Community College Review* 20 (1): 20-28.

Gabelnick, F., J. MacGregor, R. S. Matthews, and B. Leigh-Smith. 1990. Learning communities: Creating connections among students, faculty, and disciplines. *New Directions for Teaching and Learning*, no. 41. San Francisco: Jossey-Bass.

Gandara, P. forthcoming. Staying in the race: The challenge for Chicano/as in higher education. *Harvard Education Review.*

Halpin, R. L. 1990. An application of the Tinto model to the analysis of freshman persistence in a community college. *Community College Review* 17 (4): 22-32.

Kraemer, B. A. 1997. The academic and social integration of Hispanic students into college. *Review of Higher Education,* 20 (2): 163-179.

Kuh, G. D., J. H. Schuh, E. J. Whitt, and Associates. 1991. *Involving colleges: Successful approaches to fostering student learning and development outside the classroom.* San Francisco: Jossey-Bass.

Levin, M. E., and J. R. Levin. 1991. A critical examination of academic retention programs for at-risk minority college students. *Journal of College Student Development,* 32, (4): 323-334.

Mayo, J. R., and Associates. 1995. Social integration and academic performance among minority university students. *Journal of College Student Development,* 36 (6): 542-552.

Moss, R. L., and R. B. Young . 1995. Perceptions about the academic and social integration of underprepared students in an urban community college. *Community College Review* 22 (4): 47-61.

Mow, S., and M. Nettles. 1990. Minority student access to, and persistence and performance in, college: A review of the trends and research literature. In *Higher Education Handbook of Theory and Research*, no. 6, edited by J. Smart. Bronx, N.Y.: Agathon.

Nora, A. 1993. Two-year colleges and minority students' educational aspirations: Help or hindrance? In *Higher Education Handbook of Theory and Research,* no. 9, edited by J. Smart. Bronx, N.Y.: Agathon.

_____. 1987. Determinants of retention among Chicano college students: A structural model. *Research in Higher Education* 26, no. 1: 31-59.

Nora, A., L. C. Attinasi, and A. Matonak. 1990. Testing qualitative indicators of precollege factors in Tinto's attrition model: A community college student population. *Review of Higher Education* 13 (3): 337-356.

Pascarella, E. T. 1980. Student-faculty informal contact and college outcomes. *Review of Educational Research* 50 (4): 545-595.

Pascarella, E. T., and D. W. Chapman. 1983. A multi-institutional, path analytic validation of Tinto's model of college withdrawal. *American Educational Research Journal* 20 (1): 87-102.

Pascarella, E. T., J. C. Smart, and C. A. Ethington. 1986. Long-term persistence of two-year college students. *Research in Higher Education*, 24 (1): 47-71.

Pascarella, E. T., and P. T. Terenzini. 1980. Predicting freshmen persistence and voluntary dropout decisions from a theoretical model. *Journal of Higher Education* 51 (1): 60-75.

Pascarella, E. T., and P. T. Terenzini. 1991. *How college affects students*. San Francisco: Jossey-Bass.

Rendon, L. I. 1994. Validating culturally diverse students: Toward a new model of learning and student development. *Innovative Higher Education* 19 (1): 33-51.

Stage, F. K. 1989. Reciprocal effects between the academic and social integration of college students. *Research in Higher Education* 30 (5): 517-530.

Tinto, V. 1975. Dropout from higher education: A theoretical synthesis of recent research. *Review of Educational Research* 45 (1): 89-125.

_____. 1993. *Leaving college: Rethinking the causes and cures of student attrition*. 2d ed. Chicago: University of Chicago Press.

Tinto, V., and P. Russo. 1994. Coordinated Studies Programs: Their effect on student involvement at a community college. *Community College Review*, 22 (2): 16-25.

Voorhees, R. A. 1987. Toward building models of community college persistence: A logit analysis. *Research in Higher Education*, 26 (2): 115-129.

APPENDIX

Abbreviated Form of the Interview Schedule

1. Why were you going to college, at the time you were taking this course? Were there some other specific goals for taking this course?
2. Why did you complete this writing course?
3. If you had it to do over again, would you make the same decision to stay and complete the course?`
4. Did your writing skills change in any ways during the course?
5. What kinds of things or activities happened in the course that helped you to improve your writing? During the writing course, how often did the teacher divide the students into small groups and ask you to work together as a group on some writing task? What kinds of things did you do in these small groups that you liked or that you found to be helpful to you? Were there things that happened in these groups that you did not like?
6. Were there other things in the course that made it difficult for you to improve your writing? Were you as successful as you wanted to be in this course? Thinking back to the readings in the course, what did you think of the readings? Were the readings too difficult or too easy?
7. Did you feel like an important member of this class, or did you feel like an outsider in this class? How did the teacher make you feel as a member of the class or as an outsider? Did the teacher call you by name in the class?
8. During the time you were in the course, did you ever meet the teacher outside of the class to discuss your work? During the time you were in the course, did you ever stop and talk to the teacher after class? Did the teacher ever call or write you at home?
9. Did you meet outside this class with other students from the class to study for the course?
10. In this course, did you feel that your culture was given enough attention in the assignments, readings, and discussions in class?
11. What things would you like to have changed in this course?
12. What parts of the course seemed especially important to you and should be kept?

Note: The full schedule for the interview included a brief introductory section, and a variety of suggested probes for use in elaborating the responses.

18. Observing the Spirit of Resilience: The Relationship Between Life Experiences and Success in Higher Education for African American Students

Cheryl Getz

Introduction

Currently, the dominant culture controls the majority of educational institutions in this country and as a result, institutional and cultural racism, even though it may be unintentional, exists (Bennett, 1995). Quite naturally, White educators view the world through their own experiences which constantly shape their perceptions, which in turn shape their reality. However, those working in and for institutions of higher learning, ought not to assume others' experiences are always similar, and subsequently dismiss the perceptions of others such as African American students. The African American students in this study remained challenged by their own perceptions of how they believed others viewed them as well as the reality of their experiences and interactions with others and how this may have affected their sense of resiliency.

Research designed to focus on voices that have generally been silenced was important in efforts to improve the quality of education for African Americans and other marginalized students in this country (Anderson & Herr, 1994; Maher & Tetreault, 1994).   Traditional education in the twentieth century has not adequately reflected the perceptions and views of students who were not members of the dominant culture.   Some (Nieto, 1996; McLaren, 1989) believe that further explanations of schooling grounded in students' perspectives are needed so that professors, administrators and policy-makers can better understand how educators fit diversity and student characteristics into the framework of the institutions they represent.   Quite often, educators' perceptions of reality have been dominated by the worldview of the Anglo culture.

     This paper has been organized into five sections. The first section begins with the purpose of the study, the next section is the background of the study which provides the reader with an overview of the relevant research topics in resiliency, self-efficacy and spirit. The third section includes the methodology used for this study. The next section is the findings that illustrate and illuminate the data analysis. The conclusion provides discussion and recommendations for the future.

Purpose
Some African American students with challenging early life experiences appear vulnerable to failure in higher education. This vulnerability may be exacerbated when educators fail to recognize the relationship between the life experiences of African American students and their academic performance and college success. When students' experiences outside of school are not validated as part of their school experience, then it can work against their ability to be successful in our current educational system. African American students are challenged further as they attempt to successfully adjust to collegiate environments, which often do not validate them or their experiences.

     The primary purpose of this study was to investigate the challenges these students perceive and examine how their life experiences enhance their success in higher education. A secondary purpose was to learn how these students developed their sense of resiliency and how they thought this knowledge could be utilized to promote their own greater self-efficacy. Therefore, the overall purpose was to engage selected African American students in order to learn from them directly about their perceptions of the connections between life experiences and success in higher education.

Observing the Spirit of Resilience: The Relationship   459
Between Life Experiences and Success in Higher Education
for African American Students

Background of the Study
African American youth in general face many barriers to academic achievement and success in life. Nevertheless, while some African American youth succumb to these pressures and risk factors, others go on to achieve despite overwhelming odds (Ford, 1994). Students who are able to overcome these barriers appear to be resilient individuals. Resilient students are often self-efficacious: they believe in themselves and their ability to succeed. These qualities along with several others are key ingredients for successful resilient African American student achievement.

Resiliency
There are many experiences in the lives of African American students that contribute to their sense of resiliency. The qualities may be perceived differently by every student; however, this study attempts to find common explanations from among the eight African American students selected. The students in this study perceived these qualities differently from others who were not raised in similar environments and because of their particular position in our society (Ogbu, 1987).

Resiliency, self-efficacy and other qualities were attributes that many successful students exhibited (Farrell, 1994; Garmezy, 1991; McMillian & Reed, 1994; Rutter, 1987). These students' expressions of resiliency are supported by various writings in the literature on resilient children and adults. Thus this study supports recent resiliency research which points to an increasing awareness that individuals growing up in stressful environments often develop an increased sense of personal proficiency in many areas of their lives (Wolin, 1993; Werner & Smith, 1992). The students in this study were resilient and they all had to overcome various stressful life experiences before they entered the university or college environment. In addition, they were further challenged by their experiences away from home and on their respective campuses.

The increased awareness of children's coping mechanisms under difficult life circumstances led to the discovery of protective factors that are present in resilient children (Rutter, 1987; Garmezy, 1991). Resilience and protective factors, which are the positive counterparts of risk factors, modify a person's reaction to a situation that in ordinary circumstances may lead to maladaptive behavior (Werner & Smith, 1992). Educators continue to revisit their positions with respect to students raised in stressful environments from students who enter college as "at risk" students exhibiting resilience. Children who start off in troubled environments do not necessarily continue having bad experiences (Rutter, 1984). Much research is focused on translating negative risk factors into positive educational outcomes (Williams & Newcombe, 1994; Benard, 1993; McMillan & Reed, 1994; Winfield, 1991; Sagor, 1996). Educators must continue to address these students and the issues that affect them with positive insights about the strengths they bring to our educational institutions. If professionals in higher education can find ways to support and strengthen various protective factors exhibited by resilient African American students, these students are more likely to be successful.

<u>Self-Efficacy</u>

In the social learning theory, Albert Bandura places emphasis on one's ability to handle demands in life (Lahey, 1995). Self-efficacy is the perception that one is capable of doing what is necessary to reach a goal. In addition, it is the sense of knowing what to do and being emotionally able to do it. Moreover, "people who perceive themselves as self efficacious accept greater challenges, expend more effort, and may be more successful in reaching their goals as a result" (Lahey, 1995, p. 472). The term "perception" is key to understanding self-efficacy in African American students.

The perception that a student is capable of accomplishing a given task may be learned from what others say about them or their direct experiences of success and failure (Lahey, 1995). Efficacy beliefs influence individuals' thought patterns and emotional reactions (Pajares, 1996). African American students who may not believe they are capable of reaching their goals may learn something about themselves through environmental influences in the educational setting or elsewhere, that can contribute to or destroy their self-efficacy. According to Edward "Chip" Anderson (1989), "underrepresented students are more likely to experience prejudice as well as discrimination and alienation. With prejudice comes all of the unfavorable, negative, and demeaning judgments that, if internalized, could negatively affect motivation, commitment, and self-efficacy" (p. 238).

The messages sent by the dominant culture can influence the ways in which African American students perceive their own ability to achieve academically. African American youth have historically been confronted with many challenges to their self-concept that have negatively influenced their physical and psychological development (Steele, 1992). As a result of their subordinate position, Blacks have

Observing the Spirit of Resilience: The Relationship   461
Between Life Experiences and Success in Higher Education
for African American Students

formed an identity system that is perceived and experienced as different from and in opposition to the social identity of the Anglo culture (McLaren, 1989, p. 212). Furthermore, since the mainstream experience is often characterized by the value systems of the dominant culture, African American students are influenced to adapt to Anglo norms, values and expectations that often contradict their own cultural experiences (Nieto, 1996). Given this experience, African American students may find it difficult to seek out support in many higher education institutions because educators and other students in the environment may be perceived as hostile and in some instances may be, in fact, hostile. A student who does not believe the environment supports one's achievement, loses some belief in one's own abilities (Gorden, 1995).

Spirit as a Source of Self-Efficacy; Self-Efficacy as a Source of Resiliency

Educators must find ways to understand and translate the experiences of African American students in ways that could promote their self-efficacy and thus academic success. All students including African American students could benefit from environments that nurture their positive qualities and work to promote protective factors (Comer, 1980). However, strategies for improving academic performance among Black children often occur in isolation without adequate attention to the social contexts in which they occur (Haynes and Comer, 1990, p. 112). Educators who respect, listen and try to understand the experiences of African American students may be more able to support them and contribute to their sense of self-efficacy and thus resiliency.

     The African American students in this study continued to believe in themselves and appeared to maintain a strong sense of self-efficacy despite environments that they described as unfavorable. In fact, they all displayed an inner strength, sense of self and focus, which in this study was referred to as spirit, that continues to motivate them. Spirit can be defined as a life-giving force or vivacity and enthusiasm for life. According to Native American teachings, the spiritual dimension of human development is the capacity to have and respond to realities that exist in a non-material way such as dreams, ideals and goals. And, as is the case with these students, the capacity to use this symbolic expression to guide future action – action directed toward making what was only seen as a possibility into a living reality (Bopp,

J., Bopp, M., Brown, L. & Lane, P., 1984). It has been my experience over the last fifteen years in higher education, that many resilient African American students are able to achieve tremendous goals partly because they possess something intangible that is not easily defined. For years, I have witnessed African American students whom I knew to be resilient, that were never able to actually define this inner source of strength they possessed.

Spirit reveals itself through the actions and energy of human beings (Locust, 1998), however, the spiritual basis of human existence is ultimately unconscious (Frankel, 1975). This might explain why the students in this particular study did not speak specifically to the term spirit. The experiences they described and the actions and behaviors they exhibited as a result of these experiences demonstrated that spirit might be a source of their self-efficacy and thus resiliency.

For many African Americans, expressions of a deeper ability to triumph over tremendous obstacles are often reflected upon as spirit (Taylor, 1993). Many consider the "spirit" of African Americans the life force that holds individuals within the community together (Nobles, 1997; hooks, 1993; Angelou, 1986; DuBois, 1961). Moreover, many resilient African American students appear to maintain a strong belief in themselves (Garmezy, 1991; Rutter, 1987). It is proposed that the source of the students' resiliency may be self-efficacy and perhaps the source of these students' self-efficacy is spirit, which ultimately has a grand effect on the success of some African American students. If this hypothesis is correct and the source of these students' resiliency is self-efficacy, it may be very difficult for African Americans to remain resilient in institutions of higher learning when they perceive the environment as hostile. Since their perceptions shape their reality, students' sense of self-efficacy and thus their spirits, are further challenged by their own evaluation of barriers, real and perceived, in and out of the institutions they attend.

METHODOLOGY
Research Questions
The research questions for this study were designed to explore how students view their own sense of resiliency and how this self-awareness contributes to their sense of self-efficacy and success in higher education. The questions serve as a guide to support a qualitative approach and facilitate participant exploration. The questions are also intended to aid in the use of grounded theory methodology.

Two questions were explored: (1) what can we learn from African American students about life qualities such as resiliency, self-

Observing the Spirit of Resilience: The Relationship   463
Between Life Experiences and Success in Higher Education
for African American Students

efficacy, and perhaps other qualities, that may relate to their own sense of success in higher education? And, (2) what educational theory might emerge to guide teacher and student relationships, given the grounded theory that comes from this study?

Selection of subjects

Students were selected from solicitations to eight schools in the San Diego area. Six colleges and universities responded affirmatively to a request to identify students at their institutions. Therefore, a variety of colleges and universities in the San Diego area were represented by the subjects in the study: six (total) colleges and universities, two private four-year schools, one four-year state school and three community colleges. Three of the six schools were predominately White and three represent mixed populations: one was predominately Hispanic, one predominately African American and the third had a very diverse student population.

Students were not randomly selected. They were recommended for the study by administrators, faculty or students at their respective institutions. Participants were evenly distributed by gender and included four women and four men.

The eight students selected for this study were: (a) of African American descent; (b) sophomores or juniors in college; (c) between the ages of eighteen and twenty-two; (d) attending a college or university in the San Diego area at the time of the individual interview; (e) lived through or are currently living in what they referred to as difficult, stressful or challenging life situations; and (f) were willing participants.

For the purposes of this study, the fifth criteria -- living through difficult or stressful life circumstances -- was established by each of the eight individual African American student participants. Since one of the purposes of this study was to learn about resiliency, students were deliberately sought out who had come in direct contact with disruptive elements as they grew up. Obviously, this has not been the experience of all African Americans, but the students in this study believed they were resilient because of the difficult, stressful and challenging environments they were exposed to and able to overcome. These challenging experiences described by the students included more than one of the following: violence in their home and/or neighborhood; drug and alcohol abuse by parents and/or other family members; sexual abuse, homelessness, gang involvement, incarceration, or emotional abuse; parents' separated or divorced or single-parent families; and constant moving from one home to another.

The subjects' level of exposure to various disruptive elements varied. Two of the students had limited exposure (compared to the other six students in the study) to disruptive elements during childhood and were raised in homes with two parents. However, they too described incidences of drug abuse, emotional traumas and instability in their environments. The other six had a variety of exposures to factors that were extremely disruptive to their emotional, social and intellectual development.

Research Design
Data was gathered through the process of two individual interviews with each student, informal discussions and a group interview. Two sets of questions were developed. Before the first round of interviews took place with subjects, a pilot interview was done with four colleagues who served as advisors throughout the study. These were African Americans who were raised in what they described as difficult and often hostile environments. Three were women ages twenty-four through thirty-one and one was a male in his sixties. All four were working with students in higher education settings. Several suggestions were made to improve the open-ended interview questions that were incorporated in the final study (appendix A).

Credibility in this study was established by using open-ended questions and interviewing each participant twice as well as another method Lincoln and Guba (1985) labeled as "member checking." In this study, the preliminary analysis was given to each subject prior to their second interview to ensure clarity and exactness. This also gave the participants an opportunity to revisit some of the issues that were discussed, prior to their second interview. Some of the subjects provided additional feedback based on the analysis, while others said the analysis was accurate and they had nothing new to add. The complete analysis at the end of the data collection phase was also given to each participant for review and additional feedback.

The purpose of the open-ended interview approach was to remain flexible as the interview process unfolded, so the questions were often modified during the interview. The questions were designed to reflect individual variations in the participants' responses during the interviews.

Several other methods of data collection were utilized for this study including a group interview, the observance of verbal and non verbal behaviors and the literature review. All served as sources of

Observing the Spirit of Resilience: The Relationship   465
Between Life Experiences and Success in Higher Education
for African American Students

triangulation to enhance transferability. Written notes were taken throughout the data collection phase in a separate notebook and on the interview transcriptions as well. These notes, along with participant observations, also served as overlapping methods noted by Lincoln and Guba (1985) as measures of dependability. Confirmability was established through the audit trail technique (Lincoln & Guba, 1985), as critiques were solicited from colleagues throughout the process who served in an advisory capacity. This advisory committee also provided frequent interpretations of the data to ensure its consistency and reliability. Members of the researchers dissertation committee also acted as additional external auditors who provided feedback on written and verbal data analyses.

At the conclusion of all individual interviews, a group interview was arranged. Six of the eight student volunteers participated in the group interview. The initial themes that emerged from the data based on the total number of individual interviews were shared with the sixteen subjects during the group interview. During that time, their feedback was sought and used to expand upon several of the initial topics.

FINDINGS
Students Sense of Resiliency
Achievement for these students involves more than the development of skills and knowledge. The people that came into contact with these students at their respective schools and universities expected them to look, think and behave a certain way. This seemed to be especially difficult for the four male students. The following two statements from two of the men regarding situations that occurred on their predominately White campus:

> People just start expecting me to be just like what they see on TV. I remember we went to a party, and somebody got in a fight and they thought we were doing it. And we were nowhere near it. It was two white guys. People said to us "what are you guys starting trouble for?"

> I have been pulled over three times since I have been back to school. Three times! I didn't get a ticket any of the three times. Once, I had three African American friends with me, and I guess we seemed out of place.

All of the students agreed that dealing with discrimination and learning to cope with negative bias was a matter of survival. They explained that they did not want to let other people's perceptions of who they were affect them or their self-esteem in negative ways. So, in many instances the students chose to block things out.

Blocking things out
All of the students spoke about experiences dealing with stereotyping and misconceptions about them. They perceived they were constantly judged by the color of their skin. The student who was stopped by the police three times, tried to explain that if he didn't block things out, he would have been negatively affected by how other people treated him:

> As far as college, being African American, people act a certain way toward you. You gotta pretty much block that out, too. You have to get used to blocking stuff out. Or like, not really block it out -- not let it bother you. Cause if you take it personally, let it get to you, then it's going to slow your day down. It makes you tired and it'll start to really bother you and you really start to second-guess yourself and other people. And then it will bring a whole lot of problems to you that you don't need.

For some of the students ignoring discrimination or *blocking it out* was necessary for them to get along with their White peers, professors and others. Both of the following students spoke about how they contended with these difficult situations. Here they explain how they coped when they were confronted by people who made assumptions about them:

> I tend to block a lot of things out. Like when somebody says something to me that I really don't like. Most of the time, I just block it out. Act like it was never said. Act like it never happened.

> You just feel like you're a rat in a cage, you know; it's nerve-racking. Here, if I do run into some kind of a problem like that, I try to block it out because I know I'm here to do work and try to do good in the course and to move on. I don't let it bother me now. I think I've grown to be able to deal with it.

There was a great deal of discussion concerning this phenomena during the group interview. One student said she's learned to deal with racism and rise above the ways she is often perceived by others:

Observing the Spirit of Resilience: The Relationship   467
Between Life Experiences and Success in Higher Education
for African American Students

> If I run into a problem -- what the teacher is saying on a
> racial level, I don't think I'm going to take it to heart.
> Because if I take it to heart, it's going to affect me bad. So I
> try not to let it get to that level, and try to deal with it.
> Because if every time something came at me and I let it
> affect me, I think I would be crazy.

Other students also thought it was better to find ways to deal
with difficult situations. They insisted that if a student continued to
block things out, they were holding in reality, things in and keeping a
part of themselves suppressed. During further discussions in the group
interview, several of the students revealed that as African Americans
they sometimes have to put up a front and just deal with situations. One
student disagreed:

> One teacher told me it starts with you. Once you refuse to
> accept it, buy into it and feed off of it, it will stop. And I
> think that includes addressing racism head on instead of
> just blocking it out, letting it go or putting on a mask. It
> starts with yourself.

Following this response, one of the students who previously said she
chose to block things out too, changed her perspective:

> I think it's better to deal with something than to try to block
> it out. If you try to block it out, it's going to come back at
> you full force, and you're going to have to deal with it in a
> worse way.

It is clear that these eight students had to find mechanisms to deal with
hostile pressures associated with being African American students.

Making choices
The subjects in this study were acutely aware that the choices they
made directly affected their success in the future. The students accepted
responsibility for their actions and the consequences of their mistakes.
They believed that they were able to manage their lives and influence
their environment. This resilient quality indicated a strong internal
locus of control.

The students were very clear about how they perceived their own roles in determining the direction of their life. On many occasions throughout the interview process, the students mentioned they didn't want to use their life experiences as an excuse to fail. Two students explained that regardless of past experiences, they had a choice to make their lives meaningful and productive. For example, one stated:

> Everything in life is either -- you can take it for good or you take it for, you know, what it's worth. You have an option to go forward or you have an option to be stuck or you have an option to go backwards. It's whatever you choose.

Another student also explained:

> Your environment can keep you from succeeding, but it would be, like, a personal choice. Everything in life affects you. So I don't think people should make excuses for themselves.

Some of the students were critical of the choices that their mothers or fathers made. In these instances, the student's felt breaking away from their families was essentially their only choice for a more productive future. One male student suggested:

> It's really not my friends that are holding me back, usually it's my family. Both of my brothers. One's in juvenile hall and my dad's in jail. And this is just a re-occurring cycle -- what they see at home is how they act. Growing up, I was my own leader and my own parent and stuff like that. I just had to get around that and go off on my own and do my own thing.

The other was a female student who confirmed the previous statement:

> I figured there had to be something more than what I was going through or how I grew up. I've seen lots of violence that was in the home, in addition to the violence that was in the streets. And I just didn't want to be a part of that. I mean, I saw all the drugs that my mother was on and I saw all the drug-addicted people that she used to hang out with, and just all that -- that kind of pushed me away.

Observing the Spirit of Resilience: The Relationship   469
Between Life Experiences and Success in Higher Education
for African American Students

Maintaining a sense of their own identity along with an ability to act independently in spite of circumstances appeared to be consistent among these students. Making the break from their families (even though in some cases it was not permanent) was necessary for these students to focus on their educational goals and aspirations.

Setting educational goals

All of the students were driven by the belief that school success was important to future happiness. Getting an education was the assurance that they would realize the goals toward which they aspire. This was especially poignant for the following two students in this study who intuitively knew that getting an education was one way of ensuring that their lives would not emulate past experiences. The following student left home at the age of eleven, because his father and brothers were always getting in trouble. He explained:

> I want to be where I can be comfortable and my family could be comfortable and my kids could go to school and not worry about things. And I don't have to worry about things and my wife doesn't have to worry about things. That's what motivates me. Accomplish more and more before I die because, well, I don't want to have to struggle in life like I did growing up. I feel like when I get to that point where -- not that I'm super rich; I don't think that's all that important -- where I can just feel secure and have my family around.

Another student, who had been homeless and was very critical of her mother's choices, said:

> I don't really ever remember liking school, ever. But I always knew that I had to go through it, if I didn't want my kids to grow up the way I grew up. I knew that school and an education was the only way that I could get out of it.

Experiences shaping perceptions

Along with the stresses present for every student in the context of higher education, African American students face additional pressures of being perceived as less capable than their White peers. Being valued as significant, productive and capable was important to all students including those who were African American. Claude Steele (1992) states that society is conditioned to see the worst in African American students. He further notes that Black students quickly learn that acceptance will be difficult to earn. The responses from the students in this study supported this statement as they described their perceptions of how others in the college environment regarded them.

The following student talked about how he felt at the predominately White institution that he attended. He mentioned that people made statements about quotas. He was frustrated because he believed these statements were made about him, but the people who made the statements did not really know him. He didn't understand why people at his school don't see that he had something positive to offer. He thought that people use these types of statements because they do not want African American students at his school:

> I'm just here to meet a quota. I have heard that. Why? The way I see it is why don't they think I have anything to offer [school]? Why? Why, just because I am Black? Why can't you just be satisfied that I am here and you know me? And leave it at that?

Many of the students remarked that people constantly perceive them as less than capable. The following two students suggest how they handle knowing that others view them this way:

> It's just the whole way that I think people look at us. I don't think they think we should be here. We should probably be on a street corner somewhere. I think that's what they want to think. But I try not to worry about what other people think. I mean, I'm here. And I'm not going anywhere. So that's it.

> Even though my White friends are -- I'm pretty sure half of them think they're better than me. But I look past that, you know? 'Cause I may be thinking the same thing about them. 'Cause I think myself, I'm a good person; that's what makes me better than them.

All of the students expressed feelings of disappointment and frustration about how they believed they were perceived by, in most instances, many of the White people on campus. However, half of the students noted that people on their campuses were also helpful and supportive. This following statement was made by the same student who previously talked about his White friends thinking they were better than he was. He later said:

Observing the Spirit of Resilience: The Relationship   471
Between Life Experiences and Success in Higher Education
for African American Students

> For the most part, a lot of people here are nice. All that I've
> encountered, just about. I've met a lot of people, have a lot
> of friends. I've gotten nothing but support.

Some of the students perceived their college environments as
supportive in one instance and hostile the next. There was ambivalence
in the students' perceptions of their experiences on campus. Even
though they were able to find support from people in their schools, they
still perceived the campus environment as sometimes exclusionary,
indifferent or hostile.

Each one of the students at one time or another talked about
having a feeling that a professor was treating them differently because
they were Black. Sometimes the students talked about getting too much
attention because they were the only African American in class. Most
of their comments indicated that their thoughts and frustrations created
an additional challenge for them to overcome:

> Sometimes I am kind of slow at learning things because, I
> go back to that, you know: "Oh, I can't do it." That type of
> thing. And paranoia, mainly; it's like: "Oh, they're going to
> think I'm stupid because I'm Black." Sometimes I actually
> think that. And I try not to let that hinder me.

Remaining self-efficacious in spite of these negative messages is a
formidable task, and one that these resilient students were generally
able to accomplish.   However, they were often frustrated with the
knowledge that for them, getting an education required much more than
studying hard and getting good grades. As the following student stated,
for them, academic success required prevailing over the ignorance and
perceptions of the dominant culture:

> If I'm reading a book in my South African class, my
> teacher, I mean she's a nice lady, but everybody in class
> looks at me every time she says anything about African
> Americans. I'm learning just like they are. The teacher, she
> is teaching me. I'm not teaching the class. So you can't
> look at me for answers. And there are people that expect
> me to get upset if the teacher says something about
> apartheid or this and that, or expect me to raise my hand.
> And if I raise my hand, I can say something totally

ludicrous and people will still agree with it just because
they think that I'm supposed to automatically know.

Working harder and acting better

All of the students were adept at handling challenges such as this one
because they possessed the insight that they would learn from and
become successful despite the attitudes and perceptions of their peers,
professors and fellow students. However, these students also believed
they had to *work harder* and *act better* than their White peers to be
successful:

> Nobody knows how it feels to be that one race except you.
> And I found that my first couple years that was very
> intimidating. Especially being in that class, being the only
> race, you find yourself having to put more effort into your
> work and try to get over that.

Most of the students agreed with this statement. In addition, several
noted that there may have been other barriers for them to contend with
that could have affected their classroom achievement:

> I know they [White students] have to work just as hard in
> the classroom as I do to get their grades. It might help them
> that they don't have other things to worry about, like is dad
> going to be all right, is dad coming home, things like that.
> So they don't have to fear for anything.

Not only did the students feel like they had to work harder, but they
expressed concerns about being constantly aware of their actions in and
out of the classroom and how this affected the perceptions of others.
This next student had the insight that people tended to judge his
intelligence by his actions and behaviors. However, he was keenly
aware that he was capable of future success because he believed this
insight gave him a distinct advantage over other less aware White
students.

> It's hard because I feel that if I was to do anything stupid, it
> would be like stereotypical: "I knew that would happen," or
> something like that. That is why I take it upon myself not to
> do that, and be looked upon as, up there as one of the better
> students. I mean, not as far as in the classroom, but as a
> person. Because I know some real bad people. Some White
> guys here are real bad, but they are still great in the

Observing the Spirit of Resilience: The Relationship   473
Between Life Experiences and Success in Higher Education
for African American Students

> classroom. I wouldn't say I was so great in the classroom,
> but I know I am a better person altogether."

Being the only African American in class

Being the only African American student in the class was a common occurrence for six of the eight students in this study. All of the students expressed how difficult this experience was:

> I took a physics class last semester and I was the only Black person in the class. So I looked around, like, man, I'm the only Black person here! I don't mean to do it, but I see myself doing it sometimes. And I'm trying to get out of that because once I get to the upper level, with the classes that I want to take, there might not be any African Americans in the class. So I'm trying to get out of that way of thinking.

> It's, like, you're in a class of maybe thirty-five, forty people, and then you have only one Black student, you know? Where is all the collective work? Where is everything?

When asked about how he felt in his first week of school, one student responded:

> Everybody has been stereotyped. I mean the only thing is where is anybody like me at [this school]? You know, that is how you basically feel, out of place at first.

This same student continued his response and shared with me how he relied on his life experiences when searching for ways to find comfort in this environment. He believed he had learned favorable ways of adjusting, whereas some of his other African American friends had not:

> But as far as myself, I make friends, as many friends as possible. Growing up where I did, I got bussed to a rich neighborhood again. It is sort of the same thing that I did here. I look past all of the racial things 'cause by no means do I have anything against any race or anybody. I settled in fine. Some people wouldn't, like some of my friends.

Relating to African American Students
Every student talked about people in the college environment relating
to them. Some of the students were more able than others to verbalize
how it felt when others did relate to them. They spoke often about the
relationship between themselves and their professors. The students
expressed a desire to be treated just like everyone else in the classroom.
Most of them had come to the conclusion that this was not possible. All
of the student's had, at one time or another, a professor with whom they
could relate. It was during these periods when the students said they
learned the most and felt valued in the classroom.

When asked directly, some of the students said that the
professors did not need to know anything about them or their
background. However, those same students later mentioned the types of
professors they thought were most effective and those they were most
comfortable with. In nearly every instance, the students described
professors who spent time getting to know the students, who made
themselves available to students and who appeared as though they
really cared. The statements below display how the students believed
having positive relationships with professors were beneficial to them
and aided in their own motivation and learning:

> Some of my professors, they make a lot of eye contact and
> they do a lot of stuff to kind of affirm your presence in the
> classroom; well, my Black teachers do a lot of that. They
> do a lot of eye contact, they smile a lot and they talk to you
> a lot after class and they interact with you a whole lot as if
> you were part of the family, like they really care.
> Sometimes that makes a big difference in class.

> If you go in there and talk to him about Algebra and about
> yourself at the same time, how you feel about that class, not
> just, how you do this problem; can you show me; I'm a
> little confused. But if you also go in there and tell him how
> you feel about that class, how it contributes to your outside
> life, then he can learn more about you because he can see:
> "Okay, well he's this kind of person." Because perception
> is life. At least he will be closer to perceiving you as to the
> way you are than he will be without you doing that.

> I know that when that happens [when the professor gets to
> know the students better], the student/teacher relationship is
> a lot better. My English teacher really got to know us. And
> you knew you couldn't get over on him, so you've got to
> do something 'cause he's going to put you to the test all the

Observing the Spirit of Resilience: The Relationship   475
Between Life Experiences and Success in Higher Education
for African American Students

> time, because he knows what kind of person you are. And
> if you come in one day and you're feeling down, he knows
> what gets you going.

In the students' view, the ideal professor / student relationship was
forged when the professors could relate to the students. Some of the
students thought that African American professors could relate to them
better than White professors could. Other students believed that race
was not as important if the professors could find ways to understand all
students, regardless of race:

> I think that if teachers could just relate to students. They
> don't have to have your life experience, but just relate on a
> certain level. I mean, not making a student feel like they're
> stupid because they ask a question that might not sound
> intelligent, you know? In their eyes, it might sound
> intelligent.

> I guess they [professors] could give us a little bit more
> understanding about certain stuff. Not special attention, but
> just understanding. Like, it's different here, you know? We
> are three percent of about ninety percent of the different
> colors on the campus. After a while it takes its toll and
> sometimes you just try to second guess and start to feel
> certain ways.

It was difficult for many of the students to verbalize how they thought
professors should respond. I suspect that it was a feeling that was
difficult to express. The experiences they had with many of their
professors were neither negative nor positive. It was often a feeling, a
nonverbal communication that expressed to one the essence of whom
they truly were. The professors may not have committed racist acts, or
make disparaging remarks. But it was the human connection between
two people that had a direct effect on the student's spirit. This student
seemed to understand this connection, and he spoke directly to it:

> If you're going to be an understanding teacher to African
> Americans, be understanding out in public. I don't really
> know the words I'm looking for. Just kind of live your life
> and try to live your life the way you would teach it. The
> way you would teach it in class. Don't just be extra nice to
> African Americans just because he is African American.

> Just be aware of everybody else's culture. Just don't be
> stuck in yours.

He may sound as if he was talking about how professors should be. But
to capture the essence of what he is saying, one must look beyond the
spoken words. If professors really want to understand all of their
students, then for some this is a life change. He suggests that for some,
this means embracing and accepting difference as a part of who you are
as you live your life every day.

Not expecting special privileges

At one point or another, every student in the study said they did not
want to be treated any differently than any of the other students in the
classroom. They did not want to be treated unfairly and they did not
want any special privileges because of their race. They expressed their
desire to engage in the learning process like all of the other students in
the classroom. However, they realized that people are not color-blind,
and they would like the professors to acknowledge the difficulties that
race causes. Yet as this student noted, they would prefer to be treated
like everyone else:

> I don't want any special privileges because of my race. I
> feel I should be just taught like anybody else. Once you get
> into the classroom, then everybody should be seen as
> students.

> [Professors should] Treat me like everybody else in the
> classroom. Just try to know what it is like being one of the
> few African Americans that go to this school. Just only
> think about it and sympathize with me, and don't treat me
> any differently. Just treat me like Joe, you know, don't look
> at me weird or do anything. I am just another student trying
> to get a good education, just like Joe sitting next to me.
> That would help my success if I didn't have to worry about
> a professor and if he is going to treat me differently
> because I'm Black. I shouldn't have to worry about that.

Many of the students wanted their professors to know that they were
motivated to learn. The students often saw the professors as the enemy
who did not believe in them and did not trust that they were motivated
and interested in the learning process.

This particular student was fearful that if she talked to the
professor about getting extra help, she would be viewed as someone
who wanted an extra benefit:

Observing the Spirit of Resilience: The Relationship   477
Between Life Experiences and Success in Higher Education
for African American Students

> Professors need to know that me and other African
> American students are motivated to do well. I don't expect
> instructors to make exceptions for, quote, unquote, minority
> students, but to think of everyone as an individual, not a
> number, and offer assistance to those who need it and who
> are willing to work to improve.

A significant paradox exists in the students' perceptions of professor /
student relationships. The students would like to develop a rapport with
the professors. However, institutional racism and the students'
perceptions of racism seem to be barriers to this endeavor. For instance,
if these students approach professors for help, they are fearful that they
will be judged harshly and be looked upon as expecting special
privileges. On the other hand, if they do not develop rapport with the
professors, that faculty member does not have the opportunity to
understand the students' needs.

The Importance of Learning about African American culture
One of the most important school experiences these students discussed
was learning about their own culture. For some, the experience was
powerful because it was the first time they would be in a college
classroom with many other African American students:

> If I'm taking an African American culture class, it seems
> like I can relate more, like, on a social level with the people
> in those classes. I don't really feel like I can relate to a lot
> of the people that are in my classes now.

The students were asked what made them feel happy their first few
weeks of college. Two of the students said that what made them feel
happy was looking forward to learning more about their culture:

> I was looking forward to taking some African Studies
> classes, which I never had in high school. I've always
> wanted to find out more about me and where I came from,
> where our people come from, what we did and all that stuff.

> I was happy that I was going to be in a Black studies class
> and it was fun. When you're in school for twelve years all
> you learn is Eurocentric history. And you don't get to learn
> the other side. All you see in the books is about some

> pilgrims. You see slaves and then you see all these things
> that White men have contributed.

The significance of this information is underscored by the statements of
this student, who grew up with negative feelings about his family, his
race and his own sense of who he was:

> As I was growing up, I know all the Black people were
> seen as lowlifes and we were nothing and everybody else
> was, like, raised up and they were feeling better. And I was
> kind of ashamed of being Black. I was like [dismissive
> sound] "I could probably pass for something else, I'm kind
> of light-skinned." I always used to think that. But as I got
> older and started learning more about my culture and what
> we've been through, it made me proud to be Black.

Self-Efficacy as Spirit

In utilizing many of the principles of grounded theory methodology, the
data was analyzed and integrated to generate a theory that was
grounded in the specific experiences of the eight African American
students involved in this study. The emergence of *spirit* came from the
data analysis in the advanced stages of this work. The term spirit
encompassed every previous theme and seemed to best describe the
students interviewed for this project. As new ideas continued to unfold,
this theme became a prominent framework for the analysis.

As resilient people, the students' spirits were wounded from
previous life experiences. However, they all refused to allow negative
experiences influence their commitment to succeed. This supports the
view that resilient people are able to learn from and seek out the
positive forces in life. When the students arrived on campus, all of
them were hopeful that their school experiences would be positive and
meaningful.

All of the students dealt with various life challenges growing
up, and as African Americans, they were burdened with the additional
requirement of meeting the Eurocentric institutional norms of the
college environment. In spite of the difficult personal and intellectual
tasks that the students in this study spoke about, they appeared to
maintain a sense of hope that their future and the future of their families
would be productive, peaceful and healthy. They were the kind of
survivors who had spirits that could be injured but not broken. In fact,
in many instances their spirits were strengthened by problems
surmounted in the past and present. This strength continued to reinforce
their spirits into adulthood.

Observing the Spirit of Resilience: The Relationship   479
Between Life Experiences and Success in Higher Education
for African American Students

Hopeful Spirit

As they entered into educational settings that appeared intimidating and frightening, these eight students were hopeful that their school experiences would be positive. Most of the students knew that getting an education was essential for a secure future. They realized that college would be difficult, but it was something that they looked forward to. The following statements were made in response to a question about their first week of school. A few of the students expressed excitement and anticipation. One student said:

> I was kind of excited because it just seemed like a whole
> new beginning.

And another one noted:

> I felt good because I was finally here! I'm on the road to
> being where I want to be in life. I was excited about it,
> finally getting my life started.

Some of the students expressed other feelings about entering the college environment. Among those who had different feelings was the following student, who had some prior gang involvement. He felt pain because he was reminded of all that he had endured before he came to college:

> A whole new world opened for me when I came here. And
> a lot of happiness. I also felt pain when I came here. I just
> felt pain because I was happy to be here but then when I
> thought about what I had to go through to get here, you
> know, to realize that this is where I wanted to be, it hurts.

Other students felt alienated and insecure upon arrival at college. This is discussed further in the following section. Even those students who initially felt alienated and alone, were hopeful that their school experiences would be more positive than some of their life experiences. One student explains how she feels about being in school:

> It's just; I don't want to be there, so this is the only
> alternative for me. This is the only way. So far, my school

> experiences have been positive and my life experiences
> have never been positive.

This hope that the students have was founded on the belief that getting an education was synonymous with success. Most of these students were the first in their families to achieve such a goal. Yet, despite the obstacles and challenges they faced, the students in this study continued to have hope that they would live happy and prosperous lives.

Challenged Spirit

Throughout the study, the students' responses indicated that they were aware that their lives were more arduous than many others who attended their college or university. Initially, some of the students were anxious and fearful. It was difficult for these particular students to feel good about entering the university environment. The following student attended a predominately White institution. She describes how she felt out of place and alone when she arrived on campus:

> When I first came here, I felt like a foreigner in a new
> country or something. I felt a little confused, lonely, like I
> didn't belong there, this particular setting, initially. The
> transition from high school was hard. I felt lost, like
> something going down the drain, in a whirlpool or
> something like that. People looked at me funny. I also saw
> a lot of White students. Didn't see too many that looked
> like me.

Unlike the previous student, the next student felt very happy when he arrived on his campus, which was also predominately White. However, feelings of happiness were soon replaced with disappointment when he realized that people did not really accept him. He began to notice some of the behaviors of the people around him. He eventually realized that racism was something that he would have to endure while he was in college:

> The first couple of days I felt pretty happy. I didn't feel
> alienated any kind of way. Everybody came to me with
> open arms, it seemed like. But after a while it progressed. I
> started to see things different ways. I mean, after a while
> you live with somebody for a while or live next to
> somebody you get to see the ways that they really are. At
> first, I wasn't noticing it at all because I was so joyful.

Observing the Spirit of Resilience: The Relationship   481
Between Life Experiences and Success in Higher Education
for African American Students

It appears that many African American students are affected at some point and in some way by racially hostile environments. It was clear that the students who attend predominately White institutions were much more likely to experience racism on campus. But others who did not attend predominately White institutions, were also stereotyped and judged by someone in their current or previous educational institution. All of the students had learned not to succumb to the destructive verbal and nonverbal messages they received. Although they realized that these messages were generally based on ignorance, disruption of one's self-esteem and confidence was inevitable. These students were challenged by the perceptions others had of them and, in addition, they were challenged by their own perceptions of how they believed others viewed them. Within weeks, many of them became aware that they would be challenged repeatedly and their spirits wounded once again.

Nurtured Spirit

Some of the students did not initially believe that they could or would be successful. Even though they perceived that they were more able to adapt than many of their peers, sometimes they were shaken by old belief patterns based on past experiences. More often than not, when they arrived on campus, they were unsure of themselves and their abilities to succeed. Once they realized that college was not as complicated as it appeared, their motivational levels began to increase. These same students became more confident with each success.

One student described how his confidence was bolstered when he understood how the college system worked:

> I know when I first came to school, I thought everyone was smarter than I was. And it turns out a lot of people are, because a lot of people went to private schools. Not really smarter, but they know how to apply themselves better. Initially, you just think that you can't handle it. You can't compete with everybody here. Once you get here, you realize it's just something that you just didn't know about. It's unknown. But then once you figure it out and get to know what it is, then it's not as bad as it seems to be.

Another student remembered that he was not very motivated in high school and this knowledge kept him from believing in himself when he first began college. However, he realized that if he took a risk and put forth some effort, he grew less intimidated:

> At first, I felt like I didn't know if I was going to be able to make it. I was just, like, going through the motions. Because I knew the kind of student I was in high school. I was lazy and I didn't want to do anything. So, I was like, will I really learn anything? Kind of hesitant. So, I was, just worried at first. But, once I got going, it was all right.

This very same student found that he was motivated by experiencing positive feedback through good grades. When he received his first exceptional grades, he truly believed in himself and now expects he will continue to earn good grades:

> I remember the first time I finished a whole semester here, I was, like: "Wow, I got good grades!" It was like something I was really proud of. And after a while you start to get into school. It's like something that's expected of you; it's like run of the mill.

Several other students related how positive educational experiences gave them the confidence and belief that they could make it in higher education. Positive educational experiences include academic achievement, as well as social adjustment and verbal and tacit acknowledgment. The acknowledgment of the achievement, no matter how subtle, increases student motivation. This also had an effect on the students' expectations of themselves and influenced the expectations of others.

For example, the following student's family did not even expect her to go to college. When it was obvious that she was becoming successful in her academic endeavors, the family expectations increased and in turn, became a motivating factor for her achievement:

> I want to be successful and I didn't come from a successful family. Or a successful environment or whatever. That pushes me. And the fact that now, I have a lot of relatives who expect me to do a lot of stuff now. Whereas, before I really didn't, so that's a motivating force.

The multiple dimensions of nurturance are reflected through the family as well as the college community. Nurturing can be complex because of

Observing the Spirit of Resilience: The Relationship 483
Between Life Experiences and Success in Higher Education
for African American Students

the contradictions present in the students' relationships on and off campus.

Nurturance takes place on campus, which spawns another contradiction. Throughout the interviews and in the transcribed documents, there existed a contradiction between attitudes and feelings. A significant number of students described what appeared to be a continuing paradox. An ambivalence existed in the students' expressions of their feelings about their experiences on campus. There was a continuous fluctuation between affirming attitudes by others versus the disheartening and negating behaviors they often experienced. The first part of this paradox was touched upon in the remarks about the numerous negative experiences these students had encountered. The second part of the paradox was described here with an example of the notable expression of positive experience and contact the student had with people on campus.

One student agreed and stated:

> I met so many different people also on this campus that actually helped me progress. Like, I have a lot of multi-colored friends, and they are just people. It worked out perfect, like my best friend, John. He's White and from a total opposite culture. But we both came to the same place. So stuff like that helps me grow.

The aspect of nurturance is highly important in maintaining and healing the students' spirit. They are more able to succeed when there is nurturance of their strengths as resilient people. Support for these resilient qualities comes from all segments of the college community and family. Recognition of the need to establish a nurturing environment is critical.

Discussion and Recommendations
The students in this study revealed how they perceived their environment. Furthermore, they believed the difficult experiences they encountered made them stronger than others who did not have similar challenges. The majority of these students were hopeful and happy about being in college. However, they became disappointed and frustrated because they did not always feel the institution understood nor embraced them. They then relied on their strengths as resilient students to master the collegiate experience.

The institution becomes strong when it nurtures the strengths that these students bring with them. The institution can demonstrate its support by nurturing these students and modeling acceptance. Moreover, there is a reciprocal value for the institution when it recognizes the need to provide a community for all students to learn and develop. Most importantly, professors and college personnel can model and support the numerous attributes that make a successful student. This model in the college community will not only support African American students, but all students.

The implications for professionals and educators working in higher education are many. Professionals in higher education need to find ways to improve the learning environment for African American and other underrepresented students. This can be done with careful consideration and dialogue about why these students often have difficulties at institutions of higher learning. Changes in the curriculum, faculty development programs, collaboration with outside communities, and the inclusion of nontraditional teaching practices may place colleges and universities one step closer to ensuring that all students learn in an environment where their views, experiences, and cultures are welcomed. When this occurs, more students may begin to recognize the importance and value of having not only their own, but other student perspectives in the classroom and on the campus.

Transforming the educational system is not an easy task, and some would say that it is not necessary. This research, along with other similar studies, demonstrates the need to make structural changes in the programs and practices that are currently utilized in higher education. This can be achieved if colleges and universities are serious about changing the institutional inequalities that exist in higher education.

At many colleges and universities around the country, changes are taking place. Culturally and ethnically diverse students are often provided programs whose goals are to enrich their experience and provide them with ways to connect with other diverse students and staff on campus. While these programs are a tremendous first step and they can provide students with opportunities to connect with others, they currently have little effect on the *majority* students on campus. Furthermore, some of these programs create hostility due to limited understanding between White students and students of color. In addition to these programs, the agenda in higher education must include curriculum expansion (or even transformation), pedagogy, and faculty development (Bennett, 1995).

Changing demographics in this country and in the schools has prompted many professionals and theorists involved in educational

Observing the Spirit of Resilience: The Relationship   485
*Between Life Experiences and Success in Higher Education
for African American Students*

research to reexamine traditional educational approaches in favor of educational reform efforts that are much more inclusive and empowering for all students. Because educational institutions in the United States reflect the power relations that exist within the broader society (McLaren, 1989; Giroux, 1989; Durodoye & Hildreth, 1995), the interests of the dominant culture class are often implied in the teaching practices used (McLaren, 1989) and the institutional policies and practices employed. "Teachers and teacher educators, need opportunities to examine much of what is usually unexamined in the tightly braided relationships of language, culture, and power in schools and schooling" (Cochran-Smith, 1995, p. 500).

Educators in the new millennium will be faced with these issues and many more challenges at every educational level. The dialogue about America's schools and how to improve them must continue. While opinions vary on how to facilitate progress, there is a general agreement that schools need many structural changes to address issues pertinent to the needs of today's youth (Smith & Kaltenbaugh, 1996). Often schools and universities focus primarily on cultural sensitivity and engage in programming efforts such as weekly special events to honor and recognize different cultures. These are laudable practices; "a focus on cultural sensitivity in and of itself can be superficial if it fails to take into account the structural and institutional barriers that reflect and reproduce power differentials in society" (Nieto, 1996, p. 49).

The vision of educational reform depends on making opportunities and resources available for professors to learn how to support new learning for an increasingly diverse population of students (NCRTL: National Center for Research on Teaching and Learning, 1995). After all, the attitudes and actions of the professoriate are among the greatest influences on curriculum and student life on campus (Lewis & Altbach, 1997). There are two areas of concern to address with faculty members on campus. Specifically, curriculum development, and teaching styles and practices used by the professors. Both reform efforts would require a strong commitment from the president or governing body of any institution.

Staff and student development programs are currently in place on many campuses across the country. These programs generally include a diversity component with goals of increasing awareness and improving understanding among all members of the university community. However, although these programs are not specifically

designed to work with professors to improve teaching effectiveness, they could equip professors with skills to work with a diverse student population. The cultivation of effective faculty development programs should include a variety of perspectives from the campus community, including students, human relations and student affairs staff members and other faculty members who support educational reform efforts. Collaboration among all constituents would ensure a variety of perspectives and rich dialogue, which would increase the likelihood of program effectiveness. Faculty development programs should be preceded by assessments of faculty readiness and attitudes toward change (Katz, 1991). The pursuit of community amid diversity involves the entire community
(Bennett, 1995).

Those in higher education must continue to find ways to address the diversity of cultures, experiences and learning styles of the students who attend colleges and universities. As we enter the 21st century, schools that do not promote the diversity of students and the student experience may not continue to prosper. Colleges and universities may be more likely to flourish if they include students from all segments of the population, and then provide meaningful experiences for them once they arrive on campus. These institutions may thus become stronger as others begin to recognize the value of knowing and learning from all people.

References
Anderson, Edward "Chip". (1989). What would we do if we really loved the students? In Gorden LaVern Berry & Joy Asamen (eds.). Black Students (pp.218-242). Newbury Park, CA : Sage.
Angelou, Maya. (1986). All Gods Children Need Traveling Shoes. New York, NY: Random House
Anderson, Gary L., & Herr, Katherine. (1990). The micro-politics of student voices: Moving from diversity of bodies to diversity of voices in schools. In Catherine Marshall (eds.), The New Politics of Race and Gender (pp.58-68). The Falmer Press.
Benard, Bonnie. (1993). Fostering Resiliency in Kids. Educational Leadership, 51 (3): 44-48.
Bennett, Christine. (1995). Research on Racial Issues in American Higher Education. In James Banks & Cherry Banks (eds.), Handbook of Research on Multicultural Education. (pp.663-682). New York, NY: Simon and Schuster Macmillian.

Observing the Spirit of Resilience: The Relationship   487
Between Life Experiences and Success in Higher Education
for African American Students

Cochran-Smith, Marilyn. (1995). Color Blindness and Basket Making are not the Answers: Confronting the Dilemmas of Race, Culture, and Language Diversity in Teacher Education. American Educational Research Journal,32,(3): 493-522.

Bopp, Judie., Bopp, Michael., Brown, Lee., & Lane, Phil. (1984). The Sacred Tree Book. Four Worlds International Institute for Human and Community Development. Alberta, Canada.

Comer, James. (1980). School Power. New York,NY: The Free Press.

Delpit, Lisa. (1988). The Silenced Dialogue. Harvard Educational Review, 58: 280-298.

Dubois, W.E.B. (1961). The Souls of Black Folks. New York, NY: Fawcett Publications.

Durodoye, Beth & Hildreth, Bertina (1995, Winter). Learning Styles and the African American Student. Education, 116 (2): 241-247.

Farrell, Edwin. (1994). Self and School Success: Voices and Lore of Inner-City Students. Albany, NY: State University of New York Press.

Fine, Michelle (1989). Silencing and Nurturing Voice in an Improbable Context: Urban Adolescents in Public School. In Henry Giroux & Peter McLaren (eds.), Critical Pedagogy, The State and Cultural Struggle.(pp. 125-152). Albany, NY: State University of New York Press.

Frankl, Victor. (1975). The Unconscious God. New York, NY: Simon & Schuster.

Ford, Donna F. (1994). Nurturing Resilience in Gifted Black Youth. Roeper Review. [on line], vol.17, 80, ff

Giroux, Henry (1989). Schooling as a Form of Cultural Politics: Toward a Pedagogy of and for Difference. In Henry Giroux & Peter McLaren (eds.), Critical Pedagogy, the State, and Cultural Struggle.(pp. 125-151). Albany, N.Y: State University of New York Press.

Garmezy, N. (1991, March/April). Resiliency and Vulnerability to Adverse Developmental Outcomes Associated with Poverty. American Behavioral Scientist, 34 (4): 416-430.

Giroux, Henry (1981). Ideology Culture and the Process of Schooling. Philadelphia, PA: Temple University Press.

Gordon, Kimberly A. (1995, Aug.). Self Concept and Motivational Patterns of Resilient African American High School Students. Journal of Black Psychology. [on line], vol. 21, 239, ff.

Haynes, Norris, M. & Comer, James P. (1990). Helping Black Children Succeed: The Significance of Some Social Factors. In Kofi Lomotey (eds.), Going to School: The African American Experience. (pp.103-112). Albany, NY: State University of New York Press.

hooks, bell (1993). Sisters of the Yam. Boston, MA: South End Press.

Katz, J. (1991). White Faculty Struggling With the Effects of Racism. In P.G. Altbach & K. Lomotey (eds.), The Racial Crisis in American Higher Education (187-196). Albany NY: University of New York Press.

Lahey, Benjamin B. (1995). Psychology: An Introduction. Dubuque, IA: Brown and Benchmark.

Lewis, Lionel., & Altbach, Philip. (1997). ACADEME. July/August. The Dilema of Higher Education.

Lincoln Y.S.,& Guba E.G.,(1985). Naturalistic Inquiry. Beverly Hills, CA:Sage.

Locust, Carol. (1988). Wounding the Spirit: Discrimination and Traditional American Indian Belief Systems. Harvard Educational Review, 58: 315-330.

Maher, Frances., & Tetreault Thompson, Mary Kay. (1994). The Feminist Classroom. New York, NY. Basic Books.

McLaren, Peter., (1989). Life in Schools: An Introduction to Critical Pedagogy in the Foundations of Education. White Plains, NY: Longman Inc.

McMillan, James H. & Reed, Daisy F. (1994, Jan./Feb.). At-Risk Students and Resiliency: Factors Contributing to Academic Success. The Clearing House 67 (3): 137-140.

NCRL: National Center for Research on teacher learning (1995). Learning to Walk the Reform Talk, A Framework for the Professional Development of teachers. College of Education, Michigan State University.

Nieto, Sonia (1994, Winter). Lessons From Students on Creating a Chance to Dream. Harvard Educational Review, 64 (4): 392-426.

Nobles, Wade (1997). African American Family Life. In Harriette Pipes McAdoo (ed.). Black Families. (pp.83-93).Thousand Oaks, CA: Sage.

Ogbu, John (1987). Variability in Minority School Performance: A Problem in Search of an Explanation. Anthropology and Education Quarterly, 18: 312-334.

Pajares, Frank. (1996). Self-Efficacy Beliefs in Academic Settings. Review of Educational Research, 66, (4), 543-578.

Observing the Spirit of Resilience: The Relationship   489
Between Life Experiences and Success in Higher Education
for African American Students

Rutter, Michael, M.D. (1987). Psychosocial Resilience and Protective Mechanisms. American Journal of Orthopsychiatry, 57 (3): 316-333.

Rutter, Michael, M.D. (1984). Resilient Children. Why Some Disadvantaged Children Overcome their Environment and How We Can Help. Psychology Today, 57-65.

Sagor, Richard (1996, Sept.). Building Resiliency in Students. Educational Leadership, 54 (1): 38-43.

Smith, Deborah & Kaltenbaugh, Louise (1996). University-School Partnership:Reforming Teacher Preparation. In Comer, James., Haynes, Norris., Joyner, Edward., & Ben-Avie, Michael.(eds.). Rallying the Whole Village. The Comer Process for Reforming Education. (pp. 72-97).New York,N.Y: Teachers College Press.

Steele, Claude (1992). Race and the Schooling of Black Americans. Atlantic Monthly, 269 (4): 68-78.

Taylor, Susan. (1993). In the Spirit. NY.,NY: Harper Collins.

Werner, Emmy E. & Smith, Ruth S. (1992). Overcoming the Odds: High Risk Children from Birth to Adulthood. Ithaca, NY: Cornell University Press.

Williams, Belinda & Newcombe, Ellen (1994, May). Building on the Strengths of Urban Learners. Educational Leadership, 51 (8): 75-78.

Winfield, Linda F. (1991, Nov.). Resilience, Schooling and the Development in African-American Youth, *A Conceptual Framework*. Education and Urban Society, 24 (1): 5-14.

Wolin, Steven J. & Wolin, Sybil (1993). The Resilient Self: How Survivors of Troubled Families Rise Above Adversity. New York: Villard Books.

APPENDIX A – FIRST ROUND INTERVIEW QUESTIONS

1. What does this definition of resiliency mean to you?
2. Do you see yourself as someone who is resilient, why?
3. What experiences have you had that challenged you or provided you with opportunities to grow?
4. How do you rely on your experiences now to help you succeed in college?

5. Do you view your life experiences and school experiences as separate or connected? How? In what ways?
6. What specific things frustrate you about being an African American in a college setting?
7. In what ways could others in your college make your experience more valuable?
8. In what ways do you think your life experiences are similar to the other students in your classrooms?
9. In what ways do you think your life experiences are dissimilar to the other students in your classrooms?
10. If I were looking out from your eyes, on your first few days of college, what kinds of things would I see occur? If I could feel what you were feeling, how would I feel?
11. What do you think your teachers should know about the value of your experiences that could contribute to your success in the classroom?
12. How could your overall experience help someone else in the college setting?
13. In what ways could teachers and administrators learn better to help African American students become more successful in the classroom?
14. What attributes, skills or traits could be taught to students like you, through the university or college system that could help them be more successful?

19. *Improving Learning Outcomes for At-Risk Multicultural Community College Students*

Sheila T. Gregory and Otis O. Hill

INTRODUCTION

In 1996, 24.6 million (9.3 percent) of the U.S. population were foreign-born. This number has fluctuated from a high of 14.7 percent in 1910 to a low of 4.8 percent in 1970, but since that time the percentage has steadily increased. Among all immigrants, nearly one-half do not speak English well and 28 percent live in households where very little English is spoken (American Council on Education, 1994).

The United States population is projected to grow from 249 million in 1990 to 355 million people by the year 2040. Currently, almost half of the population of Los Angeles (Fix & Passel, 1994) and nearly half of all students attending the City University of New York (CUNY, 1995) do not report English as their native language. Furthermore, the 1994 United Way Survey of Los Angeles revealed that one-third of the county's population (2.9 million people) was born outside of the United States (Stein, 1994).

At the City University of New York, there are a significant number of recent freshman students who are born outside of the United States. Those trends as well as recent immigrant trends into New York City are illustrated in Figure 1 (CUNY, 1995). Figure 1 juxtaposes the proportion of first-time freshman in 1990 and 1991 born outside the U.S. who come from each country, with the proportion of immigrants to New York City during the 1982-1991 period who come from the same country. Data are shown for the 17 most significant source

countries for both CUNY and New York City. The correlation (.90) is
high between the number of immigrants by country residing in New
York City and the proportion of recent CUNY freshmen from those
specified countries.

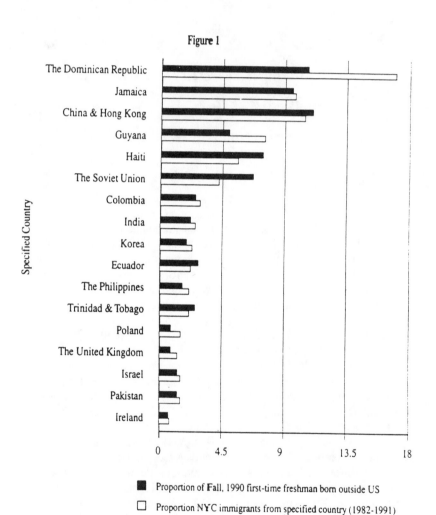

Figure 1

The population of foreign-born persons in the U.S. are not homogeneous. There are many differences based on country of origin, how long they have lived in the U.S., and whether or not they have become American citizens. For example, foreign-born persons who arrived in the U.S. more recently are more likely to have lower incomes and higher unemployment rates than U.S. born persons, although foreign-born persons who have resided in the U.S. for more than 6 years usually recover from poverty (U.S. Department of Commerce, 1997). Due to increases in immigration and high ethnic birth rates, the U.S. population is expected to grow from 250 million in 1990 to 355 million by 2040. Immigrants arriving since 1990 will account for two-thirds of that growth.

The University of Michigan was perhaps the first to anticipate and plan for the increasing wave of foreign and immigrant students when they began investigating the role of an English Language Institute. In 1941, The University of Michigan opened a very prestigious Institute whose original purpose was to provide ESL for tourist and foreign visitors, but soon shifted the focus on academic ESL for students of the University. The mission of the Institute was to provide a variety of courses in English for academic purposes for non-native speakers enrolled at the University (Morley, 1991).

For all students, starting college can be an experience filled with feelings of anxiousness and anxiety. But for foreign students this overwhelming transition can be frightening because of the need to adjust academically, socially, and culturally (Dillard & Chisolm, 1983; Schram & Launerm, 1988).

Typically, freshmen around the country perceive themselves as being capable of reaching their academic goals, which for many are graduation. However, research indicates (Chickering & Reisser, 1993) that there is often a gap between freshman optimism and the commitment necessary to academically succeed. This gap is often caused when a student has a difficult time adjusting to college life, especially during the freshman year where attrition is the highest. This problem can be exacerbated for under-prepared students.

Many would argue that community colleges are perhaps the most capable of developing and maintaining special academic programs to meet the needs of culturally and academically diverse students, although evidence of such is inconsistent (Cuseo, 1991; LeBlanc, 1991). However, regardless of the type of institution attended, the most critical period of adjustment for students is during the first academic year, particularly the first semester. Under-prepared students who require remediation, rarely have developed the life skills necessary to effectively and directly influence their ability to academically succeed.   Institutions can positively influence student persistence and retention by helping them to develop these life skills as well as help strengthen basic academic skills.

Several factors have been identified that directly affect the intellectual development and academic achievement of multicultural students.   Some of these factors include: cultural bias of tests; equivalence of test items; student motivation and attitudes towards test taking; familiarity with test taking; poor study strategies; external locus of control; lower self-esteem; rural versus urban environment; level of education; preprimary education; early and current nutrition; cognitive and social stimulation; and a host of socioeconomic factors (Stevenson, 1985).

REVIEW OF THE LITERATURE
There has been an increased concern in recent years about how to identify and address the academic needs of "at-risk" cross-cultural college students to help improve learning outcomes. This issue has become a growing concern in light of the increasing numbers of foreign (Dunn and Griggs, 1995), immigrant, and minority students (Carter and Wilson,   1992)   who   are   either   academically   underprepared, economically disadvantaged, non-native speaking (Mentzer, 1993), or students with learning problems in discipline-specific areas.   While there is little disagreement that institutions need to develop new and innovative strategies to target the needs of this increasing student population, few agree on what should be done to improve learning outcomes (Clark-Thayer, 1987; Cook, 1989; Dunn, Bruno, Sklar, Zenhausern and Beaudry 1990; Mickler and Zippert, 1987).

Parker (1998) found that seven primary barriers affected the retention of community college students based on ranked responses by college administrators. These included: job and family responsibilities of students; locations of colleges outside urban areas; lack of minority faculty and administrative staff; lack of college funds for intervention purposes; inability to afford college; lack of appropriate social and cultural activities; and unsupportive surrounding communities. The ten major factors most often cited for affecting retention included: positive faculty-student relations; positive relationship or collaborations between college and community organizations that work with people of color; public support of the minority communities role as a critical part of the overall taxpaying community; leadership within the college; retention   service   organized   as   a   unit   to   give   more   visibility, accessibility, and importance; special courses and support services for new and returning students; orientations planned especially for minority students; identification of at-risk students before they encounter serious academic problems; a campus atmosphere that support minority students ability to learn; and overcoming the barriers of institutional racism that exist throughout American society.

Research supports the notion that students of higher socioeconomic status have numerous advantages over those less fortunate.   Typically those of higher socioeconomic status, by definition, have greater income, higher education, and better access to quality education. Additionally, people of higher socioeconomic status have fewer divorces, enjoy longer life expectancies, and report themselves to be happier than people who of lower socioeconomic status (Collier and Smith, 1982). A 1981 extensive study of high-risk students in 58 different colleges and universities across the nation described two trends that illustrate the relationship between socioeconomic status and risk (Coulson et. Al., 1981; Carroll, 1987). First, the findings indicated that students whose parents earned higher incomes experienced less risk of all types and had higher rates of persistence, higher GPAs, and higher rates of progression.   Second, similar patterns existed for students who received large amount of financial aid and students who received more compensatory services.

There has been some evidence that the risk associated with socioeconomic disadvantage can be ameliorated.   In 1987, Murdock examined more than 30 research studies that addressed the relationship between financial aid and persistence.   The study reported that the presence of financial aid reduced risk among lower-income students to almost the same level of those among middle-and upper-income students.

In addition to systematic factors explaining academic performance, other individual factors such as poor study habits, academic preparation, student self-esteem must also be considered. Academic under-preparedness and poor study habits illustrate failure by a student to obtain needed skills, as well as failure on the part of teachers to adequately prepare students.   In addition to environment forces, teachers' negative attitudes towards students can also lead to low self-esteem, which in turn affects academic performance.   Several researchers have been successful in documenting this relationship.   In a 1988 study, Geary found that although high risk students who succeeded perceived themselves as self-confident and self-motivated, teacher's attitudes were found to have a much stronger effect on academic performance than either the student's or the teacher's perceptions of the student's ability (Holliday, 1985). Another study (Graham, 1984) explored the relationship between teacher's affective cues and the self-perception of sixth graders by race and socioeconomic status. In that study, middle-class African American children displayed the most positive self-concept in the pretest, but all racial and socioeconomic groups in the sample changed their self-perceptions in response to teacher's affective cues.

Grimes (1997) described a study comparing the characteristics of college-ready and academically under-prepared community college students. She reported that under-prepared students demonstrated lower levels of course completion rates, greater attrition, higher levels of test anxiety and a more external locus of control than college-ready students but did not differ from college-ready students in self-esteem, grade point-average, or learning-study strategies.

In a 1996 (Campbell and Blakely) longitudinal study of over 3,200 students at a midwestern, suburban community college, cumulative grade point average and number of remedial courses were the two greatest predictors of persistence and remediation. Furthermore, early remediation, taking remediation in the first year, and a degree-seeking intent were also significant predictors of persistence, particularly for those students most under-prepared for a college level curriculum. In addition, the variables, age, ethnicity, gender, and degree-seeking intent were significant predictors of academic performance (cumulative GPA) for under-prepared community college students.

In a 1996 study, Douzenis used the Community College Student Experiences Questionnaire (CCSEQ) to ascertain the relationship between students' quality of effort and estimated gains in knowledge in college. The study found that participation in academic activities was a more important predictor of students' perceived academic achievement than participation in social activities.

In a 1994 study of nearly 100 community college freshman, Rendon found that students were more likely to persist if institutions helped them to be successful in negotiating the transition to college, becoming involved in campus (in and outside of the classroom) as well as in academic and social life, and developing positive attitudes about their learning ability. Successful students reported remembering incidents when they experienced validation and when faculty, staff, friends, or family members actively reached out to them and affirmed them as capable.

Terenzini (1992) conducted a study that explored community college students transition to college through focus group interviews with 132 students at four different types of higher education institutions--a community college, a liberal arts college, an urban university, and a residential research university. Terenzini reported that some of the 22 students in the community college focus group expressed feelings of self-doubt, but positive experiences in and outside of the classroom reinforced their self-esteem and perceptions of themselves as learners. Terenzini also reported that community college students in the study became involved and excited about learning when they participated in class activities.

IMPLICATIONS OF CULTURAL DIFFERENCES
Unlike American mainstream culture that stresses independence and individualism, many non-Anglo community college students come from families and traditions that value interdependence and collective contribution. In other words, many of these students do not attend college solely for themselves but for the benefit of their families and communities. Therefore, the selection of majors and educational objectives may likely be a collective decision between a student and their family rather than an individual choice. In some cultures, students may be pressured by their families to do well so they can transfer to a prestigious college of university. For some Asian students whose families leave their native countries to seek a better life in the states, the pressure can be tremendous (Gregory, 1997). In addition, because of the lack of knowledge about career choices, the nature of the job market, and job opportunities in the United States, parents may encourage them to pursue careers that students really have no interest in.

Another aspect with cultural implication is the different approaches to learning. In many countries, such as China, Korea, Laos, Thailand, Vietnam, Iran and Latin America students utilize their right-brain functioning in the classroom, which governs the nonverbal, intuitive, and experimental functions of thought. By contrast, American students favor left-brain functions that tend to be analytical, verbal, and linear modes of thought. Thus, some students from culturally different backgrounds may likely encounter greater difficulties with school-work due to lack of experience and preparation (Do, 1983).

Dunn and Dunn (1993) define learning styles as the way each individual begins to concentrate on, process, internalize, and remember new and difficult academic information or skills. They generally describe learning styles in terms of a person's ability to master this knowledge   environmentally,   emotionally,   sociologically, physiologically, or globally versus analytically.

The structure of most American tests are a third concern. Many tests in the U.S. are objective and multiple-choice as compared to comprehensive essay exams in many other countries. Furthermore, listening carefully in class while simultaneously taking copious notes from an instructor is not an easy task for any student. Yet foreign students must cope with these demands while often trying to translate the English language of the instructor at the same time. In addition, many undergraduate students from foreign counties are not typically required to complete research papers. When they come to the U.S., they may lack the research and library skills most American students have experienced.

METHOD

The model used for the study is an adaptation of Chickering's (1993) model of student development. The Chickering model is based on two assumptions. The primary function of higher education is to encourage student development and the most effective programs provide opportunities for close and sustained relationships between students and faculty in which students are actively involved in planning and carrying out their own education through a mix of experimental learning and classroom activity. The model suggests that there are seven vectors of development that involve students differentiating and integrating thought and behavior. They include: achieving intellectual, social and physical competence; managing emotions; becoming autonomous; forming an identity; freeing interpersonal relationships; clarifying purpose; and developing integrity. In earlier work, Chickering and Gamson (1987) provided examples of good academic approaches, which included; learning groups of five to seven students who meet regularly during class to solve problems set by the instructor; active learning using structured exercises, discussions, team projects, and peer critiques; and mastery learning; and contract learning. Most of these principles were employed during the study.

With the goal of developing a new skill-based pilot program based on Chickering's model of student development, a three-year longitudinal study was conducted of 30 cross-cultural "at-risk" college students in the College Discovery (CD) Program at Kingsborough Community College (KCC)-City University of New York (CUNY) located in Brooklyn, New York. The program was primarily designed to enhance reading, writing, speech, and Math skills, raise academic performance, motivate students, and encourage persistence and matriculation

Kingsborough Community College is a CUNY comprehensive community college where in a typical semester, 15,218 students are enrolled. Roughly 55 percent (or 8,331) are part-time and 45 percent (or 6,887) are full-time. The mean age for the student population is 25 and nearly 65 percent of all students are female. The racial background of students at KCC are not unusual. Forty-seven percent are White, 30.2 percent Black, 13.8 percent Hispanic, 8.3 percent Asian and .1 percent Native American. However, what is unique about KCC is that 45.8 percent of all students were born outside the U.S., 57.5 percent are the first in their generation to attend college, 53.5 percent receive PELL grants, and 16.5 percent are married. Furthermore, 11.7 percent of full-time students also work full-time and 30.1 percent work part-time. Of part-time students, 29.3 percent work full-time, while 22.8 percent work part-time. Sixty percent of all full-time students have a household income of less than $20,000 and 58 percent of part-time students have a household income of less than $30,000 per year.

Students in the College Discovery (CD) Program from which the study was based, reflected some of the academically and financially disadvantaged students in the university. Through the CD program, they receive the support they need to stay in college and graduate. In a KCC report (1994), 90.3 percent of first-time CD students came from families with annual incomes between $0-$20,000 and 53.6 percent were on public assistance. Over half of the students in this study had ESL needs. In the home, only 44 percent spoke English regularly and 74.1 percent indicated that neither parents had received a college degree. Seventy percent lived with their mothers, while only 40 percent shared the home with their fathers as well.

In order to qualify for the CD program, students must have a high school diploma or GED, rank in the 65th or lower percentile, have received remedial or ESL assistance in high school and determined to need continuing help, and lack math and science requirements. In the CD program, students receive remedial, compensatory, and developmental instruction in basic skills, a semester long orientation introducing them to college life, inter-session classes, special tutoring, intensive counseling and comprehensive academic advising, and a financial aid package.

RESEARCH QUESTIONS
1. What effect did the learning outcomes program have on their academic performance?
2. What were the distinct characteristics of students whose GPA significantly improved?
3. What were the motivations of students to do well academically?
4. What were student's greatest concerns in their academic and personal lives?
5. What major problems were students currently experiencing?
6. What things should be considered when developing a learning outcomes program?
7. What identified factors contributed to the academic success of students?

SAMPLE

The purpose of this study was to determine what factors contributed to better learning outcomes for students in the program. A random sample was conducted and from that sample, 30 students self-selected themselves to participate in the program and 30 additional students were placed in a control group. At the time of selection, all 60 students had a GPA of 2.0 or less and/or were on academic probation. The 30 students in the experimental group signed a contract promising to complete assignments, meet one-on-one and in group settings, maintain a portfolio of their academic work in all their classes and a journal of all activities, be tutored, discuss problems and issues openly, and complete pre and post-tests.

Of the 27 experimental group participants whom successfully completed the three-year study, 8 were African American, 7 Latino, 3 West Indian, 3 Anglo, 1 Chinese, 1 Korean, 1 Russian, 1 Native American, 1 Lebanese, and 1 Greek student. Therefore, over half the students had ESL needs and CD students as a whole came to the university with more academic and financial difficulties to overcome than the average student. At the conclusion of the research study in April 1997, 27 out of 30 students had complied with the contract and fully completed the study.

The treatment group was given an array of assignments to identify and measure their motivators, characteristics of achievement, short-term and long-term goals, study habits, greatest achievements, concerns and problems, sources of support, effort, self-esteem, etc. These assessments along with a comprehensive 55-item pre and post-tests, student portfolios, and their participation in a series of activities served as the data collected and measured for this study.

VARIABLES AND INSTRUMENTS

Gender, Age, and Ethnicity. The gender (50% male and female), age (M=23) and ethnicity of participants were designated by a self-report measure obtained in a 55-item pre-test questionnaire. Ethnicity included 8 African Americans, 7 Latinos, 3 West Indians, 3 Anglo, 1 Chinese, 1 Korean, 1 Russian, 1 Native American, 1 Lebanese, and 1 Greek student.

Cumulative Grade Point Average (GPA). GPA was taken directly from the student transcripts of the experimental group (n=30, M=1.68, SD=.67) and the control group (n=30, M=1.65, SD=.72) at the beginning of the study and at the end of each Fall and Spring semester until the three-year study had completed.

Academic Standing. Academic standing was taken directly from the transcripts of the students. All students in the study had a GPA of 2.0 or less, and/or were on academic probation. There were three categories for academic standing for full-time students: Good Academic Standing (GPA of 2.0 or above); Academic Probation (GPA of 1.99 or below the first semester); and Academic Dismissal (repetitive GPA of 1.99 or below) which is determined on a case-by-case basis.

Motivation/Self-Esteem. A pre-piloted Motivation/Self Esteem Survey was used to measure 38 different items on the inventory. The factors were identified and placed on a form and members of the experimental group were asked to select and rank only ten.

Greatest Concerns in Academic and Personal Lives. A survey was developed to identify those academic and personal areas where students had the greatest concerns. The survey items were selected from a pilot study that was conducted on a similar population of at-risk students. The items were groups in two major categories: academic life and personal life. Students were also given the opportunity to freely list other concerns they may have experienced that were not identified in the previous questions. Internal reliability for these items was $\alpha=.71$.

Current Major Problems. A survey was developed to identify those current issues students considered to be major problems. The instrument was composed of ten blank lines where students were asked to list the most serious problems they were currently experiencing. The composite score for each item was determined by the number of times each item was listed by individual students. The higher the score, the greater the problem. All students ranked at least ten items and eight items were listed numerous times.

PROCEDURE

A series of data including motivations, academic concerns and current major problems were collected in and outside of class, one-on-one and in group sessions from experimental group participants and one-on-one with control group participants. Although there were several methods used to evaluate improved learning outcomes--including self-evaluation, rate of credit accumulation, rate of credits to contact hours, persistence, and graduation--the primary measure discussed in this article is grade point average. A pre and post-test survey was administered to the experimental and control group as well as a vast number of exercises, surveys, activities, focus groups and other data collection measures. All surveys were piloted prior to implementation in this study. The data was examined and direct comparison between initial and baseline data were revealed. The authors reflected on other qualitative data mentioned above. Based on this data and current research, the authors provide recommendations for things to consider when developing a program for at-risk students and offer identified factors that contributed to academic success.

RESULTS

Results indicated that many experiences were common among the experimental and the control groups, however, there were striking differences. In September 1994, the 30-member experimental group possessed a median grade point average of 1.68. The 30-member control group had a median grade point average of 1.65 and did not receive treatments other than those given to all CD students. In the Fall of 1995, the experimental group maintained a stronger grade point average of 2.05 (an increase of .374) as compared to the control group members who maintained a grade point average of 1.88 (an increase of .031). In Spring of 1997, the 27 remaining members of experimental group maintained a GPA of 2.71 (a gain of 1.03) as compared to 2.23 for the remaining 25 members of the control group (a gain of .58).

The participants whose GPA's improved the most were primarily from the experimental group and possessed several common characteristics. The students tended to be younger with fewer dependents, studied more often in the library, sought academic advising and tutoring, missed fewer classes, joined study groups at test time, were more self-motivated, most often participated in small group cooperative learning environments and reported that they believed if they tried harder, they would do better.

A series of pilot tests were randomly administered to over 150 students who were asked to list 10 factors that motivated them the most. Slight modifications were made and the revised instrument was utilized on the group in this study. Thirty-eight factors were identified and placed on a form and the experimental group was asked to select only ten. Those motivators most often selected in rank order was: success, money, interest, career-future, goals, self-esteem, enjoyment, independence, challenge, and recognition/ acknowledgement.

Students were also asked to indicate those areas of greatest concern to them in their academic and personal lives. Those items most commonly listed in rank order included: passing their courses; not doing as well as their families expect them to do; having enough money to stay in school; knowing how to study effectively; worrying about tests; finding some courses difficult; not having enough time to study; finding a job when they graduate; and choosing the right major.

Students were also asked to identify up to 10 major problems they were currently experiencing. Many students listed more than ten items and the average number of items listed was twelve. The items which appeared the greatest number of times included: finding time to study; short attention spans; low self-esteem/self-confidence; poor time management; getting along with their families ("bad vibes in home life"); having the discipline to study; and fitting school, work, and play into one day.

The experimental group gained more on all measures. Self-reports indicated that academic achievement (cumulative GPA) significantly improved more than the control group and students in the experimental groups were aware of the importance of study strategies and the significance of their effort on performance.

DISCUSSION
The ultimate goal of this study was to provide academic, social, and institutional support to increase the GPA of at-risk, probationary, community college students and remove them from probationary status to good academic standing. In the study, several interventions were used both in and outside the classroom that appeared to encourage student motivation and persistence. By the end of the three-year study, close to a third had not yet graduated with their associate's degree, however, some indicated that obtaining a degree was not their intent. Overall, the interventions significantly increased the academic

performance of the experimental group as compared to the control group.

One specific detail that was noted during the process was the differences in learning styles among students. Some responded better when working independently while others worked best in groups or with individual tutors. Once students became comfortable with one another, most responded well to assistance being offered from the instructor, counselor or fellow classmates.

The specific results, if viewed by GPA alone, would indicate a significant improvement of learning outcomes for students who participated in the experimental program, as compared to those in the control group. At the same time, however, it is important to note that although these techniques can assist students to develop their own learning potential, they can best do so in a carefully managed setting that is sensitive to individual student learning problems and discipline-specific areas. According to a European study (Parsons and Meyer, 1990), learning behavior intervention for academically "at-risk" students takes place only after students have altered their perceptions about the context of learning. In addition, if students are to get the most out of a learning session, they need to know: 1) why the topic is important and interesting; 2) it's relation to other topics in the course; 3) what they need to know already to make the best use of the material provided; and 4) the defined learning objectives in view. Many students need to simply learn how to learn, therefore, emphasis should not only be placed on skill but on facilitating a personal awareness of strengths and weaknesses (Gregory, 1997).

WHAT TO CONSIDER WHEN DEVELOPING A LEARNING IMPROVEMENT PROGRAM

There are several things institutions should consider when developing a program. First, assess the need of students and identify long-term and short-term goals that can be attained in a realistic period of time. Second, consider developing a new paradigm with established boundaries that provide fixed rules for success within an institution that focus on learning as an ongoing process. Third, establish learning outcomes which can be measured and ensure that the learning strategies are task-related. This will help to empower students by allowing them to take responsibility for their own learning. Fourth, utilize student teams for problem-solving and brainstorming activities and provide conducive learning environments that promote cooperative learning, curiosity, acceptance of others and their ideas, and individual commitment. Fifth, be aware of student perceptions about the environment and try to identify personal approaches for studying in order to offer alternative strategies. And finally, apply real-world problems and concepts in the classroom and try to construct meaning from a diverse set of materials.

Community colleges need to help build learning communities where students are validated and motivated to do their best. This must be done early in the academic process and can be done by offering encouraging words, building upon strengths, personalizing the environment, providing one-on-one feedback and a hospitable campus atmosphere, a positive classroom environment with affirming relationships between faculty and students, a diverse curricula, and an opportunity for self-expression in a non-threatening environment.

Today, most institutions address the needs of "at-risk" students by simply admitting them and providing them with reduced academic curriculums and some remedial and/or ESL coursework. This patchwork method fails to embrace legitimate concerns of individual differences with respect to learning styles, academic strengths and weaknesses, and learning behaviors as manifested within a particular course, say Math or science. In order to truly make a difference at some simplistic level, institutions need to develop a conceptual model of quality learning tailored to their specific student population which reflect the strategies presented in this article as well as address qualitative learning differences (Meyer and Muller, 1990). For those institutions thar are either unable or unwilling to do so, they may opt to only admit those students whose needs they are prepared to meet through their current programs and services.

IDENTIFIED FACTORS THAT CONTRIBUTE TO ACADEMIC SUCCESS

There are eight identified factors that contribute to the academic success of minority, immigrant, and international the students, particularly those who are not native speakers of English. They include: early assessment and placement; remediation; mainstreaming; supplemental instruction; acculturation; academic counseling and advisement; personal and career counseling; and faculty and staff development.

Obviously, assessments are important because they provide us with tools to evaluate a student's academic skills. Assessment and placement programs for this diverse group should include assessment of language for integrated proficiency and be tied to instruction and curriculum. All assessment/basic skills tests (reading, writing, Math) could be translated into the major languages of the ESL population and students could have the option of taking it in their native language or in English. Students scoring below a specific number would be required to re-test in their native language. By taking the tests in their own language, institutions would have the added advantage of avoiding cultural bias and providing more help in identifying the exact type of ESL instruction needed. With regard to placement, a list of courses could be developed that would include all the courses open to ESL students according to a student's ESL level and their score on the placement tests. However each test, for example the reading test, would only be used as one measure for placement along with the others and movement from each level of ESL would be based on multiple measures. Tests such as writing, would be kept and used for comparison purposes for evaluators and students to see improvement. Low level ESL students would be placed in reading classes specifically designed for ESL students, taught by ESL specialists, and re-tested after each semester. In one study, (Gray, et. Al., 1996) inadequate language skills was reported as the greatest barrier immigrants faced in acquiring postsecondary education. One problem often occurs when faculty are reluctant to discount a student's grade or successful completion of a course because of difficulty with English language skills. In some cases, this has led to large numbers of foreign students graduating who failed to demonstrate these basic skills (Gray et. Al., 1996). The primary goal of assessment and placement is early intervention so students can be moved into academic programs as soon as possible.

Remediation is often thought of as intense classroom instruction using drills and other repetitive forms of learning. Often students remain in remediation long after they have mastered the materials because instructors, many of which are not well-trained to work with ESL students, are not aware that the material has been learned. To overcome this problem, courses in reading, writing, and Math could be grouped into four categories--non remedial, low remedial, middle remedial, and high remedial--according to subject area. All students, regardless of discipline or ESL status, could be given the opportunity to collaborate through small group discussion, peer group editing, 'study gangs,' and other activities that foster meaningful communication. Such collaborative efforts would also foster communication between native and non-native speakers of English.

Mainstreaming is considered early participation in the regular college curriculum, although it rarely integrates language instruction and academic support with a wide array of courses in the regular curriculum. Integration is critical and should include: collaborative teaching where content is tied to language; and collaborative learning where informal study groups, peer discussions, writing groups, and peer tutoring take place on a regular basis. In a 1993 study, Hirsch found that peer study groups involving collaborative talk and writing, enhanced content and language learning. As with assessment and placement, credit-bearing courses that ESL students could take while at each level of ESL, would need to be available and listed by department. Co and pre-requisites for discipline courses could be identified by level of proficiency in reading, writing, and Math. Since language instruction is more effective when offered within the context of the disciplines, students could be given a structured program where courses and programs contain the appropriate mix of English language and subject matter instruction. These courses should be designated to promote swift, steady, and substantive academic progress.

Supplemental instruction in course content includes such things as peer tutoring and recruitment from prior ESL students in courses, such as Freshman Composition or "sheltered" sections of 100-level distribution courses. These courses could be run like seminars with limited enrollment providing students with the opportunity for more verbal interaction with peers and the professor. It could include such things as the preparation of videotapes of introductory lectures that are designed as writing, reading, or speaking intensive. Extra academic support such as tutoring, would not be limited to ESL and remedial learners, but would also be offered to those students whose native language is not English when they take academic courses. Students who have not completed ESL and remedial courses would also greatly benefit from supplemental tutoring in lower division courses and advanced students from various disciplines could be encouraged to serve as role models and as mentors in established peer instructional tutoring programs and new programs which make use of their talents and abilities.

Acculturation (or student orientation) has been identified as one factor which can impede the academic progress of immigrant and international students who are not familiar with the American system of higher education (CUNY, 1994; Gregory, 1997). All students would be required to take at least one American history or civilization course and incorporate materials from other cultures. With regard to instruction, faculty would need to be clear when asking students to present arguments, analyze the text critically, or to debate with the instructor because these are not common practices in many other cultures. Definitions and examples of honesty and dishonesty must be not only written in the handbook, but discussed at orientation and at the beginning of each semester in the classroom. In many cultures, learning is a joint process and students are encouraged to work together to find answers to all the questions in homework and on tests. It is not unusual to find some students offering answers to other students when they are not sure of the correct choices. These and other cultural differences can be addressed by providing and encouraging students to meet with personal counselors when they are tying to cope with these types of issues and conflicts that emerge while they are trying to make the cultural transition. If needed, rap sessions could also be provided for students to discuss and deal with racial tensions on campus. Since cultural orientation is critical to academic success, ESL and international students should be given help in acquiring the cultural knowledge and skills required in dealing with a new environment.

Unfortunately in our current academic environment where resources and funding are scarce, academic counseling and advisement monies are often one of the first to be reduced. Yet the need for academic counseling and advisement has never been greater and has been shown to be a significant factor affecting retention (Gregory, 1997). Therefore, it should be convenient and accessible, especially for non-traditional and ESL students who are subject to greater stress (Villella and Hu, 1991). In many Asian countries, there were no counselors in colleges and universities, and therefore some institutions may find that their Asian students do not take advantage of counseling and advising services. Not only do these types of students have the greatest need for these services, but they are mostly likely to be unaware of certain resources and avoid seeking help (CUNY, 1994). For ESL students, however, academic advising should facilitate a successful integration into the mainstream as well as increase the potential for higher academic performance. Since the greatest need for academic counseling and advising occurs during registration periods when non-native students feel at a particular loss because of the unfamiliarity with the system, and for some with limited English, extra assistance needs to be provided at this time. Whenever possible, counselors who speak one of more of the languages of the largest immigrant and international groups should be hired to give help to those who struggle with the language and are unaware of American academic culture and custom. In addition, the advising process should be facilitated by and made more cost effective through the use of trained peer advisors.

As with academic counseling and advisement, coordinated personal and career counseling programs should be strong to help non-native students make well-informed decisions about the future of their academic careers. In many countries, a student has little choice, if any, about what they will study and changing majors or transferring to another institution is unheard of. Many cultures believe in education for education's sake and do not understand the link between college study and preparation for the workplace. Therefore, many students are unprepared to select a major let alone a career. Specifically, students need to know where to go, whom to see, and what to ask for. It would be most helpful if literature could be developed and written in several languages so students could share the materials with their families. These materials might include a list of majors, program requirements, guide in instructional resources, registration instructions, and general administrative procedures. In addition, a professionally trained, multilingual, culturally sensitive, full-time counseling staff and peer advising staff could be available in each unit to integrate the delivery of academic, personal, career, transfer, and financial aid information and advising to the second language population, for evening as well as day students.

Finally, faculty and staff development workshops should be initiated across disciplines with ESL staff to integrate language and subject matter teaching. With institutions across the country witnessing increases in immigrant and international students, faculty recruitment, development, and evaluation needs to be revisited. Due to the changing composition of student culture and language within groups, faculty and counselors need to be continuously retrained to keep abreast of issues and changes. Staff development initiatives should be broad based to promote a greater understanding and awareness of cultural differences between native and non-native students. Opportunities for dialogue must be provided for faculty to examine their pedagogical methods critically and to develop teaching strategies to meet the challenges of non-native students. Institutions should set aside adequate funds for faculty, counselor, and staff workshops and recruitment funds for multilingual faculty and counselors. Finally, the goals of the institution with regard to retaining and graduating multicultural students, should be directly tied to annual faculty and counseling evaluations addressing contribution to the school's mission so everyone is held accountable. It is also important to point out that although the wave of immigrant and foreign-born students continue to place many demands on institutions, the benefits of this increasing population compensate for the costs associated with these changes.

The academic success students achieved in this study should serve as a reminder that all students, if given the opportunity and resources, have the ability to achieve academically. The responsibility for improved learning outcomes and academic success should be shared between the student and the institution, which includes faculty, administration and student affairs professionals specializing in counseling, student activities, admissions, and student support. Only through meaningful collaboration can we significantly improve student learning outcomes.

REFERENCES

American Council on Education. 1994. *Minorities in Higher Education.* Office of Minority Concerns: Washington, D.C.

Campbell, J. and L. Blakely. 1996. *Successful Community College Recruitment and Retention: Case Studies.* Paper presented at the Annual Meeting of the Association of Teacher Educators, St. Louis, MO., February 12, 1996.

Carroll, D. 1987. The Effects of Grants on College Persistence. *OERI Bulletin.* Washington, D.C.: Center for Educational Statistics. ED 280 355. 9 pp. MF-01; PC-01.

Carter, D. and R. Wilson. 1992. *Minorities in Higher Education.* American Council on Education: Washington, D.C.

Chickering, A.W. & Z. Gamson. 1987. Seven Principals for Good Practice in Undergraduate Education. *AAHE Bulletin,* March, p. 3-7.

Chickering, A.W., & L. Reisser. 1993. *Education and Identity.* San Francisco, CA: Jossey-Bass.

City University of New York. 1995. *Immigration/Migration and the CUNY Student of the Future.* CUNY: New York, NY.

City University of New York. 1994. *Report of the CUNY ESL Taskforce.* CUNY: New York, NY.

Clark-Thayer, S. 1987. The Relationship of the Knowledge of student-Perceived Learning Style Preferences, and Study Habits and Attitudes to Achievement of College Freshmen in a Small Urban University. (Doctoral dissertation, Boston University, 1987) *Dissertation Abstracts International,* 48, 872A.

Collier, B.J. and W.D. Smith. 1982. Distributive Injustice: A Psychosocial Process Analysis. *Universal Renaissance* 3(1): 37-40.

Cook, L. 1989. Relationships Among Learning Style Awareness, Academic Achievement, and Locus of Control Among Community College Students. *Doctoral Abstracts International*, 49(03), 217A.

Coulson, J. et. al. 1981. *Evaluation of the Special Services for Disadvantaged Students (SSDS) Program: 1979-80 Academic Year*. Santa Monica, CA.: System Development Corporation. ED 214 412. 262 pp. MF-01; PC-11.

Cuseo, J.B. 1991. *The Freshmen Orientation Seminar: A Research-Based Rationale for its Value, Delivery, and Content* (Monograph No. 4). Columbia, SC: University of South Carolina. National Resource Center for the Freshman Year Experience.

Dillard, J. and G. Chisolm. 1983. Counseling the International Student in a Multicultural Context. *Journal of College Student Personnel* 24: 101-105.

Do, V. T. 1983. Cultural Difference and their Implications in the Education of Vietnamese Students in U.S. Schools. In V. Smith and M.B. Dixon (Eds.), *Second Lives* (pp. 43-46). Costa Mesa, CA: South Coast Repertory.

Dougherty, J. W. 1990. *Effective Programs for At-Risk Adolescents*. Phi Delta Kappa Educational Foundation.

Douzenis, C. 1996 The Relationship of Quality of Effort and Estimate of Knowledge Gain Among Community College Students. *Community College Review*, 24(3): 27-35.

Dunn, R. and K. Dunn. 1993). *Teaching Secondary Students Through their Individual Learning Styles*. Boston, MA: Allyn & Bacon.

Dunn, R., J. Bruno, R. I. Sklar, R. Zenhausern and R. Beaudry. 1990. Effect of Matching and Mismatching Minority Developmental College Students' Hemispheric Preferences on Mathematical Scores. *Journal of Educational Research*, 85(5): 283-288.

Dunn, R. and S.A. Griggs. 1995. *Multiculturalism and Learning Styles: Teaching and Counseling Adolescents*. Westport, CT: Praeger Publishers.

Fix, M. & Passel, J.S. 1994. Who's on the Dole? It's Not Illegal Immigrants. *The Los Angeles Times*. August 3, p. B11.

Geary, P. 1988. *Defying the odds? Academic Success Among At-Risk Minority Teenagers in an Urban High School*. Paper presented at an annual meeting of the American Education Research Association, April 5-9, New Orleans, Louisiana. ED 296 055. 9pp. MF-01; PC-01.

Graham, S. 1984. Communicating Sympathy and Anger to Black and White Children: The Cognitive (Attributional) Consequences of Affective Cues. *Journal of Personality and Social Psychology* 47(1): 40-54.

Gray, M., G. Vernez, and E. Rolph. 1996. Student Access and the New Immigrants: Assessing their Impact on Institutions. *Change* 28(5): 40-47.

Gregory, S. T. 1999. *Black Women in the Academy: The Secrets to Success and Achievement,* Updated and Rev. Ed. University Press of America: Lanham, MD.

Gregory, S. T. 1997. Planning for the Increase of Foreign-Born Students. *Planning for Higher Education,* 26, 1: 23-28.

Grimes, S. 1997. Under-Prepared Community College Students: Characteristics, Persistence, and Academic Success. *Community College Journal of Research and Practice,* 21:47-56.

Guthrie, L.E. 1991. *School Improvements for Students at Risk.* ERIC Document Reproduction Service Number ED 342135.

Hirsch, E.D. 1993. The Core Knowledge Curriculum--What's Behind's it's Success? *Educational Leadership* 50(8): 23-30.

Holliday, B.G. 1985. Differential Effects of Children's Self-Perceptions and Teachers' Perceptions of Black Children's Academic Achievement. *Journal of Negro Education* 54(1): 71-81.

Jones, D.J. and B.J.Watson. 1988. The Increasing Significance of Race. *In Poverty, Race and Public Policy,* edited by Billy J. Tidwell, Lanham, MD.: National Urban League Press.

Kingsborough Community College. 1994. *Department of Student Development 1993-94 Annual Report.* CUNY Press: New York, NY..

LeBlanc, C. L. 1991. *Minutes of the Orientation Task Force Meeting.* Gainsville, FL: Santa Fe Community College, Office for student Development.

Mentzer, M. 1993. Minority Representation in Higher Education. *Journal of Higher Education,* 64(4): 417-433.

Meyer, J.H.F. and M.W. Muller. (1990). Evaluating the Quality of Student Learning. I - An Unfolding Analysis of the Association Between Perceptions of Learning Context and Approaches to Studying at an Individual Level. *Studies in Higher Education,* 15, 131-154.

Mickler, M. L. and C. P. Zippert. 1987. Teaching Strategies Based on Learning Styles of Adult Students. *Community/Junior College Quarterly*, 11, 33-37.

Morley, J. 1993. Perspectives on English for Academic Purposes. In J.E. Alatis *Georgetown University Round Táble on Languages and Linguistics*, 1991 (pp. 143-166). Georgetown University Press.

Murdock, T.A. 1987. It Isn't Just Money: The Effects of Financial Aid on Student Persistence. *Review of Higher Education* 7(1): 75-101.

Parker, C. 1998. Cultivate Academic Persistence – Now! *Black Issues in Higher Education*, 14(26): 104, February 19.

Parsons, P.G. and J.H.F. Meyer. 1990. The Academically "At-Risk" Student: A Pilot Intervention Program and its Observed Effects on Learning Outcome. *Higher Education*, 20, 323-334.

Rendon, L. 1994. *Beyond Involvement: Creating Validating Academic and Social Communities in the Community College.* Keynote address at the National Center on Postsecondary Teaching, Learning, and Assessment, University Park, PA.

Schram, J. and P. Lauver. 1988. Alienation in International Students. *Journal of College Student Development* 29: 146-150.

Slavin, R.E. 1981. Synthesis of Research on Cooperative Learning. *Educational Leadership,* 38(8):655-660.

Stein, D. 1994. Overwhelmed by our Generosity. *The Los Angeles Times*, August 8.

Stevenson, Z. 1985. *Assessing Basic Skills Needs of High School and College Students.* Evaluative Feasibility Report.

Terenzini, P.T. 1992. *Out-of-Class Experiences Research Program: The Transition to College Project: Final Report.* University Park: The Pennsylvania State University, National Center on Postsecondary Teaching, Learning and Assessment.

United States Department of Commerce. 1996. *The Foreign Born Population: 1996.* Journey to Work and Migration Statistic Branch. United States Government Printing Office (PPL-59), March 1997.

Villella, E. F. and M. Hu. 1991. A Factor Analysis of Variables Affecting the Retention Decision of Nontraditional College Students, *NASPA Journal* 28(4): 334-341.

*I*ndex

About the Editor

Sheila T. Gregory is Director of Marketing and Public Relations, and assistant professor of higher education/educational leadership in the College of Education at the University of Memphis. She received a B.A. degree in Communications and Journalism from Oakland University, an M.P.A. degree in Health Care Administration from Wayne State University, and a Ph.D. in Higher Education Administration from the University of Pennsylvania where she graduated with highest distinction. She received a dissertation award in 1995 from the Black Caucus of the American Association for Higher Education (AAHE) and has been the recipient of numerous grants. She is the author of three published books and over a dozen articles and book chapters. In the past three years she has been awarded two Visiting Research Scholar Appointments at the University of the West Indies System and the American University in Cairo, Egypt. Her major research interests are in the areas of faculty and student recruitment and retention, professional leadership and development, and academic achievement with a special emphasis on race, ethnicity, class, and gender. She has also lectured and consulted with numerous universities, community colleges, school districts, and tribal associations.